Advance Praise for
Fallout

"This book very effectively details how a Russian domination strategy was deployed in the United States with the very willing support and cooperation of the Obama administration. These were very important and serious events that every American should fully understand. As the title suggests, the 'fallout' from this unchecked assertion of power and greed, still lingers largely in today's current affairs."

—**Scott Melbye**, thirty-five-year veteran of the uranium and nuclear energy industry and former Executive Vice President of Marketing at Uranium One, Inc.

"Putin despises Democrats and Republicans alike. What scares him the most is democracy. He wants us all to be sick from the Kremlin's discoverable influence operations."

—**Daniel Hoffman**, former CIA officer and Moscow station chief

"The full Uranium One saga is one of the most important untold stories in American politics and these authors have captured it and turned it into a fascinating thriller. Anyone who still thinks the Uranium One story has been 'debunked' *must* read this book."

—**James G. Rickards**, former advisor to the CFIUS Support Group of the Director of National Intelligence and *New York Times* bestselling author of *Aftermath*, *The Road to Ruin*, and *Currency Wars*

"More than three years ago, John Solomon and I talked about how the Russia scandal was a big onion of deceit that needed to be peeled layer by layer. He and I and a small ensemble of journalists did just that, exposing the greatest political scandal of our generation. *Fallout* is the extraordinary last chapter in John's and Seamus's mission to give the American people the truth."

—**Sean Hannity**, Fox News host

FALLOUT

FALLOUT

NUCLEAR BRIBES, RUSSIAN SPIES, AND THE WASHINGTON LIES THAT ENRICHED THE CLINTON AND BIDEN DYNASTIES

JOHN SOLOMON
SEAMUS BRUNER

BOMBARDIER
BOOKS

A BOMBARDIER BOOKS BOOK
An Imprint of Post Hill Press

Fallout:
Nuclear Bribes, Russian Spies, and the Washington Lies that Enriched the Clinton
and Biden Dynasties
© 2020 by John Solomon and Seamus Bruner
All Rights Reserved

ISBN: 978-1-64293-571-4
ISBN (eBook): 978-1-64293-572-1

Putin Cover photo credit: Kremlin.ru

Post Hill Press
New York • Nashville
posthillpress.com

Published in the United States of America

DEDICATION

This book is dedicated to the real whistleblowers—
the men and women who risk their careers, their reputations,
their liberties, and their lives to speak the truth.

Thank you.

CONTENTS

FOREWORD

By Peter Schweizer

Uranium One is a story about powerful politicians seeking money and rich people buying power. It is about reformers who fall into corruption, and about journalists who are too lazy to challenge the lies and spin they get from the powerful, the rich, the corrupted.

I have been writing books about cronyism in politics for more than fifteen years. It is, I'm sorry to tell you, very fertile ground. Where political power is great, the temptation to use it to help oneself and one's friends becomes greater still. Even in societies like ours, where we hate this kind of self-dealing and pass laws to prevent graft and bribery, the ingenuity of the truly corrupt still seems to find a way.

In the United States today, this means that exposing corruption or cronyism is a complicated task, buried under layers of connections and transactions that politicians are careful to mask, lest they become obvious. It rarely shows up as a single, highlighted line in a tax return or an eye-popping entry on a financial disclosure form. Rarely is a politician as careless as former U.S. Representative William Jefferson (D-LA), who—infamously—was caught by the FBI with $90,000 in cash bribes neatly wrapped in foil and placed in the back of his freezer.

But such frozen treats are the exception, not the rule. As a journalist, I can tell you that it takes months of hard work to connect the dots that sneaky politicians take pains to obfuscate. There is no "smoking gun" to sniff out, only a shadowy trail of money and "coincidence." That trail is a little different every time; it might start with finding an investment here that might lead to a brother-in-law there who has a company somewhere that got a no-bid contract from a government agency that just happens to be overseen by that politician you began with. Oh, and maybe the original investment at the top of this trail is actually held by the politician's spouse, or by his or her children. Certainly not by him or her—the deceit is rarely clear and often legal.

I founded the Government Accountability Institute (GAI) eight years ago because I realized I couldn't do this kind of work on my own. Based in Florida and with a very small staff, we began investigating these kinds of stories because we noticed how rarely the mainstream media, which no longer seemed to have the appetite to look into them deeply, covered them. We noticed that because of Watergate and various other "*-gate" scandals, the public understood the need to expose these misdeeds. Congress and the rest of official Washington have passed many laws designed to make it harder to cheat, to get rich through their positions, and to steer political and financial favors to their biggest donors—all in exchange for large campaign contributions to scare off serious challengers. And the laws they passed certainly have helped. At least, up to a point.

Maybe they really did mean well, but what was supposed to force them to declare their earnings and confess their conflicts of interest has instead created a market where corruption is brokered through third parties. The standard for identifying these sorts of pay-to-play schemes has long been to look for the straight line, the "quid pro quo" like frozen cash in a congressman's freezer. Today's corruption is rarely this simple. The gun no longer smokes.

Instead, we are left with a question: How do you prevent this when the "quid" happens in broad daylight, almost untraceable to the "quo" that lies behind shell companies, international banking secrets, the children of politicians, cronies, foreign business partners, and various "charitable organizations" set up by the politicians themselves?

The sale of Uranium One to a Russian government-controlled company called Rosatom is that kind of story.

Our 2015 book *Clinton Cash: The Untold Story of How and Why Foreign Governments and Businesses Helped Make Bill and Hillary Rich* focused on the connections between the people who wanted that sale to happen and the Clinton Foundation, the multibillion-dollar chari-table organization set up by the former president and his wife. Hillary Clinton, while Secretary of State, was in a position to make sure that it did. Uranium One, and its connections to the Clintons, comprised just two chapters of that book—one example of many that showed how the Clintons used the *power* of their office and the cover of their philanthropy to enrich themselves and their friends through many different "pay-to-play" schemes.

Documenting these connections took us to Ukraine, Russia, Kazakhstan, Canada, and other places. Our team, and especially Seamus Bruner, tracked the money trail of massive contributions to the Clintons and connected them to the players and the timeline of the Uranium One deal. All of it was distilled into thirty-six pages of *Clinton Cash*.

Seamus found more information than we could use in that book. His gut told him there was a lot more going on, enough for a whole book. I was skeptical at first, but he was right, and the complex, interconnected web of interests, strategic mistakes, and coincidences is all laid out in detail here for the first time. As you will see, the Uranium One story sprawls across multiple U.S. administrations and reaches the highest levels of the Kremlin, where it becomes a key part of the long-held ambition of Russian President Vladimir Putin to corner the world market for atomic energy.

This book tells, as the late radio commentator Paul Harvey used to say, "the rest of the story."

The sale of Uranium One to Rosatom in 2010 (and finalized in 2013) was a bad deal for U.S. national security and should never have been approved. What was said at the time in defense of the deal has been proven not to be true, and most of what its critics feared has come to pass. Yet the *Washington Post* recently described this criticism as "debunked," despite having published its own news stories confirming what we uncovered back in 2015. Something is amiss.

The best that we as independent journalists can do with these kinds of stories is to find and expose the patterns that strongly suggest corruption. Reporters at mainstream media outlets apply this standard routinely to their political coverage of everything from gun control bills to health care, by noting how the timing of campaign contributions received by politicians matches up with those decisions. But for this story, with its cast of characters in Russia, Ukraine, Europe, and the United States, these same media outlets want to move the goalposts.

After the Uranium One story emerged, we called for official investigations—ones armed with subpoena power and the ability to gather information we could not hope to get ourselves. We were optimistic when, in 2017, then-Attorney General Jeff Sessions asked John Huber, the U.S. attorney in Utah, to look into concerns that the FBI had not fully pursued cases of possible corruption when the U.S. government decided not to block the sale of Uranium One. Huber's "investigation," finally released in 2020, was a disappointment, as it was simply a review of the FBI's earlier insufficient efforts. His team called no witnesses, did no interviews or investigations of its own, and, after more than two years, left all these questions unanswered.

As investigative journalists, we don't have the *power* or the soapbox that mainstream news organizations do to press for the truth. But that *is* their job. Part of doing this work—and why we document our facts so precisely—is our faith that those reporters, editors, congressional overseers, and executive branch prosecutors will pick up where we left off. And if they do not, it is fair to ask: Why not? Many of our friends in major news organizations tell us that they get sucked into what I have called "the Trump Vortex," the fixation by the media on President Donald J. Trump's actions, tweets, and possible misdeeds. I don't question the importance of covering those stories.

But that singular focus leaves other important corruption stories ignored. America's adversaries, in China, Russia, and elsewhere, have done business for years by working through back channels to sway those who are temporarily in office in the United States, regardless of political party. We wrote about those techniques before and will no doubt do so again. The interconnected worlds of international commerce and global strategic competition introduce temptations for our political representatives to compromise themselves and our country, and in ways far more dangerous than frozen stacks of cash in a congressman's freezer.

In this book, Seamus Bruner and John Solomon will show those dangers, detail those temptations, and expose those dark worlds.

CHAPTER 1

PUTIN'S NUCLEAR CONQUEST

The Uncanny Origins of Trump's Impeachment

After multiple late-night marathon sessions, the U.S. House stood at the precipice of impeaching America's forty-fifth president, Donald J. Trump. The chamber bore all the markings of solemnity—the marble walls, the parliamentary formality, and the endless reverential talk about the U.S. Constitution. But the gravity of America's most famous political scandal, Watergate, seemed lacking. In fact, the moment unfolding in Washington several days before Christmas 2019 seemed much more like daily politics than the rare rebuke that the Founding Fathers had envisioned impeachment to be.[1]

Much of America had already tuned out from the hearings, despite the potentially historic consequences. On the House floor, nerves were frayed and voices were hoarse. For the third time in America's history, one of its chief executives was going to be stained by impeachment. Majority Democrats had the votes.[2]

As the drama inside the Capitol wound down, Representative Doug Collins, a bespectacled Republican from Georgia, dutifully stepped to the microphone for one last shot at informing history. His words, however partisan, provided a succinct summary of what the country had endured for three tiresome years.[3]

"I've said it before, and I will say it again: I do not believe, no matter what was said today and even what has been said, this is not a solemn occasion," Collins barked.[4]

The congressman continued:

When you go looking for something for three years, and especially this year, since January, you ought to be excited when you found it… Why do we keep calling this a solemn occasion when you've been wanting to do this ever since the gentleman was elected?[5]

Collins' statement was painfully and obviously true. From the moment the billionaire bad boy Donald Trump had emerged as a viable prospect to become president in the spring of 2016, his opponents in the Democratic Party, inside the machinery of the FBI and Justice Department, around the government bureaucracy, amongst foreign allies, and inside the never-Trump wing of his own Republican Party. They threw the kitchen sink at him, to first derail his campaign and, when that failed, to cripple his presidency.[6]

The mission was accurately summed up in a private exchange between two FBI lovebirds who played an essential role in this effort. "We'll stop it," then-counterintelligence agent Peter Strzok texted bureau lawyer Lisa Page, clearly referring to Trump's election in 2016.[7]

Facts, accuracy, rule of law, and normal bureaucratic and parliamentary processes took a backseat. The political outcome was more important.[8]

As has now been well established, the Trump opposition campaign started with a research project funded by Hillary Clinton's campaign and the Democratic National Committee (DNC). These actors hired a research intelligence firm known as Fusion GPS, which in turn hired the British ex-spy Christopher Steele to produce a now-infamous dossier painting a portrait of a Trump campaign colluding with Russia to steal the election.[9]

Though assiduous efforts were made to leak this tainted opposition research, there were no takers at the time in the press. It took some artful machinations on the part of then-FBI director James Comey and his allies in the intelligence community to bring the dossier to light and make it public—a political espionage effort known as "Spygate."[10]

The opposition campaign kicked into high gear with Special Counsel Robert Mueller's investigation, which failed to find evidence of collusion and then pivoted to make a case for obstruction of justice. When Mueller's evidence failed to meet the threshold for prosecution in the eyes of Attorney General William Barr, the campaign shifted to a new attack fueled by an anonymous whistleblowing bureaucrat who alleged that Trump had tried to leverage Ukraine to start an investigation of Joe Biden, his likely 2020 rival, by withholding U.S. aid to the former Soviet republic.[11]

After a notably rushed and nakedly partisan hearing, Trump was impeached in the House and then acquitted by the Senate in a matter of weeks, both on party-line votes. Four House Democrats broke ranks and decided not to vote with their party. Just one Republican, Senator Mitt Romney, did the same.[12]

It is hard to find a winner in the aftermath of that three-year, vitriolic rollercoaster ride. The country's deep partisan wounds are packed with painful salt. Attention and appreciation for the historic progress of the U.S. economy (among other things worth celebrating) had been completely diverted, and American trust in essential institutions like the FBI, the Congress, and the media has been deeply, perhaps fatally compromised.[13]

Meanwhile, the true victor in this sordid episode resides thousands of miles away in Moscow, where the seeds of this profound domestic discord were first sown several years earlier.[14]

The old Soviet hands who developed the Cold War strategy of sowing division probably never imagined a scenario quite like this one. With just a few twenty-first century interventions—$150,000 in Facebook ads, a few thousand hacked emails, a couple of energy power plays, and some classic disinformation—Russia had all but paralyzed its American adversary for three long years.[15]

In short, Russia succeeded beyond its wildest dreams. But even this does not explain the actual goals of Vladimir Putin's campaign. Lost in all the partisan hysteria about Trump's presumed relationship to Putin is the question of what Putin hoped to gain from it.[16] Did he really think that he could influence the outcome of an American election?

Yes, the Russian government has an interest in destabilizing American politics and miring its leadership in pointless partisan strife.[17] But given the absurdity of the case against Trump, many Americans sense that we are not being told the whole story. Something else is going on. Why is this really happening, and why does the same cast of characters from the Clinton-Obama "Deep State" keep popping up in this divisive theatrical drama?

In order to understand the actual roots of impeachment, we have to view it in the larger context of Putin's longterm strategic goals and interests—particularly, as it turns out, his interest in the U.S. uranium industry.[18]

This, then, is the story of the real Russian collusion, and it begins, as it must, with Vladimir Putin and his quest to return Russia to glory. It is a complex story that has never been fully explained. But without it, we cannot understand what is happening in American politics today.[19]

In this book, we are going to fully unpack the Obama-era scandal known as Uranium One. First exposed in Peter Schweizer's 2015 bestseller *Clinton Cash*, this underplayed scandal turns out to be the tip of an iceberg of corruption and subterfuge by Putin and his surrogates in the American uranium and nuclear-powered utility industries. The latter, as we will show, was an industry with which President Barack Obama had deep ties going back to his days as an Illinois state senator.[20]

This book reveals the larger story behind that scandal and explains its hidden links to the subsequent political attacks on Trump, including spying on his campaign, the Mueller probe, and the Trump-Ukraine impeachment scandal.

First, however, we have to understand the motives, the training, and the tactics of the wily, hidden actor behind these machinations.

The basic facts of Vladimir Putin's rise to power are well known. From a young KGB spy living in East Germany, he rose to become the head of the FSB, the KGB's successor agency, and eventually the ruler of Russia.[21]

Along the way, he became experienced in asymmetrical "cold warfare." He became an expert in compromising his opponents through corrupt financial deals. He also learned how to keep his rivals (and lieutenants), whose insolence was a recurring theme, in order.[22]

Our story begins in 2000, when Putin ascended to the Russian presidency. At that time, the former Soviet empire was in ruins. The Cold War had, by 1991, crushed the U.S.S.R. and changed the entire eastern European landscape. One by one, all fifteen Soviet republics split off to become independent nations.[23]

Unlike previous Soviet leaders, Putin was not a Marxist ideologue but a ruthless pragmatist. Yet he was also a nationalist and super-patriot who dreamed of rebuilding the empire that had been the goal of every Russian ruler since Peter the Great, whom Putin idolized. For Putin, this meant primarily recapturing or regaining control over Georgia and Ukraine and the Baltic "republics," as well as Crimea and other former Soviet states.[24]

Since the post-Soviet state was economically and militarily decimated, Putin knew that he had to get creative. Like many great rulers before him, he used every tool in his grubby, broken-down toolbox to once again command respect and fear.[25]

After the Berlin Wall fell, Boris Yeltsin's administration had made diplomatic inroads with the U.S. under President Bill Clinton—ties that Clinton's successor, George W. Bush, tried to maintain as hopes kindled for a long-term future of friendly relations with Moscow. History will likely show that such optimism was misplaced, overlooking both Putin's ambitions and the inevitable consolidation of Russia's major industries by a handful of politically connected billionaires—a shadowy group known as "the oligarchs."[26]

The rise of the oligarchs began before 1990 under the chaotic restructuring of the Soviet economy known as *Perestroika*. This kleptocratic rise accelerated during Yeltsin's privatization era and continued after Putin's election in 2000.[27]

The Americans had wistfully embraced *Perestroika* and privatization as the paths toward fashioning a free market-based, democratic society in Russia. But Putin seized it for a far different opportunity: creating a Soviet-style oligarchy dominated by a handful of industrialists whom he could both enrich and exploit in pursuit of his ultimate goal: to rebuild Russia's empire through the control of global energy resources.[28]

By 2006, Putin had begun his march toward regional (and nuclear) domination when he formed his state-owned atomic umbrella corporation, Rosatom.[29]

The post–Cold War thaw had all but evaporated. The five-day Russian military conflict in 2008 with neighboring Georgia, a key American ally, dashed any remaining hopes inside the Bush administration for a permanent rapprochement with Russia.[30]

Georgia had declared its independence from the Soviet Union in 1991, and its relations with Russia remained tense because of two Russian separatist communities in South Ossetia and Abkhazia. In summer 2008, the Russian military invaded Georgia to take temporary control of the separatist communities. This move forced thousands of non-Russian Georgians to flee before a ceasefire was reached five days later. Eventually, the Russians withdrew, having forever changed the balance of power in the separatist regions.[31]

Putin made it clear that fateful week in August 2008 that he was willing to use military force to meddle in, or outright annex, regions in former Soviet republics that housed large numbers of Russian-separatist populations. The muted response from the West—including a lack of NATO action—only heightened Putin's confidence, as former Secretary of State Condoleezza Rice lamented in a 2018 *Washington Post* op-ed on the tenth anniversary of the Georgian military crisis.[32]

"We could not deter Moscow in this case. But we did act, and Georgia survived. It is still a sad story," she wrote, "and perhaps Putin did take the wrong lessons from it."[33]

Putin indeed learned and recalibrated. He understood that military interventions, like those in Georgia in 2008 (and later Ukraine in 2014), could only be used in limited circumstances under the guise of protecting Russian separatists. Further military invasions risked demonizing him and unifying the West and its NATO alliance against him. Over time, Putin switched tactics. He resumed the tried-and-true method of pursuing his neo-imperialist agenda by leveraging Russia's vast energy resources as a geopolitical weapon.[34]

Putin instinctively saw Russia's vast natural energy resources as a competitive edge—whether within Russia or in the former Soviet states. Putin, like many Russian leaders before him, leveraged Russia's energy resources to reward his friends and punish his enemies.[35]

Through the corrupt privatization of Russia's energy assets and subsequent crony adventures, Putin, his immediate family, and dozens of his closest oligarchs have amassed staggering sums totaling in the tens—or perhaps hundreds—of billions of dollars. An incalculable amount of money was laundered and then stashed in secret accounts all over the world.[36]

Putin also used energy policy as a strategic weapon to threaten his geopolitical friends and foes. Putin has strong-armed entire nations through lopsided energy deals, such as the ones that left neighboring Ukraine so dependent on Russian gas supplies that Kiev was essentially powerless against the invasion of Crimea in 2014. His blatant self-enrichment schemes and blood-soaked crackdowns on dissent are equally alarming.[37]

Putin's power play began with natural gas, a bountiful commodity in Russia that was essential to survive the cold, harsh winters that grip many of the former Soviet republics. Moscow had both the supply and the pipeline distribution system to make its neighbors dependent on Russian gas, which gave Putin the sort of leverage he sought.[38]

Within a few years, Putin expanded the economic battlefield to include the fuel powering commercial nuclear reactors. Uranium was a logical extension. This is where the U.S. comes in.[39]

After the collapse of the Soviet Union, President George H.W. Bush's administration crafted a novel program that incentivized Russia and the other Soviet republics to dismantle their nuclear weapons and convert the uranium from their warheads into peaceful reactor fuel to be bought by American utilities. The senior Bush announced the so-called "Megatons to Megawatts" program in summer 1992, and Bill Clinton formally implemented it the following year. The well-intentioned program empowered Russia to corner a portion of the American energy supply, but, after two decades, Russia's nuclear profits were in jeopardy when the program was poised to sunset in 2013.[40]

In 2008, while the United States was mired in the all-consuming Iraq and Afghan wars, and its worst economic downturn since the Great Depression, Putin and his team secretly began to implement a multiyear plan for the nuclear energy company, Rosatom, to dominate the global uranium market.[41]

As part of Putin's plan, Rosatom created a U.S. shell company (Tenam) to spread goodwill in the form of millions of dollars in gifts, investments, and contracts to American political elites (and to hopefully acquire raw uranium assets in Kazakhstan and the United States). He also used the old KGB tactic of exploiting compromising information—or *kompromat*—to entrap some Americans into corruption. One of the prized assets the company acquired was a nondescript Canadian mining company known as Uranium One.[42]

What no one foresaw was that Putin's nuclear domination scheme would set in motion a decade of cascading political scandals that would stain Democrats and Republicans alike, including the impeachment of America's forty-fifth president. The unlikely dominoes, falling one after the other, exposed just how readily America's ruling classes could be bought, just how easily the U.S. intelligence community could be manipulated by inaccurate information like the Steele dossier, and just how unexpectedly American nuclear security could be compromised.[43]

The seemingly disconnected chain of events leading from the Uranium One scandal to the more recent efforts to take down President Trump came into focus in 2018, shortly after the Democrats made their bombshell revelation that Hillary Clinton's campaign and the DNC had paid for the notorious Steele dossier. This discredited document wove a deceptive tale of Trump-Putin collusion that unleashed a full FBI investigation into Trump's campaign and his early presidency.[44]

The unlikely origins of America's latest standoff with Russia trace back to Obama's November 2008 victory. The forty-fourth president was ushered in by a wave of whimsical hope and shattered one of the last glass ceilings in American politics. The upbeat mantras of "Hope and Change" and "Yes We Can" had sparked an irrepressible optimism inside the Democratic national security establishment. They believed that many of the world's most vexing problems—from Iran to Russia—could be solved by negotiation, reason, and dialogue rather than the strategy of confrontation and warfare embraced by the military-industrial establishment and neoconservative darlings like John McCain, Dick Cheney, and Donald Rumsfeld.[45]

Obama's new national security team was certain that it could reset relations with Moscow after the Georgia crisis, especially with Putin ceding the Russian presidency (temporarily, as it turned out) to a youthful and seemingly Western-friendly politician named Dmitry Medvedev.[46]

In February 2009, Vice President Joe Biden was the first to proclaim the administration's desire to "press the reset button" with Russia. Obama's National Security Council (NSC) advisor Michael McFaul (who later served as Obama's Ambassador to Russia) was the architect of the policy, and Hillary Clinton, as the new Secretary of State, was named to quarterback the reset. Clinton infamously pressed a *literal* red button in a March 2009 meeting with Putin's chief diplomat, Sergey Lavrov. The PR stunt made headlines when Lavrov informed Clinton that she "got it wrong" and used the incorrect Russian word on the "reset" label (McFaul was apparently to blame for the shoddy translation).[47]

Over the next three years, Team Obama pursued policies designed to prop up the Medvedev regime and assist Russia's economy. They facilitated the creation of a Silicon Valley–like city called the Skolkovo Innovation Center. They approved the sale of Uranium One to the Russians. And they replaced the Megatons to Megawatts program with billions of dollars of new guaranteed uranium sales to American utilities.[48]

Medvedev, it turns out, was only a political front man for Putin and not the crusading reformer that the Obama administration had assumed. Under the reset, Medvedev was able to advance Putin's agenda—all under the guise of diplomacy. Among the concessions that the Obama administration made were the following:

- Scrapping plans for missile defense in Europe.
- Slashing U.S. strategic nuclear defense capabilities.
- Surrendering substantial American uranium assets.
- Signing off on billions in new nuclear utility contracts.
- Transferring Silicon Valley technology to the Kremlin.

As it turns out, all of these items were high priorities on Putin's wish list.

Thus, Obama's reset weakened the United States while advancing Putin's plan for domination of global uranium markets and strengthening Russia's economy with new business and technology.[49]

By the time that Rosatom's corrupt activities were exposed by an undercover FBI operative named William Douglas Campbell—a crucial behind-the-scenes player whom we will meet later on—it was already too late. Putin had already usurped all that he wanted and returned to military aggression, this time invading the Crimean region of Ukraine in 2014.[50]

Before the reset was exposed as a failure, though, the crafty Putin had managed to compromise numerous Americans. For example, one of the main U.S. trucking companies entrusted with transporting uranium to nuclear energy facilities was implicated in a Russian bribery scheme. Along the way, several U.S. nuclear utilities (and their unwitting customers) became dependent on Russia's cheap fuel supply (not to mention the American lobbyists and consultants who raked in millions from Kremlin interests).[51]

Bill Clinton took a $500,000 speech fee in Moscow, and his Clinton Foundation accepted sums in excess of $150 million in cash and in-kind contributions (or commitments) from people and entities directly tied to Russia or the Uranium One transaction. And Hillary Clinton's 2016 campaign chairman John Podesta wound up on the board of a "clean energy company" that got a billion-ruble ($35 million) Russian investment.[52]

The cloud of foreign deals, missing emails, and peddled influence had already left a suspicious odor around the Clinton Foundation as Hillary Clinton launched her 2016 presidential campaign. The odor became a stench when Putin's pay-to-play politics was laid bare in 2015 by Peter Schweizer's book *Clinton Cash*, along with a front-page story in the *New York Times*.[53]

The Clintons tried to counter the narrative, claiming that Schweizer's revelations had been debunked. But the facts unearthed by *Clinton Cash* remained unassailable, and soon Trump made the Uranium One episode a centerpiece of his "Crooked Hillary" attacks on the campaign trail.[54]

The "Russian reset" was now a major political liability in the 2016 election, and Clinton's team needed to neutralize the issue. It was this desire, according to one Clinton insider, that led Democrats to launch a massive multipronged opposition research project in late 2015 aimed at tying Republicans to Russia.[55]

"We knew Republicans had their own Russia issues and we wanted to get those out there," the insider told John Solomon in a 2019 interview. The insider said that the research efforts began in a loose, ad hoc way, scouring media articles, creating timelines, and doing basic Google searches like opposition researchers often do. In spring 2016, a DNC contractor took on a more formal effort to organize reporters and activists in Ukraine to look for dirt on longtime GOP lobbyist Paul Manafort.[56]

A top priority for the Clinton campaign was to investigate Manafort's past foreign lobbying activities once he became a senior Trump campaign official. (A DNC official updated the Clinton campaign on the progress of the Ukrainian contractor's efforts, according to a leaked May 2016 email.)[57]

But the anti-Trump effort became more formal and focused in mid-2016 when Fusion GPS, run by a former journalist named Glenn Simpson, approached the Clinton campaign and the DNC with a significant body of research tying the likely GOP nominee to unsavory figures in Russia and a proposed business deal. Fusion GPS was hired by the Clinton and DNC law firm Perkins Coie, and Simpson brought in the former MI6 spy, Christopher Steele, to compile his now-infamous dossier.[58]

What had started as a political neutralization initiative grew far bigger in early July 2016 when Steele brought his lurid mess of unsubstantiated Trump allegations his FBI handler in London, and then to his friend Bruce Ohr—a high-ranking Justice Department official. Soon, the FBI launched an unprecedented counterintelligence investigation targeting Trump, whose subsequent assertions that he was being "wiretapped" were dismissed as a paranoid delusion, at the time, by the national media.[59]

Simpson claims that the campaign did not know about Steele's contact with the FBI until much later, but that some senior campaign officials were briefed by lawyers on some of Steele's findings in early fall 2016 as the campaign was heating up.[60]

After the election, the investigation grew bigger (instead of ending after no evidence was found to support the allegations against Trump). It ultimately led to the firing of FBI Director James Comey and gave rise to the appointment of Special Counsel Robert Mueller. Thus ensued a multi-year political drama that paralyzed the Trump presidency at times with relentless media coverage of what often turned out to be baseless conspiracy theories. Nevertheless, Mueller managed to ensnare a number of former Trump campaign officials in his net, leading to several high-profile convictions.[61]

Prominent Obama intelligence officials like James Comey, James Clapper, and John Brennan lent their prestige to the Russian collusion narrative (with a steady drumbeat of support from Democrats and the national press). The threat of impeachment was made early and often by attention-seeking Democratic members of Congress like Maxine Waters and Jerry Nadler. Adam Schiff went further and stated that Trump could "face the real prospect of jail time."[62]

Even before Mueller released his report, which found no actionable evidence that Trump or his surrogates had colluded with Russia, former New York City Mayor Rudy Giuliani (now the president's hard-charging private attorney) had fatefully turned his attention to the question of whether Democrats had tried to leverage Ukraine to influence the 2016 election or create the false collusion narrative.[63]

Ukraine, a Russian neighbor, was the place where an explosive document called the "black ledger" surfaced during the height of the 2016 election, forcing Trump's then-campaign chairman Manafort to resign over allegations that he had collected millions from pro-Russian politicians in Ukraine.[64]

The ledger's mysterious appearance was suspect from the beginning, but soon became ammunition (along with the Steele dossier) for the Democrats' Trump-Putin collusion theory. Eventually, Manafort's former partner, Rick Gates, would tell Mueller's team that the ledger was a fake. But by that time, the political damage had been done.[65]

In the end, Giuliani's relentless efforts to launch an official investigation on issues related to Ukraine prompted the whistleblower complaint in summer 2019 that, in turn, gave rise to the impeachment proceedings against Trump. When the "whistleblower"—an Obama NSC holdover—heard about a phone call that President Trump made to Ukrainian President Volodymyr Zelensky, he must have panicked.

Trump and his personal attorney may have been dangerously close to the heart of *multiple* corruption scandals that occurred under Obama and Biden. The whistleblower filed a formal complaint and coordinated its weaponization with Congressman Schiff's staffers (more Obama NSC holdovers). Trump was flabbergasted when the whistleblower's complaint led to impeachment proceedings since he believed that it was "a perfect phone call." The irony was striking: as with Uranium One in 2016, Trump was seeking to expose corruption and got blasted for it.[66]

In sum, what started as a straightforward (if typically underhanded) bid by Vladimir Putin for nuclear energy superiority had evolved into a series of full-fledged scandals that posed some of the greatest modern challenges to America's democracy and its revered institutions, including the FBI, the State Department, and even the presidency.[67]

The weakening of America and the enrichment of Putin's cronies during the Obama administration's Russian reset have significantly altered the geopolitical horizon. The failure by America's ruling elite to navigate such treacherous waters, *and* the media's reckless (albeit unwitting) complicity in obscuring Putin's plot, allowed the Russian ruler to rebuild his empire. As we will see in the ensuing chapters, these cascading events will have repercussions for decades to come.[68]

***

In April 2020, we contacted many of the major players mentioned throughout this book: George Soros, John Podesta, Frank Giustra, Ian Telfer, Jose Fernandez, Theodore Kassinger, Amos Hochstein, Eric Ciaramella, Sean Misko, Abigail Grace, Glenn Simpson, Exelon Corporation, and Fusion GPS (among others). We requested an interview with these parties and provided sample questions via email. Most did not respond.

However, we are grateful to Mr. Podesta, Mr. Hochstein, Mr. Kassinger, Mr. Giustra, Mr. Misko, and Ms. Grace for their detailed replies. Mr. Podesta's spokesman provided the following statement: "The Uranium One conspiracy theory has been thoroughly debunked, and John had no involvement with the issue while working in the White House. He does not recall ever discussing the company with his brother or anyone from his firm. John has not had any involvement with the Podesta Group in nearly two decades, and only learned of their work on the subject when it became fodder for baseless political attacks." Mr. Giustra and the others responded similarly.

We would like to emphasize that we do not believe Mr. Giustra (or any private individual) broke any laws nor do we allege that they engaged in criminal or unethical activity of any kind. We simply state verifiable facts. These claims are reinforced by more than one hundred pages of citations (including more than 1,200 endnotes citing official government records, corporate filings, primary source documents, and corroborating reports from legacy media outlets). Thus, our assertions can easily be confirmed.

CHAPTER 2

PUTIN AND THE OLIGARCHS

How Putin Used the Soviet Playbook and Weaponized Energy Deals

"We destroyed everything, all our communications, our lists of contacts and our agents' networks. I personally burned a huge amount of material. We burned so much stuff that the furnace burst. We burned papers night and day.... The materials were destroyed or sent into the archives. Amen!"[1]

—VLADIMIR V. PUTIN, 2000
(on his final days as a KGB officer in East Germany)

"Russian Nuclear Energy Conquers the World," exclaimed the *Pravda* headline on January 22, 2013. The former Soviet propaganda rag celebrated Russian President Vladimir Putin's latest coup.[2]

The Russian atomic energy agency, Rosatom, had just taken full control of a Canadian company called Uranium One Incorporated. Uranium One had a substantial mining portfolio with assets stretching from the United States to Kazakhstan. The takeover brought Putin closer to achieving his goal of owning the largest nuclear company in the world and controlling much of the global uranium supply chain.[3]

Putin achieved this nuclear coup after years of aboveboard lobbying efforts and through surreptitious influence operations.[4] The Uranium One purchase was a blatant muscle-flex by a man who likes to play with tigers, swim with dolphins, and ride bare-chested on horseback through Siberia.[5]

Putin had set his sights on global nuclear domination before President Barack Obama took office and then, just two days after Obama's second inauguration, Putin had achieved a near virtual monopoly (producing more uranium than all American miners combined).[6] In a single purchase, he had gained full control of one of the world's largest uranium mining companies and a nuclear foothold in the land of his greatest adversary.

Uranium One was headquartered in Canada but mined uranium all over the world. The uranium mines in Kazakhstan were Uranium One's crown jewels, and Putin had been eyeing them for nearly a decade.[7] The mines in Wyoming, Texas, and Utah were prized too, but Putin had other, more sinister plans for Uranium One's American assets.[8]

Russia and the Soviet Union before it had mined the other precious yellow metal for nearly as long as the Americans had—more than fifty years.[9] Uranium is well known for its use in nuclear bombs due to its ability to create an explosive chain reaction of devastating power. But it is also used for civilian energy generation and medical purposes. Once uranium ore is extracted from the ground, it is refined into a commercial product known as yellowcake powder. Yellowcake is then enriched to varying levels depending on the end use: low enriched uranium (LEU) for civilian purposes and highly enriched uranium (HEU) for weapons.[10]

The *Pravda* article detailing Russia's nuclear conquest was not just propaganda. Rosatom had already doubled its nuclear fuel sales and shown "impressive results, conquering new markets and penetrating into the markets of competitors." The advantages that Rosatom had over its American, French, and Canadian competitors were significant.[11]

In 2012 alone, Rosatom's portfolio grew by more than $18 billion. American companies like Westinghouse and Honeywell, French company AREVA, and Canadian company Cameco could not compete with Rosatom's variety of products and services, which included mining and enrichment services, power plant construction, and operation.[12]

Rosatom, which Putin had launched in 2007 through a massive restructuring of Russia's many nuclear assets, had the full backing of the Kremlin. Rosatom was neither a federal agency nor a private corporation. It was a public-private hybrid entity.[13]

As a quasi-state-owned enterprise, Rosatom enjoyed advantages that its Western competitors did not: its expenditures were subsidized, its profits were privatized, and its losses were socialized.

Putin's nuclear powerhouse basically had a blank checkbook from the Kremlin while retaining the autonomy and privacy of a corporation. As such, Rosatom dominated the entire nuclear fuel cycle in ways no private competitor could dream of doing.[14]

Western competitors at this time were suffering from "Fukushima syndrome," and their governments placed nuclear projects on hold. Putin doubled down on nuclear energy and sent Rosatom on a buying spree. Acquisitions like Uranium One were just part of Putin's strategy—the supply side. He also dominated the demand side by building nuclear power plants, particularly in regions fraught with controversy.[15]

Crucial to Putin's nuclear strategy was the development of Iran's Bushehr reactor, a project that previous American administrations had deemed unacceptable. Putin completed the construction of the Bushehr reactor in 2012, all with U.S. President Obama's blessing (despite hard evidence that Iran was secretly continuing an illegal nuclear weapons program).[16]

Putin's strategy was to create new customers for Rosatom in China and Venezuela as well. In addition to his desire for nuclear partnerships with brutal, anti-American dictators like Iran's Hassan Rouhani, China's Hu Jintao, and Venezuela's Hugo Chavez, Putin even worked with Syria's Bashar al-Assad on developing Syria's nuclear program.[17]

Despite these troublesome dealings with American adversaries, Putin was able to convince the Obama administration that Russia was America's friend. Putin was somehow able to extract concessions from Obama for both Russia and Putin's friends in Iran and Syria.[18]

Not only did Putin win considerable nuclear concessions from Obama (Uranium One, the 123 Agreement, New START, and other nuclear agreements), he also got help from Obama in the military space as well—particularly bolstering Russia's cyber capabilities.[19]

The potential damage to America's national security as a result of Obama's "Russian reset" was incalculable.[20]

Putin's successful cornering of the global uranium market was entirely predictable, driven by his quest to restore the Russian empire and turn the post-Soviet rubble into a great power. It was the culmination of his entire career, which has made him a highly disciplined, focused wielder of power.[21]

The untold tale behind that story is one that involves not just the Russian president, but also a current and a former American president, and the candidate who wanted to be the successor.

Putin's Rise to Power

On New Year's Eve, 1999—the day before Y2K—men, women, and children around the world waited nervously, counting down to the digital apocalypse. But not Vladimir Putin. For Putin, December 31, 1999, was the day he seized full control of one of the largest atomic arsenals in the world, thanks to his appointment from the outgoing President Boris Yeltsin. The nuclear button, quite literally, was finally within Putin's reach.[22]

Growing up in the city known in the Soviet Union as Leningrad, Vladimir Vladimirovich Putin had wanted to be a spy since he was a teenager. In 1968, while patriotic Czechs led the unsuccessful "Prague Spring" uprising against the Soviets, the young Vladimir was captivated by the KGB heroes in the new Soviet spy thriller movie, *The Shield and the Sword*.[23]

At almost sixteen and still in high school, Putin showed up at the door of KGB headquarters in his hometown. He was initially turned away by KGB officers for lack of experience, but walked away with the hope that his chances of being accepted might increase if he were to go to law school. He was warned not to contact the agency again, but he did not have to: a KGB recruiter came to him about seven years later.[24]

Against his parents' wishes, Putin enrolled in Leningrad State University's law school in 1970. As he was finishing his studies, the KGB recruited him. Putin was *officially* a KGB asset from 1975 until August 1991, when he retired with the rank of lieutenant colonel.[25]

From 1975 until the early 1980s, Putin spent his time spying on foreigners for the KGB. Sometime after 1980, Putin was "summoned to Moscow…to attend the elite [Soviet] foreign intelligence training institute."[26]

He did well. Putin was promoted to director of a Soviet-German friendship society in the KGB station in communist East Germany beginning in 1985. Operating from Dresden, Putin worked with Matthias Warnig, a comrade spy working for the East German secret police (or "Stasi"). Both Warnig and Putin worked in counterintelligence. One of Putin's final KGB assignments in Dresden was recruiting Westerners.[27]

In the tense days after the fall of the Berlin Wall, crowds surrounded Putin's office in Dresden. Putin recalled going outside to try to calm the rioting crowds and to prevent looters from ransacking his office, thereby "saving the lives of the [double-agents] whose files were lying on my desk." Putin said he and his KGB comrades "burned so much stuff that the furnace exploded."[28]

The Cold War had, by 1991, crushed Russia. Defeated militarily and depressed economically, the former empire was in shambles. Compounding the misery, the First Chechen War broke out between November and December 1994 and, on New Year's Eve, Yeltsin's forces stormed Grozny, the capital city of Chechnya.[29]

The brutality and bloodshed that followed was described as an "unimaginable catastrophe" by international monitors, and even former Soviet leader Mikhail Gorbachev called the conflict a "disgraceful, bloody adventure." Amid the post-Soviet chaos, Putin's spy craft evolved into statecraft.[30]

When Putin returned to his hometown in 1990, he was still a KGB officer, waiting like so many others for his next assignment in the "active reserves." The Leningrad he returned to was a very different place: an absolute free-for-all was underway, and the city soon changed its name to St. Petersburg. So much money and natural resources were leaving the country that a complete accounting would prove impossible.[31]

By some estimates, the outflow of raw materials alone included "60 tons of gold, 8 [tons] of platinum, 150 [tons] of silver," as well as an immense amount of oil, believed to be worth "between $15 billion and $50 billion."[32]

For an ambitious and well-traveled KGB officer like Putin, opportunities were ripe for the plucking.

Mayor Anatoly Sobchak became Putin's mentor and a ticket to the summit of power. While working in the St. Petersburg mayor's office, Putin took full advantage of the position "as he rose through the ranks."[33]

Putin and his cronies would steal and launder enormous sums of public money out of St. Petersburg, through Germany and other countries via questionable energy and real estate deals.[34]

In 1996, Sobchak lost his mayoral reelection after his opponent received powerful support from Moscow.[35] Shortly after Sobchak's defeat, Putin was "rather harshly" evicted from his plush office, and Sobchak fled the country.[36]

For Putin, it was only a temporary setback. He retreated, too, but not so far away. Putin moved out of the city to his lake-front *dacha* (or "mansion") on the shores of Lake Komsomol'skoye. Putin allegedly acquired the lakefront estate by evicting the local villagers. An investigation found that "the person who bought the land, scared the local residents, burning down their little houses if they refused to sell them, was a St. Petersburg officer who turned out to be none other than Vladimir Vladimirovich Putin."[37]

It was here that the soon-to-be notorious Ozero (translates to "lake") Cooperative was headquartered. Putin's neighbors built their palatial dachas around him. They were his cronies from St. Petersburg, including at least one member who was linked to Russian organized crime.[38]

Security for the ritzy, lakefront Ozero neighborhood was reportedly provided by a company called Rif-Security, which was run by a well-known mafioso named Vladimir Barsukov (the alleged head of the Tambov gang and sometimes called Kumarin) and Ozero's leader Vladimir Smirnov.[39]

It is perhaps no surprise that former spies and Russian mafia operators found each other and built alliances. During Russia's chaotic transition toward capitalism, KGB veterans and organized crime lords shared two crucial advantages over other Russians: they had business experience, and they were risk-takers. These qualities helped turn these otherwise unremarkable men into billionaires, almost overnight.

Soon Putin's social circle would fill with notorious oligarchs. Together, they would plunder their country's resources. Before Putin's kleptocracy could be fully realized, there was another setback: Putin's lakeside dacha burned to the ground in August 1996.[40]

Putin admitted later he was able to "force" his contractors to rebuild the Ozero dacha "even better" than the original.[41]

Putin's retreat did not last long. He had signed on to work for President Boris Yeltsin's 1996 re-election campaign, and following Yeltsin's victory, Putin moved to Moscow. He soon found himself in the good graces of the Russian president.[42]

Putin's success under Yeltsin catapulted his career—and spread his reputation as someone willing to sacrifice anyone and anything to attain power.

One of Putin's many strengths is his ability to use tragic events to his best advantage. As he had done with his burned dacha, Putin would find a way to come back stronger. Like the famous Slavic legend of the firebird, time and again, Putin rose from the ashes in a way that can only be described as meteoric.[43] His new boss, Boris Yeltsin, would not be so lucky.

The First Chechen War had been a disaster, draining economic and military resources, as thousands of Russian troops and tens of thousands of civilians perished in the conflict.[44]

The fledgling Russian economy was also in tatters, and its transition to some form of market economy was agonizingly slow. Into these challenges jumped a young reformer named Anatoly Chubais with a scheme to hasten this transition by privatizing state-owned property.[45]

Chubais' early privatization efforts attracted both wealthy investors and average citizens who were looking to participate in Russia's new capitalist experiment.[46] But the program would wipe out middle-class savings while foreign investors and emerging Russian oligarchs (dubbed "the kleptocrats") seized billions. Chubais allegedly allowed his cronies to unfairly acquire Russia's prized assets.[47]

One of Chubais' first efforts in 1995 was a creative auction program called "Loans for Shares." This program was the primary scheme that created many of the first post-Soviet oligarchs.[48]

As Harvard economics professor Marshall Goldman explained it, Loans for Shares was how "[Mikhail] Khodorkovsky got a 78 percent share of ownership in Yukos, worth about $5 billion, for a mere $310 million, and how Boris Berezovsky got Sibneft, another oil giant, worth $3 billion, for about $100 million." As ordinary Russians suffered in the turbulent economy, Chubais came under fire from Yeltsin's nationalist opposition, who viewed his auctions as more corruption and kleptocracy.[49]

The new Russian oligarchs weren't the only ones who capitalized on Chubais' privatization schemes. Billionaire financier George Soros saw the potential as well. The man who had previously made a fortune speculating on the British pound and was commonly referred to as "the man who broke the Bank of England" invested at least $2.5 billion during the Russian privatization era.[50]

Soros and Harvard University's endowment management company were the only foreign investors allowed to invest in Chubais' Loans for Shares program in 1995, and both quickly became top shareholders in Russia's second-largest steel mill, an oil company with reserves that rivaled Mobil, and Russia's growing bond market.[51]

In 1997, a Soros-led consortium snapped up a 25 percent stake in one of Russia's largest telecom companies, a move he would soon regret. At the time, Soros praised Russia for "moving away from robber-baron capitalism to a law-abiding capitalism where shareholders rights are protected." Later he declared it "the worst investment" of his career.[52]

Chubais had become a darling of Western officials and investors who celebrated the capitalist feeding frenzy, but Russians soon grew tired of his schemes. Yeltsin became critical of Chubais and sacked the young reformer in January 1996. "How those auctions were fouled up," Yeltsin moaned, "[o]ur enterprises were sold for next to nothing!"[53]

Shortly after he fired Chubais in an official capacity, though, Yeltsin (who needed all the help he could get) quietly rehired "the reformist" to manage the 1996 reelection campaign.

Despite rapidly sinking approval ratings, Yeltsin's alliance with Western leaders like President Clinton kept him afloat. In 1996, Clinton deployed a battalion of his own closest veteran political advisors, like Dick Morris and Richard Dresner, to help keep Yeltsin in office. When accusations of American meddling went public, Yeltsin's team implied that Clinton's political consultants had limited or no contact with Chubais or other top Yeltsin campaign officials since "when all the real decisions were made, they were not present."[54]

Indeed, while Clinton's political strategists did help the Yeltsin campaign with polling and research, "it was money that tipped the balance."[55]

Clinton, with the help of British Prime Minister John Major, French President Jacques Chirac, and German Chancellor Helmut Kohl, pressured the IMF to provide Yeltsin with more than $10 billion in loans. Critics claimed that the Americans, British, French, *and* Germans had effectively meddled in the 1996 election in an attempt to keep communist Gennady Zyuganov from winning, and destroying their capitalist dealings.[56]

During Yeltsin's two terms in office, the IMF would provide around $40 billion in loans to Russia. Like other untold billions in Russia, much of the IMF money simply vanished.

At least some of the missing IMF money is believed to have made its way into Yeltsin's campaign coffers. Russian presidential candidates' private financing is capped at $2.9 million. Yeltsin campaign officials *admitted* they spent at least $100 million. His opponents believe it was actually anywhere from $500 million to more than $2 *billion*.[57]

Yeltsin's emissary to the IMF was none other than Anatoly Chubais. During the 1996 campaign, Chubais was excoriated by Russian media when two associates were arrested carrying boxes filled with $538,000 in cash out of the main Kremlin office.[58] Chubais later acknowledged that Russia had taken advantage of the IMF and other Western lenders, stating that "we conned them out of $20 billion."[59]

Yeltsin won reelection with 53.8 percent of the vote despite single-digit poll numbers in the months before the election. Critics claimed that the election was rigged, and the Russian economy still stagnated despite the billions from the IMF.[60]

His so-called "reformers," Prime Minister (PM) Sergei Kiriyenko and Vice Premier and financial guru Chubais, among others, came under fire after their privatization schemes built an über-wealthy oligarch class while ordinary Russians suffered.[61]

The missing IMF money did not entirely thwart the reformist's career trajectory—quite the opposite. Chubais was named "Finance Minister of the Year" by the Western magazine *Euromoney* in 1997. In March 1998, Yeltsin promoted Kiriyenko from minister of energy to PM (replacing longtime PM Viktor Chernomyrdin).[62]

In August 1998, the massive debts Russia had racked up finally caught up with them and the market crashed—almost overnight. Yeltsin had no choice but to fire his entire cabinet, including Chubais and Kiriyenko.[63]

All in all, it was a year of turmoil for Yeltsin before he eventually settled on a PM of his liking in August 1999: a relative unknown named Vladimir Putin.[64]

Putin's Rise to the Presidency

In July 1998, Yeltsin installed Putin as the new head of the Federal Security Service (FSB), the successor to the KGB.[65] Putin swiftly restructured the entire organization and installed his old KGB comrades and friends from St. Petersburg. He also eliminated two crucial directorates that were tasked with investigating white-collar financial crimes—the kind that implicated oligarchs and members of the Yeltsin family.[66]

Putin's loyalists—Sergey Chemezov, Sergey Ivanov, and Nikolai Patrushev, among others—were placed in charge of various subagencies within the new FSB. Later, when Putin became president, Chemezov, Ivanov, and Patrushev were put in charge of Russia's intelligence and military-industrial complex.[67]

Details of Putin's rapid rise to Yeltsin's inner circle are hazy. Given the KGB's intense secrecy, this is no surprise. A senior fellow at the conservative Cato Institute named Andrei Illarionov was once Putin's chief economic advisor but was dismissed in 2005 for criticizing the administration's policies. Illarionov had a falling out with Putin and his crew of ex-KGB spooks whom he now calls "Siloviki Incorporated." According to Illarionov, Putin's SI operates under a strict code: they always take care of their own and abide by "the custom of omertà" (the mafia code of silence).[68]

Just a few short months after Putin took control of the FSB, his first major scandal occurred. In November 1998, Boris Berezovsky, a renowned oligarch from Yeltsin's inner circle, wrote an open letter in *Kommersant* accusing a faction within the FSB of conspiring to assassinate him.[69]

Lieutenant Colonel Alexander Litvinenko alleged that he and other FSB operatives in charge of combating organized crime groups (an alleged "death squad" unit known as "URPO") were tasked with carrying out the hit. Litvinenko was close to the oligarch, having worked for him as a bodyguard in the past. Litvinenko admitted that he warned his former boss, Berezovsky, of the sinister plot and later held a press conference that blasted Putin's predecessors at the FSB. This appears to be the first time Litvinenko dared to expose top-level corruption within the FSB. It would not be the last.[70]

After the news died down, Putin personally and publicly demonstrated his loyalty to the powerful oligarch by showing up uninvited to Berezovsky's birthday party in February 1999. At that time, Berezovsky had been implicated in the notorious $10 billion Bank of New York (BNY) money-laundering scandal. Prosecutors were out for blood.[71]

Then-PM Yevgeny Primakov was on a corruption crusade against Berezovsky and "the [Yeltsin] Family." Primakov reportedly did not like Putin and fought the latter's appointment "from the very beginning." At the birthday party, Putin reportedly told Berezovsky that he "[didn't] care what Primakov thinks," and signaled loyalty to the oligarch over PM Primakov. Putin's shrewd support for Berezovsky must have been substantial as it became mutual and further fueled Putin's rise.[72]

The Russian economy began to collapse in the summer of 1998. Meanwhile, Putin restructured the FSB to serve his and his friends' interests. Putin's boss, Yeltsin, the so-called reformers, and Yeltsin's cronies—"the oligarchs"—were deemed total failures. But Putin had been just far enough away at the FSB to avoid being blamed.

Against this unruly backdrop, Yeltsin promoted Putin to prime minister—the second most powerful position in Russia. Putin was Yeltsin's fifth PM in less than a year and was narrowly confirmed by the Duma on August 16, 1999.[73]

Despite the fact that Putin was a political novice, Yeltsin praised his "vast experience" and promised that Putin would enact reforms if elected to be his successor. Putin soon converted the Russian public's outrage over the corruption and chaos during the Yeltsin era into a new and even more powerful motivator: fear.[74]

However, despite Yeltsin's backing, Putin had minimal support in the polls (under 2 percent) at the time of his appointment. Almost immediately (and perhaps not coincidentally), Putin had the benefit of a political distraction when an army of approximately two thousand misfits—comprising Chechen rebels, Arab mujahideen, and Wahhabi fighters—invaded Chechnya's neighbor, Dagestan. Putin saw opportunity in the chaos.[75]

Within weeks of Putin taking over as Yeltsin's prime minister, Russia entered the Second Chechen War.[76]

The conflict had been stoked, in large part, by a series of bombings that rocked Russia between August 31 and September 16 1999.[77]

One of the first bombs targeted Russian military barracks in Dagestan on September 4, 1999. Dozens of Russian soldiers and their family members were killed. An Islamic Chechen separatist initially claimed responsibility (but later retracted), kicking off a Kremlin narrative blaming Chechen terrorists for each of the acts that followed.[78]

The Dagestan bombing struck a military target out of sight and out of mind of most Russian citizens. The next bomb struck at the very heart of Russia. Less than a week after the Dagestan barracks bombing, an eight-story apartment building in Moscow was blown to rubble, killing more than a hundred men, women, and children in their sleep. The Kremlin almost immediately declared it a Chechen terrorist attack.[79]

Moscow and other major cities were thrown into hysteria overnight. Virtually everywhere was on high alert. On September 13 just past 5:00 a.m., another bomb struck a separate apartment building, killing 118 Muscovites. Three hours before that blast, Russian authorities had responded to a call to investigate suspicious activity at the apartment, but somehow they overlooked the enormous bomb placed in the basement.[80]

Adding to the confusion, the head of Russia's lower parliament mistakenly reported to his fellow Duma members that a bomb had struck an apartment in the city of Volgodonsk. The misinformation appeared to be an honest mistake. Or it was prescient. On September 16, a real bomb in Volgodonsk killed eighteen more apartment dwellers. The bombings began to reek of a conspiracy.[81]

On September 22, residents of an apartment building in Ryazan, a city southeast of Moscow, were horrified when they witnessed three individuals deposit three large bags in the basement and quickly speed away. When the police arrived, they reportedly found the bags filled with explosives.[82]

A manhunt began throughout Ryazan. When the culprits were apprehended, they shockingly produced FSB credentials, usually a badge known as a *vezdekhod*, which permitted FSB agents to go anywhere, public or private, and do anything. FSB headquarters called the local authorities and asked them to release the operatives.[83]

The events that followed raised suspicions that Putin and his KGB-turned-FSB apparatchiks had perpetrated a "false-flag attack" on Russian civilians.[84]

Less than two days after that incident, new FSB director Nikolai Patrushev gave a press conference claiming that the whole thing had been a misunderstanding. There were no explosives. In fact, he said, it was all an FSB "training exercise." Residents were supposed to ignore the fact that local authorities had performed a chemical analysis proving the bags were filled with a powerful explosive called RDX.[85]

The Ryazan incident marked the end of the bombing spree, but by that point the death toll had topped two hundred and thousands more were injured. Russian citizens were sufficiently terrified.[86]

Whatever doubts were held about the official Kremlin narrative and "training exercises" were suppressed, and calls for retaliation against Chechnya reached a fever pitch. By the end of September 1999, PM Putin had become the face of the war effort.[87]

Within hours of the Ryazan incident, the Russian air force carpet bombed the Chechen capital of Grozny. Putin's scorched-earth campaign forced hundreds of thousands of civilians—more than half the population—to flee Chechnya as refugees to neighboring republics. Grozny was destroyed; witnesses compared the scene to the atomic destruction of Hiroshima.[88]

Regardless of who was really to blame for the bombings, the Russian people had been craving a decisive and fearless leader, and that is exactly what Putin offered. The Yeltsin era was marred by uncertainty, misery, economic desperation (exacerbated by external and internal plunder of state resources), and overall weakness.[89]

In his book *Deception*, Edward Lucas describes how the Russian people yearn for the respect their country once had:

> They mourn the Soviet Union's power, not its politics. They recall growing up in a great country—a superpower—defined by the size of its nuclear arsenal, its global reach, and its wartime sacrifice. In their lifetime, all that disappeared. The Soviet system became the butt of jokes—for the senility of its gerontocratic leadership, for the poor quality of its consumer goods and for the omnipresent shortages. What came next was worse: the humiliating retreat from the old empire, the acceptance of German reunification on the West's terms, and playing second fiddle to America in global politics…. Their driving concern now is to restore Russia's standing in the world, and to prevent the West from ever again exploiting its weakness.[90]

Handed another pile of rubble, Putin seized the day and used it to his advantage. Yeltsin would resign by year's end.

By early 2000, Putin was completely in control. He brought the Chechen separatists to their knees and established control over Chechnya, appointing the pro-Russian Akhmad Kadyrov as ruler of the Chechen government in June 2000. Even so, terrorist acts, suicide bombings, and skirmishes would continue—including the assassination of President Kadyrov in 2004—fueling the conflict for years afterward.[91]

Putin's reputation as a merciless ruler and fervent Russian nationalist earned the respect of the Russian people. His approval rating soared amid the bombings and their aftermath. Meanwhile, at the same time the second Chechen conflict was raging, a plan to ensure Putin would be Yeltsin's permanent replacement was already underway.[92]

In November 1999, the powerful oligarch Berezovsky traveled to Washington to meet with President Clinton's longtime friend and Russia expert, Strobe Talbott. In Washington, Berezovsky sang Putin's praises and assured Talbott that Putin would be a friend of the U.S. and the North Atlantic Treaty Organization (NATO). Financier George Soros, who knew Berezovsky, explained what the oligarch was up to:

> Berezovsky and Yeltsin's Family [i.e., his circle of associates] were looking for a way to perpetuate the immunity they enjoyed under the Yeltsin administration…Berezovsky's situation turned desperate when the scandal broke over the laundering of Russian illegal money in U.S. banks in 1999, for he realized that he could no longer find refuge in the West. One way or the other he had to find a successor to Yeltsin who would protect him. That is when the plan to promote Putin's candidacy was hatched.[93]

Talbott had already met with Putin in June of that year and publicly praised him. The week after Putin was elected president in March 2000, Talbott testified in Congress to answer the question on everyone's mind—*Who is Vladimir Putin?* Talbott's tone was complimentary, and he took every opportunity to highlight Putin's commitment to democratic ideals. However, he equivocated over whether to trust Putin and ultimately concluded, the "short answer, of course, is that we don't know."[94]

In December 1999, Putin gave a speech on "Security Organs Day" (also called "Chekist Day") at Moscow's intelligence headquarters building (called the Lubyanka). "Putin said that 'the mission of the group of FSB officers sent undercover to work in the government is being accomplished successfully.'"[95]

As time went on, it became clearer that Putin's crew of ex-KGB spooks—Siloviki Inc.—had entrenched itself in every Russian sector, from the Kremlin to private business and the media. As Putin's former chief economic advisor put it, "there are now few areas of Russian life where [Siloviki Inc.'s] long arm fails to reach."[96]

Putin's Energy Kleptocracy

With the turn of the new millennium and the final exit of Boris Yeltsin from the stage, President Putin moved swiftly and tactically re-nationalizing (or privatizing/piratizing as the case may be) Russia's strategic industries. Russia's vast natural resources—especially uranium and oil—were crucial to his geopolitical strategy.

Just as he had done with restructuring the FSB in 1998, Putin quickly appointed cronies from his inner circle to run Russia's energy and military-industrial complexes—positions of enormous power and profit—as soon as he became president.

One of Putin's earliest moves was restructuring Russia's electricity distribution network: Unified Energy System (UES). This effectively created a monopoly on the national high-voltage transmission grid and the local utility grids.

The UES supplied electrical power not just to Russia but to the neighboring republics too. The plan reportedly "angered both minority shareholders, who [feared] it could pave the way for an asset-grab, and [the opposition party], which described it as 'criminal.'"[97]

Putin placed control of Russia's *literal* power in the hands of his inner circle lieutenants (like the so-called reformist Anatoly Chubais and, later, the Siloviki Inc. head Igor Sechin). The Kremlin retained a controlling stake.[98]

Putin did likewise with other critical Russian industries, placing his close friend Vladimir Smirnov in charge of Russia's nuclear sales corporation. Smirnov was a round- and ruddy-faced man with a thick mustache. He and Putin met in Germany in 1990 and discussed early investments in St. Petersburg.[99]

They were part of a trade delegation to Frankfurt in 1992 and, by November 1996, Smirnov had become one of Putin's closest inner circle members and the leader of the notorious Ozero Cooperative. In the early 2000s, Putin put Smirnov in charge of the nuclear sales behemoth Techsnabexport (Tenex) when he began restructuring Russia's nuclear programs.[100]

Putin's so-called inner circle consisted of an assortment of old KGB comrades like Smirnov, Ivanov, and Chemezov, and licit and illicit business partners from St. Petersburg like Nikolai Shamalov, Vladimir Yakunin, Yuri Kovalchuk, and the Fursenko brothers. The Ozero group was "the inner circle of Putin's inner circle."[101]

Ozero co-founder Yuri Kovalchuk became widely known as "Putin's banker," and runs the Putin insider bank: Rossiya Bank. His son, Boris, also held Rossiya Bank stock and later became CEO and chairman of the executive board of the Inter RAO UES—one of Russia's largest and most powerful monopolies.[102]

The Kovalchuk and Shamalov families remain major stakeholders in Rossiya Bank, as do several other close associates of Putin. Putin has benefitted directly from Rossiya Bank since 1992, and the bank has been described as the "mega piggy bank of Putin's entourage."[103]

As Putin's power increased, so did his fortunes and the fortunes of his cronies. By 2005, Rossiya Bank had purchased a 51 percent stake in SOGAZ, a gas insurance company that insures all of Russian petroleum giant Gazprom's major (pipeline and exploration) projects. Rossiya Bank paid $58 million for the stake, which was valued at around $2 billion.[104]

When Putin came to power in 2000, he brought his St. Petersburg deputy Alexey Miller with him to Moscow. First, Putin installed Miller as deputy energy minister and later as CEO of Gazprom.[105] Putin reportedly owns a 4.5 percent stake in Gazprom, among other companies he and his cronies control. Under Putin's reign, Gazprom has become the world's largest oil and gas producer, consistently generating over $100 billion in annual revenue.[106]

One way for the cronies to repay Putin and demonstrate their loyalty to him, appears to be putting Putin's family members on the payroll. Shamalov's son, Kirill, would eventually marry Putin's daughter, Katerina Putina (also known as Katerina Tikhonova). Katerina's holdings via her marriage to Kirill are estimated at around $2 billion.[107]

The Shamalovs and other inner circle oligarchs (such as Sechin and Chemezov) have enriched Putin's daughter directly through several initiatives, which are funded by Rosatom and Gazprombank, among other Putin-connected entities.[108] Kickbacks are a central and recurring theme in Putin's ascent to power. Like most corrupt regimes, those who keep the dictator and his family well paid remain in his good graces.

The St. Petersburg Real Estate Holding Co. (German-registered "SPAG") and Petersburg Fuel Company (Russia-registered "PTK") were two significant kickback vehicles established by Putin and his cronies in 1992 and 1994, respectively. SPAG would later become famous for being one of Putin Inc.'s earliest money-laundering operations.[109]

Putin scholar Karen Dawisha explains how the SPAG money-laundering operation worked. In essence, Putin was a major gatekeeper in the St. Petersburg mayor's office. As the head of the city's Committee on Foreign Economic Relations ("KVS"), Putin granted licenses for foreign exchanges in and out of St. Petersburg.[110]

Putin's deputies in the KVS were Alexey Miller (now head of Gazprom) and Dmitry Medvedev, among others. Medvedev acted essentially as Putin's legal clerk and advisor. His office was right outside Putin's, and he helped mastermind some of Putin's early schemes. According to an audit by the Russian Federation, "in 1994, the humble clerk Medvedev owned 10% of Europe's largest pulp and paper mill. Even then he was a millionaire. And this was only Medvedev, Putin's advisor. Can you imagine what kind of money was already owned by his boss?"[111]

The sums of money flowing into *and especially out* of Russia at that time were massive and unprecedented.[112]

Both SPAG and PTK connected Putin closely to the Russian mafias known as the Malyshev and Tambov gangs through Vladimir Smirnov and Vladimir Kumarin.[113]

According to Smirnov, Putin's longtime close friend, they first met in Frankfurt in 1991 and returned to that city with a trade delegation in 1992 to register SPAG. Smirnov was the co-owner of two SPAG subsidiaries in Russia that also employed Kumarin. Furthermore, Smirnov and other friends of Putin's from his KGB days founded PTK in 1994. Both the SPAG and PTK operations required licenses from Putin's office, which were granted in July 1994 and August 1994, respectively. One major investor in PTK was the "personal bank" for Putin and his associates: Rossiya Bank.[114]

Vladimir Kumarin, also known as "the Night Governor," was the alleged leader of the ruthless Tambov gang, accused of money laundering, racketeering, contract killings, drug and human trafficking, and other violent crimes.[115] According to Kumarin's own estimates, "Putin had signed between eight hundred and eighteen hundred contracts during the early 1990s."[116]

In early 1995, Putin granted PTK the exclusive rights to build gasoline stations throughout St. Petersburg and to supply the city's massive fleet of municipal vehicles—every vehicle from cars and city buses to fire trucks, police cars, and ambulances. Putin also granted PTK authority to "participate in the formulation of policies of the St. Petersburg Mayor's Office in the area of [gasoline] supply."[117]

SPAG and PTK both benefitted from Deputy Mayor Putin's sweetheart deals and were run by members of Putin's inner circle (including his mayor's office cronies, Ozero Cooperative co-founders, ex-KGB comrades, and even mafiosos). Dawisha claims that Putin profited both personally and substantially. Herman Gref was another Putin crony affiliated with SPAG, and he became one of Putin's closest economic advisors.[118]

Putin was on the board of SPAG beginning in 1992 and subsequently granted Smirnov power of attorney to vote on behalf of the St. Petersburg Mayor's Office, a major SPAG shareholder. The unusual arrangement led to multiple international criminal investigations. Offices were raided and arrests were made. Somehow, Putin escaped unscathed.[119]

On May 23, 2000, shortly after his inauguration, Putin resigned from the SPAG board. But SPAG was not Putin's only self-enrichment scheme. Twentieth Trust, for example, was an entity that Putin had used to launder the kickbacks from the KVS office in St. Petersburg to international real estate ventures in at least eight countries, according to investigators. The criminal investigation into Twentieth Trust was closed three months after Putin's inauguration.[120]

It appears that as investigators closed in on one Putin scheme, Putin simply cut ties and formed a new one.

The same month Putin was inaugurated, Gunvor Trading was formally established by Putin's close friend Gennady Timchenko. Thanks to Putin's connections, Swiss-based Gunvor rapidly became one of the largest oil traders in the world. According to a now-scrubbed article in *The Economist*, Gunvor's byzantine ownership structure "looks like a Chinese puzzle...and has estimated revenues of $70 billion a year."[121]

Putin reportedly owns a 50 percent stake in Gunvor, contributing significant sums to his personal fortune, which totals about $40 billion (according to a CIA assessment). Putin, of course, denied suggestions about his wealth, calling them "rubbish picked out of someone's nose and smeared on bits of paper."[122]

The German secret police (BND) had a file on Putin's SPAG money-laundering operation. In July 2001, prosecutors in Liechtenstein indicted two of SPAG's founders, Rudolf Ritter and Eugene von Hoffer, on money-laundering charges. The BND believed that SPAG had laundered millions of dollars for the Russian mafia as well as Colombian drug cartels.[123]

But German Chancellor Gerhard Schroeder, who called Putin a "flawless democrat," apparently made the BND's case against Putin disappear. As it turns out, Schroeder was appointed to the head of the shareholders committee of the lucrative Russian gas pipeline company, Nord Stream (which supplies Germany with fuel), shortly after leaving office.[124]

But SPAG was just one of several instances where Putin's Russian and German relationships overlapped. The German connection dates back to his days working as a KGB officer in Dresden between 1975 and 1990.

It was in Dresden where Putin met then-Stasi officer Matthias Warnig. In those days, the Soviets and the East Germans cooperated closely—especially on intelligence and espionage operations. Putin and Warnig were photographed together during an awards ceremony in Dresden. Over time, Putin and Warnig became very close.[125]

Warnig went to work for Dresdner Bank—one of Germany's oldest financial institutions—in March 1990, shortly after the Stasi disbanded. In 1991, Dresdner tasked Warnig with opening a branch in St. Petersburg. As luck would have it, Warnig knew just the man to talk to.[126]

Putin plucked Dresdner Bank's application from the stack and personally authorized Dresdner's entry into the Russian banking market. Two years later, Russia imposed a moratorium on licensing foreign banks, essentially protecting Dresdner from increased competition.[127]

Warnig was reportedly an early investor in Rossiya Bank and, when Putin needed help bringing oil tycoon Mikhail Khodorkovsky to heel, Warnig facilitated the transfer of wealth.[128]

Before Putin very publicly stripped him of all his assets and dignity in 2005, Khodorkovsky was the most powerful (and wealthy) oligarch in post-Soviet Russia. His personal funds were estimated at a staggering $18 billion—the bulk of which comprised his majority stake in Yukos, one of Russia's largest oil companies.[129]

During the buccaneering days of early-nineties Russia, virtually every oligarch amassed his fortune through crooked means—including alleged kidnapping, extortion, and murder. Khodorkovsky was no exception. He was by no means the most deplorable criminal (relatively speaking), but Khodorkovsky's enterprises were known to have openly violated Russian law with impunity.[130]

Putin knew that oligarchs like Khodorkovsky held the keys to the kingdom: Russia's vast natural resources. The oligarchs that came to power under Yeltsin were skeptical of Putin, and many of them were not his biggest fans. The feeling was mutual. Putin realized, however, that to go to war with multiple oligarchs at once was a fool's errand. So, he kept his friends close, his enemies closer, and then singled out the biggest enemy of all as an example.[131]

Khodorkovsky amassed his fortune through a series of corrupt deals. In 1995, he participated in a Chubais Loans for Shares scheme. Khodorkovsky's bank loaned the cash-strapped Kremlin $159 million, and the Kremlin put up a 45 percent stake in Yukos—a prized state-owned asset—as collateral. The terms of the scheme basically guaranteed that the Kremlin would default on the loan.[132]

When the Kremlin predictably defaulted, Khodorkovsky gained nearly half of Yukos, which at the time was worth more than $3 billion—or nearly an 1,800 percent gain. Not bad. Within days, Khodorkovsky snapped up another 33 percent of Yukos from the distressed Kremlin for just $150 million. Khodorkovsky took full control of one of Russia's most prized assets for pennies on the dollar.[133]

By 2003, Khodorkovsky had turned Yukos into a global player that supplied nearly 2 percent of the world's oil and 20 percent of Russia's domestic production. Yukos was the model Russian success story. The company was the first of its kind to adopt international accounting standards and to institute Generally Accepted Accounting Principles (GAAP). Yukos even hired Western world giant Pricewaterhouse-Coopers to sign off on their audit reports. Khodorkovsky apparently thought that these reforms made him untouchable. They did not.[134]

When Khodorkovsky began accusing Putin of corruption and infringement of civil rights, he poked the bear. When Khodorkovsky started donating heavily to Putin's opponents, he woke the bear. When he set up a complex international business deal that involved Western acquisitions of strategic Russian energy assets, he had finally gone too far.

First, Khodorkovsky announced the merger of Yukos with Sibneft—an oil firm acquired by fellow oligarchs Boris Berezovsky and Roman Abramovich by way of Loans for Shares. The resulting YukosSibneft would have been far and away the largest Russian oil company, surpassing all others under Putin's control—primarily Gazprom and the other oil giant, Rosneft. That was his first mistake.[135]

His next mistake would prove fatal. Khodorkovsky thought that he could start a bidding war between Exxon and Chevron over the not-yet-merged YukosSibneft *behind Putin's back*. Khodorkovsky had become too irritating to ignore. He had crossed Putin's red line.[136]

Putin loathed the prospect of foreign companies controlling Russia's valuable domestic resources. When the Exxon CEO called Putin to make sure that the deal had the Kremlin's blessing, Putin assured him it did not. The deal was off, and Khodorkovsky was irate.[137]

During a February 2003 meeting at the Kremlin, Khodorkovsky *publicly* accused Putin's government of widespread bribery and corruption. He accused Putin of plundering state assets to give to his inner circle. Putin coolly flipped the accusation back on Khodorkovsky. How were all those valuable oil reserves acquired? Had Yukos paid all of its taxes? Were there any bribes?[138]

Virtually every oligarch tuned in, worried that Putin's "live and let live" rule might be in jeopardy. What happened next guaranteed that no oligarch, no matter how wealthy or powerful they thought they were, would cross Putin again.[139]

In October 2003, masked FSB agents stormed Khodorkovsky's plane. They threw him in jail and charged him with tax evasion, fraud, forgery, and embezzlement. The Kremlin demanded that Yukos pay $30 billion in back taxes—the first installment was due within forty-eight *hours*. Naturally, the company was unable to pay because Putin had already frozen its assets.[140]

In the blink of an eye, Khodorkovsky was broke and in prison. At the subsequent kangaroo trial that began in June 2004, the court took all the prosecution's charges at face value and refused any exculpatory evidence from the defense. Adding insult to injury, Putin made Khodorkovsky sit in a cage and broadcast the spectacle on national television. After the trial, Khodorkovsky was sentenced to nine years in prison and served most of his sentence until he was set free in December 2013.[141]

When it came to the auction of Yukos' assets, the Kremlin set terms that effectively dissuaded most viable competitors from bidding. Prospective bidders needed permission from the Russian anti-monopoly authority and had to deposit more than 49 billion rubles (or $1.7 billion) in advance.[142]

The sole qualified bidder, an unknown shell company, won the auction and paid $9.35 billion for Yukos' most prized assets, a bargain compared to its value ranging from $10.4 to $22 billion. The shell company, called Baikal Finance Group, had a meager net capital of $300 and was registered at a cell phone store outside Moscow.[143]

Within days, it was obvious what had happened. Kremlin-backed Sberbank fronted the $1.7 billion down payment to Baikal Finance Group, and Kremlin-backed Rosneft loaned the rest (nearly $10 billion). When the auction was over, Rosneft took control of Yukos' assets. Overnight, Rosneft tripled its production, quintupled its reserves, and became the third-largest oil producer in the country.[144]

Putin had sent an "unmistakable signal" when he installed his inner circle Siloviki man, Igor Sechin, as Rosneft chairman less than six months before the auction. The rigged Yukos auction catapulted Rosneft from a forlorn mid-ranking producer to a top-tier prized asset.[145]

Bringing Khodorkovsky to his knees and appropriating his billions may have been Putin's boldest (and savviest) move to date because it signaled a change in the status quo. In one fell swoop, Putin brought every oligarch to heel, silenced a powerful critic, increased the oil reserves of his favorite company, *and* scored a victory with the public, who had always wanted to see oligarchs punished for their greed. The televised trial with Khodorkovsky in a cage was an added bonus.[146]

The controlled demolition of Yukos proved that Russian energy conglomerates effectively had one manager: Putin. It also kicked off a new era in his career, and the world learned that Putin would rule Russia with an iron fist.

First, he sacked his entire cabinet, including his prime minister, in February 2004. Next, he began to restructure many of Russia's major energy producers and turned them into massive, state-owned juggernauts.[147]

With the bulk of Russian energy supplies firmly in the hands of his loyalists, Putin began amassing power and leverage outside of Russia. It was in this new era that Putin's weaponization of energy became a serious threat to his European neighbors.

CHAPTER 3

PUTIN'S COLDEST WAR

The Strategic Quest for Global Nuclear Dominance

"What amazed me most of all was how one man's effort
could achieve what whole armies could not.
One spy could decide the fate of thousands of people."[1]

—VLADIMIR V. PUTIN, 2000

When Putin became president, he submitted his "2020 Energy Strategy" for Russian Federation approval. The document outlined two phases to achieve his goals by 2020. The stated goals were to satisfy the demands of Russia's developing economy and to help Russian energy business "integrate into world energy markets." This initiative was approved in August 2003.[2]

The first phase was to reform the legal structures of the *domestic* energy industry, implement transparency and openness, and realize the "export potential of oil and gas," among other domestic policies. The second phase would increase Russia's competitiveness internationally through the "rapid use of the existing odds in nuclear power and hydro energy sectors…the support of a specialized business sector in the field of energy saving," and significant state investment in new projects, among others.[3]

Back in 1996, Putin had gotten an advanced degree from the St. Petersburg Mining Institute, which he never actually attended. His dissertation advocated greater state control of Russia's natural resources (the daughter of Putin's professor alleges that her father actually wrote Putin's dissertation with her help). It nonetheless revealed the essence of his mindset: in order to command respect globally, the state *must* control Russia's vast domestic resources and wield them as a political tool.[4]

While post-Soviet Russia's military and economy remained on life support, Putin dreamed of rebuilding the empire. One of his earliest acts as president was combining Russia's two largest weapons companies and, on November 4, 2000, Rosoboronexport was born. Putin appointed his ex-KGB comrade Sergey Chemezov to lead the new arms conglomerate. Rosoboronexport soon became the crown jewel of Putin's military-industrial complex and Russia became the second largest weapons exporter on the planet.[5]

But energy was the more important thing. As Putin's own dissertation made clear, Russia's energy resources were its strongest advantage. Leveraging energy resources as a foreign policy weapon was not a new concept, but Putin knew he needed to wield it more aggressively than his predecessors.

The Soviet Union had subsidized (or inflated) energy prices to dominate their neighbors for decades. The hook was that once a dependency had been established, "any reduction in supply threatened the stability of the regimes." When manipulating prices failed to produce intended results, the Kremlin would flat out stop shipping fuel (sometimes even in the middle of winter). Joseph Stalin did this to Yugoslavia in 1948. Nikita Khrushchev did the same to Israel in 1956, Finland in 1958, and China in 1959. Gorbachev even tried it against Latvia and Lithuania in 1990.[6]

Putin borrowed and adapted all this from the Soviet playbook, then mastered it.

Putin's Playbook: Energy Weaponization

After consolidating energy assets, Putin's regime went on the offensive. Throughout Putin's first term, he either halted or reduced the flow, or manipulated the price of energy supplies to Ukraine, Georgia, Moldova, Belarus, and other nations in his sphere of influence. The Baltic states and Finland import up to 100 percent of their natural gas from Russia (in extreme cases), making them particularly vulnerable.[7]

Gazprom was Russia's largest gas provider and thus served as the schoolyard bully in the region of former Soviet republics. Within a year of taking power, Putin had cleaned house at Gazprom and installed his St. Petersburg cronies: legal counselor and campaign chief Dmitry Medvedev became Gazprom's chairman, and advisor Alexey Miller became CEO.[8]

At one point, Putin described Gazprom as "a powerful political and economic lever of influence over the rest of the world." Russian experts concur that when Putin's neighbors "show good will towards the Russian Federation, then the situation with gas deliveries, pricing policy and former debts changes on a far more favorable note to the buyer."[9]

For Russia's international energy strategy to succeed, Ukraine's compliance had always been critical. More than 80 percent of Gazprom's gas exports are to Europe—much of which passes through Ukraine. In exchange for transporting Russia's gas to Europe, Ukraine receives a portion of its own fuel for free. But the arrangements are murky and the Kremlin has a habit of reneging.[10]

Energy disputes between the two countries sprang up almost immediately after the Soviet Union dissolved, and remained constant and unpredictable. An early example occurred when President Yeltsin used Ukraine's gas debts as pressure to extract military concessions from Ukraine's then-President Leonid Kuchma.[11]

Yeltsin leveraged Ukraine's $3 billion energy debt in negotiations for control of the Sevastopol naval base in Crimea and ownership of the Black Sea Fleet (nearly six hundred naval vessels). Control over the Crimean Peninsula (located within Ukraine's boundaries but largely populated by ethnic Russians) and its strategic naval base was of critical interest to both nations.[12]

After years of contentious negotiations, Yeltsin partially forgave or postponed Ukraine's billion-dollar debts and Kuchma conceded ownership of nearly 80 percent of the fleet to Russia, along with control of the Crimean naval base via a long-term lease.[13]

Kuchma's submissive demeanor continued under Putin. In fact, he was compliant even *before* Putin took office. Kuchma admitted in private that he had caved and illegally funneled tens of millions into Putin's campaign.

"Putin telephoned, the fuck, during the election campaign," the Ukrainian president told an administration official on a secretly recorded telephone call. "'Leonid Danylovych [Kuchma], well, at least give us a bit of money,'" Kuchma said, imitating candidate Putin's patronizing tone.[14]

Kuchma did as Putin had commanded and ordered the head of Ukraine's public oil and gas company to scrounge together $56 million for Putin's campaign coffers. When Putin won in March 2000, he repaid Kuchma's favor nearly fivefold with a $250 million transfer—allegedly via Gazprom. However, instead of the money going to pay back Ukraine's gas company, it disappeared into a dizzying structure of shadowy offshore interests.[15]

After Putin brought Ukraine to heel, the former Soviet Republic of Moldova was the next to feel Putin's aggression. By the end of his first year in office, Putin had taken effective control of Moldova's energy *and* financial sectors. Later, when Moldova thought about signing a free trade deal with the EU, Russia threatened to cut its gas supplies. Putin's deputy foreign minister even shamelessly threatened the Moldovans, stating, "We hope that you will not freeze."[16]

In 2002, Putin signed an agreement with Kazakhstan's "dictator for life," Nursultan Nazarbayev. Most of Kazakhstan's oil would be transported via Russia's transit network. In addition, Putin proposed a pipeline network creating a "single export channel" for all gas exports from Central Asia. Putin coveted Kazakhstan's vast oil and uranium reserves, and his strategic energy alliance with Soviet-era despot Nazarbayev had only just begun.[17]

By 2003, Putin had reached a similar deal with Turkmenistan, giving Russia long-term priority access to the third-largest gas reserves in the world. The plan was quite obvious: Putin was cornering the oil and gas markets in Europe and Central Asia. Combined with Russia's substantial domestic production, Putin's effective control of gas from Kazakhstan, Turkmenistan, Moldova, and other countries meant that soon all of Europe could become dependent on Russia for its energy needs.[18]

Putin's kleptocratic alliance with Kuchma and the power moves that he was making in the former Soviet republics concerned U.S. energy and diplomatic observers. The foreign policy intelligentsia in Washington had already masterminded (and refined) a counteroffensive: the so-called "color revolutions."[19]

The West's Counteroffensive: Color Revolutions

Western-backed protests had successfully ousted the Russia-allied president of Yugoslavia Slobodan Milosevic in 2000. That playbook was used again in November 2003 to spark the "Rose Revolution" in Georgia. Strategically speaking, the most threatening insurgency to Putin's energy stranglehold was Ukraine's first "Orange Revolution," which began in November 2004.[20]

Putin blamed the U.S. for fomenting the revolutions, which he considered an "unlawful way" to oust the leadership in Georgia and Ukraine. He warned that the West's attempt to create a "system of permanent revolutions" was "very dangerous." Any diplomatic gains that Putin made with the Bush administration in the wake of the September 11 terrorist attacks eroded after the successes of the color revolutions in Georgia and Ukraine.[21]

Putin and his mafia-linked security services retained significant sway in pockets of Georgia, Moldova, and Ukraine—the regions of South Ossetia, Transnistria, and Crimea, respectively.[22]

Russian journalist Yulia Latynina described Georgia's pro-Russian region as a mafia state, saying, "South Ossetia is not a territory, not a country, not a regime. It is a joint venture of Siloviki generals and Ossetian bandits for making money in a conflict with Georgia."[23]

In these regions (and in Russia generally), Putin's Siloviki retaliated against the U.S. by targeting diplomats and allied organizations with constant surveillance, overt harassment, and covert threats. To avoid a color revolution in Russia, Putin eliminated jury trials and redefined "treason" to include protests (peaceful or otherwise).[24]

In all, Putin created many enemies but demonstrated his commitment to wielding energy for greater power and control. By 2006, the Swedish Defense Research Agency estimated that post-Soviet Russia had leveraged energy policy to pressure or coerce Russia's neighbors—and by extension most of Europe—at least fifty times. Also, from 2000 to mid-2010, Putin's regime engaged in thirty-one energy conflicts affecting twenty different countries.[25]

Putin's *2020 Energy Strategy* document never specifically acknowledged his strategic use of energy as a foreign policy tool. It stated that the document had "originate[d] from the necessity of fulfillment by Russia of its international ecological commitments." Therefore, it appears that Putin's calculated efforts to showcase pro-globalization and pro-environmentalism in his *2020 Energy Strategy* were a classic case of Russian duplicity.[26]

Putin's cooperative language, as compared to his coercive actions, confirms the chasm between his *public* agenda and his *private* agenda. In the words of Russian scholar James Sherr, "It would be prudent to conclude that Putin's talk of 'globalization' is *boltovnya* [empty talk]."[27]

His successes with controlling the flow of oil and natural gas to his closest neighbors were just the first steps. Looking further at Europe, Putin knew the importance of selling nuclear energy to countries such as Germany, France, and Great Britain.

Putin's Nuclear Agenda: The Energy Playbook Goes Global

As Putin consolidated Russia's vast oil reserves into Gazprom and Rosneft, he began doing the same thing with nuclear fuel. Just as Putin used Gazprom and Rosneft to leverage his neighbors, Putin's plans for his atomic umbrella corporation Rosatom were to use nuclear *energy* to leverage the world. Putin's nuclear agenda began with Tenex and would culminate in the takeover of Uranium One.

Putin knew that Tenex was the back door through which his Siloviki could infiltrate and manipulate the American nuclear industry. He needed full control of the company that made uranium deals with the Americans, but Tenex shares had fallen into the hands of oligarchs during the failed privatization era under Yeltsin.[28]

Putin's plan for global nuclear domination began almost immediately after he took over as president. By June 2001, Putin had reclaimed absolute control over Tenex when the board ceded all private shares back to the Kremlin. Less than two weeks later, Putin signed a package of controversial laws designed to vacuum up the world's spent nuclear fuel (and billions in cash) into Russia and thereby clean up global nuclear waste.[29]

To some, it was an obvious scam. As one critic at Greenpeace had explained a few months earlier, "the fairy tales about nuclear cleanup... are nothing but public relations for [the Kremlin's] crude attempt to get Western money for an expansion of the Russian nuclear industry."[30]

Putin's brilliant plan worked: the United States aggressively lobbied the international community to pour at least $10 billion into Russia for the reprocessing of spent nuclear fuel (also known as "radioactive garbage").[31]

The plan was to ship twenty thousand tons of "potential bomb-making," enriched uranium waste under the auspices of non-proliferation (an ironic proposal given that the Kremlin had admitted to nearly two dozen nuclear heist attempts at post-Soviet facilities). The Americans even offered to match the $10 billion, for a combined $20 billion to Russia.[32]

Putin's Nuclear Inner Circle

Once the Kremlin had full ownership of Tenex, Putin installed an ex-KGB comrade to lead the nuclear corporation (just as he had with all industries critical to Russian national security). His Ozero neighbor Vladimir Smirnov was a man who could be trusted to execute Putin's agenda.[33] Smirnov's background in espionage would facilitate Putin's infiltration of the American nuclear sector.

Putin tapped Smirnov to run Tenex sometime in 2002—the year after their SPAG money-laundering operation was exposed. Smirnov's mafia-linked SPAG associates were indicted in July 2001, and *Newsweek* blew the story wide open six weeks later. In 2003, German police raided offices linked to SPAG. They were seeking to bust the St. Petersburg crime syndicate responsible for "numerous crimes, including vehicle smuggling, human trafficking, alcohol smuggling, extortion and confidence trickstering."[34]

As it turned out, Smirnov's experience setting up complex money-laundering and influence operations in St. Petersburg would come in handy at Tenex.[35]

Russian newspaper *Novaya Gazeta* reportedly obtained stolen corporate documents that revealed Tenex, under Smirnov, had set up a secretive subsidiary in Germany called Internexco GmbH to "[represent] Tenex interests in selling nuclear fuel and nuclear technology but also for the purpose of *continuing to launder money* [emphasis added]."[36]

A former FSB investigator named Alexander Litvinenko spent years documenting Putin's mafia and criminal underworld connections. He investigated Putin and Smirnov's SPAG money-laundering operation and worked with international investigators to expose Putin's "mafia state." Litvinenko was infamously poisoned by a radioactive isotope called polonium-210. The source? Litvinenko's widow alleges that the polonium trail leads directly to Smirnov-led Tenex.[37]

Smirnov was just one of several Putin loyalists entrusted with the Kremlin's nuclear secrets. At the center of Putin's nuclear ambitions with Smirnov was Sergei Kiriyenko. Kiriyenko, a brainy and bespectacled man, had been one of Yeltsin's young technocrat reformers who provided crucial political support to Putin for the 2000 election.[38]

Putin rewarded Kiriyenko with an appointment to a diplomatic envoy post in the Volga Federal District, which Putin's *2020 Energy Strategy* identified as a "main [consumer] of primary energy resources." From there, Kiriyenko headed the Kremlin's State Commission on Chemical Disarmament, eliminating Soviet-era chemical weapon stockpiles.[39]

In 2004, Putin restructured the entire Russian nuclear industry into a single, vertically integrated nuclear behemoth: the Federal Atomic Energy Agency, or "Rosatom." By the end of 2005, Putin again rewarded Kiriyenko's service by placing him in charge of perhaps the most critically important conglomerate in all of Russia, even though Kiriyenko "had been outside nuclear industry circles."[40]

Rosatom would play both a military and civilian role in Putin's nuclear strategy, and Kiriyenko understood that his assignment was "to restore the glory days of Mindredmash, the notorious secret super-industry of Soviet times that had under its purview all things nuclear."[41]

Prior to Putin's presidency, neither the mafia-linked Smirnov nor the "untested neophyte" Kiriyenko had any apparent experience running nuclear companies, let alone a conglomerate as large as Tenex (or Rosatom for that matter). Smirnov's KGB background, Kiriyenko's financial background, and their loyalties to Putin appear to be all the credentials they needed.[42]

In addition to these loyalists, Putin needed operatives with a nuclear background and technical expertise. Longtime nuclear apparatchiks Alexei Grigoriev and Vadim Mikerin had negotiated complex nuclear agreements with the Clinton administration. They were both instrumental in making a deal with Clinton to sell Russian uranium to American utility companies via Tenex and the United States Enrichment Corporation (USEC).[43]

Megatons to Megawatts

Tenex was formally established by the Soviet Union in 1963 and remains one of Russia's oldest nuclear companies. Tenex is the international trading arm of Russia's nuclear industry and sells uranium to virtually anyone willing to pay—including Iran and China.[44]

Communist East Germany partnered with Tenex's predecessor (Technoexport) to supply uranium to the Soviet nuclear weapons program throughout the Cold War. But when Tenex partnered with the French in 1971 to enrich uranium, the Russians officially entered the Western market. This marked the beginning of the end of U.S. nuclear dominance. By 1991, the Soviets had amassed an enormous strategic stockpile of uranium—two hundred thousand tons.[45]

After the Cold War ended, Russia was flush with nuclear weapons but strapped for cash. The fledgling post-Soviet regime found compliant partners in the Clinton administration, who soon began importing Russian corruption while exporting American wealth and nuclear secrets.[46]

Beginning in February 1993, Clinton's administration signed a series of deals with the Kremlin under the guise of nuclear disarmament. Commonly known as the "Megatons to Megawatts" program, it was a valiant proposal to turn "swords into ploughshares."[47] The idea had been conceived a year earlier under George H.W. Bush's administration, but it was Bill Clinton who executed the strategy.

The Clinton team's Russian counterparts agreed to ship Russian nuclear warhead materials, namely highly enriched uranium (HEU), from St. Petersburg to the U.S. There, it would be converted into low enriched uranium (LEU) for U.S. nuclear reactors. The $12 billion deal (which ballooned to over $20 billion) was hailed as a win-win: the U.S. claimed a post–Cold War victory while securing essential energy resources, while Russia unloaded more than five hundred metric tons of HEU. Thanks to Clinton's Commerce Department, which changed certain trade regulations, the terms were very favorable to Russia (and profitable to the well-connected American utility companies).[48]

This HEU-LEU program was a central core in Putin's long-term strategy to conquer the world nuclear market using dubious international nuclear deals. Grigoriev and Mikerin had negotiated the deal under Yeltsin, and Putin kept these two valuable allies and the agreement in place.[49]

Grigoriev agrees that the HEU-LEU deal "really helped" the Kremlin during those "very difficult years" when Russia's economy was in shambles. At a time when most Russian industries were crippled, the civil nuclear industry (i.e., Rosatom and Tenex) was able to "increase its production." Yeltsin's and Clinton's Megatons to Megawatts negotiations paved the way to friendlier relations and represented a post–Cold War diplomatic high point. "I think it has really helped us in our relations with the U.S. utilities as well," Grigoriev said.[50]

The relationships that Tenex built with U.S. utility companies under the Megatons to Megawatts deal were mutually beneficial and *highly lucrative*. This oft-overlooked detail will be a crucial factor to understanding how and why the Obama administration would approve the Uranium One deal a few years later.

One factor that has never been overlooked (and certainly did *not* help Russian-American relations) is Russia's nuclear alliance with Iran.

The Russia-Iran Nuclear Alliance

Russia and Iran have been strategic nuclear allies for decades—a major point of contention with the U.S. In the mid-1990s, Russia picked up where the Germans had left off in the late 1970s in building the infamous Bushehr nuclear reactor on the coast of the Persian Gulf, approximately 650 miles south of Tehran. Also, the nuclear partnership with Iran steered virtually all aspects of American relations with Russia after 1995. Washington viewed Russia's cooperation on the Bushehr reactor as a potential facilitation of Iran's atomic weapons program.[51]

Moscow did not share Washington's concerns and viewed Iran's nuclear ambitions as a potential windfall. After all, the Megatons to Megawatts program had provided much-needed cash in the 1990s, but the program was set to expire in 2013.[52] That loss of revenue likely incentivized Rosatom to build nuclear reactors (supplied with Tenex uranium) for American adversaries like Iran.

In addition to the billions generated by the construction of the massive infrastructure, building and operating nuclear power plants (NPP)—like Bushehr—created potential long-term customers that sought Rosatom's abundant low-cost supply.[53]

While Megatons to Megawatts greased the skids between Moscow and Washington, the changing administrations—especially Putin's—brought about renewed friction between the superpowers.

When George W. Bush came to power in 2001, he and Putin initially maintained a cordial rapport. Putin often bragged that he was the first world leader to call Bush after the September 11 terrorist attacks, and Bush famously said that he trusted Putin after catching a glimpse of his soul. But when Bush placed Iran firmly inside what he called the "Axis of Evil" in his 2002 State of the Union speech, Putin no doubt felt the shot across the bow.[54]

While the two leaders made some diplomatic gains on the issue of nuclear arsenal reduction, the Iran issue was an obvious and immediate impasse. When Bush slapped sanctions on a Russian arms maker for missile sales to Tehran, Russian analysts suggested that the Americans had signaled their intent to "pursue all avenues to halt Russia's involvement in the [Iran nuclear] project."[55]

Indeed, the Bush administration took a hard stance on the "Iran issue." It demanded that Putin cancel support for Bushehr. But Putin hardly budged. Only when Putin convinced the Iranians to surrender their spent fuel and transport the nuclear materials back to Russia in 2005 did Bush yield—temporarily.[56]

It was around this time that Bush's FBI tasked a longtime American intelligence operative named William Douglas Campbell with penetrating Putin's nuclear complex. In 2005, Campbell began his harrowing journey in Kazakhstan—the heart of Russia's uranium supply—and soon found himself in Moscow, infiltrating the highest levels of the Kremlin.

Campbell apprised his FBI handlers often—via written and oral briefings—to be wary of the Kremlin's nuclear acquisitions and advances in the United States and abroad. Campbell also warned the FBI of the American lobbyists who furthered those Kremlin advances.[57]

At the same time, Putin sought to seduce the Bush administration. He visited Camp David, the ranch in Crawford, Texas, and the Bush compound on Walker's Point in Kennebunkport, Maine. Putin even tried to curry favor with Bush by offering former Secretary of Commerce Don Evans—one of Bush's closest friends—a lucrative position at oil giant Rosneft. Bush was "flabbergasted," but kept his cool.[58]

In 2006, Bush came around to Putin's requests and briefly relented on the Iran issue. It appeared that Russia would get permission to advance Iran's nuclear energy program *and* get the nuclear treaty (called the "123 Agreement") that they desperately wanted.[59]

Putin's charm offensive peaked in April 2008 when he invited Bush to visit the ritzy Russian resort town of Sochi. Bush warily agreed on the condition that Putin would not ambush him in some way. This would be Bush's twenty-eighth and final official visit with Putin.[60]

That same month, NATO announced that Georgia and Ukraine "will become members of NATO." Georgia and Ukraine were not just Putin's neighbors, they were former Soviet republics and directly on his doorstep. This announcement crossed Putin's red line.[61]

As the Georgian government sought to join NATO, the Georgian breakaway regions of Abkhazia and South Ossetia sought independence. Georgia received support from the West while Abkhazia and

South Ossetia received support from Russia. Violence broke out and escalated throughout the summer. The proxy war had fully erupted.[62]

In August 2008, Putin sent troops marching into Georgia. The conflict lasted just twelve days, but thousands were killed or injured (including civilians), and nearly two hundred thousand residents were displaced.[63]

The invasion of Georgia, combined with new evidence that Iran had a secret nuclear weapons program, would re-chill the thawing U.S.-Russia relationship that Putin had tried to cultivate with the Bush administration. Once Russia invaded Georgia, Bush scrapped the deal and reached a new deal with Russia's neighbors to install missile defense systems in Poland.[64]

U.S.-Russia relations plummeted to a post–Cold War low.[65]

These events put the U.S. on alert regarding Putin's ambitions and ulterior motives. Putin had shown himself to be a canny and sophisticated authoritarian. The Bush administration had not forgotten Putin's previous career working for the KGB and setting up its post-Soviet reinvention.[66]

The Rosatom Expansion Continues

In November 2007, Rosatom was converted from a federal agency to a state-owned corporation. Putin's state-owned corporations, like Rosatom, were essentially Soviet-style enterprises where the government owns the means of production, but the operations are opaque, outside federal budget restrictions, and more autonomous.[67]

Rosatom became a sort of hybrid—a cross between a government agency and a for-profit corporation. With this crowning stroke, Putin had successfully consolidated and gained control over virtually every facet of the nuclear fuel cycle—from uranium mining to enrichment and fuel conversion to power plant construction and operation and even to waste disposal. The Kremlin supported all divisions.[68]

The net result was that the Kremlin bankrolled the unprofitable programs (such as nuclear waste disposal and cleanup of nuclear disasters) and the profitable operations were effectively separated from these costly (and toxic) liabilities.[69] What this means economically is that Rosatom is a nuclear monopolist not subject to typical market forces and can subsidize its products to beat any international competitors' prices.[70]

For international utility companies, Tenex was an attractive fuel supplier.

With Kiriyenko at the helm, Rosatom began snapping up uranium assets and planning new projects around the world. Kiriyenko's strategy was aggressive: the Kremlin planned to spend $60 billion by 2021 building dozens of new reactors *in Russia alone* (a *fivefold* increase in new reactors over the previous fifteen-year period).[71]

Putin's infiltration of the U.S. nuclear industry through diplomacy would have to await the results of the 2008 election. Russia's post-Soviet constitution prevents three *consecutive* presidential terms. This forced Putin to yield the presidency to his hand-picked successor: Dmitry Medvedev.[72] And while Putin had relinquished the presidency to his lawyer and confidante, everyone knew who was still really in charge: Prime Minister Putin.[73]

He needed a president whose ambitions (and weaknesses) would allow Russia to recapture its former position on the global chessboard. Putin dreamed of an administration he could leverage—by any means—and wanted to take America down a peg (or three).[74]

Meanwhile, Russian spies remained undercover abroad, inching closer to Washington bureaucrats, nuclear officials, and lobbyists who could persuade Bush's successor, whomever that might be, to normalize relations with Moscow.[75]

Putin Tests Obama

In November 2008, Senator Barack Obama (D-IL) was elected the forty-fourth president of the United States. A former community organizer steeped in left-wing activism, Obama was the polar opposite of George W. Bush. Instead of an assertive nationalist confident of America's leadership role in world affairs, Obama believed the U.S. needed to apologize for its past imperialism and was uncomfortable with America's supposed role as global policeman. Whether knowingly or not, these views aligned closely with Putin's.[76]

Yet the Russian president and his circle evinced nothing but disdain for Obama's Hamlet-like ambivalence and reluctance to act. As reporters David Corn and Michael Isikoff write in their book *Russian Roulette*:

> Putin and his top advisers routinely denigrated Obama and his national security team as "weak" and "indecisive"—and then, contradictorily, blamed him for meddling in Russia's internal affairs. In Putin's presence, Obama would be called a "monkey," and it was not uncommon for the American president to be referred to as the N-word.[77]

Obama's apparent weakness and disinterest in American leadership abroad emboldened Putin's energy weaponization strategy. Putin's zero-sum mindset—we win, you lose—meant that for Russia to advance, the U.S. and its NATO allies must retreat. After years of escalating tensions under Bush, Putin apparently believed that President-elect Obama would offer no resistance to his strategy.

Just days before Obama was sworn in as president, Putin tested his theory. He turned off the flow of natural gas to Ukraine, and by extension much of Europe, and millions were suddenly unable to heat their homes amid subzero temperatures. Nearly a dozen people, mostly in Poland, froze to death when temperatures reached -13 degrees Fahrenheit.[78]

Yet again, this was Putin's way of extracting concessions from his neighbors while flexing his muscles for the world to see.

How would the president-elect react? Putin's theory was correct: instead of condemning Russia's cruelty, Obama said nothing. Nevertheless, Russia opened the pipelines the same day Obama was inaugurated and, in the months that followed, crickets chirped in Obama's White House despite the January 2009 Eastern European "humanitarian emergency."[79]

Less than three months later, in April 2009, Russia tested the Obama administration again. President Medvedev gave a press conference with the pro-Russian Georgian leaders in the breakaway regions of Abkhazia and South Ossetia. They announced a military agreement authorizing Russia, which had committed more than $300 million in military support in 2009, to dispatch more troops to the Georgian borders. This was a major escalation in the Georgian crisis that had so outraged the lame-duck Bush administration.[80]

When Obama visited Moscow three months later in July, he would barely allude to Russia's recent cruelty in Eastern Europe, let alone condemn it. Instead he voiced high-flown sentiments projecting an idealized vision of a world moving away from great power confrontation toward interdependency and cooperation.

"In 2009, a great power does not show strength by dominating or demonizing other countries. The days when empires could treat sovereign states as pieces on a chess board are over," Obama preached. "The pursuit of power is no longer a zero-sum game—progress must be shared. That's why I have called for a 'reset' in relations between the United States and Russia."[81]

This was Putin's first in-person encounter with Obama. He must have been overjoyed when Obama repeatedly praised Russia's post-Soviet reforms and lauded Russia's influence on America. "We've been enriched by Russian culture, and enhanced by Russian cooperation. And as a resident of Washington, D.C., I continue to benefit from the contributions of Russians," Obama joked, referring to Washington Capitals all-star hockey player Alexander Ovechkin.[82]

Meanwhile, his silence on Russia's weaponization of energy and the military aggression in Georgia and throughout the region was deafening. In hindsight, these benign comments are more than a little ironic in light of the harsh criticism later directed at Donald Trump for his similar praise of Vladimir Putin.

Obama did hint at Ukraine and Georgia's prospective NATO membership, but he actually downplayed U.S. support, saying, "America will never impose a security arrangement on another country." Obama ultimately concluded, "And let me be clear: NATO should be seeking collaboration with Russia, not confrontation."[83]

McCain Institute senior fellow David J. Kramer, among others, glowingly praised Obama's "reset" and said Obama "deserved credit" for the strategy. But even Kramer would concede that "provocative visits to Abkhazia and South Ossetia by Medvedev and Putin respectively, Medvedev's renewed threats to target Iskander missiles against the Czech Republic and Poland if U.S. missile defense plans move forward in those two countries, and the murders of human rights activists and charity heads in Chechnya have cast a shadow over the relationship."[84]

After eight years of the confrontational cowboy George W. Bush, the Washington foreign policy establishment was ready for a change and was fully on board with Obama's America-second agenda. Their muted reservations would remain buried in the margins of think tank white papers. Indeed, Obama and the intelligentsia in Washington had big plans to collaborate with Russia. Russia's cooperation on Obama's Iran nuclear deal would be essential. The "reset" of Russian relations was only just beginning.[85]

For Putin, this was a dream come true. Iran's fledgling nuclear program was a potential cash cow for Russia and a central component of Putin's nuclear strategy. Obama's naïveté, his general apologetic tone, and his strong desire to advance Iran's nuclear ambitions blinded him to Putin's schemes.[86]

When Bush stepped down and Obama stepped up, Putin's nuclear strategy went into full swing.

CHAPTER 4

OBAMA'S NUCLEAR CRONIES

How a Young Anti-Nuclear Activist Grew Up to Become a Pro-Nuclear President

"To put an end to Cold War thinking, we will reduce the role of nuclear weapons in our national security strategy, and urge others to do the same.... We must harness the power of nuclear energy on behalf of our efforts to combat climate change, and to advance peace opportunity for all people."[1]

—BARACK OBAMA, 2009

Deep under a college football stadium at the University of Chicago, the very first controlled nuclear chain reaction took place on December 2, 1942. Physicists first harnessed uranium fission and the United States became the world's first nuclear power.[2] Chicago would later become the headquarters of Exelon Corporation—one of the world's most powerful nuclear conglomerates—and the home of the forty-fourth U.S. president: Barack Obama.

A few hundred miles south of Chicago, in Metropolis, Illinois, a conversion facility processed the Russian uranium after it had been stripped from Soviet missiles under the Clinton-era Megatons to Megawatts deal. The facility was run by Fortune 100 industrial behemoth Honeywell International Inc. Honeywell converted the Russian uranium into reactor fuel, then shipped it off to power the nuclear plants for utility companies like Exelon.[3]

The taxpayer-subsidized Megatons to Megawatts program was highly profitable for the utilities and even more so for the Kremlin. But Russia's fortunes had waned under the Bush administration, and Putin's aggression in Georgia jeopardized the nuclear dealings of the conglomerates like Honeywell and Exelon, who enjoyed the cheap fuel supply from Russia.

The Chicago and Metropolis nuclear money fueled the rise of the Obama political network.[4] The conglomerates funneled massive sums to Obama and his inner circle even before he was elected U.S. senator in 2004. When Obama ran for president, Exelon's and Honeywell's contributions and lobbying expenditures ramped up significantly.[5]

Their years of investment in Obama and his closest advisors granted the conglomerates unprecedented access to the White House and returned substantial financial benefit in the form of green energy handouts and favorable nuclear energy policies. Obama's Russia reset provided well-connected nuclear utilities an additional windfall.[6]

Like Putin and the Uranium One stakeholders, Obama's nuclear benefactors—especially Exelon—had reason to rejoice when American uranium fell under Russian control. And like the Clinton Foundation, the post-presidential Obama Foundation reaped a big nuclear payday: Exelon was among the first to donate $1 million to the Obama Foundation (they pledged an additional $10 million, also making them one of the largest single donors).[7]

While Obama seemed particularly pro-nuclear, his propensity toward all things atomic had limits. Since his college days at Columbia University, Obama had dreamed of a world without nuclear weapons. Once president, he worked toward his near-lifelong goal of "going to zero"—dismantling the nuclear arsenal through arms reductions or "disarmament."[8] Putin could not have gotten luckier and, under the reset, he secured almost every item on his nuclear wish list by exploiting Obama's weaknesses.

While Obama was stripping the U.S. of its nuclear deterrents and crippling domestic energy producers, Putin was bolstering Russia's arsenal and cornering global energy markets. Obama must have known this, but he continued to disarm the U.S. anyway via toothless nuclear treaties. All the while, Putin cheated and breached such treaties repeatedly and, furthermore, sought to create an American dependency on Russian uranium. Evidently, Putin's customers—the conglomerates like Exelon and other American utilities—were willing to trade short-term profits for that long-term dependency on Russia.[9]

An Activist Goes to Washington

In 2004, Obama was elected to the U.S. Senate. Having grown up during the Cold War, he was passionate about nuclear disarmament and had been for a long time. Even as a junior senator, Obama knew more about Russian nuclear deals than most people and, early on, made nonproliferation one of his primary goals. To boost his foreign policy bona fides, Senator Obama traveled to Russia in 2005 to inspect Soviet-era nuclear weapons facilities and materials.[10]

Obama and his delegation were detained at an airport in the Ural Mountains for hours by the Russian authorities. It is unclear if Senator Obama was already familiar with the Kremlin's notorious brinkmanship antics, but it must have been an uncomfortable introduction to U.S.-Russia relations for the junior senator. More importantly, the trip allowed Obama to confirm Putin's nuclear ambitions and his nuclear facilities in person (though Obama did not meet with Putin directly on this trip).[11]

After that trip to Moscow, Obama talked nobly (if naïvely) about collaborating with Russia "to dismantle these arms and create a more peaceful and safe future for…people all around the world."[12]

As mentioned, Putin had been forced by constitutional constraints to step aside as president. Thus, his protégé Dmitry Medvedev, who was younger and more diplomatic than Putin, became his successor. Meanwhile, Putin continued pushing his agenda behind the scenes. Medvedev gave the outward appearance (particularly to the U.S.) that Russia was moving closer toward a pro-globalist democracy.[13]

In reality, newly elected President Medvedev oversaw the Georgia invasion and even issued a presidential decree recognizing Abkhazia and South Ossetia as independent states—an action condemned by the West. This lent credence to suspicions that Medvedev was just keeping

Putin's seat warm. These skeptics included Hillary Clinton, who in 2009 assumed the role of Secretary of State.[14]

By 2009, Russia desperately needed to reset the deteriorating relationship. Hostility at home and abroad during the Bush administration had created economic uncertainty amid threats of sanctions by Western nations. But Putin needed the West. The Russian economy depended on Western money, Western technology, and the West's willingness to do long-term business with Russia.[15]

President Obama and Secretary Clinton were both essentially globalists, but Clinton was a liberal hawk with a more interventionist bent than Obama. Unlike Hillary, who is almost fourteen years older and grew up in a conservative town (and was a self-described "Goldwater girl"), Obama was a product of the postmodern left and his views were those of the liberal faculty lounge.[16]

Obama sincerely believed that the United States had shown arrogance in its relations with the world and publicly said so during his famous global "apology tour" in 2009.[17] He apparently believed that the world was entering a new era of global cooperation, such that America should cede its role as global policeman and lead not from the front, but (as his advisor put it) "from behind."[18]

But Obama's idealism was not unmixed. As the product of the Chicago Democratic machine, he also had a certain hard-edged political realism, especially where his donors and supporters were concerned. People had to be rewarded for their loyalty. It is therefore not surprising that some of the wealthiest and most loyal benefactors from his days in Chicago, many of whom had significant nuclear operations, benefitted immensely from his plans for a diplomatic "reset" with Russia.[19]

The "reset" officially started forty-five days into President Obama's administration as he dispatched Secretary Clinton to Geneva to meet on March 6, 2009, with Russian Foreign Minister Sergey Lavrov.[20] With cameras rolling to record the event, Clinton presented Lavrov with a chintzy red emergency stop button that had actually been swiped from a hotel swimming pool or jacuzzi. They stuck the English word "reset" and the Russian word "peregruzka" onto the stolen button using a cheap label-maker.[21]

"We worked hard to get the right Russian word. Do you think we got it?" Clinton asked Lavrov. "You got it wrong," said an amused Lavrov. "This says 'peregruzka,' which means 'overcharged.'" Clinton laughed sheepishly and quickly recovered, "We won't let you do that to us, I promise."[22]

Obama's deference to other world leaders and willingness to literally bow to them matched Hillary Clinton's eagerness to take their money. In short, these were people with whom Putin could do business.[23]

Spy Ring Cover-up

A year later, President Obama sat at the head of the table in the situation room and he was *furious*. Deputy National Security Advisor John Brennan called the meeting on June 18, 2010, to inform the president that his intelligence chiefs planned to bust a Russian spy ring. The top brass were all in attendance, including Obama's Defense Secretary, Robert Gates, who recalled the scene.[24] But Gates and his colleagues were not prepared for the reaction they got from the president.

"Just as we're getting on track with the Russians, this? This is a throwback to the Cold War," Obama fumed. "This is right out of John le Carré. We put START, Iran, the whole relationship with Russia at risk for this kind of thing?"[25]

The tension in the room was palpable. In Gates' account, Obama did not seem overtly angry at the Russians' duplicity; he was not raging about Putin's blatant disrespect and mockery of the recent diplomatic efforts. Instead, Obama was mad at American law enforcement officials for their audacity in creating a PR fiasco at the same time he was trying to bring Russia to the negotiating table to reduce weapons stockpiles, to increase civilian nuclear trade, and to cooperate on the upcoming Iran nuclear deal.[26]

The situation needed to be contained.

The Russian spies—operating in Washington, D.C., Manhattan, and Boston—had gotten too close to former top intelligence officials (including a Clinton administration Megatons to Megawatts negotiator and a scientist designing bunker-busting bombs). Secretary Clinton's inner circle was targeted successfully, and one of her major financial backers had potentially been compromised.[27]

Obama's advisors were divided. On one side were CIA Director Leon Panetta and FBI Director Robert Mueller. Panetta wanted to rescue their informant, a Russian asset who had exposed the domestic spy ring, and Mueller wanted to arrest the Russian sleeper agents. On the other side were the White House and the State Department, who wanted to keep the whole thing quiet.[28]

Vice President Joe Biden, National Security Advisor Tom Donilon, and the "diplomatic players" agreed with the president. Biden and Donilon strongly argued in favor of sweeping the illegal spy ring under the rug. Without a hint of irony, Biden said, "Our national security interest balance tips heavily to not creating a flap." Obama's top officials apparently believed that bowing to Russia was in the best interests of U.S. national security and that punishing Russian spies would "blow up the relationship."[29]

Everyone agreed that busting the spy ring would blindside Medvedev, who was set to meet with Obama within days. But ignoring the spies or even letting them off the hook presented a dilemma in itself. Defense Secretary Robert Gates offered a solution: meet privately with Medvedev and reveal the real names and ranks of the nearly one dozen Russian spies and demand that they be recalled to Russia quietly and immediately. Obama did not want to embarrass Medvedev and agreed to Gates' soft-touch proposal.[30]

After Obama left the situation room, the advisors deliberated a bit more and agreed that the plan would still put Medvedev in a tight spot.[31] They decided that it was probably best to quietly "exfiltrate" their informant and deport the Russian agents without informing Medvedev.[32] That way everyone was happy.

On June 27, 2010, ten of the Russian spies were quietly rounded up and deported. They returned to Russia in exchange for four Russian prisoners accused of spying for the West. It was a lopsided trade to say the least, particularly because the U.S. was unable to secure the release of a single American prisoner.[33]

Meanwhile, the Russian illegals, including the notorious femme fatale Anna Chapman, returned to Russia and Putin gave them a hero's welcome.[34] Then, in October, the spies were awarded the Order of Merit for the Fatherland—Russia's highest award—by President Medvedev.[35]

Putin's welcome home party for the agents was a direct slap in the face to the United States. Obama was desperately trying to downplay the threat they had posed, yet the Russian president gave them a very public national award ceremony. Putin even issued a thinly veiled threat to the FBI and CIA's informant (and any potential co-informants). "It was the result of treason," Putin said of whoever was responsible. "It always ends badly for traitors: as a rule, their end comes from drink or drugs, lying in a ditch. And for what?"[36]

Putin's statement was essentially a promise of retaliation against the informant(s). In fact, as more Russian officials began to die under mysterious circumstances, the word "Putincide" became the unofficial term for such deaths among U.S. intelligence circles.[37]

In sum, the Russian reset was clearly a joke to Putin, and for obvious reasons. To him, Obama's weakness was on full display, and Hillary (and Bill) Clinton's own vulnerabilities would one day be exploited.

Putin's Nuclear Wish List

As revealed by his anger in the situation room, President Obama's primary goal with the Russian reset was to achieve nuclear deals. In fact, all the major concessions that Obama gave Putin were nuclear-related in one form or another.

- Scrapping the Bush missile defense plan was tied to mitigating Iran's nuclear ambitions.
- The New START treaty was for nuclear disarmament.
- The 123 Agreement allowed Rosatom to sell nuclear materials directly to U.S. utility companies.
- The Iran nuclear deal and other denuclearization efforts in Iran, Libya, and North Korea sent hundreds of thousands of tons of uranium to Russia.
- The administration ignored multiple Russian espionage, bribery, kickbacks, and money-laundering conspiracies—all targeting the American nuclear industry.

- Even the Skolkovo project—"Russia's Silicon Valley"—had nuclear implications.
- The Uranium One purchase approval allowed Putin to all but corner the global nuclear fuel market.

Perhaps the earliest and most controversial concession that President Obama made to the Russians was scrapping an American-European cohosted missile defense program that began under the Bush administration.[38] All other concessions flowed from there.

Russia's invasion of Georgia in 2008 had made its neighbors nervous.[39] The Bush administration worked closely with Poland and the Czech Republic on a system of ground-based interceptors (GBIs) that would simultaneously keep the Russians and the Iranians in check. Poland especially welcomed the Bush plan for a European missile defense shield as essential to its national security.[40]

Yet, just a few weeks into his presidency, Obama sent a secret letter to Medvedev offering to effectively cancel the Bush plan in exchange for Russia's help neutralizing the Iranian threat. The *New York Times* first reported on the hand-delivered letter and described it as a potential "quid pro quo," but Obama disputed the characterization.[41]

Obama ordered Secretary Gates to draft a proposal that halted the expansion of Eastern European missile defense, which some viewed as a way to appease the Russians. Gates was a Republican holdover from the Bush administration, so Obama sometimes relied on Gates' credibility as political cover. Thus, Gates was trotted out to defend Obama's secret proposal when details were leaked to the *New York Times*. That leak "made us look like a bunch of bumbling fools, oblivious to the sensitivities of our allies," Gates later lamented.[42]

In fact, Gates had recommended the missile defense system to President Bush in the first place. Gates was an expert on missile defense policy, and Obama relied on his justification and public support to reverse course.[43] Gates was also a CIA man, through and through.

The CIA first recruited Gates in 1966.[44] It was around that time that the U.S. began working on robust missile defense systems to counterbalance the Soviet missile threat.[45] Gates became an officer in the Air

Force and provided intelligence briefings on intercontinental ballistic missiles (ICBMs) during the late 1960s.[46]

Nixon signed the first Anti-Ballistic Missile (ABM) Treaty with the Soviet Union in 1972, imposing strict limits on missile defenses.[47] But Ronald Reagan's Strategic Defense Initiative (also known as "Star Wars") gave U.S. missile defense a major boost in 1983. As Reagan's deputy director at the CIA, Gates played a role in the development of a "'shield' for the United States against an all-out Soviet attack."[48]

As part of the so-called "Peace Dividend" of defense spending cuts following the collapse of the Soviet Union, funding for SDI missile defense plummeted under President Clinton, who effectively cancelled the program in 1993.[49]

In 2002, President George W. Bush unilaterally withdrew from the 1972 ABM treaty amid growing threats from "rogue" nations, particularly Iran and North Korea. Robust missile defense systems were once more on the table. Putin's duplicity, the weaponization of energy, aggression toward Russia's neighbors, and assistance to hostile regimes all made missile defense a growing priority in the years before Obama's presidency.[50]

Since Reagan's announcement of the Star Wars program, most Democrats were opposed to increasing U.S. missile defenses against the Soviets and most Republicans were in favor. But by the time Obama took office, amid mounting Russian aggression and potential rogue actions by other nations, most members of Congress supported some form of *limited* missile defense.[51]

Putin viewed Bush's nullification of the 1972 ABM treaty as yet another example of U.S. bullying. He resented the West "throwing their weight around." Also, any American advance, in Putin's mind, put Russia at a strategic disadvantage.[52]

Fortunately, in Barack Obama, Putin had a president who believed that the U.S. must atone for the "darker periods in our history," as he called them. "We have not been perfect," Obama told the Muslim world just days after his inauguration in January 2009.[53]

"At times we sought to dictate our terms," he told an audience of the world's most powerful countries in April 2009. "I would like to think that with my election and the early decisions that we've made," Obama continued, "that you're starting to see some restoration of America's standing in the world."[54]

For Putin, that meant his nuclear strategy had hit a major breakthrough.

Obama had long dreamt of a world without nuclear weapons. As a college student, he wrote his senior-year thesis on Soviet nuclear disarmament. He strongly supported disarmament initiatives to turn weapons-grade uranium into civilian reactor fuel. As a U.S. senator and presidential candidate, Obama made the elimination of nukes, or "going to zero," a top priority.[55]

As president, Obama praised past efforts to take "concrete steps towards a world without nuclear weapons." Obama believed that the U.S. had a responsibility—or even a moral obligation—to do so.[56]

But Putin was unlikely to give up *all* his nuclear weapons, and any suggestion to the contrary was almost comically naïve. Nonetheless, in 2009 President Obama began negotiating a disarmament treaty that would replace the 1991 Strategic Arms Reduction Treaty, or START I.[57]

Obama signed the New START with President Medvedev on April 8, 2010. Again, Putin made a mockery out of Obama's effort. Defense Secretary Gates informed Obama, "at the exact moment of the signing ceremony, the Russian military had been conducting a nuclear attack exercise against the United States." *A nice Putin touch*, Gates thought.[58]

As Congress began debating Obama's proposed New START treaty, on May 10, the president resubmitted the U.S.-Russian civilian nuclear agreement (or the "123 Agreement"). The Atomic Energy Act of 1954 prohibits American companies from trading nuclear materials, technology, and services with foreign governments unless that government has signed a special cooperation agreement with the United States. Section 123 of the Atomic Energy Act defined the criteria for nuclear cooperation and trade, hence the nickname of the agreement.[59]

President Bush had first submitted a Russian 123 Agreement in May 2008 but scrapped the plan after Russia invaded Georgia in August 2008. President Obama reassured Congress in a letter that the situation in Georgia should no longer be considered an obstacle. Obama believed that "the level and scope of U.S.-Russian cooperation on Iran [were] sufficient to justify" the 123 Agreement.[60]

Opponents, including Representative Ileana Ros-Lehtinen (R-FL), objected to the agreement because of Russia's shady nuclear dealings with Iran. But, Obama's allies controlled Congress and the opponents were unable to block the deal, which became official on December 9, 2010.[61]

The 123 Agreement had been a major priority for the Kremlin long before 2008. The deal allowed Rosatom and its subsidiaries to sell "nuclear material, technologies and equipment, as well as services" directly to American companies. Furthermore, Obama and Medvedev agreed that the U.S. and Kremlin would *facilitate* these "commercial relations."[62]

Obama's State Department, led by Secretary Clinton, said that the agreement "will support commercial interests by allowing U.S. and Russian firms to team up more easily in joint ventures." The Uranium One deal had 123 Agreement implications, and the approval of both (after heavy lobbying) meant that the Russian nuclear complex was poised to reap substantial benefits from Obama's reset policy.[63]

But Rosatom and the Russians were not the only corporation to profit from increased nuclear cooperation. Obama's oldest and closest corporate allies lobbied for the 123 Agreement and were among its largest beneficiaries.

Obama's Nuclear Roots

With so many nuclear concessions to Putin, especially the questionable Uranium One sale, many in Washington wondered why Obama caved so spectacularly.

Obama's critics consistently hammered him on his weak Russia policy throughout his first term. As news of Obama failures continued to trickle out through 2016, former counterintelligence officer John Schindler reported, "Hillary's secret Kremlin connection is quickly unraveling." Former federal prosecutor Andrew C. McCarthy wrote that the Uranium One deal compromised U.S. national security and was not *just* a Clinton scandal, but also "an Obama-administration scandal." Even the left-leaning Brookings Institution implored their subscribers not to "rehabilitate Obama on Russia," and laid bare how the Obama administration "consistently underestimated the challenge posed by Putin's regime."[64]

The administration's explanation was repeatedly summed up in a single word: "reset."[65]

But *why* was the reset so important for Obama? Was he just being naïvely idealistic? Was he blinded by communist sympathies? Were there perhaps any commercial motivations? All appear to be contributing factors.

Before Obama got into politics, he was a local community organizer and political activist in Chicago.[66] He was also, like many on the left, a strong supporter of nuclear disarmament. Young Obama followed the antinuclear movement and interviewed the activists who attended rallies and marches calling for a reduction in U.S. nuclear stockpiles. At Columbia, he sympathized with and promoted groups like Arms Race Alternatives (ARA), Students Against Militarism (SAM), and Students Against Nuclear Energy (SANE) in the student newspaper.[67] For his senior-year seminar thesis, Obama wrote about the nuclear standoff between the U.S. and the Soviet Union, and the prospects of disarmament.[68]

In 1983, Obama penned an article for Columbia's *Sundial* student magazine promoting the Nuclear Freeze movement. "The Freeze is one part of a whole disarmament movement," Obama wrote, quoting an ARA activist. "The lowest common denominator, so to speak." The activist also suggested that diverting government spending toward social welfare programs "may dispel the idea that disarmament is a white issue."[69]

In early 1985, Obama got a job at the New York Public Interest Research Group (NYPIRG), a nonprofit think tank.[70] Antinuclear and environmental activist Ralph Nader founded the national organization, U.S. PIRG, in 1970 to research and advocate for consumer and environmental reform.[71]

Even though Obama's supervisor was impressed with his ambitions, his efforts to bring about meaningful change in the Big Apple did not bear fruit and he needed a change of scenery. Although his supervisor wanted him to stay because "it was rare to get such a thoughtful organizer," he had already made up his mind and began looking for work elsewhere.[72] Soon he saw an ad for a community-organizing job in Chicago.[73]

Jerry Kellman, a white Jewish community organizer, had been looking for a black face to appeal to communities on the south side of Chicago.[74] Kellman would become the first of several influential Obama mentors and showed him how to work the streets of Chicago, a city that has long been notorious for its corrupt political machine.[75]

Welcome to the Machine

Before Obama moved to Illinois, his nuclear stance was purely ideological. Once he entered Chicago politics, his nuclear interests soon became commercial.[76] The experience that he gained within Chicago's corrupt political culture would hone his skills of mutual back-scratching and palm-greasing to cut through the red tape of bureaucracy.[77]

Bettylu Saltzman was one of the first powerful Chicagoans to meet Obama and see his political potential. "I told everyone I knew about this guy," Saltzman later said. "Everyone" turned out to be the most wealthy and elite families in Chicago and beyond. Saltzman opened the doors for Obama to the Pritzker real estate dynasty, the Crown business empire, the MacArthur Foundation, and other influential liberal organizations. Her vast network of connections formed the financial base of Obama's political future.[78]

Saltzman also introduced Obama to some of Chicago's winning political strategists. Soon, Obama added political heavyweights like David Axelrod, Rahm Emanuel, Valerie Jarrett, David Plouffe, and investor John Rogers Jr. to his expanding "golden Rolodex."[79] Obama's new friends showed him how to make money as an activist. He learned that with enough political power, he could do good *and* do well.[80]

Young Obama had bounced from one tiny apartment to another, all in impoverished neighborhoods ("drug-ridden," as one biographer described) and with spartan décor. When he moved to Chicago, he "outfitted the apartment for monkish living," just as he had done in New York with "a bed, a bridge table, a couple of chairs, and some books."[81]

Shortly after their marriage in 1992, Barack and his new wife, Michelle, purchased a modest apartment in the city's Hyde Park neighborhood for $277,500. Twelve years (and a few electoral victories) later, the Obamas bought a three-story brick mansion *and* the adjacent lot.[82]

The "Kenwood house" was the couple's dream home, but it came with a steep price tag. The list price of the home was $1.95 million, but with the stipulation that the buyer must also purchase an adjacent empty lot listed for $625,000—a package deal totaling more than $2.5 million. But in 2005, the Obamas only paid $1.65 million, and the wife of a political donor named Antoin "Tony" Rezko paid for the difference.[83]

Rezko was among Obama's earliest and most active donors. Rezko first offered Obama a job while he was still at Harvard Law in the early 1990s. Obama declined, but when he returned to Chicago, he got a job at the Davis Miner law firm where he did legal work for Rezko's development company.[84]

Rezko was eager for Obama to run for office and raised hundreds of thousands for Obama's early campaigns. A Syrian émigré, he had an engineering background and designed nuclear reactors before betting on Chicago real estate (and politicians). The Rezko relationship gained scandalous notoriety when Obama confessed that Rezko and his affiliates had concealed more donations than originally disclosed.[85]

Rezko had also been a major donor and advisor to former Illinois Governor Rod Blagojevich. His political influence operations later led to a conviction on sixteen criminal charges ranging from fraud to money laundering and bribery.[86]

The scandal-plagued Rezko relationship and the tainted money that flowed therefrom could have destroyed Obama's presidential ambitions and possibly his entire political career.[87] He would not be so careless in the future.

Chicago's Nuclear Oligarchs

Chicago is home to some of the largest corporations in the world, notably Boeing, United Airlines, Walgreens, Kraft, Heinz, Allstate, and McDonald's. The largest nuclear utility company in the United States is also based there: Exelon Corporation.[88]

Most Americans have never heard of Exelon. Yet the company provides electricity to tens of millions of customers in forty-eight states, D.C., and Canada (about ten million residential, commercial, and industrial accounts). Eleven of the nearly one hundred nuclear reactors in the United States are in Illinois.[89]

If Illinois were a country, it would rank twelfth on the list of "most nuclear reactors"—ahead of Sweden, Belgium, and Germany. Exelon owns all of those reactors—plus half a dozen more across the United States—and fuels them with Russian uranium. With more than $30 billion in annual revenues (and over $110 billion in assets), Exelon is, by far, the largest power company in the United States.[90] However, their corporate history is rife with cronyism.

By the end of the twentieth century, the Clinton administration had dramatically transformed the U.S. electric utility industry. The changes have been described as "deregulation" on a massive scale.[91] But in reality, power utilities became more regulated than ever. This "restructuring" led to major consolidations in an already monopolistic industry. The net result was that, over time, investor-owned utility behemoths reaped billion-dollar windfalls, devoured their competitors, and produced "little discernable benefit to consumers."[92] Putin ran a similar play a few years later, but with less of the "free market" messaging.

Exelon Is Born, Swaddled in Cronyism

Exelon was formed in 2000 via merger, which was structured by Clinton's former senior advisor, Rahm Emanuel (and conveniently implemented by Clinton's former Energy deputy and FERC chairwoman, Elizabeth "Betsy" Moler, whom Exelon hired as a senior executive and top lobbyist). After Emanuel left the Clinton administration in 1998, he got a lucrative job as a managing director at the Chicago office of an elite investment banking firm called Wasserstein Perella & Co. ("Wasserstein").[93]

Wasserstein hired Emanuel "despite [his] having no previous education in finance…and no experience in investment banking." Years earlier, Emanuel had been instrumental in ramming the North American Free Trade Agreement (NAFTA) through Congress, and with his hire came the deep-pocketed clients that he met while working for Clinton.[94]

Emanuel's Democratic connections proved to be worth every penny to the Chicago investment firm, and he quickly became the point man on deals "subject to heavy government regulation."[95]

Chicago billionaire Lester Crown was an associate of Emanuel's and introduced him to Chicago's most powerful utility executive: John W. Rowe.[96] At that time, Rowe was uncertain that it was legal (or even possible) to merge multibillion-dollar utility companies.[97] "Every deal starts with a list of reasons why it can't get done," recalled an Exelon board member. "And I can't think of a deal that had more unsolvable obstacles than that one."[98]

The Clinton administration's so-called energy "deregulation" and the FERC's complex restructuring rules had not only created uncertainty in the industry, but also kicked off a feeding frenzy for utility companies. Ever the opportunist, Emanuel adroitly "deployed his skills as a born negotiator" and cashed in. According to *Politico*, Emanuel's "signature transaction was the $16 billion merger" that created the Exelon conglomerate.[99]

Emanuel navigated the bureaucratic crosscurrents and got the multibillion deal done. Rowe had pulled off an unlikely merger in near-record time.[100] The Exelon deal provided Wasserstein an equity stake in the nuclear utility, but only for a brief moment.

Suddenly, in September 2000, the German Dresdner Bank bought Wasserstein for $1.37 billion in stock. This deal happened a couple of months after the Exelon merger and netted Emanuel much of his Wall Street windfall. Over time, Dresdner began making nine-figure loans to Exelon and advising them on their acquisitions.[101]

Without Emanuel's political connections, a foreign bank's entrée into complex American nuclear financing might have been risky. Dresdner's troubling connection to Putin included the widely condemned plunder of Russia's largest oil company. In late 2004, Dresdner (which had become Dresdner Kleinwort Wasserstein) helped Putin strip Yukos of its assets. Dresdner's man in Russia—Putin's ex-Stasi comrade Matthias Warnig—worked the politically fraught Yukos takeover *at the same time* that Dresdner was saddling Exelon with debt.[102]

Very soon, Exelon was making deals directly with Putin's Rosatom. But they would again need their Chicago political connections to open the doors.

Obama's "Backroom Deal" and Axelrod's "Astroturf"

Rowe became a generous new fundraiser for Emanuel and Obama and a windfall for Obama's closest allies. Obama's old friend John Rogers Jr. became a well-paid Exelon board member. Exelon and its interests also hired Obama's top strategist, David Axelrod. Exelon's proxies paid Axelrod's firm to run a $15 million propaganda campaign.[103]

Exelon paid Axelrod to convince lawmakers that utility rate hikes were, counterintuitively, in their constituents' best interests. This sounded like, at best, a challenging feat. But with a $15 million budget, Axelrod could sell just about anything.[104]

Axelrod was an acknowledged expert at creating the appearance of grassroots support through a practice known as "astroturfing." In 2006, an Exelon subsidiary formed an organization called Consumers Organized for Reliable Electricity (CORE). CORE literature claimed that they were an innocuous "coalition of individuals, businesses and organizations," but CORE was really funded entirely by Exelon interests and staffed accordingly.[105]

CORE carpet-bombed the airwaves with subtle advertisements warning of a vague but impending "California-style energy crisis" in Illinois if the utility's rate hikes (a nearly 25 percent increase on each residential consumer's monthly bill) were not approved by legislators. Illinois Senate President Emil Jones (D-Chicago)—an Obama mentor and fellow recipient of Exelon largesse—used a procedural maneuver to allow the rate hikes to proceed.[106]

Axelrod's astroturfing strategy found its way into Obama's playbook (the technique was used to push Obamacare through, for example) and helped cement the strategic benefit of their decades-long mutual relationship that began in 1991. Exelon's top executives invested heavily in Obama as he rose from the Illinois State Senate to the White House. By 2012, Exelon executives and employees had personally donated at least $395,000 to Obama's federal campaigns.[107]

This figure does not include the potential millions that Exelon executives and board members persuaded their friends to donate (a practice called "bundling").[108] For example, Exelon board member John Rogers Jr. bundled a whopping $500,000 for Obama's campaigns (*at a minimum*). Frank Clark, Exelon's then-chairman and a forty-five-year veteran of the conglomerate, donated heavily to Obama's campaigns—$24,300 over the years. He also gave $63,000 to the DNC and to Obama's super PAC from 2008 to 2012. As of October 2011, Clark had also raised at least an additional $200,000 as an Obama bundler.[109]

By the time Obama set his sights on the White House, the leadership of Exelon had deeply ingratiated themselves with their fellow Chicagoan. On the 2008 campaign trail, Hillary Clinton even accused him of cutting backroom deals with Exelon. "Senator Obama has some questions to answer about his dealings with one of his largest contributors, Exelon, a big nuclear power company," Clinton told ABC News. She went on, "Apparently he cut some deals behind closed doors to protect them from full disclosure in the nuclear industry."[110]

Clinton was referring to backroom meetings Senator Obama and his staffers had with Exelon executives who sought to water down a nuclear transparency bill that Obama had introduced.

For years, Exelon failed to report that their operations had released more than six million gallons of radioactive tritium-contaminated wastewater outside Chicago. Exelon's failure to alert the public demonstrated "callous disregard" for public health and safety, according to the prosecutor.[111]

Obama introduced a nuclear transparency bill (S. 2348) in response to public outrage over Exelon's cover-up. The *original* draft of Obama's bill would have required nuclear plant operators to "immediately notify" local communities of any radioactive spills. Exelon took issue with the language and wanted exemptions for spills that happened on company property.[112]

Clinton insinuated that because Exelon had funneled at least $46,000 to his U.S. Senate campaign, Obama was willing to make a backroom deal with them. She was referring to the fact that Obama met privately with Exelon's CEO and top lobbyist while the bill moved through Senate committees. Exelon's chief lobbyist on the bill admitted that Obama told him to "work with" a staffer to get the language right.[113]

Obama's nuclear bill ultimately died in the Illinois Senate, but that did not stop him from touting it as a success—"the only nuclear legislation that I've passed"—in Iowa during the 2008 campaign. According to *HuffPost*, Obama's willingness "to lie to Iowans to protect his nuclear baggage, is at the very least troublesome."[114] This was an apparent effort to distance himself from Exelon's toxicity.

Hillary Clinton's accusation of Obama's crony ties to Exelon did not receive much coverage amid the media's fawning "Obamamania," and Clinton would later be criticized for the same thing after the Uranium One deal made headlines in 2015. The truth is that Obama and Clinton *both* pushed backroom Russian nuclear deals, and the Russian takeover of Uranium One benefitted both Clinton *and* Obama cronies.[115]

Exelon Becomes the President's Utility

The day before Obama's first inauguration, January 19, 2009, Exelon disclosed nearly $1 million ($877,000) in new lobbying expenditures. The disclosure revealed that Exelon wanted to make politically sensitive nuclear deals, specifically with the Russians (who, as mentioned above, had been supplying the nuclear utilities with fuel under Megatons to Megawatts).[116] While Obama had long been a friend of Exelon, other decision makers may have needed persuasion.

The same Exelon lobbyist who successfully pressed Senator Obama to weaken nuclear transparency was now pressing President Obama, his agencies, and Congress to make nuclear concessions to the Kremlin. Exelon ultimately spent more than $4.5 million on lobbying in 2009 and an astronomical $51.5 million (including lobbying by subsidiaries) over the course of Obama's entire presidency—more than double what was spent lobbying the previous administration.[117]

Exelon executives visited Obama's White House frequently. They lobbied heavily for Obama's energy programs and were strong supporters of his environmental policies, especially the ones that favored nuclear power.[118] The *New York Times* reported that Exelon's White House visits occurred "at key moments in the consideration of environmental regulations that have been drafted in a way that hurt Exelon's competitors."[119]

How did he do this? Obama pushed emissions standards that literally bankrupted Exelon's non-nuclear rivals. Obama's climate change agenda, especially his so-called "war on coal," crippled Exelon's fossil fuel competitors and simultaneously provided Exelon more than $1 billion in taxpayer-subsidized funding in the form of "clean energy" grants, special tax breaks, and loan guarantees.[120]

Exelon was not alone. Other nuclear utilities like Duke Energy, NRG Energy, and PG&E lobbied for Obama's climate change agenda as well. They were all members of the U.S. Climate Action Partnership, a coalition of energy corporations and environmental groups that pushed for "significant reductions of greenhouse gas emissions."[121]

Exelon, NRG Energy, and Duke Energy bagged over $5 billion from the same Obama energy stimulus program that notoriously included $535 million for a failed solar panel manufacturer called Solyndra.[122]

But Exelon and the other nuclear utilities wanted more. They wanted long-term guaranteed access to Russia's cheap uranium supply. Obama delivered.

Obama's State Department began to work quickly on the Russian civilian nuclear 123 Agreement and New START under the Russian reset. In mid-2009, Exelon and PG&E were among the first four U.S. utility companies to sign "landmark deals" with Rosatom's Tenex valued at more than $1 billion.[123] The most significant beneficiaries of the reset were apparently Obama's nuclear cronies like Exelon and, of course, the Kremlin.

Even liberal critics noted the disconnect between Obama's professed environmentalism and his corporate-backed environmental policies. The left-leaning outlet *Vanity Fair* blasted Obama's cozy relationship with Exelon, which they partially blamed for his failed environmental record:

> President Barack Obama's environmental record has prompted eco-minded groups to call his policies "disastrous," a "nightmare," and a "sell-out." Less well-known, however, is the fact that Obama himself has long been allied with Chicago-area pro-nuclear-energy

leaders and that several people in his core council have professionally benefited from their association with Exelon, the power company that runs America's largest nuclear fleet.

The magazine summarized the dizzying Exelon-Obama connections as follows:

> As for political clout, it's summed up by how Exelon's former chief Washington lobbyist, Elizabeth Moler (who served as deputy national cochair for the Obama campaign), described her employer to *Forbes:* "the President's utility."
>
> How Exelon acquired that title—and in the process changed the fortunes of Rahm Emanuel, David Axelrod, and State Senator Barack Obama, is—like the workings of nuclear power plants—complicated.
>
> The simplified version skips several twists. Such as: Thomas G. Ayers—father of retired Weatherman bomber Bill Ayers—having once been C.E.O. of Exelon forebear Commonwealth Edison; Bill's wife, 60s *über-*radical Bernardine Dohrn, and future First Lady Michelle Obama overlapping as associates at ComEd's principal outside legal counsel; and two other coincidences—recent Harvard Law grad Barack chairing a public-education group his friend Bill [Ayers] helped found, and both men serving as board members of a private anti-poverty foundation.[124]

"Americanizing" Putin's Agenda

As we will see, Putin took advantage of Obama's ties to the nuclear utilities like Exelon. Putin was well aware that Russian exploitation of U.S. energy policy would be a tough sell in Washington, so he sought to "Americanize" Rosatom's efforts by working with U.S. utility companies. Even while Obama was a U.S. senator, plans were hatched to exploit those mutually lucrative relationships for Russian gain.

Tenex had collaborated with the nuclear utilities in the past, under the Megatons to Megawatts program, and the American utilities had even joined forces with Tenex to sue the U.S. Commerce Department. An independent agency called the U.S. International Trade Commission

(USITC) had been monitoring uranium imports from Russia under the Megatons to Megawatts program and repeatedly warned that Russia was effectively dumping uranium into an already vulnerable domestic U.S. market.[125]

During the Bush administration, Exelon formed the Ad Hoc Utilities Group (AHUG) with other utilities to protect their cheap nuclear fuel imports from Russia, making common cause with Putin's nuclear fuel exporter Tenex to protect their mutual interests. AHUG and Tenex sued the Bush administration when the Commerce Department sought to restrict imports after the USITC and domestic producers raised concerns over Russian dumping. But soon, their lawsuit against the U.S. government became unnecessary.[126] The nuclear deals achieved under the reset granted Russia almost unfettered access to the U.S. market, effectively rendering the lawsuit moot. For the Russians, Obama was a dream come true.[127]

Beginning in 2009, under the guise of nuclear disarmament and nonproliferation, Obama was able to sell his Russian reset not just to Americans but also to the entire world. Obama claimed that he wanted to eliminate nuclear weapons, but Putin gave him no indication that Russia wanted the same thing. In fact, quite the opposite was true: Putin concealed his nuclear ambitions.[128]

Before and after the reset, American uranium producers sounded alarm bells over the fragility of their industry—to no avail. In 2012, the USITC confirmed previous predictions that Russia's aggressively priced uranium imports would have a "significant adverse impact on the domestic industry within a reasonably foreseeable time."[129] Obama apparently ignored these and other warnings from Congress urging him not to trust Russia.

The USITC's "foreseeable" prediction proved accurate. Putin's nuclear agenda was declared a success in 2013 with the finalized takeover of Uranium One. He had conquered the world, according to the Russian propaganda outlet *Pravda*.[130] The entire Obama administration approved this takeover due to the president's desire for cooperation between American utility interests and Russian fuel suppliers.[131]

Today, the USITC's warnings of adverse impacts have come to full fruition. The Commerce Department recently determined that uranium imports from Russia and other countries pose a threat to U.S. national security. More than fifty U.S. congressional representatives and domestic uranium stakeholders have urged President Trump to act.[132]

Obama and his nuclear industry cronies seemed not to care that Russia was untrustworthy, nor that American uranium producers could go bankrupt. In fact, the elimination of American producers would effectively guarantee unlimited cheap outsourced supply to Exelon and the AHUG utilities.[133] Any long-term consequences could be addressed later.

Obama Cashes In

In Obama's final years as president, he set up the Obama Foundation and appointed two Exelon men to prominent positions. Exelon became among the very first corporate donors to the Obama Foundation.[134] Their initial donation in excess of $1 million placed them in the top tier. Exelon soon pledged an additional $10 million, making them the Obama Foundation's largest single benefactor (Chicago-based Boeing—also a beneficiary of Russian reset deals—later matched the $10 million donation).[135]

The eight-year Obama administration feigned ignorance of Putin's plans. They even sought to downplay the possibility that Putin was still in charge. They pretended that Medvedev was a great reformer and not Putin's puppet—a preposterous suggestion. *Everyone* knew that Medvedev was just a placeholder "keeping Putin's seat warm." Putin never stopped pulling the strings, as was widely reported in Russia and indeed throughout Europe. Putin and Medvedev *openly* acknowledged that Putin was still in charge.[136] So did Obama's top diplomat, Hillary Clinton.[137]

As Obama took office, Russian spies were infiltrating America and harassing diplomats abroad. Russian nuclear officials were bribing American officials and seeking to corner the global uranium market. Russian military even conducted a simulated nuclear attack on the U.S. *while* Obama was signing a peaceful nuclear treaty—on and on and on.[138]

Obama not only ignored these dirty tricks, he actually provided political cover for the Russians both at home and abroad.[139]

So desperately did he want to "reset" relations with Russia that Obama seemed to look the other way on Putin and his associates' pattern of criminality—the espionage by an illegal spy ring, bribery, kickbacks, money laundering, harassment of American diplomats, and, as we will see, cyber warfare.

"Well, first of all, I think it's important for us to look back over the last two years and see the enormous progress we've made," Obama told a Russian media outlet in August 2011. "I started talking about reset when I was still a candidate for President, and immediately reached out to President Medvedev as soon as I was elected. And we have been, I think, extraordinarily successful partners in moving towards reset."[140]

That same week, Putin publicly called America a "parasite." Furthermore, Putin's threats to effectively annex Georgia's South Ossetia region—the reason Bush had abandoned Russian rapprochement to begin with—remained while Obama turned a blind eye.[141]

Obama truly believed that America had "shown arrogance" and wanted to prove to the world that "fundamentally transforming the United States of America" was an achievable goal.[142] Ironically, it was Obama who was arrogant. He was also inexperienced, and his administration at times resembled "bumbling fools." He and his secretaries admitted to this.[143]

It was abundantly obvious to anyone paying close attention: Russia did not share Obama's "citizen of the world" naïveté. Arrogance and naïveté are a very dangerous combination, and perhaps even more so in politics, diplomacy, and world affairs.[144]

Arrogance and naïveté aside, Obama's Chicago friends had indeed shown him how to do good and do well. He and his wife had "barely finished" paying off their student loans by 2005. Not long after they left the White House, they closed on a nine-bedroom mansion in Washington, D.C., for $8.1 million. Shortly after that, they scored an $11.75 million estate with thirty acres of waterfront on the posh island getaway of Martha's Vineyard.[145]

But the millions that Obama received from crony nuclear interests seeking to do business with Russia paled in comparison to the hundreds of millions received by Obama's Secretary of State Hillary Clinton.

CHAPTER 5

CLINTON CASH (Part II)

From Kazakhstan to Russia, with Love and Money

"All of my chips, almost, are on Bill Clinton. He's a brand, a worldwide brand, and he can do things and ask for things that no one else can."[1]

—FRANK GIUSTRA, 2006

On March 5, 2015, HarperCollins announced the imminent publication of an "explosive Clinton exposé" titled *Clinton Cash: The Untold Story of How and Why Foreign Governments and Businesses Helped Make Bill and Hillary Rich* by Peter Schweizer.[2]

Schweizer, an investigative writer, had already published several bestselling exposés of cronyism and self-dealing in Washington. When Schweizer takes aim at Washington, the political class ducks for cover.

Schweizer has a reputation as a serious researcher with a bipartisan interest in corruption. (Disclosure: coauthor Seamus Bruner works for Schweizer's Government Accountability Institute.)

Schweizer's newest book exposed a pattern of moneymaking by the Clintons through a combination of exorbitant speaking fees and huge donations to the Clinton Foundation. These donations, in the range of tens if not hundreds of millions, were from people whom Bill had helped or who stood to gain from decisions made or approved by the Clinton-controlled State Department.

While corruption is notoriously difficult to prove, the pattern of Clinton Foundation donations linked to Clinton State Department favors was repeated over and over again, strongly suggesting an institutionalized influence-peddling scheme of global dimensions.

Although *Clinton Cash* was embargoed—a normal practice in cases where a book's contents have explosive news-making potential—word of its contents had already begun to leak out. The Clintons' friends had apparently scored major deals in the wake of the Haitian earthquake. Their family members did too, the forthcoming book alleged. "And this is just the tip of the iceberg," HarperCollins' press release teased.

Panic at Clinton Inc.

By late March, Clinton's inner circle was scrambling to get an advance copy of the book. "Adding Kristina [Schake, deputy communications director] who is poking around as well," Clinton campaign manager Robby Mook emailed the team.[3]

"May have a line on it," wrote media advisor Jim Margolis on March 21.[4]

"That would be big," replied campaign spokesperson Jennifer Palmieri. "We are having a hard time finding it."[5]

"Feels like what Brock is good at," campaign chairman (and fixer) John Podesta finally weighed in.[6]

"Oh that's a great idea," Mook replied, "I'll get a chain going on that."[7]

Mook quickly fired off an email to their political and legal guru, Marc Elias, at the law firm Perkins Coie (Clinton's one-stop shop for all things legally or politically sensitive): "Marc, can we communicate with Brock about getting a copy of this Clinton Cash book? We need it very urgently if possible."[8]

They were referring to Clinton's longtime political consultant David Brock. Brock has been called Clinton's "psycho dirty tricks hitman," and worse. The progressive outlet *The Nation* would later describe Brock's politics as "poisonous."[9]

Even Clinton's aide, Neera Tanden (Podesta's right-hand), thought Brock was "batshit crazy," but he did have a vast network of contacts who might be able to help acquire a prerelease copy of Schweizer's book.[10]

Brock also had a media empire that consisted of a blog called Media Matters, a media machine called ShareBlue, a super PAC called American Bridge, and a think tank called Citizens for Responsibility and Ethics in Washington (CREW).[11]

Brock's entities—especially the flagship Media Matters—served as a "hit squad" for Clinton's campaign and would prove essential in the effort to assassinate Schweizer's character.[12]

Ironically, Brock had been given similar treatment as Schweizer when he published his own book on the Anita Hill controversy in 1993 (back when he was still a conservative and before he switched to Clinton's team). In *The New Yorker's* review, writers Jane Mayer and Jill Abramson had independently fact-checked Brock's entire book hoping to find his Achilles' heel or some fatal flaw.[13]

The Clinton team was starting to get desperate. There were rumors that CBS News' *60 Minutes* might run the material, and the Clinton Foundation was also scrambling to "finesse" the story.[14]

The Clinton team hoped to paint Schweizer's premise—that the Clintons had created an elaborate, highly lucrative shakedown scheme with their do-gooding global foundation at its center—as ridiculous and to remind *60 Minutes* of the previous Benghazi debacle in which a CBS producer was fired. "And of course," campaign spokesman Nick Merrill advised, "having the book would help that."[15]

Podesta weighed in again: "Shouldn't we attack the book or get Brock to attack the book as a Murdoch special. From the folks who brought you Fox News..."[16]

Podesta, an experienced political operative, should have known that attacking the book would only increase media interest in it. He also knew that the timing of large private donations to the Clinton Foundation vis-à-vis certain State Department policy decisions would not be easily explained. His close friend Brent Budowsky told him so in no uncertain terms.

On March 21, Budowsky, a longtime Democratic strategist and columnist at *The Hill*, wrote to Podesta privately:

> If there is one thing that could well bring down a Hillary Clinton candidacy it is this cycle of money issues about which I am now

feeling red alerts, loud bells, warning signals, and red flags and I am now seriously pissed off that there is a real chance that her candidacy and the Democratic Party could be destroyed by these self-created dangers that continue to proliferate the closer she gets to presumably announcing her candidacy.

Budowsky referred to the *Clinton Cash* press release and offered one final warning: "foreign donations and paid speeches and hustling gold mining deals by her brother are entirely legitimate issues that are self-created, and must [be] self-corrected before it is too late." Budowsky signed off, "I do not believe the Clintons fully understand the magnitude and immediacy of the danger...."[17]

Budowsky obviously knew enough about the Clintons and their friends' and associates' pattern of corrupt self-dealing to believe the *Clinton Cash* press release had at least *some* merit. Budowsky never mentioned the radioactive core of the now-burgeoning Clinton cash scandal that had the potential to derail Clinton's presidential ambitions: Uranium One and its approval by a committee to which Clinton's department was a party.[18]

The situation clearly needed to be contained. Secretary Clinton could avoid uncomfortable questions if someone who worked for her would be willing to take credit (or blame) for any decisions that might pose a conflict of interest or, worse, look like a bribe. Jose Fernandez, a former Clinton undersecretary, was all too willing to support Clinton *and* help her campaign.[19]

Fernandez's official State Department title was the assistant secretary of state for economic, energy, and business affairs. Essentially, he handled Clinton economic and foreign energy policy. Fernandez worked closely with Clinton—meeting regularly with the secretary and her inner circle.[20]

One week after the internal scrambling to get a copy of *Clinton Cash*, Podesta received an email from Fernandez indicating they had previously spoken and thanking him for landing Fernandez a plum appointment on the Board of Trustees of Podesta's organization: the Center for American Progress (CAP).[21]

"Thanks no doubt to your recommendation I have joined the CAP board of trustees," wrote Fernandez, "which I'm finding extremely rewarding."[22] Neither CAP nor Fernandez disclosed what he meant by "rewarding."

It was apparently the first time they had ever had email contact, according to leaked email archives dating back to the mid-2000s.[23]

On April 17, Podesta started work at Clinton's brand-new campaign headquarters in Brooklyn, where he would spend much of the next eighteen months.[24] After getting his keycard, the two most important items on his calendar that Friday were back-to-back telephone calls.

The first was with Hillary Clinton. Immediately after that, he called Fernandez.[25]

What the two discussed is not known. However, Fernandez afterwards appeared to be very excited and highly motivated. He quickly followed up in an email, thanking Podesta for taking the time to call. "As I mentioned, I would like to do all I can to support Secretary Clinton," Fernandez said, "and would welcome your advice and help in steering me to the right persons in the campaign."[26]

Fernandez reiterated his willingness to help Clinton's campaign multiple times in the same email and concluded: "Please count on me for full support within the confines of my day job. I look forward to your suggestions on what I can do to help."[27]

With Schweizer's book set for release in a couple of weeks, a perfect storm was brewing on the media horizon.[28] Clinton's team had to move fast. They needed to prepare an airtight defense for the issues that columnist Budowsky had raised with Podesta the previous month, specifically foreign donations to the foundation and paid speeches. The problem was that there was no airtight defense and *60 Minutes* was the least of their worries. The *New York Times* was now working on a story based on Schweizer's reporting.[29]

The next day, on April 18, the Clinton team finally caught a break.

In an email chain under the subject line, "The Book," Hillary's close aide and confidante Huma Abedin delivered the news that Clinton's inner circle had been waiting for:

We have a copy. It's in DC. We can get it to Tony [Carrk] asap.

Its 186 pages with 60 pages of footnotes.

Also heard that the NYT is moving their pub date to April 26th.

Book comes out May 5th and author is slated to appear [on] Hannity and Morning Joe.

Can jump on phone if you want specifics sooner.[30]

"Perfect," said Clinton opposition researcher Tony Carrk.

"BOOM," replied spokesperson Palmieri.

The fact that the Schweizer book was so heavily sourced was bad news for the Clinton team—it couldn't be dismissed as a hatchet job. Abedin followed up with plans for an in-person handoff of *Clinton Cash* and coordinated roles for an immediate prerelease teardown of the book.[31]

Meanwhile, Pulitzer Prize–winning journalist Jo Becker and her investigative team at the *New York Times* had been vetting Schweizer's findings and in mid-April, they reached out to the Clintons for comment. This was a major roadblock for Podesta's plan to smear Schweizer as a right-wing conspiracy theorist taking orders from Roger Ailes.[32]

The Clinton team certainly could not claim that the *New York Times* was in on a right-wing conspiracy.[33] No one would buy that. The *Times'* confirmation of Schweizer's findings was unfathomable to Clinton's team, and Podesta—evincing what can only be described as cognitive dissonance—called the *Times'* joint effort with Schweizer "bizarre."[34]

Nonetheless, Clinton's press secretary, Brian Fallon, immediately got to work drafting a memo to the *New York Times* to rebut the lethal exposé.[35]

The Clinton "teardown" had not produced any evidence that Schweizer's book misstated or misrepresented facts about Clinton's role in approving the sale of Uranium One to Rosatom. The best that they could do was to diffuse the issue by blaming the other Obama agencies involved in the Uranium One review and rolling out Jose Fernandez.

Fallon's April 22 memo to the *New York Times* included the following excerpt:

Apart from the fact that the State Department was one of just nine agencies involved in CFIUS, it is also true that within the

State Department, the CFIUS approval process historically does not trigger the personal involvement of the Secretary of State. The State Department's principal representative to CFIUS was the Assistant Secretary of State for Economic, Energy and Business Affairs. During the time period in question, that position was held by Jose Fernandez. As you are aware, Mr. Fernandez has personally attested that "Secretary Clinton never intervened with me on any CFIUS matter."[36]

Fallon's memo to the *Times* and his April 23 memo to Clinton's "Friends and Allies" spelled out every talking point that was subsequently used in the coordinated effort by Hillary's surrogates to deflect and discredit Schweizer's findings. The main message was that Schweizer had not produced "a shred of evidence," and there was "no smoking gun."[37]

ABC's George Stephanopoulos interviewed Schweizer and hit every point on the script drafted by Clinton's team.[38] After the interview, Clinton's team celebrated:

A Clinton staffer forwarded the transcript and said, "great work everyone. this interview is perfect. [Schweizer] lands nothing and everything is refuted (mostly based on our work)."

"This is amazing," replied Palmieri, "A pleasure to read."

One of Clinton's top advisors called the interview "therapeutic," and offered his opinion that the ABC host "destroyed him slowly but surely" throughout the interview, "culminating when [Stephanopoulos] asks [Schweizer] about A/S Fernandez confirming that HRC had absolutely nothing to do with the Uranium 1 deal."[39]

The Stephanopoulos interview confirmed that Fernandez was critical to Clinton's defense and ultimately created more questions than answers. Rather than "debunk" the Uranium One connections to Clinton, such as the undisclosed donations from Uranium One stakeholders, it revealed that Stephanopoulos had concealed his own Clinton conflicts.

Stephanopoulos never disclosed that his questions were effectively drafted by Clinton's team. He also never disclosed that he was, *personally*, a major Clinton Foundation donor. He was excoriated for his animus and bias. Schweizer called the duplicity a "massive breach of ethical standards."[40]

Stephanopoulos apologized repeatedly for not disclosing his potential bias and regretted not having "gone the extra mile to avoid even the appearance of a conflict." But the apology was too little, too late, and Stephanopoulos disqualified himself from moderating campaign debates.[41]

Asking for forgiveness rather than permission and failing to disclose conflicts of interest are a recurring problem in Clinton world. Just as Stephanopoulos preferred to keep his financial ties to the Clintons quiet, the Clinton Foundation had conveniently failed to disclose its Uranium One-linked donations.[42]

It was only *after* the media confirmed Schweizer's reporting that the Clinton Foundation finally disclosed Uranium One chairman Ian Telfer's $2.35 million and the other millions from his Canadian cohorts.[43]

Furthermore, the Clinton campaign failed to disclose that campaign chairman Podesta rewarded Fernandez and that the former Clinton undersecretary had offered his "full support" to help her campaign. Therefore, he was neither neutral nor credible.[44]

The Clinton campaign touted Fernandez's statement as proof that the story had been debunked. But they failed to disclose that Fernandez had quietly offered his full support to help the former secretary and the campaign.[45]

Therefore, just as with Mr. Stephanopoulos, Mr. Fernandez's conflicts raise serious questions about his motives and impartiality. Also, as mentioned earlier, Podesta's recommendation was presumably crucial to the former undersecretary's CAP appointment, which the latter described as "extremely rewarding."[46]

By July 2015, the Uranium One debacle had all but consumed Clinton's campaign. By 2016, FBI field offices around the country had opened investigations based on the findings in Schweizer's book.[47] Internal campaign polling research in New Hampshire found that public perception surrounding Uranium One was the single greatest threat to Clinton's campaign.[48]

Since then, none of Schweizer's findings have been debunked. In fact, everything significant that Schweizer reported was true. Furthermore, millions more in undisclosed Uranium One–linked donations have since been identified.[49]

The Clinton team was right about one thing: Secretary Clinton did not approve Uranium One all by herself.

The Uranium One deal required the approval of Obama's top Cabinet officials, including the Secretaries of Treasury, State, and Defense. That is true. And while Obama and other Cabinet officials had their own reasons for allowing the Russian takeover of Uranium One, the Clintons had more reasons than most.[50]

Under the cover of Obama's Russian reset, Bill and Hillary Clinton and their vast network of friends and donors (known colloquially as "Clinton Inc.") were able to make lucrative deals in Russia and generate millions of dollars lobbying for Putin's interests.

The Moscow Speech (Kremlin-backed Renaissance Capital)

On April 5, 2010, Bill Clinton's office asked Hillary Clinton's State Department for permission to travel to Moscow for a paid speaking event. The request came in just as dozens before had—innocuous, terse, and devoid of any substantive detail that might lead to a denial.[51]

"Renaissance Capital is an investment bank focused on the emerging markets of Russia, Ukraine, Kazakhstan, and sub-Saharan Africa," read the description offered by Clinton's legal team. Attendees would be from the private sector ("financial experts, economists, investors and representatives of various emerging markets companies"), and no government officials were mentioned.[52]

Bill Clinton's office expected a response from the State Department within five days.[53]

Just like dozens of Clinton's previous requests, the Renaissance Capital speech was approved almost instantly—approximately forty-eight hours later. But unlike most Clinton speeches, the Renaissance Capital speech was for $500,000.[54] This massive payday in Moscow was more than *double* Clinton's average speaking fee.[55]

After the request was approved, Bill Clinton's foreign policy advisor Amitabh Desai bypassed the ethics review channel and followed up directly with Hillary Clinton's right-hand woman Cheryl Mills and top aide Jake Sullivan.[56] Desai had previously served as a legislative aide to Hillary Clinton when she was a U.S. senator and was now working at the Clinton Foundation.[57]

"In the context of a possible trip to Russia at the end of June, WJC is being asked to see the business/government folks below," Desai said on May 14. "Would State have concerns about WJC seeing any of these folks [?]"[58]

As it turned out, a significant number of Kremlin officials and influential oligarchs would be at the event, including Russian Deputy Prime Minister and Minister of Finance Alexei Kudrin, President Medvedev's aide Arkady Dvorkovich, *and* notorious oligarch Oleg Deripaska, among other top Russians.[59]

Secretary Clinton's advisors initially ignored Desai's request.[60] While Bill Clinton's office was preparing to meet with Russian officials in Moscow, Hillary Clinton's office was busy preparing to advance the "reset" in Washington.

They worked particularly hard, publicly and privately, to accomplish the New START treaty, which President Obama submitted to the U.S. Senate on May 13.[61]

Putin had a way of mocking the Obama administration's weakness. As mentioned, Secretary Gates noted the "nice Putin touch" of the Russian military simulating a nuclear attack on the United States at the exact moment that Obama and Medvedev were signing the New START Treaty in Prague.[62]

The treaty aimed to reduce America's nuclear forces in exchange for mutual cuts from Russia. More than two dozen missile silos in California and other U.S. states would be shut down, as well as nearly three dozen bombers, and nearly sixty submarine launch tubes would be retired. Obama had canceled Bush-era plans for missile defense in Poland eight months prior. Now he was hoping to reduce America's nuclear defense at home.[63]

Secretary Clinton sought to persuade lawmakers in at least two formal briefings in May 2010. Her prepared statements were an obvious effort to persuade conservatives in the Senate to get on board with the reset:

> A ratified New START Treaty would also continue our prog-
> ress toward broader U.S.-Russian cooperation, which is critical
> to other foreign policy priorities, including dealing with Iran's
> nuclear program, cooperating on Afghanistan, and pursuing
> increased trade and investment. Already, the negotiations over
> this treaty have advanced our efforts to reset the U.S.-Russian rela-
> tionship. There is renewed vigor in our discussions on every level,
> including those between our presidents, our military leaders, and
> with my counterpart, Foreign Minister Lavrov. Our approach to
> this relationship is pragmatic and clear-eyed. And our efforts—
> including this treaty—are producing tangible benefits for U.S.
> national security.[64]

Beside Clinton sat her key ally Secretary Gates, a longtime Republican.[65] They worked as a tag team to persuade Obama's opponents to back pro-Russian reset priorities. Testifying beside Clinton was neither the first nor last time Gates "was rolled out to provide political cover for the Democratic president [Obama]."[66]

In her testimony, Clinton repeatedly referred to vague verification measures, which Russia would presumably abide by. She acknowledged that New START may not convince Iran and North Korea to change their behavior. Nonetheless, Clinton emphasized that "by bringing the New START Treaty into force, we will strengthen our national security more broadly," among other counterintuitive assertions.[67]

Clinton and Obama's other top officials failed to clarify *how* they planned to ensure Russia's compliance and how weakened defenses made America safer in the event that Russia decided to breach the agreement. After all, Putin had violated other nuclear treaties, so why would New START be any different?

At the same time Clinton was pushing Obama's New START, Putin repeatedly violated the Reagan-era Intermediate-range Nuclear Forces (INF) Treaty (according to former top Defense officials)—a detail that Clinton neglected to mention in her testimony. *The Wall Street Journal* noted the irony, "It is questionable whether the Senate would have approved the 2010 New START treaty had Russian noncompliance with the INF Treaty been aired at the time."[68]

Undeterred by Republican criticism, Clinton lobbied her former Senate colleagues behind the scenes, and the treaty was eventually ratified by a lame-duck Congress.[69]

Meanwhile, back at the Clinton Foundation, Amitabh Desai was growing impatient. "We urgently need feedback on this," he nudged Secretary Clinton's advisors. Despite a lack of a responding email from Secretary Clinton's staff, Bill Clinton met directly with Putin after the June 29 speech in Moscow, which indicates that permission was granted through some other communication.[70]

While at Putin's home, the prime minister thanked Clinton for the speech. Putin seemingly mocked U.S. law enforcement for busting the illegal Russian spy ring. "You've chosen the right time to come to Moscow. I hear your police have got carried away and put people in jail," Putin said. "But that's their job after all; really, they are all just doing their job."[71]

Days earlier, the president blasted his FBI and CIA directors for daring to expose the spy ring and jeopardize the reset. Obama's loyal top officials were now scrambling to sweep the illegal spy ring under the rug.[72]

As the FBI made plans to bust the spy ring, Hillary was at home and called the Russian foreign minister.[73] Within a week of that June 20, 2010, phone call, a quick and quiet swap was negotiated that sent the spies back to receive their hero's welcome from Putin himself. Secretary Clinton—Obama's chief diplomat—was unusually silent on the spy ring. Some of Obama's closest officials wrote about the incident in their memoirs; Clinton did not.[74]

The timing of the Moscow speech is significant. Just *one week* before Clinton was in Moscow, Uranium One notified regulators that Putin's nuclear conglomerate Rosatom would take a controlling stake through its mining subsidiary AtomRedMetZoloto (ARMZ).[75] This would give Rosatom a projected 20 percent of American uranium production (at the time of the deal).[76]

Uranium is a strictly controlled commodity with national security implications. As such, the deal would require the approval of Obama's top agencies. In this process, the Secretary of State had a lead role.[77]

When Becker's investigative team at the *New York Times* inquired about the secretary's role, Fallon said that "in general, these matters did not rise to the secretary's level." Instead, the spokesman offered the statement from Fernandez claiming that Clinton "never intervened with me."[78]

Such claims were mind-boggling. Why would an assistant have the authority to approve the deal on Clinton's behalf? What does "never intervened" *really* mean? Such language sounds like a Clintonian half-truth: Hillary's role in approving the sale depends on the definition of "intervene."

One thing is certain: the deal had been in the works since 2005 and would have been impossible without support from *both* Clintons.[79]

The Giustra Connection

The Uranium One deal was the brainchild of the Clintons' close friend, Canadian mining mogul Frank Giustra. Giustra is a diminutive man, with olive skin and receding, whitish Caesar-style hair. Giustra's net worth allegedly exceeds $1 billion, mostly derived from his many successful mining deals (he disputed the "billionaire" characterization and claimed that "excess money is an illusion").[80] Giustra made his fortune chasing what he calls "ten baggers"—deals that multiply his investments tenfold.[81]

Bill Clinton and Giustra claim that they met in 2005 at a charity event for tsunami relief.[82] That may be true, but Giustra experienced Clinton's ability to open political doors more than a decade before that, in Arkansas.

The Crater of Diamonds State Park is home to the oldest diamond mine in the United States and is located about forty miles from Hope, Arkansas—the birthplace of Bill Clinton.[83] The mine's commercial operations ended when it was sold in the late 1960s, and the State of Arkansas bought the land several years later for a state park. However, plans to revive the mine brought together American and Canadian mining investors in the 1990s through a company called Diamond Fields Resources.[84]

Diamond Fields Resources was founded by a controversial mining investor named Jean-Raymond Boulle. Boulle was born in Mauritius, held British citizenship, and later moved to Texas, where he kept a low profile, scouting deals in South Africa, Namibia, and other far-flung regions.[85]

Jim Blair, a friend of Hillary Clinton from Arkansas, introduced Boulle to then-Governor Bill Clinton in the mid-1980s. Blair made millions of dollars trading commodities and had a knack for striking good deals, including helping Hillary Clinton turn a $1,000 cattle futures investment into $100,000—an almost impossible bet absent some form of insider corruption.[86] Boulle pitched Clinton on what he believed "had the potential to rival any [mine] in South Africa."[87] Governor Clinton gave the project his blessing.[88]

Bill Clinton's attorney and friend Bruce Lindsey did the legal work for Diamond Fields. When Clinton was elected president, Boulle was invited to attend the inauguration in January 1993. At the first inaugural ball, Hillary wore a gift from Diamond Fields that came from the Crater of Diamonds: a 3.5 carat diamond ring. Lindsey had been Bill Clinton's 1992 national campaign director and was tapped to serve as an aide and deputy counsel in Clinton's White House. Following the end of the Clinton administration, Lindsey joined the Clinton Foundation and later became the chairman of its board.[89]

Diamond Fields' first major investor, Robert Friedland, is notorious among mining insiders. Friedland is a wiry, copper-haired man who was classmates with Steve Jobs at Reed College. They lived together on Friedland's family orchard (giving Apple Inc. its name); Friedland traveled on a pilgrimage to India and inspired Jobs to do likewise. Incidentally, Friedland had been arrested in 1970 for trafficking more than 24,000 doses of LSD. He served more than six months in jail before his release in 1972, after which he enrolled at Reed.[90]

Friedland got into the penny stock mining business and soon earned himself the nickname "Toxic Bob" for his environmental legacy. His company Galactic Resources used cyanide and heavy metals to extract and leach gold from their open-pit mine on an Indian reservation in southern Colorado starting in the 1980s. American taxpayers footed the bulk of the estimated cleanup bill, which exceeded $200 million.[91]

Friedland introduced Giustra and Giustra's close friend Ian Telfer to the Diamond Fields play, among other deals.[92] In fact, several Canadian investors in Diamond Fields went on to become major investors in Uranium One. They also donated heavily to the Clinton Foundation.[93]

Friedland, Giustra, and Telfer are living legends in the small world of Canadian mining. Some deals make them partners; others make them competitors. There is no evidence that Friedland partnered with Giustra and Telfer on Uranium One, but there is little doubt that he was aware. (Coincidentally, Friedland was in Moscow on the same day as Bill Clinton in June 2010. He was featured in two panels at the Renaissance Capital investor conference).[94]

It is possible that Giustra and Clinton were acquainted before 2005. Both men have a habit of misrepresenting details about their past mutually beneficial interactions. They blame a faulty memory or inaccurate record keeping. Nevertheless, Clinton and Giustra became fast friends and traveled the world together on Giustra's MD-87 jet nicknamed "Giustra Air." (Clinton flew on Giustra Air at least twenty-six times, for "foundation business.")[95]

Bill and Frank's Kazakh Adventure (UrAsia Is Born)

The Clintons left the White House in 2001. Hillary alleges that they were "dead broke." This did not last for long. Hillary became a powerful senator in New York, and Bill focused on making money—both personally and for their legacy project: the Clinton Foundation.[96]

On September 6, 2005, the former president was on foundation business in Almaty, Kazakhstan.[97] Kazakhstan is a country with both rugged terrain and large grassy plains. In the West, this Eurasian country is generally known for becoming part of Genghis Khan's Mongolian empire in the thirteenth century and for the 2006 fictional comedy film *Borat*. To savvy mining explorers, however, Kazakhstan held vast untapped natural treasures—an estimated $5 trillion worth—of assorted resources including oil, natural gas, chromium, copper, gold, and the other yellow metal: uranium.[98]

The reason given for Bill Clinton's visit was, allegedly, to work on what the foundation claims to do best: helping to alleviate suffering from HIV/AIDS.[99] At the time, Kazakhstan's estimated HIV/AIDS infection rate was between 0.1 and 0.3 percent. In contrast, several sub-Saharan African nations reported an HIV infection rate in excess of 20 percent—up to two hundred times worse than Kazakhstan.[100]

But instead of meeting exclusively with health officials, Clinton met with the brutal "dictator for life," Nursultan Nazarbayev. Nazarbayev had climbed the right ladders in the days of the Soviet Union and became ruler in 1990. Since then, Kazakhstan gained independence and Nazarbayev regularly won reelections with more than 90 percent of the vote.[101]

Nazarbayev is one of the richest men in the world. He and his family, which includes two of Kazakhstan's five billionaires, have stashed their wealth in a maze of businesses.[102]

Nazarbayev has long presided over atrocious human rights violations including torture, human trafficking, arbitrary detention, restrictions on freedom of speech, press, and assembly, and overall pervasive corruption, according to the State Department and the research arm of Congress.[103]

Despite the poor track record, Clinton showered the dictator with praise for "opening up the social and political life of your country." A former State Department official under President Clinton called Clinton's position "patently absurd."[104] The official State Department position on Kazakhstan was that it "failed to significantly improve its human rights record...."[105] Clinton had swerved far outside his lane as a former president, but he was not done.

Clinton publicly lobbied for Nazarbayev's appointment to head an intergovernmental human rights organization called the Organization for Security and Co-operation in Europe (OSCE). "I think it's time for that to happen," Clinton said in his unofficial nomination, "it's an important step, and I'm glad you're willing to undertake it."[106]

Nazarbayev was ecstatic and his press release proudly boasted about Clinton's support.[107] Clinton never revised or corrected his ringing endorsement, and Nazarbayev's country became head of the OSCE in 2010.[108] As Schweizer noted, "Putting Nazarbayev's Kazakhstan at the helm of the OSCE was like putting Iran in charge of the International Atomic Energy Agency. It made no sense."[109]

If Clinton was not there to meet with health officials and to help the suffering people of Kazakhstan, why was he really there? The short answer is because Frank Giustra wanted him there.[110]

Clinton arrived in Kazakhstan on "Giustra Air." Giustra's luxurious private jet had a "bedroom and shower, gold-plated bathroom fixtures, leather upholstered reclining seats, flat-panel TVs and original paintings on the cabin walls. The blankets are emblazoned 'Giustra Air.'"[111] It could comfortably sleep a dozen and a half people.[112]

Giustra calls his jet "a business tool. No more, no less."[113] Canadians cannot donate money to U.S. political campaigns, but they can lend their private jets to the spouse of a future presidential candidate. Giustra did that often. He also funneled tens of millions of dollars into the Clinton Foundation.[114]

Giustra made much of his fortune in the penny stock market in Toronto and Vancouver. The Vancouver Stock Exchange (VSE) was a veritable casino compared to the highly regulated New York Stock Exchange (NYSE).[115] The VSE was a huckster's paradise, and Giustra got rich "through a Byzantine system of shell companies, furtive share purchases and elaborate compensation schemes." Giustra's "ten baggers" were basically hyped-up "pump and dump" operations.[116]

His 2005 trip to Kazakhstan would be his grandest mission yet. He would need a former president and a shell company called UrAsia Energy Ltd. to pull it off.

Kazakhstan's mineral rights are prized possessions. Russians, Canadians, and Australians, the world's fiercest mining rivals, covet the lucrative Kazakh leases, and access is very competitive. At the time Giustra secured the leases, the global uranium market was about to boom. The Kazakh nuclear agency, Kazatomprom, was well-positioned to take advantage of the bull market.[117]

One of Giustra's associates, a Russian man named Sergei Kurzin, had done business in Kazakhstan before. Kurzin had previously worked for Marc Rich, the fugitive billionaire mysteriously pardoned by Clinton on the last day of his presidency.[118] Kurzin located several Kazakh uranium mines, and Giustra was interested. But Giustra was hardly the only one with his eye on yellowcake, and as Kurzin recalled, "timing was everything."[119]

"Everyone was asking Kazatomprom to the dance," said one senior uranium industry stock analyst. "A second-tier junior player like UrAsia—you'd need all the help you could get."[120]

The Kazakh and Russian state-owned mining companies were more than capable of extracting uranium ore. They had actual mining experience, as did Canadian miner Cameco Corporation. UrAsia Energy was an empty holding company with no mining experience and few, if any, assets. Giustra's visit with Clinton to Nazarbayev's palace changed everything.[121]

After a lavish private feast in Nazarbayev's palace, Clinton and Giustra departed on September 7. Over the next two days, UrAsia Energy signed agreements with the Kazakh mineral agency (MEMR) that gave Giustra's shell company the rights to three of Kazakhstan's largest uranium mines. Almost overnight, UrAsia became one of the largest uranium companies in the world.[122]

The $450 million deal stunned experts in the industry. "UrAsia was able to jump-start the whole process somehow," an industry observer said of the mysterious deal. Giustra's shell company became a "major uranium producer when it didn't even exist before."[123]

Giustra and Clinton had endorsed Nazarbayev's December 2005 reelection effort with their visit. Within five weeks of their departure, Nazarbayev's opposition suffered an arson attack on their headquarters and the opposition leader was arrested by the autocrat's paramilitary forces.[124]

Nazarbayev won reelection in a landslide amid allegations of ballot-box stuffing and voter intimidation.[125] "Recognizing that your work has received an excellent grade is one of the most important rewards in life," Clinton wrote, congratulating the dictator. "At the start of your new term as president, I would like to express confidence that you will continue to live up to the expectations of your people." Nazarbayev again boasted of the endorsement by the former U.S. president and published Clinton's note.[126]

Meanwhile, Giustra began funneling almost unprecedented sums to the Clinton Foundation. The first major tranche was more than $30 million, rapidly making Giustra one of the foundation's largest benefactors.[127]

Just like the Diamond Fields deal, Giustra assembled a heavyweight team of Canadian mining insiders to boost UrAsia's clout and draw more retail investors. Then he began shopping for more uranium assets to add to the Kazakh portfolio.[128]

Giustra swiftly distributed UrAsia's shares to himself and his Canadian friends. He got three million shares. Bob Cross, an old colleague, got 500,000 shares and a board slot. Telfer got 2.2 million shares, gratis, thanks to his long-time friendship with Giustra. Telfer and Giustra had a long history of promoting penny stocks before they moved to the big leagues. "I'm more of an opportunist than a visionary," Telfer self-deprecated.[129]

With the bulk of UrAsia's shares firmly in the hands of Giustra's friends, he then offered the company to the public via the Canadian venture exchange in one of "the largest [offerings] on record."[130] The Canadian firms that handled the stock placement all became major donors to the Clinton Foundation just like Giustra, Telfer, and other UrAsia investors.[131]

Uranium One Is Born

In February 2007, UrAsia Energy announced its merger with a Canadian-South African hybrid company called sxr Uranium One Inc.[132] The $3.1 billion merger required the approval of Nazarbayev's government due to the substantial Kazakh holdings that Giustra had acquired seventeen months previously on his trip with Clinton.[133]

The same month that the merger was announced, Giustra conveniently arranged for the head of Kazatomprom, a man named Mukhtar Dzhakishev, to fly to North America and meet to discuss the future of nuclear power. Giustra's hometown of Vancouver or even UrAsia's headquarters would have been an appropriate venue. Instead they met at Bill and Hillary Clinton's personal residence in Chappaqua, New York.[134]

When asked about the Dzhakishev meeting at the Clintons' home, both Giustra and the former president denied the meeting ever took place. When confronted with evidence, they again blamed faulty memory and inaccurate record keeping.[135] Later that year, Bill Clinton invited the Kazakh dictator to be a "featured attendee" at the "exclusive" annual Clinton Global Initiative meeting in New York City, and Nazarbayev was subsequently awarded the OSCE chairmanship.[136]

The UrAsia merger with Uranium One was approved, and Giustra's baby became one of the largest uranium mining companies in the world. Giustra stepped down from the board of UrAsia one day before the merger was announced "to permit the UrAsia Board to pursue this transaction without any perception of conflict, as he is also Chairman of Endeavour Financial (UrAsia's financial advisor)."[137]

UrAsia officially became Uranium One, and Ian Telfer was named the chairman. Giustra said he sold his stake in UrAsia and characterized the transaction as a takeover of his company, but, in effect, Giustra and his friends acquired Uranium One in a tricky move called a reverse merger—Giustra's buddies wound up owning 60 percent of the whole operation, and he remained involved through his company Endeavour Financial.[138] With Telfer at the helm, Uranium One began snapping up U.S. uranium assets to add to its portfolio.[139]

In June 2007, Uranium One signed an agreement to purchase Energy Metals Corporation (EMC), which owned extensive uranium mines in Wyoming, Texas, and New Mexico. EMC also owned properties in Utah, Nevada, Oregon, Arizona, and Colorado. "The combination of Uranium One and EMC will create a powerhouse in the United States uranium sector with the potential to become the domestic supplier of choice for US utilities," said Uranium One's CEO.[140]

The deal was subject to the approval of the Committee on Foreign Investment in the United States (CFIUS) because it involved foreign companies and substantial nuclear assets in the U.S. But both companies were Canadian, and the CEO highlighted Uranium One's *potential* to become a major domestic energy source (which would presumably mitigate U.S. dependence on foreign uranium).[141]

The company boasted that the merger would create "the only company in the uranium sector with production and asset exposure to each of the world's five largest resource jurisdictions, namely Kazakhstan, South Africa, Australia, the United States and Canada."[142]

The deal cleared CFIUS without any issues on July 31, 2007.[143]

Giustra and Telfer's new uranium juggernaut was one of a kind. With the merger, Uranium One had quickly become a world-class nuclear supplier with highly prized assets.[144]

At the same time that Uranium One was snapping up properties in the United States, Putin was consolidating Russia's nuclear industry under the umbrella of the Rosatom behemoth. By the late 2000s, Rosatom had its eyes on Uranium One's Kazakh and American assets.[145]

Giustra's timing was impeccable. When he started building up UrAsia in 2005, uranium prices were approximately $20 per pound. Prices peaked in 2007 at nearly $140 per pound. Uranium One began negotiations with Rosatom in 2008, just as the global financial crisis was beginning to take its toll.[146]

Rosatom was among only a few entities capable of buying a company as large as Uranium One. Selling Uranium One to Rosatom would be extremely profitable for Uranium One's Canadian shareholders, but it would not be as easy as the EMC takeover. In addition to CFIUS, other regulatory bodies would need to sign off on the deal, including the Nuclear Regulatory Commission (NRC) and a Utah mineral rights agency.[147]

The Uranium One deal was worth a premium to Putin for several reasons. First, Uranium One had top-tier assets and had quickly become one of the world's largest uranium mining companies. Second, it had multiple mines in the United States, and purchasing those mines piecemeal would be almost impossible due to scrutiny— buying in bulk would be much easier. Perhaps most importantly, Uranium One had been accepted into the exclusive world of the American nuclear industry.

A Russian entity would have likely been treated with considerable skepticism, but, as a Canadian entity, Uranium One would pose minimal threats and be welcomed into the Uranium Producers of America (UPA) and Nuclear Energy Institute (NEI) with open arms. These members-only trade associations had access to America's nuclear security information.[148]

Using Uranium One's credentials, Putin's operatives could gain access to conventions, seminars, and lobbyists without drawing intense scrutiny. Indeed, after the takeover, Uranium One hired American lobbyists (including the Clinton-connected Podesta Group) without ever filing under the Foreign Agents Registration Act (FARA).[149]

Members of Congress and the American public were outraged— not only at Putin's audacity but also at Obama's failure to block Putin's nuclear advances.[150] Why did CFIUS allow the deal to go through?

Perhaps the simplest answer is the most obvious: because the deal aligned with the Obama administration's Russian reset.

But a more sinister possibility remains. Could Putin have bribed the gatekeepers?

According to Schweizer's calculation, "the collective commitments and donations from investors who profited *directly* from the deal would ultimately exceed $145 million."[151] The donations linked directly to Giustra and Uranium One include:

- Frank Holmes, another major shareholder in the deal, wrote a check to the Clinton Foundation for between $250,001 and $500,000.[152] Holmes also listed himself as an advisor to the Clinton Foundation.[153]
- Neil Woodyer, Giustra's colleague who founded Endeavour Financial, committed to $500,000 and providing "ongoing financial support."[154]
- Robert Disbrow, a broker at Haywood Securities, which provided $58 million in capital to float shares of UrAsia's private placement, sent between $1 million and $5 million to the Clinton Foundation a few months later.[155]
- Paul Reynolds, an executive at Canaccord Capital, Inc., donated in the same range, between $1 million and $5 million.[156] For Canaccord, the UrAsia deal was "the largest transaction in our history."[157]
- GMP Securities Ltd., another large shareholder in UrAsia Energy, committed to donating a portion of its profits to the Clinton-Giustra Sustainable Growth Initiative. GMP made great money on the private placement of shares and as an underwriter on UrAsia Energy deals.[158]

- Bob Cross, who was a major shareholder and served as director of UrAsia Energy, committed a portion of his future income to the Clinton Foundation.[159]
- Egizio Bianchini, the Capital Markets vice chair and Global cohead of BMO's Global Metals and Mining group, had also been an underwriter on the mining deals.[160] BMO paid $600,000 for two tables at the Clinton-Giustra Sustainable Growth Initiative's March 2008 benefit.[161]
- Sergei Kurzin, a Russian dealmaker involved in the Kazakhstan uranium deal and a shareholder in UrAsia Energy, also made the Clinton-Giustra Sustainable Growth Initiative a $1 million pledge.[162]
- Ian Telfer, the chairman of UrAsia Energy, who would become the new chairman of Uranium One, committed $3 million.[163]

CHAPTER 6

PUTIN AND THE PASTOR

A Nuclear Bribery Plot Exposed

"Ask your politics."

—FBI COUNTERINTELLIGENCE AGENT, 2010

(on why Obama caved to Putin)

William Douglas Campbell had seen enough. For months, the affable Florida businessman had remained silent while the soon-to-be-disproven tale of Trump-Russia conspiracy ricocheted through the media. He knew a different tale of Russia collusion, one with more dire national security consequences. By fall 2017, he could no longer bear the strain.[1]

For at least six long years, he had worked inside Vladimir Putin's nuclear empire as an FBI operative, informing U.S. authorities about a jaw-dropping bribery, kickback, and extortion scheme that had compromised one of America's main uranium trucking firms. Now sickened by cancer and threatened into remaining silent, Campbell (known as Doug by those closest to him) made his move.[2]

Campbell's new lawyer, former Justice Department official Victoria Toensing, publicly chastised her former employer until it finally agreed to lift the "gag order" so he could tell his story. Campbell worked with *The Hill* newspaper and respected investigative reporter Sara Carter, a Fox News regular, and offered an unblemished accounting of his under-cover work.[3] Appearing on camera with his face shadowed to protect his new look (he had substantially changed his appearance to protect himself from resentful Russians), Campbell offered an explosive companion story to the Uranium One tale that Peter Schweizer had exposed in 2015.[4]

Uranium One, he explained, was not just a story about political cronyism that had enriched the Clinton family and represented a bad national security decision for America. It was also the tale of a nuclear bribery, extortion, and kickback investigation that had identified, but ultimately failed to punish, top-level beneficiaries in Putin's inner circle.[5]

Congress quickly seized on Campbell's revelations, giving Republican leaders fresh ammunition to combat the Democratic storyline of Trump-Russia collusion that had been foisted on the country by the Steele dossier in late 2016. Though weakened by cancer and struggling with a faulty memory that required him to rely on notes for accuracy, the silver-haired former FBI operative became an instant celebrity for conservatives, even appearing on Sean Hannity's Fox News TV show. In March 2018, he was summoned to Capitol Hill for a private interview with congressional investigators.[6]

Though Campbell's story was meticulously backed by thousands of pages of FBI documents and contemporaneous evidence, he was about to suffer one final indignity at the hands of Democratic members of Congress and Rod Rosenstein's former Maryland U.S. attorney's office.[7]

A whisper campaign was launched, first in news media articles quoting anonymous Justice Department officials and then in a congressional memo leaked by Democrats. Each sought to portray Campbell as lacking credibility. They insinuated that Campbell had been deemed unreliable by the U.S. government and that there was no evidence he had ever raised concerns about the Uranium One transaction with his FBI handlers.[8]

Michael Isikoff, the *Yahoo! News* reporter whose stories gave life to Christopher Steele's uncorroborated allegations of Trump-Russia collusion, was one of the first recipients of the leaks. Within weeks, most of the mainstream media had published the story.[9]

Nothing, actually, could be further from the truth.

* * *

As a crisply dressed Doug Campbell stepped into the elevator on the eleventh floor of the Pentagon City-Ritz Carlton, he could feel his heart pounding. At least the sudden rush of adrenaline helped clear his bleary eyes and the sensation of fatigue he had felt all morning after a sleepless night in his hotel room.[10]

It was October 2010 and the Florida businessman had been working for the FBI as an undercover operative inside Putin's nuclear giant Rosatom for about two years. That particular morning was set for a "drop," a consequential assignment in which Campbell was supposed to capture on video members of Russia's nuclear monopoly accepting cash bribes. It was either going to be a seminal moment that advanced the FBI's counterintelligence case against Russia or blow Campbell's carefully crafted cover.[11]

As the elevator descended, Campbell could feel sweat beading in the palm of his right hand, which clenched "the football," the moniker that he and his FBI handlers had given to his trusty steel-enforced briefcase. Black on the sides with numerical locks on the top, the briefcase was his portable office on the far-flung journeys he had taken across the globe. It was also the repository for whatever secrets he was carrying for the U.S. government at the moment. As such, it seldom left his sight.[12]

A few moments before he stepped onto the elevator, FBI Special Agent Tim Taylor and his counterintelligence team had left Campbell's room to retreat to the back of the swanky hotel. It was a beautiful, crisp October day, and the agents had squirreled away behind the Ritz in an unmarked black SUV loaded with sophisticated surveillance equipment to monitor Campbell's meeting with the Russians. He was to regather with them after the drop was completed.[13]

Thanks to Taylor and his fellow counterintelligence agents, the morning had already been surreal. Campbell gazed in wonder as the agents spread rubber-banded piles of hundred-dollar bills across his hotel bed. The agents counted the stacks until they were certain that they had all $50,000. Then they removed his laptop and folders from the briefcase to clear room for the cash. The bills were placed in the body of the briefcase, filling all but a few inches.[14]

From the lid, Taylor had removed one of three pens Campbell usually kept tucked in the storage pouches. In its place, he had put a sophisticated wireless camera shaped like a pen. The device was equipped with a 180-degree eye designed to capture all the sights and sounds as soon as the Russian targets opened the briefcase.[15]

Taylor was a tall, slender, and youthful agent working his first major Russian counterintelligence case. He had a young family that he adored, and he also shared with Campbell a deep Christian faith. Occasionally, the two would pray together before assignments. When it came time to assign Campbell an operative code name, Taylor whimsically chose to call him "The Pastor." The agent would joke that Campbell reminded him of those preachers on TV with the crisp suits, southern drawls, and photographic recitations of Bible verses. On weekends, that was Campbell's life. He loved church and worshipping Christ in the congregation of friends that he shared back home.[16]

Doug Campbell appeared to friends, family, and Florida colleagues as a globetrotting business consultant who successfully dabbled in agriculture products, nuclear fuel, and other commodities. Never one to settle down, he seemed every inch the model of an ambitious corporate climber, married to his job by day and to his church life on weekends. But the silver-haired businessman harbored a secret for more than three decades that even his closest friends did not detect: his frequent international travels were cover for work as an operative for the United States government.[17]

Campbell had worked undercover for the CIA and FBI for more than thirty years.[18] Campbell's dangerous work took him into meetings with members of Russian organized crime in the United States, and in Western Europe, Russia, Ukraine, Kazakhstan, and other regions around the world. Early on, the job was simple. On trips overseas, Campbell would collect information about foreign leaders and businesses who were trying to spread cash in the form of bribes to win more business inside the United States. He would report back to his handlers, who would use the information to make Foreign Corrupt Practices Act prosecutions against violators, both foreign and American.[19]

But starting in mid-2005, the feds had a more targeted assignment for Campbell. They wanted him to penetrate Vladimir Putin's burgeoning uranium sales empire. Putin was gobbling up uranium supplies across eastern Europe, and U.S. officials suspected that he was looking to build a monopoly that could dominate the global uranium market, much as Moscow dominated natural gas sales in Europe. For a country lacking a robust, diverse economy, energy was Putin's geopolitical weapon. It kept the West at bay, and nearby neighbors from the former Soviet empire dependent on him.[20]

Campbell's assignment began in Kazakhstan in 2005, around the time that former President Bill Clinton and his top aides were also focusing on the rugged, uranium-rich former Soviet republic. (As Campbell would later learn, the Clinton connection was much more than a coincidence.) Eventually, the Russians engineered a deal to get their hands on the Kazakhs' yellowcake uranium supply, as well as a large share of America's uranium in the transaction that would become known as the Uranium One scandal.[21]

By 2008, Campbell had made a strong connection with a South African nuclear executive named Rod Fisk, who had begun working with Russians to grow their uranium market in the United States. Fisk had become a top executive at an American trucking company that moved enriched uranium around the United States, including some of the nuclear fuel the Russians had sold under the Megatons to Megawatts program created after the fall of the U.S.S.R.[22]

The growing ties to Rosatom figures like Fisk convinced the FBI in 2008 that it was time to sign Campbell to a nondisclosure agreement barring him from publicly discussing his mission. (This gag order would eventually be lifted in 2017 by the Trump Justice Department after it was publicly revealed that he was being muzzled.) A team was set up to handle Campbell, including Taylor, the bureau's young counterintelligence agent, and David Gadren, a more experienced criminal investigator with the Energy Department's office of inspector general who was steeped in the ins and outs of nuclear energy.[23]

Inside Rosatom, Fisk took a liking to Campbell and brought him into the inner circle of Tenex, the Rosatom subsidiary that was the Russians' main commercial uranium sales arm. Eventually, Campbell was hired by Tenex's lead executive in the United States, Vadim Mikerin, as a consultant to help Rosatom grow its uranium sales to nuclear utilities inside the U.S.[24]

Barack Obama, a big proponent of nuclear utilities while in the U.S. Senate, was then taking over as president, and the Russians had high hopes for expansion in the American market. That is because President Obama and Secretary of State Hillary Clinton were pursuing a high-risk diplomatic "reset." As mentioned, the reset was designed to create a more peaceful relationship with Moscow after months of tension brought on by Russia's 2008 military action against the former Soviet Republic of Georgia.[25]

Campbell would soon find out that working for Tenex came with a high cost. Shortly after he signed the consulting deal, Mikerin demanded that Campbell hire a Russian consultant for training on how to write the reports for Moscow. Mikerin gave Campbell the name of the company and where he was instructed to wire $25,000. But weeks later, there was no training and not even the name of a Russian who was to advise him.[26]

Campbell became suspicious and alerted his FBI handlers. Was this Mikerin's backhanded way of demanding kickbacks, or just the Russians being slow and plodding? Campbell and his handlers eventually determined it was the first. In fall 2009, Mikerin approached Campbell again and told him that in order to keep his consulting job, he would have to kick back $25,000 of his monthly $50,000 consulting fee.[27]

The demand thrilled Campbell's FBI handlers. They knew they had criminal conduct. Now they needed to follow the money trail to see how far the scheme went. So, they gave Campbell permission to start making the payments. The Russians had set up an elaborate payment path that laundered kickbacks through a series of shadowy offshore accounts. They called it "the System." The FBI soon discovered through Campbell's undercover work that the same accounts were being used by Moscow for other illegal activities.[28]

For most of his first year with Tenex, Campbell made wire transfers every other month and otherwise kept his head down performing legitimate consulting work, seeking to help Tenex win billions in new nuclear fuel contracts from American utilities. The work was going well, and Russia was scoring some big deals.[29]

In October 2010, Mikerin needed a temporary change in the kickback scheme. Some of his senior bosses from Moscow were coming to visit Tenex's new American headquarters in suburban Maryland, called Tenam. They needed cash for shopping and partying while on the trip, so Mikerin asked that Campbell skip the normal wire transfer and bring the next $50,000 in cash.[30]

Campbell coordinated with the FBI and checked into the Ritz the night before. But he could not sleep. The notion of delivering a briefcase full of cash to a corrupt Russian nuclear official was unnerving. And for the first time during this operation, he felt that his life could legitimately be at risk. So, he tossed and turned all night, rose for breakfast, and waited for the FBI to get him prepped.[31]

Taylor assured Campbell the FBI would have eyes and ears on him the whole time. All he needed to do was stay calm and deliver the cash. The pen camera would do the rest.[32]

As the elevator hit the first floor and the doors opened to the lobby, Campbell took one last deep breath. "Walk slow. Talk slow. Don't show the nerves. And just get this over with," he told himself. That little voice in his head was all there was to calm him until he could grab a drink.[33]

Campbell walked to the hotel bar, took a table, and waited. Soon, the stout Russian with the pug, emotionless face arrived. The two ordered a morning vodka. Campbell toasted Mikerin with a quick drink—*Nah zda-rovh-yeh!* They downed their liquor and headed back to Campbell's room. Mikerin seemed nervous, perhaps by the impending arrival of his bosses.[34]

As soon as Campbell keyed the door to his room, he put the briefcase on the small table by the bed. His fingers turned the numbers to the lock and popped open the briefcase. Then he stepped back so Mikerin could peer in.[35]

"It's all there," Campbell told his Russian counterpart.[36]

"Very good," he replied. As he was thumbing quickly through the cash, Campbell peered over his shoulder to check just once that the pen-shaped spy camera was staring right at him. The camera had not moved, and Mikerin seemed blissfully ignorant of its presence. Campbell gave a faint smile. *Mission accomplished*, he thought.[37]

Mikerin quickly gathered the stashes of cash into his own bag and got ready to leave.[38]

"I've got to get back to the office," he said. "Ludmilla wants to go shopping at Saks, and I need to get this back to the vault and get her some money."[39]

Ludmilla was a high-ranking female executive from Rosatom, a key member of the visiting delegation. The vault was a large safe installed inside Mikerin's Tenam office. Campbell was familiar with it because he had photographed it for the FBI during one of his surreptitious surveillance tours.[40]

Now the FBI would have its first video evidence that the kickbacks Campbell was paying were going far beyond Mikerin, to Rosatom's top brass back in Moscow. Campbell could not wait to tell Taylor and to get assurance that the camera caught it all.[41]

Soon, Mikerin was out the door and on the elevator. Campbell walked back into the room and slumped into the chair for a moment of relief. He let about ten minutes elapse, then called Taylor on the FBI's burner phone.[42]

The agents came to his room from their stakeout location. They opened the briefcase, pulled out the camera, and confirmed they had perfect footage of Mikerin taking the kickback money.[43]

The case had just made a giant leap forward. Campbell was relieved and increasingly certain that the FBI would be able to take down this group of Russian criminals, and, more importantly, stop Putin from amassing more uranium business inside the United States.[44]

He would be sorely disappointed. An undercover mission he hoped was about to end with speedy arrests would instead stretch on for four more frustrating years.[45] The reason for the delay, Campbell would later learn, could be traced to a meeting that had occurred about 4,800 miles away and exactly one year earlier.[46]

In October 2009, in the high-tech Moscow suburb known as Barvikha, Secretary of State Hillary Clinton had met in an opulent statehouse with Putin's right-hand men, then-President Dmitry Medvedev, and Foreign Minister Sergey Lavrov, to discuss ways the two countries could improve relations.[47]

Medvedev reportedly crowed, with a smiling Clinton standing nearby, that Clinton's further discussions with Russian colleagues demonstrated "that the level of our cooperation...is gradually advancing." To which Clinton responded that the U.S. was looking forward to "deepening and broadening this strategic relationship."[48]

A key agenda item in the U.S.-Russia talks, it turns out, was a plan to accelerate commercial uranium sales to the United States. For nearly two decades, the Russians had been guaranteed a steady sale of nuclear fuel to America by disassembling old Soviet nuclear warheads and converting the uranium to a form that could be used in reactors.[49]

That "ploughshares" program, known as Megatons to Megawatts, was about to expire in 2013. Moscow's already shaky economy could suffer a significant financial blow unless Rosatom could replace the lost revenue with sales to American utility companies. But there was a rub. Old Cold War restrictions kept Moscow from selling uranium directly to utilities.[50]

George W. Bush's administration had begun lifting those restrictions with the creation of the U.S.-Russia civilian nuclear cooperation agreement. The program was on track to be ratified during Bush's last year in office when Russia suddenly engaged in a military conflict with Georgia, a key U.S. ally.[51]

Thus, Bush's carrot was immediately pulled in favor of the stick of sanctions. But by March 2009, the new Obama team wanted to go back to the carrot approach. In rapid succession, Obama restored the agreement and lifted various restrictions that let Russia start to line up billions of dollars in new uranium sales.[52]

Little did Campbell know on the day he delivered the $50,000 to Mikerin that Secretary Clinton's jaunt to Barvikha (and the reset generally) had already opened the door for Rosatom to collect unprecedented billions from the United States. These extraordinary benefits would flow even as Campbell was documenting Russian criminality in the form of bribery, kickbacks, extortion, and money laundering. The United States was rewarding a bad actor, and the FBI and the intelligence community knew it. There are procedures for informing the appropriate persons in the government.[53] Did they do so or were the procedures ignored?

Campbell was forced to keep quiet for four more years, as he gathered a raft of evidence on how Russia's corrupt nuclear machine was compromising national security inside the United States while executing a plan to dominate the American and global uranium markets.[54]

Some inside the Obama administration believed that allowing Putin this nuclear business would keep Russia closer and more dependent on the United States, much like the original ploughshares deal with Boris Yeltsin's Russia. America could account for Russia's nuclear supplies and create a more lenient business environment, one that would lower the temptation to sell nuclear materials on the black market, such as to Iran's illicit nuclear weapons program.[55]

Others saw red flags. They had seen how Putin wielded his natural gas monopoly in eastern Europe as a weapon against U.S. allies, and remembered his bad behavior in Georgia in 2008, which occurred even as the Bush administration was opening the U.S. nuclear market for Russia. They worried that Russia would dump below-market-priced uranium and drive out its global competition, and that America would lose its independent ability to quickly mine uranium. And they suspected that once Putin got what he wanted, he would start acting badly, such as by aiding Iran.[56]

By 2014, these fears were realized. The American nuclear industry was shrinking, and Putin deployed troops to the separatist region of America's most important ally in the region, Ukraine.[57]

For Campbell, the hardest pill to swallow occurred in fall 2010 shortly after the Mikerin $50,000 briefcase drop, when Campbell learned that the Obama administration had approved Rosatom's purchase of Uranium One, which owned large deposits of uranium ore in both the United States and Kazakhstan.[58]

For months before CFIUS approved the deal, Campbell had been feeding intelligence to the FBI that Uranium One was an essential part of Putin's strategy to corner uranium markets and gain leverage over the United States. He also learned that Rosatom harbored ambitions to build a uranium enrichment complex on U.S. soil.[59]

Fisk opened doors inside Tenex for Campbell and was the first to alert him about the mining deal's importance.[60] "The attached article is of interest as I believe it highlights the ongoing resolve in Russia to gradually and systematically acquire and control global energy resources," Fisk emailed Campbell on June 24, 2010.[61]

Fisk forwarded a June 21, 2010, article from Reuters on Rosatom's efforts to buy Uranium One through its ARMZ subsidiary, and relayed a conversation that Fisk had with Canadian executives of Uranium One lamenting Russia's impending acquisition. "There are a lot of concerns," Fisk wrote.[62]

By autumn, Campbell was being solicited by his colleagues to use his lobbying muscle as a Tenex consultant to help overcome Republican opposition to the Uranium One deal. Some lawmakers in uranium mining states and neoconservatives in Congress were raising concerns about the impact of the deal on domestic production and national security.[63]

Rosatom has "shown little if any inclination to effectively address the widespread and continuing corruption within Russia, particularly its energy sector," Republican House members Ileana Ros-Lehtinen of Florida, Spencer Bachus of Alabama, Peter T. King of New York, and Howard P. "Buck" McKeon of California wrote the Obama administration in October 2010, hoping to pause the deal.[64]

Fisk wrote Campbell on October 6, 2010, in an email entitled "ARMZ + Uranium One":

Good afternoon Doug,... The referenced [October 5, 2010] article may present a very good opportunity for Sigma [Campbell's company] to try and remove the opposing influences (if that is something you can do).[65]

The next day, Campbell intercepted a memo prepared for Mikerin by an American energy consultant named Cheryl Moss Herman, who would later go to work inside the Obama Energy Department's nuclear energy office. The eleven-page report, entitled "Policy/Legislative Issues Affecting the Business Climate in the U.S. for TENAM/Tenex," made clear Uranium One's importance to the overall Russian nuclear strategy and warned that the plan could be foiled by conservative political opposition.[66] Herman warned Mikerin:

Some Republicans truly fear the entry of Russia into the U.S. market, as demonstrated by the fact that they are taking steps to block the purchase of Uranium One...This effort bears watching as it may provide clues as to the likely political reaction if a Russian entity was going to participate in the construction and operation of a uranium enrichment plant in the U.S.[67]

Herman also warned that there was growing concern inside Congress that Russia's determined march into new U.S. uranium business conflicted with Western intelligence that Moscow was still aiding Iran's illicit nuclear program.[68] "There are some in Congress who believe that Russia is providing Iran with sensitive nuclear technology as well as the nuclear know-how that will allow it to proliferate a nuclear weapons program, despite Russian Government statements to the contrary," Herman wrote.[69]

Campbell forwarded Herman's memo to his FBI handlers. By that time, he had provided the FBI incontrovertible evidence that the Russians had demanded and received kickbacks from him and others dating back to 2009, had compromised the security of an American uranium trucking firm, and boasted of a plan to corner the uranium market with artificially low prices.[70] Under the circumstances, it seemed unthinkable that the U.S. government could fail to act.

Campbell's FBI handlers assured him that his intelligence had reached the highest levels of the United States government, including then-FBI Director Robert Mueller and President Obama. There was no way, Campbell thought, that the Obama administration could in good conscience allow the Uranium One sale to proceed.[71]

A few weeks later, he received an unexpected kick to the gut when he saw the first reports that CFIUS had unanimously approved the Uranium One transaction.[72]

The decision made only back-page headlines, mostly in financial and trade publications. The message was clear: CFIUS saw no national security reason to block the deal.[73]

The bewildered Campbell wondered if all his undercover work over the last two years had been in vain. Soon, he demanded an explanation from his FBI handlers.[74]

"Ask your politics," Taylor answered when Campbell questioned the CFIUS approval. The FBI operative knew exactly what his agent handler meant. The political headwinds of the Obama reset were so strong that officials in his administration would not allow a criminal bribery scheme to stand in its way.[75]

For years now, Clinton and Obama defenders have cited the unanimous CFIUS decision, which indicates that Obama's top officials saw no national security reason to block the transaction, pushing back against Campbell's account. In so doing, they insinuated that career officials who recommended approval must not have known about Rosatom's criminal conduct. The news media, likewise, picked up on that line, using it to impugn Campbell's story and calls to reinvestigate the matter.[76]

Because most of the intelligence available to the federal agencies who participated in the CFIUS review remains classified, there has been no resistance to that narrative. The bureaucracy through claims of secrecy has thwarted any scrutiny of whether CFIUS board members could or should have known about Campbell's undercover work.[77]

For more than two long years, that answer has actually been sitting in public view in a congressional correspondence file at the Nuclear Regulatory Commission, which regulates atomic power in America. Toward the bottom of a lengthy January 2018 letter to Republican Senator John Barrasso (R-WY), the NRC acknowledged that the responsible intelligence agencies had been alerted to the Rosatom investigation in August 2010—the same month that CFIUS was notified of the transaction and *well before* the Uranium One deal was approved in late October 2010.[78]

"The NRC first became aware of the investigation in August 2010, when it received a sensitive intelligence report made available to various components of the Federal Government through normal intelligence reporting channels," the agency wrote Barrasso.[79]

This is a shocking revelation and an admission that could have neutralized months of attacks on Campbell.

The Obama administration *was* warned in advance that the Russian company about to get the American assets of Uranium One was engaged in criminal behavior, just as Campbell claimed. Yet the deal proceeded anyway!

The NRC letter raises an additional troubling question: were Obama's CFIUS members so poorly informed that they did not realize that the Russian company targeting Uranium One was the sister company of a corrupt Rosatom subsidiary that was under FBI investigation? "The NRC was not aware of any connection between the investigation and the transfer of control of Uranium One to ARMZ," the response said.[80]

The extraordinary weaponization of the so-called "Russia collusion" issue against Trump has managed to obscure this glaring flaw in the CFIUS process. The Russians dealing with Campbell, meanwhile, could not have been more elated by the Obama administration's seeming blindness to Rosatom's misdeeds.[81]

A few days after Campbell delivered the suitcase full of money to Mikerin, he was invited by the Russians to the swanky Morton's steakhouse in the Washington suburb of Chevy Chase, Maryland. Campbell's role was twofold: host the vodka-laden steak dinner and pick up the $700 tab. The date was October 19, 2010. The Russians were already aware that Uranium One was about to be approved and were planning a party to celebrate the opening of the suburban Washington office of Tenam, their new American subsidiary.[82]

Mikerin was joined by a handful of Russian figures, including one tied to the KGB and another who was a declared Russian spy on U.S. soil.[83] The rowdy guests gleefully boasted about how easy it had been for Rosatom to win concessions from the Obama administration, including lifting a regulatory suspension at the Commerce Department that allowed Tenex to receive billions in U.S. nuclear fuel contracts and the approval of the Uranium One sale.[84]

Campbell would later recount to congressional investigators how he kept a straight face that night, but winced when he heard his Russian guests deride President Obama with the nickname "Bongo-Bongo," a clear racial epithet, and mock his government for its giveaways to Putin.[85]

The Russians boasted "how weak the U.S. government was in giving away uranium business and were confident that Russia would secure the strategic advantage it was seeking in the U.S. uranium market," Campbell told lawmakers in a 2018 statement.[86]

The gloating went public by January 2013. After the CFIUS approval of Uranium One and the Obama administration's arrangement of billions in Russian-U.S. utility contracts, the headline on the *Pravda* website declared: "Russian Nuclear Energy Conquers the World."[87]

Campbell became disillusioned, a feeling that only worsened as his undercover work dragged on, with no certainty that Russia's bad behavior would be punished.[88]

"I was frustrated watching the U.S. government make numerous decisions benefiting Rosatom and Tenex while those entities were engaged in serious criminal conduct on U.S. soil," his statement to Congress recounted. "Tenex and Rosatom were raking in billions of U.S. dollars by signing contracts with American nuclear utility clients at the same time they were indulging in extortion by using threats to get bribes and kickbacks, with a portion going to Russia for high ranking officials."[89]

Russian nuclear officials cryptically threatened Campbell on at least two occasions. They ominously alluded to the radioactive poisoning of ex-FSB officer (and famed Putin critic) Alexander Litvinenko to ensure that Campbell would never betray them. In 2006, Putin's operatives allegedly slipped polonium-210—a radioactive isotope produced almost exclusively at a single Russian nuclear facility—into a teapot that Litvinenko drank from. The murder was linked to Rosatom, Tenex, and Putin's Ozero comrade: former Tenex CEO Vladimir Smirnov. Campbell knew that the threats were credible. "It makes you think hard about those you love so far away," Campbell recalled of the harrowing experience.[90]

Nonetheless, Campbell trusted his handlers inside the FBI and the Department of Energy inspector general's office (DOE IG). And for three more years, he intensely worked the Rosatom inner circle to garner intelligence.[91]

He did so even as the toll of being undercover began to show. He turned to drinking to calm his nerves and was arrested more than once for driving under the influence. Eventually, he would be diagnosed with a tumor that required thirty-six extensive radiation treatments, as well as leukemia, which, as of this writing, still requires chemotherapy.[92]

His government handlers stood beside him through the good and the bad times: Taylor's prayers and Gadren's salty pursuit of crimes provided welcome motivation. Together they made significant investigative strides.[93]

Through his work uncovering the System, Campbell identified specific money-laundering channels used by the Russians (both Kremlin officials *and* organized criminals), and others inside Latvia, Cyprus, and the Seychelles. This was a significant accomplishment that led to prosecutions. Campbell also provided crucial evidence that the kick-backs he was paying to Mikerin via overseas accounts were being partly funneled to higher-ranking Russians in Moscow, a potential major counterintelligence discovery.[94]

"They refer to the money that comes in as the parcel and in Vadim's words it is delivered by hand directly to their group," Campbell wrote in one of his updates to the FBI. "No one goes to any bank and because of the political positions of the individuals in the network no one can investigate this system."[95]

Most FBI debriefings occurred in a hotel or the unmarked Chevy Suburban that would meet Campbell at a designated rendezvous point. But the undercover operative and his handlers also set up two email accounts, one on Yahoo and the other on Google, in the name of his company, Sigma, in case that cryptic instructions needed to be passed along in between the meetings. The emails made it look like Campbell was communicating with his employees. In fact, he was talking to the feds.[96]

Nuggets of intelligence kept flowing. For example, Campbell provided the FBI with evidence about the consulting work that a lobbyist named Amos Hochstein performed to advise Rosatom and Tenex as they began their conquest of the American nuclear market.[97] While legal, Hochstein's assistance to the Russians was keenly interesting to the FBI because of his frequent proximity as an advisor to such luminaries as Hillary Clinton, John Kerry, and Joe Biden. Tenex's outreach to past or future government advisors like Herman and Hochstein clearly demonstrated that the Kremlin had mastered the art of revolving-door influence in Washington.[98]

Campbell was also able to give the FBI a heads-up about a special twist in Tenex's American persuasion strategy. While Russia made much of its money from fossil fuels, it understood the need to acknowledge the climate change agenda of the Obama administration and its European allies. So Mikerin began incorporating minor environmental nods into the company's policies.[99]

"Compliance with environmental standards during production and transportation of exported uranium products TENEX both observes and will promote the following environmental policy principles,"

Campbell reported to his handlers in summer 2010. "They will require that all suppliers and counter parties must have environmental compliance certificates (Series ISO 14001) and environmental monitoring systems."[100]

As time wore on, Campbell's nerves settled down. His hands no longer trembled when he made the bimonthly kickback payments, and his integration into the Russian machine became less stressful. Thirty years of operating covertly for Uncle Sam had made playing a role, even a dangerous one, more natural.[101]

Not surprisingly, Mikerin and his Russian comrades only seemed to grow in their trust of Campbell. He could drink them under the table one day and open the door to an American utility executive the next. That trust became readily apparent when a rival lobbying firm with deep ties to the Clinton Foundation, APCO Worldwide, tried to muscle Campbell's smaller firm out of the way on a project involving the 123 Agreement. If Campbell got sidelined, the FBI's intelligence pipeline would dry up. But the Russians intervened and overruled any effort to push Sigma aside, blissfully unaware that the consultant was in fact the FBI's best mole inside their enterprise.[102]

Campbell reported to his FBI handlers that his position inside Rosatom had survived the APCO power play.[103] "APCO lobby group requested that ROSATOM/TENEX allow them to approach US utilities and assume the responsibilities of Sigma," he wrote. "The leadership of ROSATOM (Kiriyenko) and TENEX (Grigoriev) blocked this involvement and stated that the arrangement with Sigma would stand. We know why this happened (network). Clearly APCO is far more competent and far better politically wired than Sigma. This made no difference to the Russians."[104]

As the bond between The Pastor and Putin's nuclear team solidified, the FBI's appetite for inserting Campbell deeper into the Russian web also grew. In 2012, the bureau devised a plan for Campbell to use his Russian contacts to invite Putin to visit the United States during or after the election. The agents' hope was that they could spy more effectively on the Russian leader while he was here.[105]

Campbell wanted a hook that would be a sure winner, especially given the long odds of getting Putin to say yes. He knew that Putin valued his old title as a colonel in the KGB and had a penchant for horses and racing. (Putin's personal jockey left for the United States in 2013.) Campbell tried to merge the two passions in an offer that Putin could not refuse.[106]

Through his old agricultural business work, Campbell had developed strong political ties in Kentucky, which hosts the mother of all horse races. So, he reached out to aides for the state's then-Democratic governor, Steven L. Beshear, and got Putin named an official "Kentucky Colonel." The Kentuckians had no idea that Campbell was an FBI operative. He simply knew how to pull off the Kentucky Colonel designation.[107]

This designation, one of the most coveted social honors in Kentucky, comes with an official certificate. Campbell obtained the certificate signed by Beshear and sent word through his Moscow contacts that Putin had a VIP invitation to attend the Kentucky Derby in spring 2013 and would be honored as a "Kentucky Colonel." Campbell hoped that the PR stunt would be too alluring for Putin to turn down. His handlers were impressed by his creative approach. A few weeks later, though, Campbell got word from his Moscow contacts that Putin had declined.[108]

Today, all that remains of the failed FBI operation is the official certificate declaring:

> To All To Whom These Presents Shall Come, Greeting: Know Ye, That Honorable Vladimir V. Putin Is Commissioned A KENTUCKY COLONEL. I hereby confer this honor with all the rights, privileges and responsibilities thereunto appertaining.[109]

Dated October 15, 2012, the declaration bears the signature of both Governor Beshear and then-Secretary of State Alison Lundergan Grimes.[110]

The FBI's drive to gain evidence inside Rosatom of Russian complicity with Iran's nuclear program proved to be Campbell's final mission as a Tenex consultant. Throughout 2010–2012, Campbell had repeatedly provided his handlers information about Rosatom's dealings and interests in Iran.[111] Of all the worries that critics of the Uranium One deal held, illicit support of Iran's nuclear program loomed near the top, as Herman's internal memo to Mikerin correctly noted. The FBI had similar concerns.[112]

In one debriefing, for instance, Campbell related to his handling agents that Mikerin had identified a specific Russian company, TVEL, that was facilitating business between Iran and Tenex. "As I have mentioned previously they do all the uranium business between Russia and Iran," Campbell wrote of the intermediary. "Vadim is involved in the process under the same kind of payment network between Iran and the special TENEX group. I have asked him if he visits Tehran and he indicates he will not go because he feels it will cause trouble both for [U.S.] relations as well as his US travel."[113]

Such intelligence was intriguing for FBI counterintelligence, especially as the Obama administration secretly began discussions with Tehran aimed at reaching a deal to delay Iran's nuclear weapons program.[114]

In 2010, Campbell had obtained from his Russian sources a non-public report from the International Atomic Energy Agency (IAEA), the UN watchdog that was bird-dogging Iran's illicit nuclear weapons program. The public version of the May 2010 report identified current enrichment-related activities inside Iran, including evidence that UN inspectors gathered related to a uranium enrichment plant in Natanz.[115]

While U.S. officials likely already knew the contents of the report, Campbell's acquisition had provided valuable insight: an IAEA report marked "restricted" for limited distribution had fallen into the hands of Rosatom's leadership quickly. The long arm of Putin's nuclear team knew few bounds.[116]

Campbell continued to provide fragmentary intelligence on the Moscow-Tehran nuclear dealings, including additional IAEA reports that the Russians had obtained. But in early 2012, a harbinger arrived that the bureau was preparing to pull its operative out and finally close out the counterintelligence gathering part of the probe and transition to criminal prosecutions.[117]

Special Agent Taylor contacted Campbell with the most specific instruction the team had ever given him over the years: a detailed list of fifteen questions that the bureau wanted asked of Mikerin. The questions were transmitted via the secret Sigma email accounts that the bureau had set up with Campbell. All were about Iran:

- Is Iran seeking to create a weapon, either through obvious means, or through the design of their nuclear program?
- Are there any other countries, other than Russia, partnering to help Iran's nuclear program?
- If there are other countries participating, what model for security and nuclear power generation is Iran following?
- What security measures has Iran put in place at nuclear facilities to prevent the computer failures, the failure of automated systems, or a computer virus?
- What political issues are of concern to Russia if they are to continue to support the Iranian nuclear program?
- If Iran is seeking to enrich uranium to HEU, what is the timeframe in which they expect to achieve that level?
- How many Russian employees are currently working on Iranian projects?
- How many Iranian scientists are currently working on nuclear energy projects? Who are they? What are their specialties?
- What is the megawatt capacity of Bushehr? What are the long-term goals for the facility?
- Are there other facilities currently enriching uranium? Have there been requests for assistance or indications of interest in new facilities?
- How may centrifuges are currently operating at Bushehr?
- What are the safety standards to which Iranian nuclear facilities are built? IAEA standards? How is Iran prepared to ensure force protection and answer international security concerns?
- Are there concealed or restricted areas at Iranian nuclear facilities where Russians are not allowed to visit? Where are they, and what do the Russians feel is going on there?
- Are there temporary storage facilities where nuclear materials are stored? How are they secured?
- How is new and used nuclear material moved and stored, and by whom?[118]

When Campbell got this list, he joked that the FBI was signing his death warrant. The questions were too specific, the kind only an American spy might ask. Campbell had already been threatened by the Russians with polonium poisoning to ensure that he would not betray their criminal network.[119]

The FBI, however, would not back off, insisting that Campbell press ahead and corner Mikerin with the Iran questions. The agents even coached him on how he could put his Russian friend at ease while unloading this barrage of inquiries.[120]

The agents coached Campbell:

As discussed: You spoke with contacts who understand US policy. After the conversations you wrote down notes and have some ideas. You believe that Russia, Rosatom and Tenex could improve working relations with the US by being transparent about activities in Iran. You believe that it would be easier for Tenex to do business in the US if the US knows that Rosatom and Tenex have their fingers on the pulse of what is going on in Iran and can ensure that the nuclear energy is being produced responsibly and safely.[121]

It might have sounded good to the agents, but after thirty years in the business of spying, Campbell knew that these questions would blow his cover, or at the very least break the bond of trust that he had built with his Russian targets.[122]

Campbell was right. Mikerin refused to provide much in terms of answers, and soon backed away from his longtime Sigma consultant. Campbell's work for Tenex dwindled, and his access to Rosatom diminished. He still had plenty of other contacts in Moscow. And the FBI's Taylor and DOE's Gadren sought to redeploy his attention to other projects, like arranging the Putin visit to America.[123]

The relationship between the operative and his FBI handlers remained strong even as the spy work declined. But one unanswered question still loomed large in Campbell's mind: when, if ever, would the U.S. government finally bring Mikerin and his Russian pals to justice?[124] He would have to wait another two years—until 2014—for the answer.

In 2014, Campbell was whisked to a meeting in Greenbelt, Maryland, with prosecutors in the office of U.S. Attorney Rod Rosenstein, who was Obama's pick to remain the top federal prosecutor in Maryland (one of the only Bush-era prosecutors that Obama did not fire), and eventually became Trump's deputy attorney general during the Russia "Spygate" affair.[125]

After years of grueling deep undercover work and numerous rounds of chemo, Campbell's memory was not as strong as it once was. To compensate, Campbell, now in his midsixties, had made voluminous notes to keep his testimony straight. He would have to fumble through the piles of paper before answering most questions, a performance that quickly soured the prosecutors. Soon, the writing was on the wall. Rosenstein's team did not want to use Campbell as a trial witness. Period. And no more energy needed to be wasted to debate that point.[126]

Meanwhile, so much time had elapsed since Campbell had first proved the bribery and kickback scheme in 2009 that circumstances were changing. Rod Fisk, the South African nuclear expert who ran the uranium trucking company Transport Logistics International, had been a prime early target of the probe. Campbell was able to document how Fisk made hundreds of thousands of dollars in kickback payments to Mikerin all the way back to 2004. But Fisk died in 2011 after a short and sudden bout with cancer.[127]

In contradiction to its usual practice, the FBI did not execute a search warrant to obtain Fisk's computer after his death. Instead, agents secured voluntary consent from his widow to sweep the computer of information they wanted. When they returned years later, the hard drive and its potential evidentiary gold mine had been destroyed. It was another misstep certain to aid the defense.[128]

By the time Campbell was brought to Greenbelt for a second time to meet with prosecutors, a criminal indictment had been filed by prosecutors against Mikerin and another defendant, Daren Condrey, the executive who replaced Fisk at the uranium trucking company.[129]

Gadren, the DOE IG agent who worked alongside the FBI's Taylor, filed the initial affidavit in February 2015 in support of a search warrant for some of Mikerin's evidence. His affidavit suggested that the Justice

Department had uncovered a major kickback scandal and would eventually prove that some of the monies were going to Putin's inner Moscow circle.[130]

"As part of the scheme, MIKERIN, with the consent of higher level officials at TENEX and ROSATOM (both Russian state-owned entities), would offer no-bid contracts to U.S. businesses in exchange for kickbacks in the form of money payments made to some of the same offshore bank accounts to which MIKERIN was directing CS-1 to make payments between 2009 and 2011."[131]

In the end, the government pursued convictions or plea deals for just three figures: the trucking company executive Condrey, a Russian national in New Jersey named Boris Rubizhevsky whose security firm worked as a Tenex consultant, and Mikerin, who got forty-eight months in prison after pleading guilty to felony money laundering.[132]

The missed opportunity was not lost at Mikerin's sentencing hearing in December 2015. U.S. District Judge Theodore Chuang expressed his deep dismay that the Russian had been able to compromise a sensitive American asset like the uranium trucking company. For that enterprise "to be corrupted by graft is very troubling," the judge said.[133]

Mikerin's lawyer made clear what the government had suggested from the beginning. Attorney Jonathan Lopez argued that "while his client served as a conduit for the payments he was neither the mastermind nor the ultimate beneficiary of the bribes," Reuters reported. In other words, the kickback money that Campbell so meticulously tracked for the FBI for more than six years actually benefitted inner circle nuclear industry officials in Moscow. But none would be brought to justice by Obama or Rosenstein's prosecution team.[134]

Campbell took some solace in knowing that his harrowing undercover work had resulted in some convictions. His pride was further boosted when his FBI handler team invited him out for a steak dinner to celebrate. When he arrived at the restaurant, the operative got an unexpected surprise: FBI supervisors had authorized a check for $51,046.36 as a reward for his undercover exploits.[135]

Campbell was grateful. He respected Taylor, Gadren, and his other government handlers, and remained in contact with them for months afterwards. As late as 2017, Gadren continued to reach out to Campbell for assistance on cases, in one instance seeking intelligence on Trump Energy Secretary Rick Perry and some of his international dealings.[136]

But Campbell still felt like he had been left at the short end of a stick. His compensation for legitimate work for Rosatom had been gouged by Mikerin's kickback scheme, and he believed that the U.S. government should reimburse him for far more than roughly $50,000. By his calculation, he was still short about $500,000 that he had right-fully earned in consulting fees.[137]

By summer 2016, as the U.S. presidential campaigns raged, Campbell retained private counsel and filed a lawsuit seeking payment from the feds. His suit laid out his entire role in the Rosatom affair, threatening to expose the Obama administration's feckless response to Russian nuclear bribery and tainting its anticipated successor for the White House, Hillary Clinton.[138]

Within hours, Campbell's litigation set off alarm bells in the U.S. Justice Department. His lawyer was threatened by the attorneys in the Criminal Division with prosecution for violating his nondisclosure agreement. Campbell demurred and quickly withdrew the lawsuit before it attracted any media attention or compromised what he was told were other ongoing operations in Russia based on his earlier intelligence.[139]

After Campbell went public in late 2017 and early 2018, he was immediately embraced by Republicans and smeared by Democrats and the news media. Inaccurate stories and a House Democratic staff memo sought to impugn his reputation, falsely suggesting that he was unreliable even though the FBI had awarded him the bonus check. The counterattacks became so severe that Toensing, Campbell's attorney, wrote then-Attorney General Jeff Sessions' Inspector General demanding a leaks investigation. It did not happen.[140]

Eventually, the Justice Department would make statements backing away from the anonymous attacks on Campbell, acknowledging the FBI's $51,000 check and the mentions of Uranium One in the bureau files. It was too little too late. And as too often happens with the twenty-first century news media, reporters were loath to go back and correct their erroneous reporting. They could just move on to a new tale, without any consequence.[141]

Like most undercover operatives, Campbell had his flaws, whether it was his bouts with the bottle or his struggles with memory lapses inflicted by the effects of cancer treatment. He was the first to embrace those flaws, often telling people that he did not think that he would have been a good congressional or trial witness.[142]

In the end, Doug Campbell's heroic efforts to assist the FBI in building a major Russian counterintelligence case did not warrant the smear job that he received. It was yet another travesty leveled by the falling dominoes that began with Obama's failed Russian reset.

CHAPTER 7

THE GATEKEEPERS OF CFIUS

How Clinton Turned a National Security Review into a Tollbooth (and How Obama Allowed It)

"One of the fears that I hear from Russians is that somehow the United States wants Russia to be weak. That could not be farther from the truth. Our goal is to help strengthen Russia."[1]

—SECRETARY OF STATE HILLARY CLINTON,
First Channel Television interview with Vladimir Pozner
in Moscow, March 2010

Before Hillary Clinton began her first failed presidential campaign in 2008, she burnished her image as a foreign policy expert and stateswoman in the Senate. Senator Clinton landed a position on the powerful Armed Services Committee. In February 2006, the committee convened to find out why the Bush administration had allowed the takeover of American shipping terminals by a United Arab Emirates (UAE) state-owned operator.[2] A burgeoning fiasco, known as the Dubai Ports scandal, was brewing.

Senator Clinton, in her navy pantsuit, looked disheveled. Her short blond hair was mussed, and she had heavy bags beneath her eyes. She flashed a quick smile at her friend and mentor Senator Robert Byrd of West Virginia, as he hobbled over, placed his cane beside Clinton, and sat down at the Senate panel. Clinton returned to the talking points her aides had given her. The chairman and ranking member spoke first while Clinton patiently awaited her turn.[3]

Clinton began by expressing her "deep concerns" about the port deal. Those concerns seemed to focus less on the potential national security threats of that particular deal and more on the CFIUS process in general.

> The CFIUS process has been subject to several critical reports in the last several years; most recently, a Government Accountability Office (GAO) report last fall which pointed out that one of its failures was its inability to focus effectively on national security issues as the statute establishing CFIUS intended it to do. This particular decision by CFIUS raises a number of red flags.[4]

Clinton used the opportunity to slam the Bush administration over 9/11 and Hurricane Katrina, citing "inadequate funding" and "bureaucratic dysfunction." "If September 11 was a failure of imagination, and Katrina was a failure of initiative," Clinton said, "this process is a failure of judgment." Scoring political points was no doubt high on Clinton's list of priorities, but she had another priority: she wanted to understand the CFIUS *process*.

Clinton complained of "numerous problems with this review process," and wanted answers. She wanted to know exactly who was apprised of the review and who attended the CFIUS meetings. She wanted to know if state and local officials should have been consulted.

Clinton cloaked her curiosity in a vague concern for America's national security. Meanwhile, her Democratic colleagues had more specific concerns. They linked the UAE to Osama bin Laden and al Qaeda's financing of the September 11 attacks, global terrorism generally, and with nuclear material smuggling to Iran, Libya, and North Korea. But Clinton hardly mentioned the UAE and remained laser-focused on the inner workings of CFIUS.

"I want to just get additional information about how CFIUS actually operates. How many times did CFIUS meet to consider this transaction?"

Clinton continued to pepper the Bush officials with logistical questions.

"Are there quorum and proxy rules for conducting business for CFIUS?"

When a reporter for FOX News asked a Bush official for information on past deals that CFIUS reviewed, Clinton could not help but agree:

> I think it would be useful for the committee to get those [CFIUS] examples, because if this definition of "national security" is kind of a moving target, we need some idea of what the field looks like.[5]

Clinton called the review "cursory, at best." She was outraged that the CFIUS process "did not alert the President, the Secretary of the Treasury, the Secretary of Defense that several of our most critical ports were about to be transferred to a foreign government entity."

"For many of us," Clinton harped, "there is a significant difference between a private company and a foreign government entity."[6]

For her, that difference would not matter as much when Russian state-owned Rosatom purchased Uranium One in 2010.

Previously, most people had never heard of the shadowy Committee on Foreign Investment in the United States, or CFIUS. The top-secret task force was formed in 1975 to assess foreign transactions that might pose threats to U.S. national security. Today, the committee is comprised of the top cabinet agencies, including the departments of State, Defense, Homeland Security, and the Treasury.[7] CFIUS has the power to effectively make or break foreign investment deals.[8]

In 2006, CFIUS sprang into public awareness after a Middle Eastern ship port operator called Dubai Ports (DP) World sought to buy multiple ports in the U.S. The Bush administration's CFIUS approved the transaction and strongly defended it amid intense public objections from Congress.[9]

Senator Hillary Clinton was one of the most vocal critics of the deal. Clinton argued that the deal could threaten national security and condemned the Bush administration for allowing the UAE-backed company to purchase the ports.[10]

Whatever her national security concerns, Clinton conveniently failed to disclose to the committee that, at that very moment, her husband was on the UAE's payroll. Though it was not widely noted at the time, Bill Clinton had a commercial relationship with the UAE dating back to 2002. Interestingly, the former president specifically advised the UAE on the Dubai Ports CFIUS transaction at the same time that his wife publicly opposed it.[11]

The former president also delivered paid speeches in the UAE, established a Clinton scholarship program at the American University in Dubai, and set up a three-way partnership with Dubai ruler Sheikh Mohammed bin Rashid Al Maktoum and his friend, billionaire Ron Burkle. The partnership was a new sovereign wealth fund financed by the UAE, Burkle's Yucaipa Companies LLC, and Clinton.[12]

Between 2002 and 2007, the Yucaipa partnership netted the Clintons more than $15 million. Clinton's former advisor Dick Morris linked the partnership to the Dubai Ports deal and called the affair the "Clintons' UAE quid pro quo."[13] The Clinton Foundation received millions from UAE-linked entities.[14]

A DP World competitor hired lobbyists to persuade Congress to kill the deal. Soon after, Senator Chuck Schumer (D-NY) attacked the purchase based on what the media called "anti-Arab suspicion."[15] He, Hillary Clinton, and others—including then-Senator Obama—even threatened legislation specifically targeting the Dubai Ports purchase. Meanwhile, Bush redoubled his support of the DP World purchase and threatened to veto any such legislation.[16]

The Dubai Ports fiasco was the first time that CFIUS deliberations made significant headlines and sparked public discussions. Despite receiving CFIUS approval, the sale sparked enough public outcry through Senator Clinton's and others' protests to cause the port operators to renegotiate the deal.[17]

At first glance, it appeared that Senator Clinton was working against the interests of her husband's Arab benefactors. However, it is possible that the UAE never wanted the U.S. ports to begin with. First, the "U.S. operations represent[ed] only around ten percent of the $6.8 billion of the deal," and the UAE operator's primary interest in the takeover was "getting a greater presence in Europe and especially in Asia."[18] Second, U.S. port security costs skyrocketed after 9/11, and, while airports received an influx in federal funds, "only modest federal funding [had] been made available for port facility improvements."[19] Furthermore, inefficiencies caused by American union worker demands was an added deterrent.[20]

In the end, the Dubai Ports deal was neither killed nor undone. Rather, the transaction proceeded and the U.S. ports were carved out of the deal and sold to AIG Global Investment Group—a financial firm with zero port operation experience—for an undisclosed sum.[21] As it turns out, AIG closed on the port deal with DP World less than three months after pledging $5.25 million to the Clinton Global Initiative.[22]

Whether Senator Clinton's grandstanding was a demonstration of her genuine concern for U.S. national security, or an attempt to distance herself from the UAE-linked millions flowing to her husband and her foundation, or even a potential shakedown for future UAE largesse, the true reason for the Clintons' conflicting actions was never exposed. What was certain? The UAE continued to shower the Clintons and their foundation with millions long after the Dubai Ports controversy died down.[23]

By working both sides of the deal, the Clintons received significant and undeniable benefits from the Dubai Ports debacle: it simultaneously highlighted their CFIUS expertise *and* demonstrated their ability to either close or kill a CFIUS deal.

After the Dubai Ports debacle, Senator Clinton pushed for legislation to fortify CFIUS dramatically. In 2008, when she ran for president the first time, she even touted herself as "an outspoken proponent of strengthening CFIUS."[24]

If Senator Clinton tried to kill a port deal involving an allied country, surely Secretary Clinton would be concerned when an adversary like Russia tried to purchase a strategic nuclear asset like uranium through the Canadian mining company Uranium One. But, according to Clinton, the Uranium One takeover was handled by her deputy, Jose Fernandez, who (after receiving an extremely rewarding position from Clinton fixer John Podesta) claimed that she "never intervened."[25]

Clinton's defenders contend that Uranium One never rose to the level of importance deserving the secretary's attention. Ironically, then-Senator Clinton criticized the Bush CFIUS officials for similar inattentiveness and grilled them on who was "apprised" and how many meetings they had.[26]

Hillary and Bill Clinton's counterbalancing roles in the Dubai Ports deal demonstrated several important facts that relate to Uranium One. First, Hillary Clinton was a longtime CFIUS hawk. Second, Bill Clinton was willing to take foreign cash and lobby for controversial foreign governments. Most importantly, Bill had successfully advised on a contentious CFIUS review, but Hillary and her allies could blow up a deal even after CFIUS approved it. The Clintons thus proved their ability to affect CFIUS outcomes. They were the ultimate gatekeepers for foreign entities wanting to make major investments in strategic U.S. assets.[27]

Shortly before the Dubai Ports controversy began, the Clinton Global Initiative (CGI) was established. CGI convened annually in New York, providing a forum for foreign governments and industrialists to network with some of the most powerful people in the world. In return, the Clinton Foundation raked in tens of millions of dollars in donations, and hundreds of millions in "pledges" and "commitments" for charitable work. In 2004, Clinton Foundation revenue was over $57 million. Two years later, its revenues had more than doubled.[28]

New CGI benefactors were funneled into the Clinton fundraising pipeline. Their names and donation amounts were added to spreadsheets to be tallied and totaled for future donor outreach.[29] Becoming a CGI donor was only the first step for individuals seeking Clinton's favor. Next, they were encouraged to sponsor a speech by Bill Clinton, which would put money directly into Bill and Hillary Clinton's pocket.[30]

While Hillary Clinton was running for president in 2008, the Clinton Foundation's *annual* revenue approached $200 million. Obama defeated Clinton for the nomination but tapped her for the role of top U.S. diplomat. In her first year as Secretary of State, Clinton Foundation revenues hit an all-time high of nearly $250 million (after Clinton's election loss to Trump in 2016, revenues plummeted to less than $40 million in 2017—and just over $30 million in 2018, a fifteen-year low).[31]

During her Secretary of State confirmation hearing, Hillary Clinton was grilled on the massive amounts of money flowing to her spouse and the foundation in the form of speeches and donations. Clinton was easily confirmed despite the reservations of congressional Republicans and some in the Obama administration. Clinton was able to ameliorate their concerns by signing a memorandum of understanding (MOU) with Obama's presidential transition team—cochaired by none other than Clinton's fixer, John Podesta—that promised enhanced disclosures for Clinton speeches and foundation donations.[32]

The Clinton MOU proved to be toothless as Clinton violated its requirements repeatedly with absolute impunity.[33] This was particularly evident in the troubling case of Uranium One.

Many Uranium One shareholders, for example, secretly donated undisclosed millions to the Clinton Foundation.[34] These investors stood to gain substantially from the CFIUS approval as the Russians were willing to pay top dollar. Rosatom paid billions for Uranium One—including a $610 million cash "premium"—of which *at least* $479 million went directly to Uranium One's shareholders as a "special" cash dividend.[35]

But first, the Canadians and Russians would need the blessing of Obama's CFIUS gatekeepers. Hillary Clinton was in the unique position to make or break the deal.

State Department's Lead Role on CFIUS

The Dubai Ports case had thrust CFIUS under a microscope, and the national security establishment in Washington scrambled to avoid another public spectacle. The intelligence community (IC) tapped Major General John R. Landry to put together a task force to assess potential CFIUS deals being "blindsided" by "political landmines" like the Dubai Ports scandal. General Landry was a highly decorated graduate of both West Point and Harvard with combat experience. At the time, General Landry was the national intelligence officer (NIO) for military affairs—the highest-ranking military intelligence official.[36]

In May 2006, General Landry invited James Rickards, an investment guru with CIA experience, to meet at the CIA headquarters in Langley, Virginia. General Landry asked Rickards to put together a team of experts to assess future CFIUS deals from Wall Street's perspective. Rickards agreed and set about forming a task force of private sector lawyers and financial advisors to assess CFIUS deals. Rickards' team became known as "the Dirty Dozen."[37]

Rickards' Dirty Dozen team convened at Langley multiple times each year to discuss upcoming deals with national security implications and offer their perspectives. They provided valuable insight that protected American interests while supporting CFIUS' mission. Rickards' team reviewed dozens of CFIUS transactions, and their work was so successful that the Defense Department asked him to create a similar task force at the Pentagon.[38]

The Dirty Dozen had unprecedented civilian access to CFIUS proceedings, and Rickards is one of the few experts who has shed light on the secretive process. Rickards acknowledged that CFIUS decisions must be unanimous, but that fact alone does not exonerate Clinton's key role in the Uranium One decision.[39]

The CFIUS unanimity issue became Clinton's *primary* defense in the Uranium One case—amid a series of shifting and unverifiable excuses (such as Clinton "never intervened")—when the heat came down in April 2015. "The State Department was just one of nine [CFIUS] agencies" remains the primary talking point of those who declare—without evidence—that Uranium One is a "debunked conspiracy."[40] Rickards reveals why the unanimity issue is not an airtight defense:

> It is true that CFIUS has nine votes (eight Cabinet-level departments plus the president's science adviser), and that the Uranium One deal was approved unanimously. So, this Clinton defense has superficial support.
>
> But, this defense bears no relationship to how CFIUS works in practice. In fact, there are only four votes that count—the secretaries of state, defense, energy, and treasury.[41]

The Treasury Department is the designated leader of CFIUS and sets the agenda.[42] On deals with significant national security implications, the opinions (or "equities") of the secretaries of defense and state hold the most weight and "everyone else is a bystander."[43] Despite Clinton's claim that she had no undue sway over the committee, Rickards' description of how the CFIUS participants typically behave reveals that Clinton's State Department played a central role. In fact, the State Department had the ability to single-handedly approve or block Uranium One:

The Commerce Department is considered a pro-investment cheerleader and is not taken seriously. The Office of the U.S. Trade Representative and the president's science adviser can chime in but are little more than rubber stamps for what the big four want.

The Departments of Justice and Homeland Security contribute intelligence from the FBI and other collectors. This is added to collections produced by CIA, DIA, and NSA, yet those agencies seldom voice a strong view on the merits of a deal. CFIUS is a consensus-driven group.

If the secretary of state pushed hard for Uranium One, the secretaries of defense and treasury would go along because their equities, weapons systems and terrorist finance specifically, were not infringed. Other members would remain mute. If the White House did not oppose the secretary of state, then her strong support for a deal could single-handedly carry the day.[44]

Rickards was correct. Despite the Treasury Department's designated lead role, Clinton's State Department effectively ran point on the Uranium One CFIUS review and provided positive justification for the Russian nuclear takeover. Her staff linked the Uranium One CFIUS review to New START and the 123 Agreement—both major foreign policy priorities for Obama and Clinton.[45] Obama had placed Clinton in charge of coordinating the U.S.-Russia Bilateral Presidential Commission (BPC), which had significant nuclear and foreign investment implications.[46] The State Department was the logical choice for assessing the complex diplomatic and bureaucratic cross currents posed by Obama's reset. It also dovetailed with Clinton's announced interest in promoting "economic statecraft" during her tenure as secretary.[47]

Less than two months before the CFIUS review, Clinton's economic guru, State Department Undersecretary Robert Hormats, visited Putin's hometown of St. Petersburg to promote Russian investment in the U.S. He was a featured speaker at the St. Petersburg International Economic Forum (SPIEF) on June 18, 2010. Hormats highlighted the Obama administration's commitment to fostering economic partnerships with Russia.[48]

We have a very open investment environment in the United States. We do have an investment review process known as CFIUS but that really only addresses a relatively small portion of the overall amount of investment that takes place in our country and we have a very welcoming environment for investment.... We are a country that looks forward to foreign investment.[49]

Several top Russian officials and oligarchs close to Putin (including at least one Clinton donor named Viktor Vekselberg) sat beside Hormats on the panel. They listened intently to the State Department deputy as he emphasized Obama's policy of open investment. His words must have been music to Putin's ears.[50]

A Controversial Decision

Obama's reset with Russia had been widely criticized from the start—especially because it was a polar reversal of the Bush administration's chill following Russia's 2008 invasion of Georgia. By the time the October 2010 CFIUS review approached, Obama's critics had grown frustrated with his perceived weakness and his pro-Putin policies under the guise of economic diplomacy.

Obama received the most backlash for his flip-flop on missile defense, for the perceived gutting of America's nuclear arsenal, and for ensuring the safe return of Russian spies just weeks before the Uranium One approval.[51]

Several key GOP lawmakers were especially concerned with Russia's nuclear assistance to rogue regimes (particularly Iran, Syria, and Burma) due to the threats posed by weapons-grade materials in the hands of American enemies. The ranking members of the House Armed Services, Financial Services, Foreign Affairs, and Homeland Security Committees urged CFIUS to recommend that Obama block the Russian takeover of Uranium One's essential U.S. nuclear assets (which they believed posed national security risks).[52]

As president, Obama had the sole authority to suspend or block the Uranium One transaction based on the CFIUS recommendation. But in 2006, Clinton and her Senate colleagues had already proven that a coordinated media strategy could effectively derail a controversial deal like Dubai Ports. Thus, the Uranium One deal was *by no means assured or guaranteed.*

So why did CFIUS ignore the red flags surrounding Russia's nuclear ambitions?

Clinton's State Department anticipated criticism of Russia's nuclear cooperation with Iran—the primary sticking point in past U.S.-Russia nuclear negotiations—and effectively preempted it amid CFIUS deliberations. Uranium One formally notified CFIUS of the deal with Rosatom/ARMZ on August 4, 2010.[53] On September 13, State Department staffer Ari Sulby sent a memo to the Treasury Department titled "Russian Nuclear Cooperation with Iran."[54]

The memo was sent to Treasury's CFIUS chairman, Aimen Mir. Oddly, it had no header, it was unsigned, and it was undated, making attribution difficult.[55] The memo appeared to have been hastily cribbed from a 2008 State Department assessment called a Nuclear Proliferation Assessment Statement (NPAS), prepared for the Bush administration and required for any prospective 123 Agreement.[56]

"The United States has received assurances from Russia at the highest levels that its government would not tolerate cooperation with Iran in violation of its UN Security Council obligations," the State Department memo to CFIUS began. It then proceeded to list all the ways that Russia cooperated with the U.S. to keep Iran's nuclear program in check.[57]

The State Department failed to mention the red flags surrounding Russia's nuclear cooperation with Iran, which was of particular concern to the lawmakers. Instead, the department repeatedly lauded Russia for their Iranian containment efforts such as supporting the International Atomic Energy Agency's "intense investigation into Iran's nuclear program" and "condemning Iran's construction of an illicit enrichment facility near Qom."[58]

Clinton's State Department justified nuclear dealings with the Kremlin, "In light of Russia's demonstrated willingness, as outlined above, to work together with the United States and other nations to seek a resolution of the issues raised by Iran's nuclear program."[59]

The State Department memo was timely because it was sent to CFIUS only three weeks before the four ranking members implored Obama's committee to block the deal—*specifically* due to Russia's nuclear cooperation with Iran.

In Congress, the ranking members had apparently not seen the State Department's mitigation memo praising Russia's handling of Iran. Their letter directly contradicted the State Department's optimistic view. The congressional representatives listed numerous Rosatom activities that they believed "should raise very serious concerns for United States national security interests."[60]

The ranking members' red-flag letter directly contradicted the State Department memo. While the State Department asserted that Russia was instrumental in the *containment* of Iran's nuclear weapons ambitions, the lawmakers stated that Russia had *undermined* the "longstanding efforts to compel Iran to abandon its pursuit of nuclear weapons."[61]

Other red flags that the ranking members believed should disqualify the Uranium One transaction included the fact that Russian entities have been placed under nuclear-related sanctions on more than twenty different occasions since 1998. In addition, Russia has continued to sell nuclear components with dual civilian and military use to regions that could use such technology for weapons of mass destruction (WMD) and missile programs.

The State Department memo never mentioned these alarming details. Quite the opposite, the memo highlighted that Russia is not selling dual-use technologies in violation of UN Security Council Resolutions. The memo also failed to report that Russian President Dmitry Medvedev met with Syrian despot Bashar al-Assad to discuss Russia-Syria nuclear cooperation, or that Syria continued to block any investigations into their North Korean–built nuclear weapons facilities, which were destroyed by an Israeli airstrike.

"The facilities, materials, technology, and expertise that could be provided to Syria, even for a 'peaceful' program," the congressional letter warned, "would likely be used for a renewed weapons program, regardless of any assurances the Russians might provide."

Russia's nuclear alliances with Iran and Syria were particularly alarming given that both were state sponsors of terrorism.[62] The ranking members' letter concluded by criticizing the Uranium One transaction as the "take-over of essential U.S. nuclear resources by a government-owned Russian agency." They reiterated the threat to national security and urged CFIUS to block or at least postpone the deal.[63]

CFIUS apparently found the State Department's optimistic rationale more compelling; it ignored congressional pleas to block the deal.

CFIUS deliberations are held in secret and take place at the main Treasury building in what Rickards and the IC call "'Downtown' principals meetings." Rickards does not know for certain how the State Department or any other Obama agency exercised their "equities" at the Downtown meetings. Mysteriously, he and his Dirty Dozen were kept out of the loop during the Rosatom takeover review in 2010. "Uranium One was the dog that didn't bark." When Rickards learned about the secret CFIUS approval, he was mystified:

> [Uranium One] fits squarely in the realm of deals typically denied, where an adversary, Russia, is buying a sensitive asset, uranium. Strangest of all, this deal never came to our attention. Not once in any meeting, classified or unclassified, was Uranium One ever mentioned in our full advisory board sessions or one-on-ones. It's as if the deal were being handled inside the intelligence community on a special track, precisely to avoid the analysis our group was formed to provide.[64]

Rickards' observation that Obama's IC may have shepherded Uranium One on a special track presents a curious dilemma: it either supports the Clinton defense that the State Department was just one of nine agencies who approved the deal, or it suggests that Clinton's State Department was able to persuade Obama's IC to get on board with the Russian takeover of American uranium assets.

Even if Clinton or her agency did exert pressure to approve, Obama's CFIUS *and* IC had been warned of the risks and apparently failed to provide substantive pushback on those who advocated Uranium One approval.[65]

Putin began taking Uranium One private in 2013—a move that required a further 49 percent investment and could have triggered a second CFIUS review.[66] At a time when Rickards and the Dirty Dozen would have alerted Obama's IC to national security risks, their team was unexpectedly shut down. Rickards was puzzled by the abrupt dissolution. There was no credible explanation. In terms of costs and productivity, the Dirty Dozen had been highly effective.

> We were told the advisory board's termination was for budget reasons, but that never rang true. We were mostly volunteers who got paid travel reimbursements and little in the way of fees. We even passed the hat during meetings at Langley to pay for our buffet lunches. We were probably the best value for money the government ever saw.[67]

Rickards believed there was more to the story. It was rumored that the termination came from the top of Obama's IC.

> I was informed privately that another general, James Clapper, the director of national intelligence in 2013, wanted our operation shut down. I never knew why, yet always suspected there was a reason other than lunch money and a few plane tickets.[68]

As director of national intelligence (DNI), Clapper prepared the legally required "threat assessment" of the Uranium One deal. Clapper's Uranium One threat assessment remains classified.[69]

The controversy around the Uranium One approval is amplified by the fact that CFIUS ignored many other red flags not mentioned in the ranking members' letter. These red flags included multiple *separate* Russian nuclear conspiracies involving espionage, smuggling, bribery, extortion, kickbacks, and money laundering (all amounting to Russian racketeering, not only abroad but also *in* America).[70]

Obama had ended the Russian espionage operation known as the "illegals program" in July 2010, so perhaps CFIUS considered that matter unimportant. But the Tenex racketeering scheme was still in full swing.[71]

As recounted in the previous chapter, FBI operative William Campbell repeatedly warned his FBI handlers of the Rosatom subsidiary's corruption. He was told that his intelligence had reached the highest levels, including FBI Director Mueller and President Obama.[72]

In August 2010—the same month CFIUS began the Uranium One review—the Nuclear Regulatory Commission was made aware of the FBI investigation into Tenex executive Vadim Mikerin when the NRC "received a sensitive intelligence report made available to various components of the Federal Government through normal intelligence reporting channels."[73]

The NRC does not provide details on who briefed them on the FBI investigation into Tenex corruption or whether they were fully aware of what Campbell had uncovered. It remains unclear which other agencies were informed, particularly which other CFIUS agencies, in August 2010 amid the CFIUS review. The NRC only states that "various components of the Federal Government" received the report regarding the FBI Tenex investigation.

Obama's intelligence officials, including FBI Director Robert Mueller and the Department of Energy's inspector general, were all aware of the Tenex racketeering schemes well before the 2010 CFIUS review.[74]

FBI deputy Andrew McCabe and federal prosecutors Andrew Weissmann and Rod Rosenstein—all of whose names would later become familiar during the Mueller investigation—investigated Tenex bribery and money laundering. For unknown reasons, the FBI and DOJ did not bust the Russian racketeers until after the Uranium One takeover was complete.[75]

Between the August 2010 "sensitive intelligence report" regarding Tenex (acknowledged by the NRC) and the ongoing Tenex investigation by the FBI and the DOE, DNI Clapper had ample evidence of Rosatom-linked corruption to include in his mandated threat assessment.[76]

The conclusion is unavoidable: either Obama's top intelligence officials misled CFIUS on the gravity of the Russians' hostile nuclear efforts or someone gave a stand-down order—a directive that could only have come from Obama (or a very high-ranking lieutenant).

Empty Promises

Russia and Uranium One made numerous promises in order to receive CFIUS approval. To begin with, Rosatom promised to maintain the approved management and ownership structure, and that Uranium One would not be broken up.

In a July 2010 letter to the NRC, Uranium One tacitly recognized that a Russian state-owned nuclear company taking control of American uranium might be cause for alarm. After all, the Rosatom takeover would give Russia a license to possess *unlimited* quantities of radioactive material *on U.S. soil* in multiple forms, including fissile uranium (which is used in atomic bomb chain reactions).[77]

Uranium One sought to assuage NRC concerns by promising to remain a publicly listed company (which requires more transparency than a private company). According to the July 2010 letter:

> However, Uranium One is and will remain a publicly listed company on the TSX (Toronto Stock Exchange) and JSE Limited (Johannesburg Stock Exchange) and will continue to be subject to extensive and ongoing securities regulatory, corporate governance and financial statement preparation and reporting requirements under applicable Canadian laws and regulations and the rules and regulations of the TSX and the JSE.[78]

Furthermore, the "proposed transaction does not provide for or anticipate any changes to Uranium One subsidiaries in the United States or the NRC Licenses and Applications held by such subsidiaries."[79] Uranium One's mining leases in Wyoming (among other states) would remain controlled by Americans.[80]

Throughout Uranium One's change of control notice, the company promised the NRC that the transaction would have "no effect" on Uranium One's personnel; no effect on the use, possession, location, or storage of licensed materials; no effect on the organization, the facilities, equipment, and records; no effect on any of the operating or safety procedures; and no effect on the surety arrangements, bonds, and letters of credit.[81]

While some of these assurances may have been *technically* accurate, they were certainly misleading. Uranium One's ownership structure changed multiple times. So did their operations, personnel, and activities.[82] In December 2011, Uranium One issued corporate bonds valued at 14.3 billion rubles (approximately $463.5 million) on the Moscow stock exchange (MICEX). This effectively indebted Uranium One to Russian stock traders, despite the company's promise to the NRC that the Rosatom takeover would have "no effect" on bond arrangements.[83]

Between August and October 2013, Uranium One refinanced the ruble bond debt through complicated financial maneuvers on Russia's MICEX. These financial maneuvers allowed Rosatom to increase its ownership of Uranium One from 51 percent to 100 percent. The so-called "Going Private Transaction" resulted in Uranium One being delisted from the Toronto Stock Exchange. Another promise was broken. Substantial U.S. nuclear assets became wholly owned by the Russian government.[84]

During the CFIUS review, Uranium One highlighted that the Japanese would likely be taking a significant stake in the company through a complex stock arrangement (called the "2010 Debentures"). This detail perhaps led CFIUS and the NRC to believe that an allied country would be part owner of Uranium One. That proved untrue. Two months after CFIUS approved Rosatom's takeover, Uranium One "repurchased and cancelled the debenture on December 29, 2010."[85]

From the moment CFIUS approved the takeover, the Russians had full control.

Seemingly persuaded by the company's misleading assurances, the NRC assured Congress and the American public that, at least, the new Russian owners could not export any nuclear materials.[86] But beginning in 2012, Uranium One began exporting uranium from the U.S. to Canada.[87] From there, it could be shipped anywhere in the world.

For most Americans, the Russian export of U.S. uranium—particularly to Iran, North Korea, or some other hostile regime—is a frightening prospect. Clinton apologists and defenders of the Uranium One deal argue that the export process is highly controlled and subject to significant oversight.[88] CFIUS expert James Rickards argues this defense only has "superficial substance." As Rickards explains:

What this defense misses is that uranium, usually in the form of the low-enriched concentrate, U_3O_8, called yellowcake, is a fungible commodity with a worldwide market....

Uranium One has mines in Kazakhstan, the United States, and Tanzania. It has customers, directly and indirectly via parent Rosatom, around the world, including Iran, Russia, and China. Prior to the acquisition of Uranium One by Rosatom, a U.S. nuclear power plant could have been supplied from mines in Kazakhstan. After the acquisition, Rosatom could assign that supply contract to Uranium One, a U.S.-to-U.S. deal, and the Kazakhstan output would be available for shipment to Iran. In effect, the Wyoming uranium is supplying Iran through a simple substitution of suppliers in a three-party structure.[89]

The possibility that American uranium was exported by Russians to bad actors is unlikely due to one simple fact: after taking control of Uranium One, Russia "throttled back" U.S. uranium production and even mothballed some of the American mines.[90] But this outcome is perhaps even more sinister and has been eclipsed by the controversy over whether Russians exported American uranium to Iran or North Korea.

Russia's true plans for the American assets have now become clear: the controlled demolition of the American uranium industry.[91]

Russians began restricting U.S. production after they took control of Uranium One.[92] According to Rickards, this maneuver appears to have been a price manipulation strategy:

Taking the Wyoming production off the market would be costly in the short run, but the sudden shortage could increase the world price and benefit other mines owned by Rosatom. This is a price manipulation strategy that a global, government-owned player such as Rosatom could execute that would never be tried if the U.S. mines were owned by a smaller independent player.[93]

By manipulating the price of energy fuel, Russia made it difficult for smaller American miners to compete. The utility companies that Uranium One previously supplied did not care where their fuel came from. In fact, they would rather their fuel come from Russian-owned mines in Kazakhstan than Russian-owned mines in Wyoming if it saved them money. This means that the CFIUS approval of the Uranium One takeover was likely in the utilities' immediate financial interest.[94]

Months before the CFIUS approval, the undercover informer Campbell specifically warned his FBI handlers about Rosatom's strategy to undercut prices in the American market. In a black suburban that picked him up at his normal debriefing rendezvous location near the Pentagon in suburban Washington, Campbell related in July 2010 the recent discussions he had with Rosatom officials about impacting the U.S. market now that its Tenex sales arm had become number one in the uranium enrichment services marketplace worldwide.

"TENEX's share in the world enrichment services market as of July 2010 is 37% total, which places them ahead of Urenco, AREVA, USEC," Campbell wrote in the notes he prepared to share with the FBI during the ride. "This makes TENEX #1 in the world as of this month."[95]

Campbell added, "TENEX indicates they can sell cheaper in the US market than any of their competitors however they are acutely aware of selling solo that they could possibly be accused of dumping into the market."[96]

Neither the persistent warnings about dumping from the Department of Commerce nor the intelligence of the FBI informer inside Putin's nuclear empire could put a pause on the fateful decision the Obama administration was about to make. Putin's Rosatom was about to acquire another lever in its machine to monopolize the global uranium market and make American nuclear reactors more reliant on Moscow.

Influencing and Enriching the Gatekeepers

The Russia reset provided massive opportunities for perceptive investors. Preferential treatment from Obama's State Department could be invaluable. This was especially true for Putin, the Canadians from whom he bought Uranium One, and the utility companies that stood to gain from cheap Russian uranium supplies.

If Hillary Clinton was the gatekeeper, the Clinton Foundation was the tollbooth, and Bill Clinton was the operator.

As Peter Schweizer documented extensively, Uranium One stakeholders (that is, entities who benefitted from the sale to Rosatom, including *direct* shareholders, investors, and financial advisors) donated more than $145 million to the Clinton Foundation.[97]

Beginning in June 2007, individuals linked to Uranium One secretly funneled millions of dollars through a Canadian pass-through entity called the Clinton Giustra Sustainable Growth Initiative (CGSGI). The timing of Uranium One's expansion into the United States is closely tied to the establishment of the CGSGI enterprise. That is, cash flowed to Clinton coffers from Uranium One principals as their company sought CFIUS approval more than three years before the Russian takeover.[98]

Exactly seventeen days after Uranium One announced the acquisition of their first American mines, the company became a Clinton Foundation partner. On June 21, 2007, the Clinton Foundation proudly announced a $300 million commitment by CGSGI. Uranium One and several of its key stakeholders were touted among the new CGSGI partners. The next month, Uranium One's acquisition of the American mines was approved.[99]

As a Canadian entity, Uranium One's initial purchase of the American uranium assets (those the Russians would later own) was clearly not deemed to be a threat by CFIUS in 2007. This earlier CFIUS approval has gone widely unreported since it did not involve Russia and because Canadians are typically close American allies.

But the timing of Uranium One's initial purchase of the American mines and the establishment of the $300 million pass-through vehicle are crucial to understanding how Uranium One stakeholders secretly enriched the Clinton Foundation. The timing and secrecy surrounding the payments are troubling.

CGSGI was incorporated under Canadian charity laws that prioritize donor privacy. Conveniently, the Clintons failed to disclose more than 1,100 of the donors to this entity. Uranium One's chairman, Ian Telfer, secretly steered $2.35 million through his own private entity, the Fernwood Foundation, to CGSGI.[100]

Schweizer first revealed Telfer's hidden donations, which sparked widespread condemnation of the Clintons' shady disclosure practices. The Clintons quickly released a partial list of other donors they had previously failed to disclose, including Telfer and his foundation. More than one thousand CGSGI donors remain secret.[101]

While Giustra, Telfer, and other Uranium One stakeholders (including Uranium One Inc. itself) funneled potentially hundreds of millions through CGSGI, Rosatom made its first steps to begin taking control of the company. First, in mid-2009, Rosatom tested the waters and purchased 17 percent—a minority stake.[102]

This investment apparently flew under the CFIUS radar. Throughout 2010, more funds linked to Uranium One (and perhaps even Rosatom) flowed into the Clinton Foundation and into Bill Clinton's pockets in the form of speech payments. Beginning in 2010, the Clinton Foundation received more than $2.6 million from a Canadian entity called Salida Capital Foundation. In 2011, Rosatom listed a "Salida Capital" as a subsidiary. Salida Capital refused to comment on whether or not they were owned by Rosatom—a shocking development, if confirmed.[103]

Russian money did flow directly to the Clintons. Clinton directly received $500,000 for a notorious speech in Moscow for Renaissance Capital—the Kremlin-controlled bank promoting Uranium One— mere months before the CFIUS review.[104]

On top of the hundreds of millions that Giustra and his Canadian associates sent or pledged to the Clinton Foundation, the tollbooth received between $1.74 and $6.28 million from Rosatom's nuclear utility customers and partners. While Rosatom customer Exelon *partnered* with the Clinton Foundation, neither has disclosed any *direct* contributions.[105]

At the same time the Canadian mining investors and the American utility companies were pouring money into the Clinton Foundation, Rosatom's Tenex subsidiary hired an international lobbyist named APCO Worldwide.[106] One of Clinton's deputies and top energy advisors, Amos Hochstein, had worked for Tenex in the past and taught the Russians how to "Americanize" their efforts by partnering with American utility companies.[107] That strategy paid off.

Tenex hired APCO in April 2010 to promote the interests of Rosatom and used the pending 123 Agreement and New START as cover for their strategic interest in cornering supply. In September 2010, APCO sponsored a media panel at the CGI annual meeting and was listed as a CGI "meeting partner."[108] This was APCO's first *public* affiliation with the Clinton Foundation and occurred just one month before CFIUS approved the Russian nuclear takeover.[109]

APCO first signed on to CGI as an in-kind donor in 2008, just before Obama won the presidency, but its support markedly soared after Hillary Clinton became secretary of state and the firm scored its contract with the Russians.[110] In hindsight, these developments do not appear coincidental.

Public disclosures list APCO as a $25,000 to $50,000 donor to the Clinton Foundation, but internal Clinton Foundation records show APCO contributed closer to $1 million, including in-kind contributions. APCO sponsored multiple Clinton events while they lobbied for Russian interests, but their contributions were never fully disclosed publicly. This was another violation of Hillary Clinton's 2009 special ethics agreement not to commingle public and private affairs on her watch as secretary.[111]

Throughout 2010 and into 2011, APCO contacted federal and congressional officials at least fifty times on behalf of Tenex—including at least ten interactions with the State Department. APCO built Rosatom a website, www.usarussia123.com, that touted Russia's willingness to cooperate with the Americans. APCO's efforts on behalf of Russian client Tenex were effectively propaganda.[112]

"APCO Worldwide's activities involving client work on behalf of Tenex and The Clinton Global Initiative were totally separate and unconnected in any way," claimed APCO's chairwoman and founder, Margery Kraus, when asked about the suspicious connections.[113] What else could she say?

At the same time the Kremlin was paying outside lobbyists such as APCO to lobby for their nuclear interests, the Russians also hired past, present, and future Obama administration officials. Washington insiders Theodore Kassinger and Amos Hochstein served in Clinton's State Department at various times throughout her tenure. Both were on the payroll of Rosatom subsidiaries and specifically advised them on how to extract nuclear concessions from the Obama administration.[114]

Shockingly, Kassinger served as counsel to the Russians during the Uranium One CFIUS review while simultaneously advising Secretary Clinton. In addition to Hochstein and Kassinger, Rosatom employed energy consultant Cheryl Moss Herman. Two weeks before the CFIUS approval in October 2010, Herman drafted a memo for Tenex that specifically discussed the pending Uranium One takeover (as mentioned in Chapter Six). Before long, Herman was working within Obama's Energy Department.[115]

Kassinger had been a top official in the Bush Commerce Department before he hit the lucrative revolving door in Washington. He took his commerce experience to the private sector and advised foreign clients at the white-shoe law and lobbying firm O'Melveny & Myers. As a Council on Foreign Relations member, he contributed to a 2008 report titled "Global FDI Policy: Correcting a Protectionist Drift."[116]

The paper claimed the "danger of a protectionist drift…is considerable." It specifically advocated tearing down barriers to foreign investment and assuaged concerns over investments by state-owned enterprises (SOEs)—entities like Rosatom.[117] By 2009, when Kassinger served as the chairman of a State Department advisory panel, his anti-protectionist leanings were put into action.

In 2009, Secretary Clinton tasked her State Department Advisory Committee on International Economic Policy (ACIEP) to present policy recommendations dealing with foreign investment in the U.S. Kassinger was Clinton's ACIEP chairman, and his report advocated an open investment climate and welcomed investments from SOEs like Rosatom.[118]

Kassinger was the perfect man to advise the Russian state-owned nuclear corporation on investments in the U.S. He had a significant role inside Clinton's State Department and met regularly with Undersecretary Jose Fernandez—the man who claims that Clinton played no role in the Uranium One decision. Furthermore, Kassinger's role as chairman of the ACIEP meant that he was not a full-time State Department employee. Thus, while serving in this advisory role, it is unlikely that he would have been required to disclose any potential conflicts of interest.[119]

Secretary Clinton met with Kassinger and Fernandez during an ACIEP meeting on April 15, 2010, just six months before Fernandez reviewed the Uranium One sale for CFIUS. Kassinger met again with Fernandez on August 12, just nineteen days before Uranium One's shareholders approved the sale to ARMZ and shortly before CFIUS approved the transaction.[120] State Department emails reveal that on October 22, the Uranium One CFIUS approval was sent to the Russians' attorney: Ted Kassinger.[121]

The Russian agents working both inside and outside Clinton's State Department, combined with the massive sums of money flowing to the Clinton Foundation from Uranium One stakeholders, have still not been seriously investigated. An internal audit (or "governance review") of the Clinton Foundation, performed at the behest of Chelsea Clinton, revealed that several Clinton Foundation benefactors "reported conflicts" associated with the donations and "may have an expectation of quid pro quo benefits in return for gifts."[122]

The sums Clinton received from interested parties linked to Uranium One were staggering. Schweizer's original calculation exceeding $145 million has ballooned to a figure that could exceed $450 million.[123]

The FBI opened multiple investigations after *Clinton Cash* was released and FBI agents consulted with Schweizer on his findings. But those investigations were ultimately stymied by FBI leadership, including then-Director James Comey and his deputy Andrew McCabe. New details have now emerged, and the public continues to demand answers.[124]

* * *

Despite the protests from high-ranking U.S. legislators and numerous complaints from constituents, Vladimir Putin took majority control of significant American uranium assets. The deal was finalized in December 2010. Six months later, Obama signaled that such investments had his blessing:

My Administration is committed to ensuring that the United States continues to be the most attractive place for businesses to locate, invest, grow, and create jobs. We encourage and support business investment from sources both at home and abroad.[125]

Putin's takeover of Uranium One was a major coup, especially when combined with guaranteed billion-dollar nuclear fuel contracts he simultaneously secured with U.S. utility companies.[126]

While Hillary Clinton's defenders used the unanimity of Obama's CFIUS to ameliorate Clinton's role, the fact remains that Putin further cornered the uranium market and gained significant energy assets around the globe by way of a single purchase. Putin also extracted other significant nuclear concessions from Obama, including the New START treaty, weakened NATO missile defense, and the 123 Agreement concerning civilian nuclear sales.

CFIUS expert Rickards and his Dirty Dozen team were never consulted on the transaction. Had they been, they would have recommended rejection of the Russian nuclear takeover scheme. Rickards believed that this type of deal would have typically been denied. "In the end," he concluded, "the Uranium One deal went through because the secretary of state and the White House wanted it to go through."[127]

Just as Clinton's State Department could not approve the deal single-handedly, Putin could not have pulled off the Uranium One takeover by himself. Putin needed lobbyists and embedded allies in high places in Washington to pull off the deal. His nuclear operatives also partnered with politically connected American utilities by appealing to their mutual interests—primarily cheap nuclear fuel supplies. These collaborative efforts began under the Bush administration but ramped up when Obama took power.

Clinton's defenders were correct that Obama's CFIUS decision granting Putin control of Uranium One was unanimous. That argument is irrelevant because it does not exonerate Clinton. Rather, it condemns the broader Obama administration. Her earlier criticisms of the Dubai Ports deal would be more fitting had they been applied to the way CFIUS approved the Uranium One deal.

CHAPTER 8

RESET CRACKS AND SKOLKOVO HACKS

The Russian-Silicon Valley Tech Transfer

*"Our critics constantly labeled us Russophobes, but I wanted to prove
that some of us, including Obama, were Russophiles. How could a
man with a daughter named Sasha not love Russia!"*[1]

—MICHAEL McFAUL, *From Cold War to Hot Peace*, 2018 memoir

Michael McFaul was a tenured Stanford professor before Obama
hired him as senior director for Russian affairs on the National
Security Council. He had lived in Silicon Valley for most of his adult
life apart from a few stretches of living in Russia while studying abroad
at a Soviet university in 1983.[2]

Now, in June 2010, McFaul would be giving Russian President
Dmitry Medvedev a tour of his West Coast stomping grounds. As the
"architect" of the reset, McFaul had planned the trip for nearly a year
with three objectives that he wanted to achieve. First and foremost, he
wanted to show the results of the reset. Second, he wanted to emphasize
the administration's current engagement with Russia. Third, he wanted
to highlight its expanding Russian agenda (focusing on economic ties).[3]

Nuclear cooperation with Russia was the number one priority of
the reset based on the sheer number of nuclear dealings it achieved
(such as New START, 123 Agreement, Uranium One, and cooperation
on Iran, among other things). Having worked tirelessly to accomplish

the nuclear side of the reset, McFaul was excited to pivot to an area more within his wheelhouse: academia and technology.[4]

McFaul personally lobbied for the Russian president to visit Stanford (McFaul's alma mater) along with Silicon Valley. Secretary Clinton officially arranged the trip a few months prior on her April 2010 visit to Moscow. Though they did not know it at the time, Medvedev's June 2010 visit would be the final "full-fledged Russian-American summit of the Obama era."[5]

Cracks were already beginning to form in the reset, despite Obama's and McFaul's desperate insistence to the contrary.

Medvedev's trip to California was a success. He had dinner with some of the "founding fathers" of Silicon Valley. The next day, Steve Jobs gave him the newest iPhone 4G model, which had not yet been released to the public. (Two months later, Putin's old KGB comrade Sergey Chemezov unveiled a 4G Russian prototype that fueled speculation it was an iPhone copycat.)[6]

Medvedev also met with Cisco CEO John Chambers and Google CEO Eric Schmidt, both of whom pledged to increase substantially their Russian investments. Medvedev opened a Twitter account and soon began tweeting Obama and California Governor Arnold Schwarzenegger.[7]

In addition, McFaul was able to secure a private meeting with Medvedev for his former Stanford students at a nearby coffee shop. Several Russians working in the Valley attended. At Medvedev's speech to McFaul's alma mater, the tech-savvy president famously read his remarks from an iPad. McFaul was loving every minute.[8]

Days earlier and three thousand miles away, Obama was in the White House Situation Room mulling what to do about the Russian spy ring that his intelligence chiefs had just brought to his attention. The Russian spies included a beautiful red-haired woman operating under the name "Anna Chapman," and at least one of the spies was preparing to flee the country. Something had to be done or the FBI and CIA might lose them.[9]

Medvedev was in Silicon Valley promoting a high-tech project known as "Skolkovo," which was Russia's attempt to re-create Silicon

Valley. At the time, no one knew (not even Chapman) that Skolkovo would become the next mission for the Kremlin's "sexy spy."[10]

McFaul, a major proponent of the Skolkovo project, recalled Medvedev's promotion in his memoir:

> At the time, Medvedev was trying to jump-start Skolkovo, a high-tech business area just outside Moscow. Most Americans rolled their eyes at the idea of a state-led Silicon Valley in Russia, but I was a supporter. I knew the odds were long for the project, but reasoned that it could be in the United States' interest to have the Russian government invest in high tech and education....
>
> I also saw business opportunities in Russia for our high-tech firms. Cheerleading for Skolkovo seemed like an easy call.[11]

When Medvedev arrived in Washington, Obama did not want to offend him by bringing up the Russian spies who had infiltrated the highest levels of Washington (including Secretary Clinton's inner finance circle). Instead, Obama allowed Chapman and the others to operate just a bit longer and showed Medvedev around Washington while the Russian president "went on and on about the Valley's energy."[12]

At a highly publicized lunch meeting, the two leaders shared a small table at a cozy restaurant called Ray's Hell Burger. McFaul was worried that the Russians would feel offended by the casual venue, but in the eyes of Obama's team the "Burger Summit" was deemed a huge success. Next up on the two leaders' agenda was meeting the titans of American industry at the U.S. Chamber of Commerce.[13]

At home in Moscow, Putin may have found the PR stunt sophomoric, but he *must* have appreciated the subsequent meeting that Obama convened with top American technology companies who pledged their support (and funds) to Russia's new cyber project.

The companies were also excited by the package of incentives Medvedev offered to "stimulate" participation in Skolkovo. As McFaul put it, "The American Chamber of Commerce did not normally lead cheers for Obama. On this day, however, its members embraced him with glee."[14]

But it was not such a joyous time for some Obama officials. As the Burger Summit and the deal-striking meetings were taking place, Obama's hawkish foreign policy and intelligence veterans (like CIA

Director Panetta and FBI Director Mueller) were nervously hatching plans to deport the illegal Russian spies.

Furthermore, Obama's critics (particularly from human rights groups) did not like the president's choice to "tone down" criticism of Russia's atrocious human rights record—a decision McFaul advocated in 2009, in stark contrast to the Bush administration's vocal criticism.[15]

Undeterred, McFaul and the rest of the Obama administration were able to convince themselves that Medvedev was changing Russia for the better—and that Putin, the ex-KGB elephant in the room, could be ignored a bit longer. There were still more deals to be made. Clinton had selected the perfect team to get them done.[16]

The Globalist Deal Makers

One week before Medvedev's visit, State Department Undersecretary Robert Hormats delivered the keynote address at the St. Petersburg International Economic Forum in Russia. There, he reiterated the State Department's commitment to bolstering economic partnerships with Russia and welcomed Russian investment in the U.S. (and, as mentioned, he gave a wink to the secretive CFIUS review process that Russian nuclear oligarchs would soon find themselves navigating).[17]

Hormats was one of the State Department officials directly responsible for reviewing CFIUS transactions and later admitted responsibility for the Uranium One approval. When the Uranium One scandal exploded a few years later, Hormats, like his colleague Jose Fernandez, protected his former boss Hillary Clinton: "As I recall, the Secretary of State never discussed this case with me or intervened with me about it in any way."[18]

In an opinion article published after his visit to St. Petersburg, Hormats extolled the virtues of increased collaboration with Russia. He praised Medvedev and his team at the Kremlin for making "innovation a high national priority, to diversify the Russian economy and reduce dependence on energy and raw materials."[19]

Hormats specifically identified the Skolkovo project as a good way for American businesses to help Russia diversify its economy. He hoped that Skolkovo would "inspire other centers of innovation to flourish."[20]

Hormats had pushed for controversial deals like Uranium One and Skolkovo (which many believed were against American interests) his entire career. Though hardly a household name, he had been a pillar of the Washington establishment since 1969, advising President Jimmy Carter, Zbigniew Brzezinski, Brent Scowcroft, and Henry Kissinger through various posts in the State Department. He left State in 1982 to work for Goldman Sachs, spending twenty-five years there as vice chairman.[21]

In 1993, President Bill Clinton appointed Hormats to the Board of The U.S.-Russia Investment Fund—a shadowy entity that capitalized on the crooked privatization schemes under Yeltsin.[22]

Throughout President Clinton's tenure, Hormats championed Goldman's preferred policies of "widescale deregulation." This meant departing from a Cold War mindset by granting China most-favored nation status, sponsoring China's accession to the WTO, and bringing China and Russia into the West's economic embrace.[23]

Before rejoining the State Department in 2009, Hormats served as a director at the Council on Foreign Relations (CFR) from 1991 to 2004. His official title in the Clinton State Department was Undersecretary of State for Economic Growth, Energy, and the Environment. In this role, he was the direct supervisor of CFIUS decider Fernandez and worked closely with McFaul.[24]

Like many of Obama's appointees and Clinton's State Department advisors, Hormats, McFaul, Fernandez, and Rosatom's CFIUS agent Ted Kassinger were card-carrying globalists. Some associate the term "globalist" with wild conspiracy theories. In reality, self-described globalists are proud of the label.

According to the founder of *The Globalist*, a publication to which Hormats contributed his insights, "Globalists are patriots who have a worldview that is not limited to the political boundaries of one state," and "by no means an elite circle of business or political leaders determined to push forward their agenda in a rapid-fire fashion."[25]

The Obama administration figures in charge of crafting and executing U.S. foreign investment and energy policy shared this common linkage: they were proud globalists and members of the CFR—

an international membership organization where globalists seem to congregate.[26]

Like Kassinger, Hormats had advised the CFR on foreign investment in the U.S. before joining the Obama State Department. He also contributed to a CFR report after the Dubai Ports fiasco that warned legislators to "use a scalpel, not a chain saw" in their CFIUS reforms.[27]

The report recommended looser restrictions and an open investment stance, stating that "when investments are blocked, politicized, or unnecessarily delayed, the United States sends a negative signal to the rest of the world about the openness (or lack thereof) of its markets."[28]

When Secretary Clinton tapped Hormats to be her economic guru, she likely knew that he would push globalist policies that favored foreign entities like Rosatom, just as she likely knew that Kassinger would advise such entities. Both men had been openly working for foreign and multinational interests for decades. It was not a secret.

As Clinton's undersecretary, Hormats was in frequent contact with Russian officials, oligarchs, and their lobbyists seeking favorable treatment from Obama. The Russian Federation retained Ketchum Inc., which paid another lobbying firm, Alston & Bird, to meet with Hormats and Vice President Biden's advisor, Antony Blinken, in September 2011.[29]

Russia's lobbyists sought to convince Hormats and Blinken to facilitate meetings for Igor Shuvalov, whom Putin had tapped to be Russia's chief economic negotiator.

According to a Senate report, Shuvalov was central to formulating Putin's "energy superpower" strategy and the weaponization of energy deals.

> Mr. Putin's *Kremlin employs an asymmetric arsenal* that includes military invasions, cyberattacks, disinformation, support for fringe political groups, and the *weaponization of energy resources*, organized crime, and corruption…
>
> As Putin's sherpa to the 2005 G8 summit, *Shuvalov developed a new energy policy approach for Russia* and proposed that the Kremlin make the European countries an offer at the upcoming G8 summit:

Moscow would take care of ensuring a flow of fuel sufficient to supply every house in Europe, and in return Europe would show friendship, understanding, and loyalty.... [emphasis added][30]

According to the Senate report, this strategy would "make Putin the energy emperor of Europe."[31]

Meanwhile, shortly after meeting Hormats in September 2011, Shuvalov made headlines for being linked to questionable deals involving the purchase of U.S. assets by his own offshore holding companies.[32]

So, when Clinton put Hormats in charge of the "Innovation Working Group" of the U.S.-Russia Bilateral Presidential Commission (BPC)—the group that dealt specifically with Skolkovo—it was clear to Western globalist investors and Russian oligarchs alike that this was a man they could do business with.[33]

Governor Schwarzenegger threw his support behind the Russian technology transfer project as well.

Just days before CFIUS approved the sale of Uranium One, Putin dispatched some of his top economic and business leaders to San Francisco to promote Skolkovo at an event sponsored by the U.S.-Russia Business Council. A Russian venture company paid Chicago-based lobbying firm Edelman Imageland LLC, which in turn engaged Governor Schwarzenegger, to deliver the pro-Russian talking points.[34]

Schwarzenegger's speech, just ten days after touring Moscow for an official visit, was largely about climate change and highlighted nuclear power as "a non-CO2-emitting energizer."

The "Governator" praised Obama and Medvedev's efforts to reduce nuclear weapons:

But everyone is trying to—every country is kind of concerned about how do you get—how do you reduce that? Because there are those in America that are trying to flex their muscles and pretend they're ballsy by saying, "we've got to keep those nuclear weapons." That's very rugged, when you say that. It's not rugged at all; it's an idiot that says that. It's stupid to say that.[35]

Schwarzenegger also advocated for admitting Russia to the World Trade Organization (WTO)—a top priority for Medvedev given the trade advantage WTO members receive.[36]

At the Burger Summit, Obama had promised to elevate Russia into the WTO within three months, but there were several delays. Georgia objected because of its 2008 conflict with Russia, and in 2009 Putin "abandoned" his WTO aspirations, saying he wanted joint entry with Kazakhstan and Belarus. Nevertheless, Russia would officially join the WTO in 2012 and Kazakhstan in 2015.[37]

In his speech, Schwarzenegger showered Medvedev with praise, calling the Russian leader "a great visionary" and an "action president." He called Russia a "gold mine" for foreign investors and pledged, "We want to do what we can as Californians and as Americans because it is in our interest to make Russia successful.... We don't see Russia as an enemy. We see Russia as our friend."[38]

This mindset surrounding the reset allowed Skolkovo (and related espionage operations) to flourish, both in Moscow and in Washington.

Skolkovo: Russia's "Silicon Steppe"

Skolkovo was perhaps the Kremlin's boldest maneuver yet. Envious of America's technological success, the Russians sought to re-create the West Coast high-tech industrial hub in the suburbs of Moscow. But unlike the bottom-up innovation that defines Silicon Valley, where computer geniuses like Bill Gates and Steve Jobs pinched their pennies and built the first personal computers in their garages, Skolkovo was a top-down state-run project that sought to replicate decades of trial and error seemingly overnight.

It was also a ploy to steal American intellectual property and transfer technological secrets to the Kremlin.

Former federal prosecutor Andrew C. McCarthy described the Skolkovo scam best: "The project was like an espionage operation in broad daylight, openly enhancing Russia's military and cyber capabilities."[39]

Indeed, multiple Defense Department (DOD) agencies and the FBI condemned Skolkovo as an espionage front that posed a clear and present danger to U.S. national security.

In 2012, the U.S. Army Foreign Military Studies Program at Fort Leavenworth examined the security implications of Skolkovo and concluded that Skolkovo was an apparent "vehicle for worldwide technology transfer to Russia in the areas of information technology, biomedicine, energy, satellite and space technology, and nuclear technology."

The Kremlin and the Obama State Department praised the civilian endeavors of Skolkovo and its "clusters"—information, energy, biomedical, and even space technology (among other seemingly innocuous initiatives). The promoters of Skolkovo in Moscow and Washington conveniently neglected to mention the military applications.

According to the Army's Fort Leavenworth report:

> The Skolkovo Foundation has, in fact, been involved in defense-related activities since December 2011…the [Kremlin's] operation of Skolkovo and investment positions in companies will likely provide [Russia's] military awareness of and access to [American] technologies.[40]

The FBI's Boston field office sent warning letters to American companies involved with Skolkovo alerting them to the possibility that they had fallen prey to a Russian espionage trap. Assistant Special Agent in Charge Lucia Ziobro went so far as to publicly announce that Skolkovo "may be a means for the Russian government to access our nation's sensitive or classified research, development facilities and dual-use technologies with military and commercial applications."[41]

DOD's European Command (EUCOM) posted an alert that stated, "Skolkovo is arguably an overt alternative to clandestine industrial espionage—with the additional distinction that it can achieve such a transfer on a much larger scale and more efficiently."

Then EUCOM asked the obvious question: "why bother spying on foreign companies and government laboratories if they will voluntarily hand over all the expertise Russia seeks?"[42]

Former National Security Agency analyst John Schindler was a Navy officer and professor at the War College with deep contacts in the Pentagon. "It's an obvious Kremlin front," Schindler's Pentagon source told him regarding Skolkovo. "In the old days, the KGB had to recruit spies to steal Western technology, now they do deals with you. The theft is the same."[43]

Skolkovo *publicly* announced numerous events and programs involving some variation of the word "hack," including a cash prize "Hackathon," a "RoboHack," and the RoboCenter even had a place for Skolkovo visitors to work called a "hackspace."[44] Each event was, on the surface, rather benign, but the shadowy appeal to actual Russian hackers was undeniable.

Less benign was Skolkovo's promotion of a hacker conference in St. Petersburg called Positive Hack Days (PHD).[45] The hacker conference made a valiant effort to appear innocuous by stating (in the header), "We do not teach hacking, we learn to protect by understanding the mechanisms of hacking…"[46]

However, the PHD hacker conference clearly *did* teach hacking. Each of the seminars had obvious cyberespionage implications, such as Sergey Gordeychik's "How to hack into telecom and stay alive" class and Andrey Kostin's "PostScript: Danger!" class on hacking PCs—both at noon.[47]

Alexander Peslyak taught "Password protection: past, present and future" at 2 p.m.

The "Using radio noise for hacking…" seminar at 3 p.m. certainly sounded ominous.

Also at 3 p.m., Miroslav Stampar taught "Data Leaks Through DNS," and advised attendees to "use sqlmap."[48]

More alarming still, the hacker conference was sponsored by Kaspersky Labs—accused of "helping the Kremlin spy on the U.S. intelligence agencies as part of its 2016 election meddling."[49]

Kremlin-owned Sberbank (Russia's oldest and largest bank) later became a sponsor of the PHD hacker conference. Sberbank was particularly close to Putin and bankrolled his oil giant, Rosneft, during the plunder of Yukos oil in 2004.[50]

Sberbank also provided financing for Rosatom investments and enterprises. When Sberbank underwrote a Rosatom affiliate bond offering in 2009, Putin's nuclear giant obtained newly available funds to finance its investment in Uranium One.[51]

"Sberbank is the Kremlin," according to a former senior U.S. intelligence official. "They don't do anything major without Putin's go-ahead, and they don't tell him 'no' either."[52]

The Kremlin—through Sberbank and other entities—sought to influence the Obama administration. They did so through Obama's right-hand man (and longtime Clinton "fixer"): the legendary political guru John Podesta.

Podesta Incorporated: Kremlin Lobbyists and Russian Agents

Obama tapped John Podesta as a top advisor and Counselor to the President in December 2013. Podesta would later become Hillary Clinton's campaign manager and oversee the campaign's unexpected and spectacular defeat, which he, Clinton, and their allies all blamed on "RUSSIA!"[53]

Podesta's and Clinton's outrage over Putin's alleged collusion in 2016 rang hollow. Indeed, as one Hudson Institute fellow surmised, the "sinister yarn" that Trump's opponents wove was merely "a textbook case of denial and projection."[54]

Podesta profited substantially from Kremlin-backed projects while working on Obama's reset. And his brother Tony (and the eponymous lobbying group they cofounded, Podesta Group) was one of the Kremlin's favorite agents in Washington.[55]

John Podesta met with newly minted Russian President Vladimir Putin in 2000. Podesta joined President Clinton for an evening with the new leader of Russia. "We saw Putin and then we had the evening free," Podesta told a reporter in 2014. "We went to the Café Pushkin in Moscow, and as is habit in Moscow, we started drinking vodka shots," Podesta recalled. That night, the three drank so much vodka that Podesta could not recall how he managed getting out of bed the next morning. "I wouldn't even describe myself as hungover; alcohol was still pouring out of my pores."[56]

More than a decade later, Podesta again fell prey to Russian wiles.

On October 23, 2010—just *one day* after CFIUS approved the Rosatom takeover—Podesta was tapped for a board position by Joule Unlimited, a small energy company based near Boston. By July 2011, Podesta had also joined the board of Joule's holding company, which was based in the Netherlands. Podesta technically served on the "executive board," according to corporate records. Joule was founded in 2007 and bragged that it could create "Liquid Fuel from the Sun," using a far-fetched process involving biofuel produced from algae.[57]

One of Joule's notable investors was a controversial and reclusive Swiss billionaire named Hansjörg Wyss, whose company was charged by the Justice Department with performing illegal human experiments, causing at least three deaths. Podesta had consulted for the Swiss billionaire, and Wyss donated up to $5 million to the Clinton Foundation.[58]

In his 2014 federal government financial disclosure, Podesta listed stock options from Joule. However, the disclosure does not cover any Joule transaction activity during the years 2010 through 2012. Podesta reportedly owned seventy-five thousand shares in Joule, and there remains some uncertainty about whether he fully divested them before joining the Obama White House (it appears that he transferred his Joule shares to a new shell company conveniently controlled by his daughter).[59]

Any potential *direct* payments from Joule are not known, but the Swiss billionaire Joule investor paid Podesta more than $87,000 (through a foundation) while Podesta was on Joule's board. When the *Daily Caller* reported on the shady nature of Podesta's Joule transfers, the outlet received a cease and desist letter. In the letter, Podesta's attorney (notorious Democrat legal guru Marc Elias of Perkins Coie) called the story "entirely false" and claimed "Mr. Podesta actually reported more than was required."[60]

Podesta had minimal, if any, experience with energy and certainly no biofuel expertise. Rather, Joule "gained the strategic insights and support of a long-time government expert who can help Joule build the lasting relationships needed for long-term success." Shortly after Podesta joined the Joule board, Secretary Clinton placed him on the State Department Foreign Affairs Policy Board. As a key advisor to Secretary Clinton (and later President Obama), Podesta certainly opened doors to relationships needed for long-term success. So did former Assistant Secretary of Defense Graham Allison, who also joined Joule's board.[61]

Shortly after Podesta joined the board, state-owned nanotechnology conglomerate Rusnano invested one billion rubles ($35 million) in Joule Unlimited. The Government Accountability Institute concluded that "it is hard to underestimate how close Rusnano is to the political-military elite in Russia." In February 2012, Putin's so-called "reformer" and chairman of Rusnano, Anatoly Chubais, joined Joule's board of directors.[62]

Rusnano's billion-ruble investment in Massachusetts-based Joule—made while Podesta was on the board—was among their largest U.S. investments. In October 2011, Rusnano's U.S.-based subsidiary had promised to deliver "cheap money" to U.S. businesses in need of capital.[63]

The Boston FBI's warning about Skolkovo seemed to be aimed directly at entities like Rusnano: "The FBI believes the true motives of the Russian partners, who are often funded by their government, is to gain access to classified, sensitive and emerging technology from the companies."[64]

Rusnano played a central role in all aspects of the Skolkovo project, which the FBI warned could be a massive Kremlin-backed economic espionage scheme or cyber counterintelligence operation.[65]

Furthermore, Rusnano's sizable investment in a company advised by John Podesta created yet another commercial link between Putin's nuclear complex and Obama's and Clinton's inner circles. Rusnano also had extensive dealings with Rosatom—the company that was seeking approval to acquire U.S. uranium assets.[66]

Did Russian Interests Funnel Money to Podesta's Think Tank?

Podesta's Russia connections did not stop with Joule. While Podesta's progressive think tank, the Center for American Progress (CAP), championed Obama's reset policy, substantial funds flowed through a byzantine network of shell corporations that ultimately linked back to Moscow. Between 2010 and 2013, CAP reportedly received $5.25 million from a shadowy entity called the Sea Change Foundation, which had received $23 million from a Bermuda corporation linked to Russia.[67] It appears that the Sea Change Foundation was a pass-through entity.

The connections were dizzying and bore resemblance to the signature obfuscation of Russian money laundering. But the obvious question is this: Why would international shell corporations pass millions through Caribbean tax havens (thus bypassing disclosure requirements) to fund a think tank founded by the secretary of state's close advisor and future campaign chairman?

Podesta has refused to comment substantively on the Russian connections and denied that any untoward activity occurred. In 2016, Clinton's campaign was asked to comment on its chairman's relationship with Joule and the apparent divestiture, disclosure, and timing discrepancies.[68] The campaign issued the following statement:

> When Podesta went back to the work at the White House, he worked with White House counsel to personally divest from Joule and ensure he was in full compliance with all government ethics rules.
>
> He transferred the entirety of his holdings to his adult children, resigned all positions with the company and filed the appropriate forms which were then certified by the appropriate ethics officials. As an additional step, he recused himself from all matters pertaining to Joule for the duration of his time at the White House.

But the statement hardly assuaged legitimate concerns and raised more questions. Does transferring ownership to your children *actually* remove the appearance of conflicts of interest or is it merely a technicality? What "matters pertaining to Joule" did Podesta recuse himself from? Was this recusal also an apparent technicality? Why did Joule executives remain in contact with him after he "resigned all positions"? We may never know.[69]

Ultimately, the timing of Joule's incorporation, Podesta's involvement, and Rusnano's subsequent investment track closely with the Russian-linked donations to the Sea Change Foundation, and the latter's donations to CAP suggest that there might be more to the story.

Not only was Joule funded by Russia, it was linked to Skolkovo corporate espionage. John Podesta tried to hide his stake by transferring it to his daughter (who did not have to disclose the Russian-backed asset the way her father would).

Podesta's Double Standard on Russian Influence

President Donald Trump's 2016 campaign manager Paul Manafort was sentenced to seven-and-a-half years in prison and faced solitary confinement at Rikers Island (a horrific New York City prison typically reserved for serial killers, mob bosses, and cop killers).[70]

In fact, Manafort had several business associates in Ukraine, including the Podesta Group. John Podesta and his brother Tony cofounded the Podesta Group in 1988. Since then, the group has lobbied for dozens of countries that run the gamut from American allies to adversaries—including multiple contracts with Kremlin interests.[71]

The Podesta Group raked in more than $1 million (combined) from Kremlin interests such as Sberbank, Uranium One, and the Ukrainian political group tied to the pro-Putin President Viktor Yanukovych. As Reuters reported, Tony Podesta was "among the high-profile lobbyists registered to represent organizations backing Ukrainian President Viktor Yanukovych."[72]

Astonishingly, the Podesta Group did not register as foreign agents for any of these state-owned (or state-backed) entities. In an insulting display of Washington's double standards, the Podesta Group *retroactively* filed Foreign Agents Registration Act (FARA) disclosures years later and only *after* Trump's campaign advisor Manafort was forced to resign the campaign in August 2016. The Podesta Group filed *more* retroactive disclosures two months before Manafort was indicted for violating FARA (among other crimes).[73]

The double standard was particularly egregious since Manafort secretly lobbied for the exact same Ukrainian client as the Podesta Group—the European Centre for a Modern Ukraine (ECFMU). But instead of letting Manafort disclose the decade-old work retroactively with a quiet mea culpa (like Podesta had done), federal prosecutors threw the book at him.[74]

The Steele Dossier Reveals the Obama State Department Double Standard

Adding insult to injury, Clinton's campaign contractor Fusion GPS paid ex-MI6 operative Christopher Steele to highlight Manafort's connection to the Ukraine lobbying scheme that Fusion founder Glenn Simpson had reported nearly a decade prior in the *Wall Street Journal*. The infamous "salacious and unverified" (and now-debunked) "Steele dossier" ominously stated:

> Ex-Ukrainian President YANUKOVYCH confides directly to PUTIN that he authorized kick-back payments to MANAFORT, as alleged in Western media. [Yanukovych] Assures Russian President however there is no documentary evidence/trail.[75]

While Steele's sinister (and largely falsified) reports were circulating around the Obama State Department in 2016, so were Podesta Group requests to help their Russian client. In July 2016, a Podesta Group lobbyist emailed the State Department seeking assistance on Sberbank's dire situation due to Obama's 2014 sanctions imposed after the Crimea debacle:

> Since imposition of US and EU sanctions, Sberbank has discontinued its operations in Crimea, Donetsk and Lugansk. Sberbank continues to operate elsewhere in Ukraine—with more than 3 million clients—despite attacks on its branches. In February 2016, Sberbank assisted Ukraine's Ministry of Finance with a $367 million debt restructuring for two state-owned companies.
>
> In May Helen Teplitskaya, a senior adviser to German Gref, Chairman and CEO of the bank, was in Washington and met with PDAS Warlick. At the end of the meeting PDAS Warlick suggested that when Helen returned to Washington she seek a meeting with you to discuss the impact of sanctions on the bank....Would you have time in the next few weeks to see Helen?[76]

Within hours, more than a half dozen State Department staffers were peppering each other's inboxes with suggestions on how to satisfy the Podesta Group request. Deputy Assistant Secretary Kathleen Kavalec weighed in: "Happy to meet with Sberbank together or separately—they have not approached directly as far as I know."[77]

It is worth noting that Kavalec appeared to have played a very central and secretive role in laundering (for lack of a better term) the Steele dossier through the State Department. She received a detailed briefing from Steele in October 2016, before the first Foreign Intelligence Surveillance Act (FISA) warrant targeting the Trump campaign was granted.[78]

To recap, the Podesta Group was paid more than $1 million by Russian state-owned Uranium One, Russian state-owned Sberbank, and pro-Putin Ukrainian President Yanukovych's political outfit. Tony Podesta's firm advanced Putin's interests by lobbying the State Department on sanctions relief (the exact sin that Steele falsely accused other Trump campaign staffers of committing) at the height of the 2016 campaign while Podesta's brother, Clinton campaign chairman John Podesta, was accusing the Trump campaign of colluding with Russia.[79]

Worse, Obama State Department deputies quickly acted to help the Podesta Group's Russian client at the very same time colleagues were promoting the now-debunked Steele dossier as gospel truth. Ironically, Steele's paid sources included anonymous *former FSB officials* who may have been pushing Russian disinformation. Steele's allegations against Manafort pertained to decade-old undisclosed pro-Russian lobbying and *directly* implicated the Podesta Group which, unlike Manafort, had since taken on controversial Russian entities, Uranium One and Sberbank, as new clients.[80]

John Podesta, for all his outrage over now-debunked Trump-Russia collusion conspiracy theories, concealed his own Russian interests. While his brother's firm was raking in fees from Russian clients, John Podesta was profiting *directly* from a company backed by the Kremlin.

Obama Advances Russian Cyber Capabilities

Just before Obama's reelection, in October 2012, the Department of Justice indicted a Russian agent named Alexander Fishenko, ten other Russian agents, and two corporations for conspiring to ship controlled high-tech electronics to Russia. The FBI accused Fishenko of illegally shipping $50 million worth of sensitive electronics to "Russian military and intelligence agencies." A secretive FSB branch called the "3rd Directorate" was implicated. Meanwhile, Obama and Clinton were *still* helping Russia re-create Silicon Valley in Moscow and singing the praises of the Skolkovo tech transfer project.[81]

The very same month that Russians agents were indicted for stealing American technology, Clinton dispatched her economic guru Hormats to the hub of the Skolkovo complex (called the "Hypercube"). At the Hypercube, Hormats again enthusiastically extolled the virtues of U.S. collaboration with the Kremlin. The Fishenko fiasco was yet another blow to the reset, but, seemingly undeterred, Obama continued to try to mend the crumbling relationship.[82]

McFaul was starting to get nervous. Tensions were escalating between the two countries. After several years with minimal tangible results, would Obama's reset policy ultimately be deemed a failure? Of course, they could always spin the policy as a success, and the media had cooperated with them thus far.[83]

Past and present officials from the Pentagon and other agencies did not like the appeasement strategy of Obama's State Department toward the Russian satellite agency that wanted to install "monitoring stations" on U.S. soil, the deals with Russian nuclear companies, or the flagrant espionage and corruption demonstrated by the Kremlin. And they certainly did not like Obama's desire to sweep the Russian illegals program under the rug.[84]

Eight months after the Fishenko tech transfer scheme was busted, Obama and Putin established the BPC Cybersecurity Working Group. The group was supposed to address issues relating to cyber security, espionage, and warfare.[85]

The Obama administration welcomed Russian Security Council official Nikolai Klimashin to the State Department to work with American cybersecurity officials. Klimashin, who was also the former chief of the FSB's secretive "3rd Directorate," chaired the first Cyber Working Group meeting with his American counterpart.[86]

Between the time that Putin and Obama initiated the Working Group and the 2016 primaries, Russia repeatedly hacked sensitive parts of the White House network and the State Department and tried to install monitoring stations throughout the U.S.[87]

In November 2013, the *New York Times* reported that a Russian space agency wanted to install antennae on buildings in the U.S. These monitoring stations could have been used to spy on America and would have given Russia improved guided missile technology and accuracy while operating on American soil.[88]

Obama's State Department apparently thought that granting Russia the ability to compromise U.S. national security might "help mend the Obama administration's relationship" with Putin.[89]

But as tensions between Moscow and Washington rose, so did Putin's cyberattacks. For months, the Russian hackers gained unauthorized access to sensitive White House information—including the president's nonpublic schedule. The FBI, Secret Service, and other intelligence agencies described the White House intrusions as "among the most sophisticated attacks ever launched against U.S. government systems." The State Department email hack was reportedly the "worst ever."[90]

In September 2015, Fishenko pleaded guilty to all nineteen charges. Then-Assistant Attorney General for National Security John P. Carlin stated, "Fishenko illegally acted as an agent of the Russian government in the United States and evaded export laws by sending microelectronics and other technology with military applications to Russia."[91]

In July 2016, Fishenko received a $500,000 fine and was sentenced to ten years in prison.[92]

Shockingly, Klimashin (co-chair of the Obama-Putin Cyber Working Group) ran the *exact* FSB Directorate reportedly involved in the Fishenko conspiracy. Why did the Obama administration welcome him to Washington eight months after the Fishenko ring was busted? Furthermore, *another* Russian operative on the Cyber Working Group would, by 2016, reveal a top-secret Kremlin program that he insinuated was the electronic equivalent of a nuclear bomb.[93]

The Russian BPC Cyber Working Group co-coordinator, Andrey Krutskikh, was one of Putin's top advisors on cyber issues. In February 2016 (while Fishenko awaited sentencing for the electronic espionage conspiracy), Putin's cyber official delivered a private speech in Moscow to a group of Kremlin insiders and security experts. In his speech, Krutskikh hinted ominously that the Russians were working on some kind of powerful electronic weapon.[94] The cyber official's leaked notes read:

You think we are living in 2016. No, we are living in 1948. And do you know why? Because in 1949, the Soviet Union had its first atomic bomb test. And if until that moment, the Soviet Union was trying to reach agreement with Truman to ban nuclear weapons, and the Americans were not taking us seriously, in 1949 everything changed and they started talking to us on an equal footing.

I'm warning you: We are at the verge of having "something" in the information arena, which will allow us to talk to the Americans as equals.[95]

How did Krutskikh know what the Americans had in the "information arena" and why was he so confident that Russia could so easily rival the country that created Silicon Valley?

In January 2017, the *Washington Post*—likely still reeling from the election of Donald Trump—suggested that the Russian cyber official's ominous warning nine months prior to Election Day might have been legitimate. Based on information from an anonymous Obama source, the Russian cyber official's warning may have been a precursor to Putin's new doctrine for information operations.

The anonymous Obama official told the *Washington Post*: "In the U.S., we tend to have a binary view of conflict—we're at peace or at war. The Russian doctrine is more of a continuum. You can be at different levels of conflict, along a sliding scale."

The *Post* failed to mention that Obama's reset had allowed Krutskikh to exploit the inner circles of Washington in the first place as the coordinator of Obama's and Putin's Cyber Working Group.[96] In addition, the working group's initial meeting was cochaired by Klimashin, the Russian Security Council official.

Worst of all, at the time of the Cyber Working Group meeting in Washington, the Justice Department surely suspected that Klimashin was linked to an FSB scheme to steal controlled technology and microelectronics. The *Post* ignored those details despite the benefit of hindsight (and Google).[97]

Had the *Post* mentioned Krutskikh's (and Klimashin's) very recent history, it would have been obvious to their readers that Obama had allowed Russia to steal U.S. technology between 2008 and 2012, and then rolled out the red carpet for two Kremlin cyber officials linked to sinister plots against the U.S. Then the *Post* would have had to acknowledge that it was Obama, not President-elect Trump, who had advanced Russian information warfare capabilities (to make no mention of the nuclear handouts like Uranium One).[98]

Perhaps the *Post* was merely being sloppy. Or perhaps, the paper was covering its own involvement in and glowing coverage of Obama's disastrous Russian reset.

Through the cyber and media working groups (particularly the journalist exchange program), Obama and Secretary Clinton opened the doors to potential Russian spies, hackers, and propagandists. The *Washington Post* and many others in the Obama-Clinton orbit participated in these initiatives. Somehow, they were all shocked when Russia exploited these cooperative Obama initiatives to (predictably) meddle in the 2016 election.[99]

* * *

Skolkovo was not just a massive security threat to the United States; it turned out to be a potential gold mine for well-connected entrepreneurs and politically connected profiteers to cash in on their connections to Clinton and Obama. Ironically, those who profited from Obama's reset would later accuse then-candidate Trump and his associates of foreign lobbying and endlessly decry Trump's ever-elusive ties to Russia.

Their scapegoat was Manafort, and the location of the frame-up was Ukraine.

CHAPTER 9

THE UKRAINE BOOMERANG

Obama's Russia Failures Unleash New Chaos and Cronyism in Ukraine

"I'm telling you, you're not getting the billion dollars. I said, you're not getting the billion. I'm going to be leaving here in, I think it was about six hours. I looked at them and said: I'm leaving in six hours. If the prosecutor is not fired, you're not getting the money. Well, son of a bitch. He got fired."[1]

—VICE PRESIDENT JOE BIDEN,
to the Council on Foreign Relations, January 2018

In late January 2020, the outcome of President Trump's impeachment was already cast. An acquittal was a fait accompli. Democrats had failed to make a case with wide bipartisan appeal. And all the House impeachment managers could hope to score was a single Republican defector on the jury, Senator Mitt Romney of Utah.[2]

The House Democrats voted to impeach Trump (though they failed to win over a single Republican member) after an impassioned closing argument from Congressman Adam Schiff.

Schiff's spirited speech roused the liberal faithful and their media acolytes, whose desperate three-year obsession to rid the White House of Donald J. Trump had come to this final, failed moment. But in Schiff's closing utterances, Trump defenders found a rich irony: much of the arguments the California Democrat laid out seemed to apply to the prior administration and the failed orchestrations of the Obama-Biden team in Eurasia a few years prior.[3]

Yes, a U.S. administration had indeed leveraged foreign aid to force the Ukrainians to do something. (Joe Biden even admitted it on video!) They had created the appearance of a conflict and personal gain. (Indeed, Biden and his son had.) Career bureaucrats were concerned about the conduct. (Deputy Assistant Secretary of State George Kent testified he even had tried to raise it with Biden but was rebuffed.)[4]

For conservatives and security experts truly in the know about what transpired in Ukraine—and not trapped in the prevailing media narrative—Schiff's final summation was the clearest evidence that the impeachment process had really been a defensive maneuver by Democrats to neutralize the impact of their own failures in the region. To the Trump faithful, Schiff's words almost seemed to be a projection of those Democratic failings upon the current occupant at 1600 Pennsylvania Avenue. In fairness, Trump had given them an opening with some of his comments and actions. But there was no provable crime, just a political question.[5]

That question, Schiff argued to the senators, is whether President Trump "will put his personal interests ahead of the national interests?" If so, it cannot be tolerated, Schiff insisted.[6]

"There's no Mulligan here when it comes to our national security," he said, using the golfer's favorite term for a do-over.[7]

Perhaps not a do-over. But maybe a makeover. Democrats were trying to rewrite the script from a decade of Russia and Ukraine policy failures so that Trump owned it all heading into the 2020 election. But in so doing, they had unintentionally educated the American public about Joe Biden's own family foibles and had elevated the Burisma Holdings episode with Hunter Biden into a powerful symbol of American cronyism overseas.[8]

The very political figures that Schiff's mission seemingly had sought to protect had now become its casualty.

The extraordinary boomerang began a decade earlier, when a youthful president with a penchant for domestic policy, and a yawn for foreign affairs, first tried to reboot America's relationship with Moscow.

Former speechwriter and security advisor Ben Rhodes summed up Obama's approach to foreign affairs in a poignant anecdote in his book.

> "What's the Obama doctrine?" [President Obama] asked aloud. The silence was charged, as we'd always avoided that label. He answered his own question: "Don't do stupid shit." There were some chuckles. Then, to be sure that he got his point across, he asked the press to repeat after him: "Don't do stupid shit."[9]

Those who watched the Obama doctrine unfold across Russia and Ukraine ultimately concluded his simple rule appeared to have been voided, including by the family of his Vice President Joe Biden, in whom he had entrusted Ukraine policy starting in 2014.[10]

After Russia had secured billion-dollar deals (at great expense to American taxpayers and national security), it was Ukraine's turn.[11]

Just as in Russia, the favors that the Obama administration granted Ukraine benefitted politically powerful oligarchs—notorious for cultivating the culture of corruption, bribery, extortion, kickbacks, and money laundering. Obama's bailout to Ukraine allowed its oligarchs to plunder not only its national resources but America's as well.[12]

Politically connected Americans like the Clinton and Biden families—among myriad others—mysteriously (or perhaps not) landed lucrative deals with these oligarchs and some of the same foreign entities who capitalized on American taxpayer-funded aid.[13]

Publicly, Obama and his diplomats tried to preserve the Russian reset through 2013. Privately, Hillary Clinton and Moscow Ambassador Michael McFaul had begun meddling in Russian and Ukrainian affairs by 2012. In Russia, the State Department funded opposition groups and fomented protests against Putin and his allies (arguably the equivalent of Putin directly funding political groups in the United States).[14]

The Maidan revolution—which began in late 2013—provided the perfect opportunity for the West to reduce Putin's influence over his neighbor by showering Ukraine with cash while simultaneously pushing vague "reforms"—alleged anti-corruption measures that the Ukrainians came to see for what they were: ironic at best.[15]

In Ukraine, the State Department sought to oust the Putin-friendly leader Viktor Yanukovych and install a pro-Western administration.

The installation of President Petro Poroshenko (with his willingness to accept foreign aid money into his country and his own pocket) alienated Russia and swiftly brought Ukraine into the Western sphere of influence.[16]

As the reset fizzled, the Obama team pivoted toward Ukraine in an apparent attempt to foil Putin's energy dominance and cyber warfare strategies. Putin sought to counter their efforts, especially in Ukraine. Obama and his top officials had officially botched the Russian reset.[17]

The exact date that the reset completely collapsed was February 22, 2014, with the ouster of pro-Russian Ukrainian President Viktor Yanukovych. A proxy war broke out in the Ukrainian Donbass region shortly after.[18]

Putin and his maneuvers in Crimea would become a scapegoat, but even the architect of Obama's Russia policy—Ambassador McFaul—knew that the beginning of the end occurred long before Crimea. In fact, two years before war broke out, the reset was in tatters.[19]

Obama and his team blamed Putin's years of aggressive meddling in Ukraine for the diplomatic breakdown, but the truth is that Obama and his diplomats were meddlers too.[20]

In September 2012, Putin took steps to eliminate their influence.

Reset Failure Led to Damage Control in Ukraine

On September 18, 2012, Putin expelled the U.S. Agency for International Development (USAID). USAID had operated in Russia since 1992—ramping up dramatically under Bill Clinton's administration—and has provided nearly $3 billion in funding to various groups that presumably advanced the U.S. agenda. Putin singled out one USAID-funded group called Golos ("vote" in Russian) for its election activities. Indeed, Golos had backed protests against Putin.[21]

McFaul was defiant. "Many people have asked me whether USAID departure will mean an end to our support for these important initiatives," McFaul wrote on his blog. "It will not." This marked the beginning of the end for the reset.[22]

USAID had partnered with the liberal billionaire investor George Soros on international advocacy projects for more than a decade. Soros had operated in both Russia and Ukraine since before their post-Soviet separation. His Open Society Institute (and his vast network of affiliate nongovernmental organizations—"NGOs") had entered both Soviet Russia and Ukraine before 1990.[23]

As one of the most influential globalists in the world, Soros had previously experienced Putin's protectionist tendencies and declared that his investment in the nationalist country was the worst of his career.[24]

After USAID's expulsion, Soros had lost a major co-financier. And now he had a major axe to grind.

By November 2012, Soros and his network were cognizant that their operations could be Putin's next expulsion. Russia "can do so anytime, legally or illegally," Soros' operatives acknowledged in a November 2012 meeting. So, they began ramping up efforts to diminish Putin's power.[25]

Soros believed that Russia and Ukraine were suffering from the same problem: a dilemma he termed the "original sin." The ruling class in both countries had been involved in government corruption for at least a decade. They were all "infected" with the original sin. So, in the event of a coup, any new administration would just be seen as "the bastard child of the old regime" and "a rotting element."[26]

As it turned out, Ukraine would be the key in Soros' pivot.

With all pretenses of the reset largely dispensed, the Obama administration set out to counter Putin's advances in Ukraine. Even before Clinton left Foggy Bottom in February 2013, the State Department was adapting its democracy-building strategy (the play that had been used to upend the Middle East during the "Arab Spring") for Ukraine.[27]

In November 2013, the Maidan Square protests—backed in part by Soros and the State Department—were in full swing. Three months later, pro-Putin leader Viktor Yanukovych was still refusing to sign an agreement to build closer ties with the West.[28]

On February 20, 2014, the violent protests turned deadly as gunshots rang out from the rooftops overlooking the Maidan Square in downtown Kiev. Snipers (whose identity and affiliation remain unknown) picked off anti-Yanukovych protesters *and* pro-Yanukovych police forces alike.[29]

By the time the smoke (and tear gas) had finally cleared, more than fifty protesters and four police officers had been killed. Almost immediately, Western media alleged that the snipers were acting on Yanukovych's orders and an arrest warrant was soon issued for the deposed leader. The dead—now called the "Heavenly Hundred"—from the mob of irate protestors became martyrs.[30]

Within forty-eight hours, the pro-Putin government in Kiev had been overthrown.

War in Ukraine

Putin's disbelief could hardly match his fury. The ouster of the democratically elected Yanukovych was the final straw. From fury, action soon followed from Moscow. Russians had always fretted about the future safety and independence of their ex-patriates in Ukraine's semi-autonomous and strategically important Crimea region. Soon they would act to change the balance of power.

Putin refused to recognize the new Western-backed government in Kiev, seeing it as the offspring of an "unconstitutional coup."[31] Instead, he plotted with his Siloviki (security service chiefs) through the night of February 22, 2014, to rescue Yanukovych and whisk him to safety in Russia. Yanukovych was in mortal peril, he believed, and was grateful that Putin "saved [his] life."[32] By 7:00 a.m. the next day, Putin—no doubt weary from the all-nighter—had decided, "we must start working on returning Crimea to Russia."[33]

On February 27, Putin dispatched thousands of heavily armed troops—"little green men"—to the capital city of the Black Sea peninsula called Crimea (a move he initially denied, but later acknowledged).[34] Putin's little green men stormed the Crimean parliament building and raised the Russian flag—a universal declaration of capture.[35]

Crimea was a strategic outcropping of land in a sea that borders Russia, Ukraine, Georgia, Romania, Bulgaria, and Turkey. Through the Bosporus Strait, the Black Sea connects to the Mediterranean and thus all of Europe and the Western world. Once under Soviet control, the Crimean Peninsula remained majority Russian-speaking and hosted the ex-Soviet Black Sea Fleet.[36]

A series of treaties governed Russia's and Ukraine's claim to the Black Sea territory and, in 2010, a partition treaty guaranteed Russia's use of the Sevastopol port and the right to station up to twenty-five thousand Russian troops there. The 2010 treaties re-upped Russia's claims to Crimea through the year 2042 and allowed 24 artillery systems, 132 armored vehicles, and 22 military planes in addition to the troops. In exchange, Russia paid the equivalent of hundreds of millions of dollars to maintain the fleet and offered Ukraine discounted natural gas.[37]

But by early 2014, Putin apparently felt that the rapidly Westernizing Ukrainians could no longer be trusted and the treaties were as good as ancient history. He thus signed a reunification treaty with the Crimean city of Sevastopol on March 18, 2014, and the so-called annexation of Crimea was officially underway.[38] War between Russia and Ukraine seemed imminent.

Indeed, a firefight broke out in the Ukrainian Donbass region less than one month after Putin signed the reunification treaty in Crimea.[39]

Earlier in March, Kremlin-backed media had leaked a bugged phone call between two European diplomats that undercut the sniper narrative being pushed throughout Western media. On the call, the Estonian foreign minister told the EU foreign affairs chief that "there is a stronger and stronger understanding that behind snipers it was not Yanukovych, it was somebody from the new [Western-backed] coalition." Years later, questions still lingered over whom the snipers were *actually* working for.[40]

Perhaps the war in Ukraine was just a spontaneous combustion of long-volatile relationships, or perhaps Putin's provocations during the reset and Obama's (and Soros') revolutionary reprisals in Putin's backyard (or vice versa) had made violent conflict inevitable. According to analysts, one thing is certain: February 22, 2014, marked the time of death for Obama's reset.[41]

Billion-Dollar Bailouts

On the other side of the world, President Obama tapped Vice President Joe Biden to be his Ukraine point man. Biden rose to the occasion and was on the ground in Kiev in April 2014 to help usher in the new pro-Western regime after the bloody Maidan Square clashes.[42]

Once Yanukovych was out, and Poroshenko and Arseniy Yatsenyuk (party rivals) were installed as Ukraine's new pro-Western president and prime minister, respectively, Biden acted as "marriage counsel[or]" to resolve their political differences. Biden persuaded them to join forces, to unify their factions to combat Putin's advances. In addition to this advisory role for Ukraine's political leaders, Biden coordinated the coming deluge of financial assistance to Ukraine.[43]

Ukraine's energy debts to Russia were substantial. Furthermore, corrupt oligarchs had plundered billions from Ukraine. Over the years, money simply vanished from Ukraine's coffers into the byzantine web of shell corporations and offshore accounts in known money-laundering hot spots like Latvia, Cyprus, and Seychelles (as mentioned, FBI operative William Campbell's Russian contacts called this informal network "the System").[44]

The first major financial life rafts to cash-strapped Ukraine came in the form of a $1 billion loan guarantee from the U.S. with an additional "U.S. crisis support package" (plus security assistance) totaling $58 million.[45]

In March 2014, the White House called on Congress to approve a $1 billion loan guarantee to Ukraine. Congress quickly delivered and appropriated the funds by April 14. Within a week (on April 21), Biden announced the $58 million aid package. Days after Biden announced this *first* wave of U.S. aid, the IMF approved an additional $17 billion loan package.[46]

But this funding was only the beginning. By June, the U.S. financial package tripled to more than $184 million (including $23 million in nonlethal "security assistance").[47]

The Man Behind the Billion-Dollar Bailouts

A leaked Open Society Foundations (OSF) memo (from a hack attributed to the Kremlin) revealed that, in late March 2014, Soros and his lieutenants met with Obama's diplomats in Kiev along with Ukrainian officials from the ministries of health, education, and justice (among others). Soros and his NGO operatives discussed a variety of issues ranging from financial assistance to HIV/AIDS initiatives.[48]

Soros openly acknowledged that his efforts had created momentum for the rebellion. He proudly believed that "the rebellion wounded Putin in his Achilles heel." Indeed, Soros worked in tandem with Obama's State Department to help fund the protesters in 2013.[49]

Now, in March 2014, his NGO network must build on that momentum. The leaked memo made certain that Ukraine had become the "main priority" of the entire Soros network.[50]

Soros met with U.S. ambassador to Ukraine Geoffrey Pyatt on March 31 and impressed upon the ambassador that Obama's weak Russia policy was a problem. Pyatt was eager to hear Soros' recommendations and told the billionaire that "Secretary Kerry would be interested to hear [Soros'] views on the [Ukraine] situation directly."[51]

"Obama has been too soft on Putin," Soros told the ambassador. Soros suggested that the U.S. and EU should now play dual roles in the front against Putin. The U.S. should play the "bad cop role" by imposing "potent smart sanctions."[52]

American efforts to install a friendly government in Ukraine—especially in coordination with the EU—were a delicate issue at the time of Soros' visit. One month prior, in February, Pyatt's phone call with State Department deputy Victoria Nuland had leaked, revealing that Pyatt and Nuland were orchestrating the installation of U.S.-approved Ukrainian leadership. The controversial recording was widely condemned as obvious evidence of U.S. meddling in Ukrainian affairs.[53]

Nuland's explicit comments regarding the EU were especially scandalous. She suggested they bring in a UN undersecretary general to assist with the so-called "puppet regime" scheme. Nuland, a Bush-Cheney holdover who won the confidence of the Obama administration, wanted the UN undersecretary general "to help glue this thing and to have the UN help glue it and, you know, Fuck the EU." "Exactly," replied Pyatt.[54]

"We could land jelly side up on this one if we move fast," Pyatt said but it would help to have someone "with an international personality to come out here [to Ukraine] and help midwife this thing." Nuland confirmed that Obama's point man was on board. "Biden's willing," she said before they hung up.[55]

The casual tone Nuland and Pyatt used, behind the scenes, while discussing the fate of a nation on the brink of violent revolution exhibited an ivory tower detachment at which the public does not often get a glimpse.

Soros and his team exhibited similar detachment when discussing ways to further enmesh their network in the Ukraine crisis, as revealed in the hacked memos. They were especially eager to help the Ukrainians with HIV/AIDS and other public health matters (such as opioid addiction). Soros personally offered to send an Open Society expert to "help with the [drug] procurement," and suggested ways to optimize health budgets "in partnership with the Clinton Foundation."[56]

The Clinton Foundation had set up the Clinton Health Access Initiative (CHAI) branch in 2002 to focus on HIV/AIDS. By 2003, Soros and Ukrainian billionaire Victor Pinchuk had set up HIV/AIDS programs in Russia and Ukraine. Over the years, Soros and Pinchuk had become Clinton mega-donors, and their HIV/AIDS work often intersected.[57]

As previously mentioned, when Clinton and Giustra flew to Kazakhstan in 2005 to procure the Uranium One mines, their stated reason for the visit was to discuss HIV/AIDS (despite Kazakhstan's infinitesimal infection rate).[58]

The connection between HIV/AIDS and large sums of money flowing to the politically powerful who conduct complex business deals remains unclear. In Ukraine, the Anti-Corruption Action Center (AntAC) and the Soros/Clinton/Pinchuk-backed HIV/AIDS network would later become embroiled in a controversy surrounding suspected embezzlement and missing aid money. On February 17, 2020, the National Police of Ukraine opened an investigation into the possible theft of aid money flowing through the NGO network—the missing funds in question exceeded $140 million in just two years.[59]

Soros capped off his trip to Ukraine with a dinner attended by the board of his International Renaissance Foundation (IRF)—the largest branch of the Open Society network in Ukraine. The Soros operatives spoke candidly and thanked the billionaire for all he had done for the revolution in Ukraine.[60]

Soros returned the compliments to his operatives stating that "his merit is the IRF's merit." Soros was proud of the work they had done—it could become a new model. But there was still more work to be done. "Ukraine is in grave danger," Soros conveyed, "because Putin knows he cannot allow the new Ukraine to succeed."[61]

Soros had a carrot-and-stick strategy for the Ukraine-Russia conflict: he wanted the EU (the good cop) to fund Ukraine and the U.S. (the bad cop) to hit Russia in the wallet. Soros said that the U.S. should target Putin's inner circle banks with sanctions and strategically dump oil reserves on the global market to "depress the price of oil." Soros suggested hitting Putin financially for ninety days or until he accepted the new pro-Western Ukrainian government (whichever came first).[62]

Less than one month after Soros' trip to Ukraine, Obama slapped sanctions on Putin's inner circle. Among the twenty-four individuals and entities listed were Rosneft's Igor Sechin, and Putin's ex-KGB comrade Sergey Chemezov.[63]

At the same time, plans to prop up Ukraine's economy were still underway. Obama invited President Poroshenko to the White House in September 2014 to discuss *further* financial assistance.[64] At the press conference, Obama announced that the U.S. had supplied, and would continue to supply, Ukraine with "significant financial assistance" in addition to the billion-dollar loan guarantee and the "hundreds of millions of dollars that we've provided in assistance."[65]

Obama also promised to provide "additional assistance, both economic and security assistance to Ukraine to make sure that not only are they able to weather this storm economically, but they're also going to be able to continue to build up an effective security force to defend themselves from aggression."[66]

But after a year of war and upheaval, Ukraine's economy was still spiraling out of control. By 2015, anti-Putin hawks were urging the Americans and other generous Western benefactors for a bigger bailout.[67]

Soros Pushes for Bigger Bailouts

In January 2015, Soros thought he might know where to find more billions for Ukraine. In an opinion article, Soros urged the EU to dig deep in their pockets to produce far more than the meagre $17 billion from 2014. Soros recommended a whopping $50 billion in emergency relief to Ukraine. "Europe needs to wake up and recognize that it is under attack from Russia," Soros wrote. "Assisting Ukraine should also be considered as a defense expenditure by the EU countries."[68]

Soros was instructing the EU to redirect their funds previously earmarked to help stabilize EU members (Ireland, Portugal, Romania, and Hungary)—and cobble together the next bailout for Ukraine (a non-member). "The additional sources of financing I have cited should be sufficient to produce a new financial package of $50 billion or more."[69]

The EU funds Soros cited were likely paid for by EU taxpayers but, "needless to say, the IMF would remain in charge of actual disbursements, so there would be no loss of control."[70]

Within weeks of Soros' article, IMF chief Christine Lagarde announced an assistance package totaling about $40 billion. Lagarde said that approximately $17.5 billion would come from the IMF and the remainder would come from "additional resources from the international community."[71]

"The economic and political success of Kiev would be a major blow to the Kremlin's narrative on Ukraine," said former Russian Duma member Ilya Ponomarev—a renowned dissident and strong Putin critic. "The West has a chance to show the world—and Russians in particular—what it has to offer," Ponomarev believed, but "unfortunately [the West] is missing this opportunity."[72]

And yet, Ukrainian Finance Minister Natalie Jaresko *still* did not believe the IMF's latest tranche would be enough to stabilize Ukraine's fragile economy.[73] Ponomarev agreed and presciently added that corruption in Kiev could siphon funds off the Western aid package, resulting in even less impact.[74]

By March 2015 (just one month after the $40 billion IMF announcement), Soros announced his intention to invest in major Ukrainian development projects. "There are concrete investment ideas, for example in agriculture and infrastructure projects. I would put in $1 billion. This must generate a profit," he told an Austrian newspaper. He claimed he would not benefit personally, but his foundation would.[75]

Soros' January 2015 EU bailout plea did not mention that he would be seeking a financial stake in Ukraine's agriculture and infrastructure.[76]

But Soros was not the only politically connected Westerner scouting deals in Ukraine. Obama's inner circle would soon do the same.

Commercial Deals: The Burisma Connection

As Biden was flying to and from Kiev amid the Maidan revolution in early 2014, an oligarch who had founded one of Ukraine's largest natural gas companies—Burisma Holdings—got an idea. Perhaps Burisma (or even the oligarch himself) could curry favor with Obama or his vice president by putting people close to them on the payroll—corruption by proxy.[77]

The oligarch, Mykola Zlochevsky, had acquired his Burisma gas assets through suspicious—or even criminal—means. Furthermore, he had allegedly looted large sums of money from the company. Now, in April 2014, international investigators were hot on Zlochevsky's trail.[78]

By April 22, Burisma had tapped an American named Devon Archer—a close associate of the Biden and Kerry families—for the position of independent director. Archer and the vice president's son, Hunter, were close friends and business partners in an investment fund called Rosemont Seneca Partners. Archer had also worked on Secretary of State John Kerry's 2004 presidential campaign and was the roommate of Kerry's stepson, Chris Heinz, while they studied at Yale.[79]

Financial statements obtained by the FBI and Ukrainian investigators reveal that exactly one week before Archer *publicly* joined Burisma as a director, Burisma began funneling substantial sums to bank accounts linked to Devon Archer and Hunter Biden.[80] The very next day, April 16, 2014, Archer visited the Obama White House to meet directly with Vice President Biden.[81]

Within a week, the vice president met with Ukrainian Prime Minister Yatsenyuk to discuss ways to eliminate reliance on Russian gas. Biden urged Ukraine to boost its energy production and said that an unspecified American team was "currently in the region" and that "more teams are coming to support long-term improvements." The Ukrainian prime minister thanked Biden (and the American taxpayers) for their generous support.[82]

On April 28, 2014, the reason for Burisma's peculiar political hire of Archer began to make more sense. The Serious Fraud Office in the U.K. froze certain assets belonging to Zlochevsky and Burisma (worth about $23 million). The U.K. authorities suspected that the money was transferred out of Ukraine *fraudulently* (Zlochevsky and Burisma have denied any wrongdoing).[83]

On May 13, 2014—less than one month after Archer was appointed and the *first* Burisma payments had entered U.S. accounts—Burisma announced that Hunter Biden had officially joined his friend on the board (his bio on Burisma's website was deleted, but archives indicate that Biden may have *quietly* joined in April). Within forty-eight hours, Burisma's sizable twin payments began to flow to the Morgan Stanley account of Rosemont Seneca Bohai (Biden and Archer's firm).[84]

Secretary Kerry's stepson, Chris Heinz, was clearly uncomfortable with his friends' Ukrainian arrangement. The same day that Burisma announced Hunter Biden had joined the board, Heinz quickly put his concerns in writing to officials at his stepfather's agency: "I can't speak to why they decided to [join Burisma]," Heinz wrote his contacts at State, "but there was no investment by our firm in their company."[85]

Starting on May 15, 2014, two separate payments of $83,333.33 (for a total of $166,666.66) landed in Biden and Archer's account. Like clockwork, Burisma's transfers continued for more than a year.[86]

While Secretary Kerry's stepson may have been uncomfortable with the Burisma arrangement, Kerry's press secretary, Jen Psaki, did not appear to have any issues with the appearance of Hunter Biden making big bucks from Kiev while his father oversaw U.S.-Ukraine policy. "No, he's a private citizen," Psaki responded coolly at a routine State Department briefing on May 13. The reporter pushed back, likening Hunter Biden's private citizenship to that of an oligarch. "No, there are not [any concerns]," Psaki said conclusively.[87]

Secretary Kerry's former chief of staff David Leiter had no apparent qualms either. Less than one week after Hunter Biden joined the board, Burisma hired Leiter as their lobbyist. Burisma paid Leiter's firm

$90,000 to lobby his former boss' department (and Congress) through-out 2014.[88]

Burisma also hired a Democrat-linked outfit named Blue Star Strategies to help the Ukrainian gas company shed its controversial image. Blue Star Strategies lobbyists dropped Hunter Biden's name in communications with the State Department and tried to "leverage" the son of the vice president to get key meetings and "burnish" Burisma's image.[89]

Part of Hunter Biden's Burisma duties included advising the company on legal and corporate governance issues. While providing moonlight advice to Burisma, Biden also worked at the law firm Boies Schiller Flexner LLP. When Archer asked Biden to recommend a law firm to counsel Burisma, presumably on their frozen asset dilemma, naturally, Biden recommended his own firm.[90]

Burisma's first payment to Boies Schiller occurred on May 7 in the amount of $250,000. Burisma made another payment to the firm—for $33,039.77—less than five months later. Burisma's payments to Boies Schiller apparently bought the Ukrainian gas company a report (prepared by Nardello & Co.) that concluded Burisma was not under any international investigations.[91]

This conclusion proved to be false.

The Point Man's Point Man

As a senior senator serving on the foreign relations committee, Biden had been instrumental in creating a new "Special Envoy" position at the State Department to combat Putin's maneuvers against his neighbors.[92]

In 2007, Biden and his colleague Senator Richard Lugar wrote a letter to then-Secretary Condoleezza Rice stating, "Russia's attempt to consolidate its control over energy resources presents unacceptable security and economic risks to the United States and our allies." They urged Secretary Rice to appoint a "special representative" to the regions bordering Russia and the Caspian Sea.[93]

When Secretary Clinton took over the State Department, the "Special Envoy" position that Senator Biden helped create in 2007 underwent significant changes. In October 2011, Clinton created a new bureau of energy resources and appointed an ally named Amos Hochstein to help develop the special energy envoy position.[94]

Secretary Clinton tapped Hochstein as a deputy assistant secretary for energy diplomacy and created the Bureau of Energy Resources (ENR). At the same time, Clinton placed "Special Envoy" Carlos Pascual (a former Ambassador to Ukraine) in charge of the new bureau (under the oversight of Undersecretary Robert Hormats).[95]

There were few men or women in Washington as knowledgeable about global energy issues as Hochstein. Between stints working as a lobbyist for international energy corporations, Hochstein had advised senators and members of Congress; then he advised Secretary Clinton and her successor Secretary Kerry. During his last federal assignment, Hochstein worked as Obama and Biden's point man on the Ukraine-Russia standoff.[96]

On July 8, 2014, Hochstein was, as always, impeccably dressed for his appearance in front of the Senate Foreign Relations European Affairs subcommittee. He appeared like an image from a Brooks Brothers' catalog, his periwinkle-with-pearl striped repp tie, his snappy pinstripe suit, and jet-black hair greased back—hardly a strand out of place.[97]

Hochstein was prepared, physically and mentally. His statement (which he had practiced delivering in one form or another since April—several weeks after the Ukraine crisis began) was careful, crisp, and punchy. Hochstein and his colleagues from the Defense Department and USAID were there to discuss how Russia's conflict with Ukraine affected energy security in the region and to inform senators how Russia had leveraged—and at times weaponized—their energy resources for geopolitical gain.[98]

Hochstein began with an update on the energy crisis in Ukraine. Russia had ceased gas supplies less than one month prior, on June 16, and Ukraine and the European Union were negotiating with Russia to resolve their energy issues. Russia had demanded repayment from Ukraine for past energy debts before any further negotiations could take place. "The situation is urgent," Hochstein warned.[99]

Part of the solution, according to Hochstein, was Ukraine's integration into the EU energy market. "However," Hochstein cautioned, "before this integration can happen successfully it is essential that Ukraine reform its energy sector." Without reform, and "if corruption and inefficiency continue along with crippling energy subsidies for consumers," Hochstein believed, "Ukraine will be right back where it started."[100]

Two weeks later, Hochstein again testified to a separate Senate Foreign Relations subcommittee on energy security vis-à-vis Russia's conflict with Ukraine. In his written testimony, Hochstein reiterated the Russian threats to energy security.[101]

After quickly mapping out the geopolitical energy landscape generally, Hochstein issued the same caveats he had two weeks prior. "Ukraine and Europe's dependence on Russian gas is a clear example of the danger of relying on a dominant supplier," Hochstein told the lawmakers. "The situation is urgent for Ukraine," he warned and while he did not believe Europe was in *immediate* danger, a crisis "may be just around the corner."[102]

Three days later, Hochstein got promoted to the "Special Envoy" position. As "Special Envoy" and coordinator for international energy affairs, Hochstein led "the U.S. Government's efforts to combat the use of energy resources for political leverage while promoting a vision of energy cooperation and collaboration."[103]

Hochstein was right about Ukraine. In the months leading up to the February 2014 ouster of Ukrainian president Victor Yanukovych, Putin's oil giant Gazprom had rewarded Ukraine for walking away from the EU. Yanukovych rejected an EU trade deal and, in December 2013, Gazprom unilaterally reduced the price of gas for Ukraine by a third. Putin *personally* and publicly announced the Gazprom discount—a clear demonstration of his approval that Yanukovych had distanced Ukraine from the EU.[104]

However, three months later, after the Maidan revolution and Yanukovych's ouster, Putin unleashed his fury: Gazprom jacked up Ukraine's prices by 81 percent.[105]

At one event hosted by the Atlantic Council (an entity funded by Soros *and* Burisma), Hochstein again warned that Russia's weaponization of energy was predictable and must be counterbalanced:

When the gas was shut off from Russia to Ukraine on June 16th [2014], that was not a unique event. It happened in 2006 and it happened in 2009 and, therefore, it happened again in 2014. And there is no reason to believe it will not happen again. The way to prevent it from happening again is to…[create] new infrastructures that can allow for energy, for gas and for other sources of energy to come into Europe from other places to compete with Russian supplies.[106]

Between his visits to Congress (and well-connected think tanks) to apprise decision makers of Putin's energy antics, Hochstein was Biden's right-hand man on visits with various world leaders. He frequently flew to Ukraine (and other nations) with Biden to work out energy deals.[107]

But Hochstein had a secret.

Russia's Best Energy Lobbyist

Time and again, Biden's advisor failed to mention that he had witnessed Putin's energy strategy first hand. Hochstein communicated Putin's energy dominance strategy in the oil and gas sectors very effectively, but he never mentioned Russia's attempts to corner the global uranium market. It was something he had assisted personally.[108]

While working as a U.S. lobbyist in the private sector, Hochstein had advised Rosatom's subsidiary: Tenex.

Hochstein became a revolving door extraordinaire early in his Beltway career. As he weaved in and out of the private sector, his positions (and profits) rose substantially. From 2001 to 2007, Hochstein worked in various capacities at Washington lobbying powerhouse Cassidy & Associates. In 2006, then-Governor Mark Warner (D-VA) hired Hochstein to serve as a senior policy advisor. Hochstein *purportedly* left Cassidy in January 2007 to join Connecticut Senator Chris Dodd's presidential campaign, according to a press release by the firm.[109]

In a 2006 *Washington Post* interview, Hochstein was asked about his lobbying efforts on behalf of the brutal regime in Equatorial Guinea. "But when you meet with Obiang, do you think to yourself: This guy has done awful things?" reporter Michael Grunwald asked Hochstein.

"No, I really don't. Our meetings have all been very businesslike. He's convinced me of his deep care for his people," Hochstein replied.[110] Hochstein helped overhaul the corrupt nation's image (where the *police* raped and tortured the citizens, according to State Department reports).[111] When asked about the $120,000-per-month fees, Hochstein acknowledged that lobbying is not "charity work."[112]

Indeed, Hochstein continued to work for Cassidy's deep-pocketed foreign clients, even while he was employed by Governor Warner and Senator Dodd's presidential campaign. In 2006, Russian nuclear corporation Tenex asked Campbell (unaware that he was an FBI operative) to find a Beltway lobbying powerhouse to help further their interests. By March 2006, Campbell found himself meeting with Hochstein, who ensured that Tenex hired Cassidy & Associates. Cassidy claims that Hochstein left the firm in January 2007, but Hochstein continued to meet with Putin's top nuclear officials throughout 2007 and 2008 while he was working with powerful Democrats.[113]

Did Warner and Dodd know that Hochstein was simultaneously serving Russian interests? Hochstein's public bios make no mention of his work on behalf of Tenex, although he does acknowledge returning to Cassidy in August 2008 (and remaining there until 2011).[114]

Before long, he was directly advising Secretary of State Clinton, her successor John Kerry, and Vice President Biden (and even President Obama). His LinkedIn profile is meticulously manicured to show no overlap between his public and private sector gigs, but, in fact, Hochstein advised multiple public officials *and* simultaneously worked to advance foreign interests while on the payroll of Cassidy.[115]

According to the Obama White House's visitor records, Hochstein visited more than 150 times between December 2010 and September 2016, including several trips to the Situation Room. His first visits occurred while he was still working with Cassidy.[116] Did Hochstein disclose his past lobbying relationships on behalf of Kremlin interests when he visited the Obama White House?

Furthermore, Hochstein's current LinkedIn profile states that he stepped down from Cassidy in March 2011. But, an archived version indicates that he left in July 2011, and Cassidy continued to list him on their website through August 2011. This is significant because he began communicating with Clinton's top lawyer at the State Department, Cheryl Mills, no later than May 10, 2011.[117] Did Hochstein advise Clinton or her State Department on energy matters while employed by a lobbying firm that had represented Russian nuclear interests?

Nevertheless, Hochstein's global perspectives were clearly appreciated within the State Department, and he soon found himself regularly meeting with Secretary Clinton and her inner circle directly. As Clinton's "Special Envoy" at the ENR, he traveled the globe promoting Secretary Clinton's energy agenda. "I have been privileged to help build and lead the bureau since its creation," Hochstein said.[118]

After Clinton left State, Hochstein initially advised Secretary Kerry and traveled overseas with him to work on EU energy issues.[119] While advising Kerry, Hochstein worked closely with other Obama officials including Assistant Secretary Victoria Nuland, Special Coordinator Jonathan Winer, National Security Council (NSC) Senior Director Charles Kupchan (each of these individuals played starring roles in Obama's Russia and Ukraine operations *and* they later helped perpetrate the political dirty tricks against Trump).[120]

Hochstein soon found himself in the good graces of Vice President Biden. He traveled around the world with Biden—numerous times to Ukraine, and they also visited Turkey, Cyprus, Romania, and even the Caribbean. At an Atlantic Council summit in Istanbul, Biden praised the special energy envoy and announced that he had put Hochstein in charge of European energy security efforts.[121]

As "Special Envoy" and advisor to Biden, Hochstein met with an impressive number of top foreign officials on trips to Europe, the Middle East, Latin America, and the Caribbean (including Ukraine, Egypt, Israel, Saudi Arabia, Lebanon, Qatar, Azerbaijan, Turkey, Greece, Croatia, Colombia, Argentina, and Kuwait). He also came under fire from the department's inspector general for, among other things, his attendance and poor record keeping.[122]

The State Department inspector general (IG) investigated the ENR and published the findings in February 2016. The report blasted the ENR generally, and Hochstein in particular.[123]

The IG found: extended absences of top ENR officials were deemed detrimental to ENR's operational effectiveness; weak institutional procedures, in particular information sharing and communication, as well as the bureau's organizational structure, hampered internal operations and coordination with bureau partners; the strategic planning process was not inclusive and lacked rigorous prioritization of objectives; the Bureau of Energy Resources lacked an effective security program to ensure the protection of sensitive information.[124]

Regarding Hochstein's attendance specifically, the IG found:

> The Special Envoy, in particular, travels a great deal and is frequently away from the Department. The official records for his travel and time and attendance indicate that he has not been physically present in ENR for almost two-thirds of regular working days between August 2014 and the beginning of the OIG on-site inspection in May 2015.[125]

Despite Hochstein's poor review from the inspector general, he was embraced by his superiors, including Biden.

Firing the Prosecutor

In December 2015, Vice President Biden was preparing for his next trip to Kiev. His aides were bracing for "renewed scrutiny of Hunter's relationship with Burisma." Hochstein allegedly "raised" the Burisma issue with Biden but did not recommend Hunter step down from the board.[126]

On December 6, Biden departed for Ukraine in his capacity as Obama's point man. He had been sent to "announce that there was another billion-dollar loan guarantee." But en route to Kiev aboard Air Force Two, Biden had an idea.[127]

Obama's point man had previously asked the Ukrainian leadership to "take action" against a prosecutor that was investigating Burisma. When they failed to do so, Biden apparently decided to take matters into his own hands. But he would need to leverage the loan guarantee that he was scheduled to announce. He would need to scrap that language from his upcoming speech. His aides did as they were instructed and edited the speech, removing any references to the billion-dollar loan guarantee.[128]

Biden's aides had been right to worry about the Burisma situation. On December 8, two days after Biden and his delegation landed in Kiev, James Risen at the *New York Times* ran a blistering exposé on the Hunter Biden-Burisma connection stating that "the credibility of the vice president's anticorruption message may have been undermined by" his son's connection to Burisma.[129]

Biden decided to hit two birds with one stone: he could deliver a strong anti-corruption message and eliminate the pesky prosecutor investigating Burisma. The latter could bolster the former and it was a low-risk gamble: Prosecutor General Viktor Shokin "had become widely reviled" by U.S. officials and media (after he began investigating a Soros-funded Ukrainian NGO for diverting U.S. aid). After less than ten months on the job, Shokin had made enemies more powerful than his allies.[130]

Biden used the visit—his latest of what became approximately one dozen trips to Kiev—to leverage the American aid money against Ukraine and extract concessions. Biden specifically leveraged the aid "as a pressure tactic to force the firing of a prosecutor he did not like."[131]

In the wake of the revolution, Biden's message to Ukraine's parliament was simple, according to one aide: "If you don't get your shit together, your country is doomed."[132] By December 2015, Biden's approach had hardly changed. As a Ukrainian parliamentarian put it, Biden's tone "was like the big brother coming to tell the little brother what to do—a recommendation that you can't ignore."[133]

According to Biden's recollection:

> I had gotten a commitment from Poroshenko and from Yatsenyuk that they would take action against the state prosecutor. And they didn't. So they said they had—they were walking out to a press conference. I said, nah, I'm not going to—or, we're not going to give you the billion dollars. They said, you have no authority. You're not the president. The president said—I said, call him.
>
> (Laughter.)
>
> I said, I'm telling you, you're not getting the billion dollars. I said, you're not getting the billion. I'm going to be leaving here in, I

think it was about six hours. I looked at them and said: I'm leaving in six hours. If the prosecutor is not fired, you're not getting the money. Well, son of a bitch. (Laughter.) He got fired. And they put in place someone who was solid at the time.[134]

Biden's threat was effective. By March 29, 2016, prosecutor Shokin was out. The loan guarantee—linked to Ukraine's efforts to implement reforms and reduce corruption—was finally announced by the U.S. Embassy in Kiev in June 2016.[135]

A Not-So-Solid Prosecutor Buries Burisma

The position of prosecutor general is the Ukrainian equivalent of the U.S. attorney general. It is a very powerful position, especially due to systemic corruption among the politically connected billionaire oligarch class. The Prosecutor General has the ability to investigate and indict lawbreakers, and effectively end (or exonerate) an oligarch's reign of corruption.[136]

In the tangled Obama-Ukraine saga, there are at least two prosecutor generals worth noting—Viktor Shokin (the one Biden wanted fired served from February 2015 to March 2016) and Yuriy Lutsenko (the one Biden called "solid" was not even a lawyer—he served from May 2016 to August 2019, despite attempting to resign in November 2018—Poroshenko refused).[137]

The irony of Biden's recollection was that he claimed this unusual incident was an example of his efforts to prevent Ukraine from "backsliding" into a culture of corruption. Hochstein agreed and vehemently denied that Biden forced Shokin's firing because the prosecutor was investigating Burisma and Hunter Biden. "Many of us in the U.S. government believed that Shokin was the one protecting [Burisma founder] Zlochevsky," Hochstein said.[138]

Apparently, Hochstein did not realize how ludicrous such an assertion sounds in retrospect. Was Hochstein really suggesting that Biden *wanted* his son's Ukrainian paymaster investigated? Was he actually suggesting that if Shokin protected Burisma, then Biden would want him fired?

Whether Shokin was corrupt or not is of minimal importance given what happened next. In Biden's oft-quoted CFR video recollection, one piece is often overlooked: Biden claimed that Shokin's replacement (at the time) was "solid."[139]

This crucial afterthought is even more ironic. Shokin's replacement was *far* from solid.

The new prosecutor, Yuriy Lutsenko, was a former Ukrainian minister with a checkered past (to put it mildly). In 2006, Lutsenko was removed from his post in parliament on charges of corruption. In 2008, he was accused of assaulting the mayor of Kiev. While drunk in an airport in 2009, Lutsenko was arrested by German authorities for making a scene. That same year, he lost a libel suit (he was known for disparaging his opponents).[140]

Shortly after Yanukovych took power in February 2010, Lutsenko was charged with public corruption (charges he denied) and sentenced to four years in jail. Yanukovych pardoned Lutsenko in April 2013, and he was released from prison. Soon after his release and by November 2013, Lutsenko became one of the top organizers of the Maidan protests. He was injured during a clash between protesters and riot police in January 2014.[141]

After the coup, Poroshenko appointed Lutsenko as a top advisor to the new pro-Western administration. He became the head of the Poroshenko bloc political party and held that position until late August 2015. As a Poroshenko loyalist with experience behind bars, Lutsenko knew the consequences of falling out of favor with the administration. Clearly Poroshenko trusted Lutsenko. *Euromaidan Press* said that the close relationship "casts a shadow" over Lutsenko's appointment because Lutsenko would be "unlikely to take steps which contradict the President's views."[142]

It remains unclear why Biden deemed Lutsenko "solid," but six months after Lutsenko's appointment, the Shokin-era investigations into Burisma disappeared.[143]

After Trump saw Biden's explicit quid pro quo *on video*, he asked Ukraine to investigate the Burisma situation. Was Shokin investigating Burisma when Biden demanded his ouster? Why would Biden say Shokin's replacement, Lutsenko, was solid? Did it have something to do with the fact that Lutsenko quashed all Burisma investigations within months?[144]

These were reasonable questions. Even one of Trump's most virulent critics, Congressman Adam Schiff, would acknowledge that Lutsenko was "widely viewed to be corrupt."[145]

Schiff and the Ukrainian Arms Dealer

Initially, President Obama's assistance to Ukraine was largely financial. He later came under fire for failing to send military assistance.[146]

Schiff (D-CA), meanwhile, was enthusiastic in his support for Ukraine military assistance. During the impeachment proceedings against Trump, Schiff repeatedly blasted the president for allegedly placing conditions on military aid to Ukraine.

What Schiff failed to mention throughout the impeachment debacle was that he played a key role in appropriating military assistance funds to Ukraine to begin with. Schiff cosponsored a bill in early 2015 that would provide Ukraine with *direct* military aid. One of Schiff's fundraisers stood to gain substantially from his efforts.[147]

On February 12, 2015, the House introduced H.R. 955: "To authorize assistance and sustainment to the military and national security forces of Ukraine." Schiff had long been an advocate for the interests of the American military-industrial complex.[148] In theory, providing Ukraine with new protective gear and weaponry—from Kevlar vests to firearms and ammunitions or even Javelin rocket launchers—could be a windfall for defense contractors.[149]

One of Schiff's constituents in California, a Soviet-born American named Igor Pasternak, had a company that had received favorable military contracts since the mid-nineties. Pasternak, who claims to be Kazakh-born and is "proud to forever call [himself] a Ukrainian-Jewish-American." He played a mysterious role in the Maidan revolution and flew to Kiev in "the final hours of the Yanukovych presidency....for diplomatic reasons in response to the outbreak of violence...."[150]

It remains unclear what those "diplomatic reasons" entailed, but Pasternak flew back and forth to Kiev in the aftermath of Yanukovych's ouster. For his efforts, he received an award from Ukraine's Embassy in the U.S. and soon began hustling Ukrainian-American defense contracts (which began to flow more freely shortly after the Ukraine bailout billions became available).[151]

Pasternak founded a company called Aeros Ltd. in Ukraine after he graduated from Lviv Polytechnic University's engineering school. When he immigrated to the U.S. in 1994, he founded Worldwide Aeros Corporation ("Aeroscraft" or "Aeros"). Aeroscraft manufactures lighter-than-air ships—blimp-like structures that float through the sky on surveillance and reconnaissance missions.[152]

Aeroscraft's ships were designed to vacuum up radio signals while hovering high above the ground, out of sight. The company had grabbed multimillion-dollar contracts from NASA, the U.S. Air Force, and other defense agencies interested in Aeros' patented advanced blimp technology.[153]

The crisis in Ukraine brought new opportunities for Pasternak's company.

Pasternak's first lobbying disclosure was filed March 27, 2014—even before the ink had dried on the bailout packages to Ukraine. His initial lobbying disclosures were generic, though USAID was mentioned as an agency Pasternak sought to target. Once the specific Ukrainian assistance resolution (which Schiff cosponsored) was introduced, Pasternak's disclosures got more specific.[154]

As H.R. 955 was meandering through House committees in early 2015, Pasternak aggressively lobbied for its adoption. On April 20, Pasternak's company disclosed its lobbying efforts on issues that included: "Continued efforts on gaining support and promoting Aeroscraft and lighter-than-air (LTA) product line, including integrating surveillance equipment," and "Promoting HR 955 the Ukraine Support Act, which will help provide funding for defensive weapons to Ukraine." Less than sixty days later, Pasternak's lobbying had apparently paid off.[155]

In mid-June 2015, Pasternak's Aeroscraft signed a deal with Ukraine's defense conglomerate Ukroboronprom. Aeroscraft and Ukroboronprom would be partnering to produce (or retrofit) assault rifles for Ukraine compatible with NATO-standard ammunition (5.56mm rounds).[156] This would allow Ukraine to retire their antiquated Kalashnikovs (Soviet-era compatibility) and adopt NATO standards by 2020.

Pasternak highlighted the ramifications: "when you see a Ukrainian soldier with a NATO weapon in his hand, it is a strong political message to Russia."[157]

Pasternak was thrilled at how quickly his company became a major player in the Ukrainian defense sector. His Washington connections had paid off.

"This is the first time in my practice when the decision to grant a license for the production of weapons in another country was provided by the U.S. government that quickly," Pasternak boasted at a press conference in January 2017. "We got a license in three weeks and we are already working on setting up production of NATO weapons production in Ukraine."[158]

The West had been pushing for reforms in the Ukrainian defense ministry since the 2014 revolution at least. Over time, those reform efforts paved the way for increased Ukrainian cooperation with U.S. and NATO defense contractors (a contentious issue). As a sign of the increased cooperation, the Obama Defense Department invited Ukroboronprom's CEO, Roman Romanov, to the United States to meet with American defense officials and attend a prestigious weapons conference.[159]

There was just one problem: Ukroboronprom was a hotbed of corruption and could not be trusted to manage aid money properly.[160]

International monitors were growing increasingly concerned with the billions (and counting) in missing Ukrainian aid money. By late 2017, the lack of transparency—particularly in Ukrainian defense budgets—was becoming an unavoidable issue.[161]

At a Commission on Security and Cooperation in Europe (or "CSCE," which is also known as the U.S. Helsinki Commission) hearing in the Dirksen Senate Office Building in Washington, the issue of Trump's military aid to Ukraine vis-à-vis ongoing corruption arose.[162]

An attendee from the Center for International Policy (among several Soros-funded NGOs in attendance) asked: "As we're awaiting President Trump's decision to transfer defensive weapons to Ukraine, are there any concerns about this affecting current anti-corruption efforts going on in the country, and is there any anti-corruption body that is prepared to oversee this?"[163]

The moderator asked who the question was directed to. The attendee replied, "Whoever wants to answer it." "Give it to Orest [former CSCE policy advisor]. He'll answer anything," the moderator quipped.[164]

The former CSCE policy advisor acknowledged that the defense sector was still undergoing reform, but that transparency problems in the procurement process remained. "You have this secrecy law on procurement which even includes things like buckets and socks, for instance, so there's a lack of transparency...."[165]

He emphasized that Ukrainians, particularly decision makers, were growing frustrated with the opaque nature of the defense sector, and he specifically identified Pasternak's partnering entity as central to the problem. Efforts were supposedly underway to make the "whole process more open and transparent, especially also when it comes to Ukroboronprom."[166]

A report from the Carnegie Endowment for International Peace found that the Ukrainian defense sector was plagued by a "lack of internal coordination between structures; lack of civilian and parliamentary oversight of the armed forces; incomplete integration of volunteers into the regular army; impunity and abusive behavior in the conflict zone; and systemic corruption and non-transparency of budgets."[167]

The Carnegie report concluded that Ukroboronprom was a primary driver of corruption:

> The problem is exacerbated by the fact that one state-owned conglomerate, Ukroboronprom—variously referred to as a "monster" and a "parasite"—enjoys a de facto monopoly over Ukraine's defense industry.[168]

Indeed, the Trump administration was beginning to view Ukroboronprom as a center of corruption in the Ukrainian defense sector.

By mid-2018, the Trump administration was digging into corruption in Ukraine (President Trump was especially concerned with misspent U.S. foreign aid). Trump's State Department specifically identified Ukroboronprom as a corrupt entity.[169]

"Ukroboronprom remains very much an umbrella group that provides many of the opportunities for corruption in the military security sphere in Ukraine," Deputy Assistant Secretary Jorgan K. Andrews said at a foreign press briefing on June 26, 2018. "This umbrella organization [Ukroboronprom] was created to provide kind of this overarching cover for all of the other defense industrial enterprises," Andrews went on. "And so that middleman doesn't need to exist, and that middleman provides opportunities for corruption."[170]

The State Department deputy left little doubt that Trump's State and Defense Departments were "working closely with Ukrainian counterparts to recommend serious, profound reforms to the defense industrial sector."[171]

Why was Schiff so concerned with Trump seeking to investigate corruption in Ukraine? How many other impeachment-obsessed Democrats had taken money from Pasternak or other Ukrainian interests? Would placing a hold on military aid to Ukraine affect Pasternak's contracts with Ukroboronprom?

These questions and so many others demand answers.

Uranium One Cover-up and the 2016 Collusion Delusion

The allegations of Trump-Russia collusion are rooted in Ukraine and center around Trump's former campaign manager Paul Manafort. On August 14, 2016, the Ukrainian efforts to sabotage the Trump campaign went public.

The *New York Times* published a report titled "Secret Ledger in Ukraine Lists Cash for Donald Trump's Campaign Chief." The report was based on anonymous sources who alleged that Manafort was implicated in a bribery scheme (evidenced by secret payments documented in the so-called "black ledger"). The report was published on a Sunday night, and by Monday morning the allegations had gone viral internationally.[172]

Then the Clinton spin machine sprang into action. Clinton's friend, fundraiser, and confidante David Brock used his Media Matters blog (another recipient of Soros' largesse) to blast the Manafort story and pressure the media to do likewise.[173]

On the morning of Friday, August 19, 2016, CBS News interviewed Serhiy Leshchenko, the Ukrainian who worked with the National Anti-Corruption Bureau of Ukraine (NABU) and the DNC operative

Alexandra Chalupa on the dubious black ledger story. Coincidentally, Leshchenko worked with Soros operatives and was at the March 2014 meeting in Kiev (per the leaked OSF memo), and Chalupa was a long-time Clinton ally (and former Clinton White House staffer) working to advance her candidacy.[174]

During the interview, CBS News aired small snippets of the alleged black ledger on screen. After the interview, Leshchenko quickly posted a link to the interview (uploaded by Clinton-linked Media Matters) on his Facebook page. His comment read:

> Our morning's report on Yanukovych's money for Manafort…hit the morning news of the American TV channel CBS News. I think this was the last nails in the cover of Manafort's coffin. I hope that Trump is with him. (translation)[175]

Before lunchtime, Manafort had resigned from the Trump campaign.[176]

It did not take long for the Chalupas to take a victory lap. Alexandra's sister Andrea emailed her colleagues: "Exciting day: Paul Manafort resigned from the Trump campaign and will likely face an investigation for not declaring being a foreign agent while lobbying for Yanukovych and his party."[177]

Chalupa's and her Ukrainian colleagues' efforts—which she admitted to—helped fan the flames of an FBI operation already underway code-named "Crossfire Hurricane." The Crossfire Hurricane operation (run by the FBI's top officials, including James Comey, Andrew McCabe, and FBI "lovebirds" Peter Strzok and Lisa Page) was examining possible collusion between the Trump campaign and Russia. That FBI probe ultimately led to a special counsel investigation headed by former FBI Director Robert Mueller. But after many months (and millions spent), Mueller came up with no evidence of collusion.[178]

Unsatisfied, Trump's opponents prepared for their next effort to remove him from the White House. This time, Trump was accused of abusing his power by questioning Ukraine's ongoing corruption and raising doubts over whether foreign aid to Ukraine was being misused—completely valid concerns.

The impeachment case that Schiff and the House managers presented was flimsy. Impeachable offenses must meet the constitutional threshold of "high crimes and misdemeanors," but the Democrats' charges—"abuse of power" and "obstruction of Congress"—were not even real crimes (which the Democrats openly acknowledged). The allegation was that Ukrainian President Volodymyr Zelensky had been pressured to investigate the Bidens and Burisma or risk losing its U.S. aid.[179]

It took less than two months for Trump's legal team to expose the weaknesses in that evidence and defeat Schiff's impeachment effort.

Trump Exonerated

On February 5, 2020, President Trump was acquitted on both charges leveled against him by the House managers. The so-called "Schiff Show" had finally ended. The impeachment inquiry formally began on September 24, 2019, but efforts to remove Donald Trump began literally minutes after he was inaugurated in January 2017.[180]

Trump maintains that his interaction with Zelensky was a "perfect phone call," and the transcript released by the White House contains no apparent quid pro quo (an allegation that Schiff repeated ad nauseam).[181]

To understand Trump's motives, some context must be applied. The very real problem of corruption in Ukraine dates back decades—since the fall of the Soviet Union, Ukraine has consistently ranked among the most corrupt countries in Europe (and possibly the world).[182]

The specific issues that Trump asked Zelensky to get to the bottom of were allegations of Ukrainian interference in the 2016 election and possible bribery involving Biden.

The allegations that Ukraine meddled in the 2016 election were first publicized by *New York Times* reporter Ken Vogel (at *Politico* at the time). Vogel and his colleague David Stern reported that the Ukrainian *government* worked closely with DNC operatives to support the Clinton campaign. The alleged bribery efforts involving Burisma and Biden date back to the collapse of Obama's Russia reset and subsequent efforts to perform damage control on Obama's disastrous Russia policy via Ukraine. While at the *New York Times*, Vogel reported on the Biden allegations as well.[183]

The allegations that Trump asked Zelensky to investigate implicate numerous individuals (including Biden and Clinton) and their tangled web of cross-border relationships that span continents and decades. Obama was at the center of this web. Obama, his former officials, and their cronies circled their wagons around Clinton first and then again around Biden. The implications are manifold.

Not only was Trump exonerated and cleared of the charge that his campaign colluded with Russia, but in an ironic twist, DNC operative Chalupa reportedly solicited Ukrainian officials for dirt on Trump stating that the "DNC wanted to collect evidence [proving] that Trump, his organization and Manafort were Russian assets." Chalupa supplied Clinton's team with Trump dirt after coordinating with Ukrainian officials—in other words, they colluded. Chalupa tried to distance herself from her previous statement, but more evidence indicates she was correct the first time. Furthermore, current and former government officials close to Vice President Biden attempted to conceal the Ukrainian collusion along with Biden's alleged corruption.[184]

For example, the alleged "whistleblower" who kicked off the Trump impeachment inquiry in September 2019 was a thirty-three-year-old CIA operative named Eric Ciaramella. Ciaramella was an Obama NSC holdover who reportedly expressed hostility toward Trump and sought to undermine the president beginning in 2017. Three of Ciaramella's NSC colleagues—Ukraine-born Lieutenant Colonel Alexander Vindman and staffers Sean Misko and Abby Grace—played major roles in the impeachment effort. Misko and Grace left the NSC to join Congressman Schiff's staff in 2019. Vindman reportedly relayed the July 25 Zelensky call to Ciaramella, who then worked with Schiff's staff on the complaint against Trump (an allegation that Schiff's office denied).[185]

A further shocking development was that Ciaramella (a Ukraine analyst who advised Biden) met with DNC contractor Chalupa during the 2016 campaign as she investigated then-candidate Trump. The proximity of these obscure relationships is unsettling and has compelled lawmakers and government watchdogs to demand further investigations.[186]

Had the Democrats not promoted the Trump-Russia conspiracy theory so vigorously, it is possible that House Republicans and President Trump's legal team would have left the 2016 election in the past. Ironically, during the efforts to defend Trump against baseless accusations of being "Putin's puppet," investigators uncovered a broader and more convincing case that the Clinton campaign (with help from Obama officials and the DNC) colluded with *multiple* foreign governments—primarily Ukraine, the U.K., and Australia—to influence the 2016 election campaign.[187]

Obama's doctrine had proven to be little more than an elusive aspiration. The Democrats had overplayed their hand. And it had boomeranged.

CHAPTER 10

URANIUM ONE, SPYGATE, AND IMPEACHMENT
What They Portend for the Future

Robert Mueller had been at the witness table several long hours when Congressman Will Hurd finally chimed in. Now in his midseventies, Mueller, the Justice Department special counsel who oversaw the Trump-Russia probe was not quite the same crisp-speaking Marine whom Americans had come to know as their FBI director during the aftermath of the September 11, 2001, terror attacks through his retirement in 2013.[1]

But his experience still loomed as an asset, especially when it came to the art of refusing to bite on politically loaded questions. He had just finished a five-minute, rapid-fire round of questions from Representative Joaquin Castro (D-TX) that clearly had frustrated the Democrat's effort to pin him down on questions about former Trump fixer Michael Cohen.[2]

Mueller's answers were classic dodges. "I can't adopt your characterization," he answered Castro at one moment. The next, he added: "I can't speak to that." A few seconds later he threw in "I'm not certain I could go that far," and finished with, "I defer to you on that....I can't get into details....I can't speak to that." Castro yielded back his time, unsatisfied by his effort to get Mueller to bite on his preferred story line.[3]

Hurd, a Republican from Texas, was up next. A former CIA officer, he shared a common intelligence community experience with the former FBI director. But the odds that he would fare better than Castro in extracting new information from Mueller seemed equally long.[4]

Over the first few hours of the nationally televised hearing, the prosecutor had tenaciously stuck to the text of his four-hundred-plus page report, which had concluded a few months earlier that the Trump campaign had *not* demonstrably colluded with Vladimir Putin to hijack the 2016 election.[5]

Hurd was a few seconds into his Q and A when he sprang a question that uncharacteristically got Mueller to stray outside the confines of his report.

Hurd knew that Mueller had not addressed in his final report anything about the widely reported rumor that Trump's campaign may have used a computer server inside the Alfa Bank of Russia to secretly communicate with Team Putin during the 2016 election.[6]

It was an odd omission given how much attention that allegation had been given in the court of public opinion over three years, contributing to the relentless media narrative of Trump-Russia collusion.

The tale appeared to start in the summer of 2016 with a computer blogger who went by the name "Tea Leaves" and an Indiana University computer sciences professor (and Hillary Clinton supporter) named L. Jean Camp. The data they published supposedly demonstrated mysterious computer pings between the Trump Tower in New York and Alfa Bank in Moscow.[7]

By early fall, FBI General Counsel James Baker had brought similar allegations into the bureau's counterintelligence team, courtesy of a data dump he got from a lawyer who represented the Democratic National Committee (DNC).[8] (No political motive there!)

About the same time, Christopher Steele, the former MI6 operative working as a Hillary Clinton opposition researcher for Fusion GPS, walked the Alfa Bank allegation into a senior State Department official, Kathleen Kavalec. She immediately forwarded it to the FBI (though she also cast doubt on its veracity).[9]

Glenn Simpson, the former *Wall Street Journal* reporter who ran Fusion GPS, did his best to sell the same rumor to senior Justice Department official Bruce Ohr during an early December contact. Ohr shipped it to the FBI as well.[10]

And numerous media outlets—Slate, CNN, *The New York Times*, and *The New Yorker* among them—peddled the allegation over two years.[11]

While the FBI had tried its best to shut down the Alfa Bank rumor for months—its agents had debunked it early on as nothing more than routine computer pings, most likely from marketing spam—Mueller's team had been silent on the issue. So, Hurd took a crack at getting an answer.[12]

"On October 31st, 2016, Slate published a report suggesting that a server at Trump Tower was secretly communicating with Russia's Alfa Bank, and then I quote, 'akin to what criminal syndicates do.' Do you know if that story is true?" the congressman asked.

"Do not. Do not," Mueller answered rather hurriedly.

Hurd was not satisfied, convinced that Mueller's team must have examined such a high-profile claim.

"You do not?" he replied in a surprised tone.

"…know if it's true," Mueller answered.

"So you did not investigate these allegations that are suggestive of potential Trump/Russia…" Hurd began to ask before Mueller cut him off.

"Because I believe it not true doesn't mean it would not be investigated," the silver-haired prosecutor snapped back. "It may well have been investigated. Although my belief at this point, it's not true."

Hurd had created one of the few newsworthy moments in the hearing, extracting from Mueller a tidbit of information that fell outside the findings specified in his report.[13]

Two words. *Not true.*

Those words summarized not only Mueller's assessment of the Alfa Bank allegation. They might as well have been the title for a bad Broadway musical celebrating the decade-long fiasco that began with the 2009 Russia reset and ended with Trump's impeachment in 2019.

Time and again, government, political, and media elites made declarations to the American public that turned out to be false.

The Obama-Clinton team declared that their "reset" (an appeasement strategy that gave away America's nuclear business to Moscow) would make Russia a close friend. Obama said that the strategy succeeded.[14]

Not true.

Hillary Clinton and Ambassador Michael McFaul declared Skolkovo the solution to creating a peaceful spy-free technology partnership with Russia.[15]

Not true.

Steele declared in his infamous dossier that his sources had told him that there was a "well-developed conspiracy" between Trump and Putin to hijack the 2016 election.[16]

Not true. And even his primary intelligence source disowned much of what had been attributed to him in the dossier.[17]

James Comey and Rod Rosenstein, two creatures of the permanent Justice Department (DOJ) bureaucracy, declared that the information submitted to secure a Foreign Intelligence Surveillance Act (FISA) warrant targeting the Trump campaign in October 2016 went through a rigorous process to ensure that it had been verified.[18]

Not only was this claim not true, the DOJ inspector general identified fifty-one claims that the FBI and DOJ made in the warrant applications that were demonstrably false, misleading, or unsubstantiated.[19] Comey would later admit his defense of the FISA warrant was misguided. "I was wrong," he told Fox News' Chris Wallace.

The FBI declared that there was good reason to believe that Trump advisor Carter Page was influenced by the Russians.

Not true. Page was actually a CIA asset providing intel on Russia matters, and an FBI lawyer had to alter a document to hide this fact from the FISA judges.[20]

Joe Biden declared that there was nothing untoward with his son Hunter taking a job with a Ukrainian natural gas company (Burisma Holdings) that had a reputation for corruption while the vice president oversaw U.S. policy in that country.[21]

Not true. A State Department official testified that he and his colleagues saw the appearance of a conflict of interest and even tried to block some federal business from going to Burisma on Hunter Biden's watch because of corruption concerns.[22]

House Democrats in their impeachment proceedings declared that there was evidence that Trump withheld foreign aid in a July 2019 call with Ukraine's president as pressure for an investigation of the Bidens.[23]

Not true. Ukrainian prosecutors had already opened the investigation months earlier, and there was no mention of foreign aid being tied to a Biden investigation in the call.[24]

Politics has always involved degrees of lying, exaggeration, and mistruths. As comics like to joke, "show me a good politician and I'll show you a good liar." But the ten-year period that began with the Obama presidency in 2009 was a far more consequential *Decade of Deceit.*

Some of that deceit came from a new mastery by foreign adversaries of the ancient spy craft of disinformation. As Russia showed with its intervention in the 2016 American election, the 2010s opened a new era of social media manipulation, information insecurity, and manufactured news that could be hijacked to foment social and political unrest. The United States is a prime target for all those foreign adversaries that resent the success of our economy and the freedoms afforded by our democracy.[25]

U.S. military and intelligence chiefs are right to raise the alarm about this trend, and American high-tech companies are justified in seeking new fortifications to this advanced form of warfare.

But the more consequential deceit of the last decade came from institutions—the FBI, the Justice Department, the State Department, and the mainstream media—where truth had once been mandatory for the bedrock trust the American public placed in them.[26]

For the first time, we saw in the 2010s a systematic effort by players in these institutions to knowingly and willfully promote falsehoods to achieve bureaucratic and political outcomes or, possibly, to foment division in America.[27]

This institutional dishonesty had proliferated faster than North Korean missile tests, Iranian enrichment sites, or mating bunnies. And the advent of social media and "Big Tech" companies added digital warfare to the arsenal. False stories could be propagated at the speed of light on the information highway, and dissenting voices were stifled through digital censorship unseen in any prior era.

At the same time, nonprofit institutions funded by a new generation of American billionaires like George Soros could wage information and disinformation campaigns to achieve ideological outcomes sought by their benefactors. And the American public would accept the incoming data because of the good-sounding name of the group, the reputation of its billionaire founder, or the hipness of its social media appeals.[28]

Just as alarming, a financially weakened and less-experienced journalism profession began to aid and abet disinformation in ways that would make Walter Cronkite turn in his grave.

Can you remember a time when an FBI lawyer was caught doctoring an official government document to deceive a court? It happened during the Trump-Russia collusion case.[29]

The boldness of this new generation of federal bureaucrats to impose their own will cannot be overstated. Not when you consider the crafty dishonesty employed by the FBI in sustaining the myth of the Steele dossier.

It turns out that the FBI interviewed Steele's primary source in early January 2017—just a few months into the Trump-Russia investigation. The source disowned much of the intelligence attributed to him in the Steele dossier and admitted that the claim of Trump being compromised by a Russian prostitute was a "rumor and speculation," not fact.[30]

Justice Department Inspector General Michael Horowitz's December 2019 report lays bare just how definitively the source knocked down the Steele dossier, which at the time provided much of the justification for the FBI's FISA warrant targeting the Trump campaign.

The January 2017 interview "raised doubts about the reliability of Steele's descriptions of information in his election reports. During the FBI's January interview, at which Case Agent 1, the supervisory intel analyst, and representatives of NSD were present, the [source] told the FBI that he/she had not seen Steele's reports until they became public that month, and…made statements indicating that Steele misstated or exaggerated the [source's] statements in multiple sections of the reporting."[31]

In earlier generations, such a reversal of an informer's evidence essential to a court proceeding would have led to an immediate alert to the judges, the end of the wiretapping and surveillance, and the likely shutdown of the entire investigation. But not inside this FBI, run by James Comey and Andrew McCabe.

Instead of shutting shown its FISA operation, the bureau renewed the surveillance warrant three more times to cover the next nine months. This made it look to the court as though Steele's source had actually substantiated the dossier, when in fact the source had disowned it.[32]

As Horowitz observes, "We found no evidence that the Crossfire Hurricane team ever considered whether any of the inconsistencies warranted reconsideration of the FBI's previous assessment of the reliability of the Steele election reports."[33]

This was not any old whopper. It had far-reaching consequences. The FBI was allowed to spy, without justification, on Page and the Trump apparatus for nearly a year, and the entire country was allowed to suffer through the Trump-Russia scandal for two more years even though it had been mostly contrived. Meanwhile, Trump's nascent presidency was handicapped out of the gate by a manufactured scandal driven by epic falsehoods.[34]

Such institutional dishonesty was exposed across the political landscape by the Trump-Russia collusion narrative, from the *New York Times* false story in February 2017 that U.S. intelligence had corroborated collusion between senior members of the Trump campaign and Russian intelligence, to Adam Schiff's repeated assertions after FBI briefings that evidence had been collected of a Russia-Trump conspiracy. Neither (among so many other false bombshells) was true.[35]

Not even Putin, in his wildest dreams, could imagine how some computer server hacks and $150,000 spent on social ads in 2016 would be amplified by a bogus scandal propagated and sustained for three years by America's own institutions.[36]

At the dawn of a new decade, there is one overarching lesson that America must digest from the progression of the failed Russia reset to the Uranium One scandal to allegations of Trump-Russia collusion, and, eventually, impeachment.

We are entering a new era of information warfare, and foreign adversaries are not the only perpetrators. American institutions, long trusted to give us the truth neutrally, are now active participants in misinformation, deceit, or shading of the facts. The consequences are far reaching, and the solutions are not easily devised.

There is reason to suspect that the political divide that has separated left and right in America in recent years may be worsened by this trend. What cost will this new era of institutionalized disinformation impose on American democracy, unity, and sovereignty?

This is but one lesson of the *fallout* from the last decade.

Vladimir Putin began the 2010s with his KGB skills and a nuclear arsenal but little else to leverage for regional or global advantage. He had a weak economy, technological gaps, and little influence or capital outside Eastern Europe.

Now, thanks to the giveaways of the failed Obama-Clinton reset, Putin begins the next decade with gas and uranium monopolies that prop up his economy and make both Europe and the United States more dependent on his resources. His strategy to weaponize Russia's energy sector as a geopolitical game changer has been all but accomplished.

Thanks to the bungled Skolkovo experiment, his country has access to far more Western technology with half the need for espionage, as evidenced by the Russian president's prized new hypersonic missiles that travel at twenty-seven times the speed of sound.[37]

His military has been rebuilt and is flexing its muscle in far more places than a decade ago, including Syria and Ukraine. And he faces an America torn from within by a series of political scandals—some funded by Democrats or furthered falsely by U.S. bureaucrats and the news media—that have tarnished both U.S. democracy and its most trusted institutions.

Irrefutably, Putin is more firmly in control of Russia's destiny at the dawn of the 2020s because of America's many failures to combat his asymmetric aggression in the preceding decade. Putin is not invincible, though, as the Trump sanctions and the limited economic options for Moscow still expose. But vigorous American leadership will be required to execute a far more coherent and strategic Russian policy than the one that Obama began with in 2009.

Finally, the American experience with Iran, Syria, North Korea, and the Russian reset have created a poignant body of evidence that a

U.S. foreign policy that relies heavily on appeasement and blind trust in adversaries and "frenemies" only weakens the United States.

This is an instinctual lesson that Trump embraced early as he crafted his *America First* agenda that appealed to a large plurality of Americans. And it is a bitter pill that some liberal security revisionists are now beginning to swallow when it comes to looking back at the Obama reset with Moscow.

In March 2018, the reliably liberal Brookings Institution sought to provoke such a debate on the left by republishing an article from a month earlier entitled "Don't Rehabilitate Obama on Russia." The article warned readers "not [to] slip into collective amnesia over the Obama administration's weak and underwhelming response to Russian aggression."[38]

Throughout his presidency, Obama consistently underestimated the challenge posed by Putin's regime. His foreign policy was firmly grounded in the premise that Russia was not a national security threat to the United States. In 2012, Obama disparaged candidate Mitt Romney for exaggerating the Russian threat—"The 1980s are now calling to ask for their foreign policy back because the Cold War's been over for 20 years," Obama quipped.[39]

This breezy attitude prevailed even as Russia annexed Crimea, invaded eastern Ukraine, intervened in Syria, and hacked the Clinton campaign and the DNC. Obama's response during these critical moments was cautious at best and feckless at worst.

Even the imposition of sanctions on Russia for its invasion of Ukraine was accompanied by so much propitiation and restraint elsewhere that it did not deter Russia from subsequent aggression, including the risky 2016 influence operation in the United States. Obama, confident that history was on America's side, for the duration of his time in office underestimated the damaging impact Russia could achieve through asymmetric means.

What is so remarkable about the sustained Democratic effort to destroy and/or end Trump's presidency is that inherent in its many manufactured attacks are clear projections of the party's own foreign policy missteps when it governed during the Obama era.

For instance, the impeachment articles accuse Trump of withholding U.S. foreign aid to force a decision in Ukraine. Yet Vice President Joe Biden did just that in 2016 when, by his own admission, he ordered Ukraine's president to fire the country's chief prosecutor or lose $1 billion in U.S. loan guarantees. And the Clinton-funded Steele dossier accused Trump of conspiring with Russia to the detriment of America, something that the Uranium One, nuclear fuel, and Skolkovo giveaways *actually* achieved.[40]

Meanwhile, even as Trump has been accused of being Putin's puppet, he has been far firmer and more aggressive in his dealings with Putin than Obama ever was. Trump's sanctions on Russia are far tougher than Obama's, and the forty-fifth president did something that his predecessor had not: he gave Ukraine lethal aid to resist future Russian aggression. Yet none of this is acknowledged by the media, since it would fatally compromise the Russian collusion narrative.[41]

If Trump survives and wins a second term, he should be armed with a mandate to create his own Trump Doctrine. Such a foreign policy could eradicate the failings of both George W. Bush's endless wars and Barack Obama's appeasement at all costs. As such, it could return America to an era of *peace through strength* that typified the presidencies of Ronald Reagan, George H.W. Bush, and Bill Clinton. During his first term, Trump has flashed some pillars of such a potential doctrine.

One tenet is that if America draws a red line, it must act when crossed. Obama waffled on such foreign policy delimiters, often turning them into dotted lines that emboldened bad actors. Trump has declared that his red lines will remain red, as he demonstrated when he executed Iran's top general with a drone strike in January 2020 after Tehran refused to stop perpetrating attacks on U.S. personnel in Iraq.[42]

A second pillar is that America will never stop seeking the return of its hostages but at the same time will not pay cash for such returns. Trump's commitment and success with hostage negotiations involving North Korea, Iran, and the Taliban have been born in part by a clear policy. The enemy knows what to expect going in, and coming out.

Trump's clarion call for other nations to step up and fund or man security operations across the globe is another potential tent pole for his foreign policy doctrine. Trump is not an isolationist as some have

215

claimed, but he also does not believe in endless wars or that America must always be the global cop. And just because America can do something militarily now, or has done something in the past, does not mean that it should necessarily be done in the future. Military action as a *potent but last resort* is Trump's comfort zone.[43]

Similarly, the forty-fifth American president understands that all deals are not the same. Some do not have to be consummated, officiated, or credited to American leadership. They can be fostered in secret and even executed by allies. As America's self-proclaimed "dealmaker in chief," Trump grasped early in his presidency that sometimes a too visible American role can be detrimental to negotiations.[44]

America can lead, even when it is quiet or invisible. And the regional dealmaking that Trump quietly fostered in the Middle East starting in 2019 may have far more long-term consequences for America than the Hail Mary throws for a global Middle East deal that always proved elusive.

Whether it is Trump or a new president, the most important challenge of 2021 is to create a coherent long-term strategy that defines the American interest, globally and regionally. For most of the twentieth century, nearly every president's foreign policy began with a definition of the American interest.

The values and objectives in the American interest definition guided not only the U.S. security and diplomacy bureaucracies, but also the expectations of both allies and foes abroad. But in recent years, particularly under Barack Obama, foreign policy decisions became more fungible and episodic, detached from the larger values, interests, or objectives defined by the American interest.[45]

Obama's lack of a consistent foreign policy doctrine led to the unnecessary destabilization of Libya, where Muammar Gaddafi had been providing U.S. counterterrorism assistance. It also led to a complete misread of the Arab Spring uprising and the missed opportunity to ride the 2009 Green Movement in Iran to a regime change that would oust the ruling mullahs. Finally, the excessive giveaways of the Russia reset cannot be traced to clear American interests. They benefited Putin far more than the domestic interest.[46]

The geopolitical continuum that began with Obama's bungled Russian reset and ended with Trump's impeachment cannot be repeated in the next decade. The challenges abroad and at home are too vexing, and the costs of failure too great.

The America of the 2020s must eschew the mistakes of the past decade and chart a new course that strengthens America abroad and unites it at home. The only question is whether America's current leaders can embrace and execute the mission.

ENDNOTES

Chapter 1

1   Jeremy Herb and Manu Raju, "House Judiciary Holds Marathon 2-Day Debate Ahead of Committee Impeachment Vote," CNN, last updated December 11, 2019, https://www.cnn.com/2019/12/11/politics/house-judiciary-committee-markup-impeachment/index.html; Nicholas Fandos, "Pelosi Is Prepared to Send Impeachment Articles to Senate, Just Not Yet," *New York Times*, January 9, 2020, https://www.nytimes.com/2020/01/09/us/politics/impeachment-articles.html.

2   Stephen Dinan and Valerie Richardson, "Rates Fall Flat As Most Americans Tune Out Impeachment Spectacle," *Washington Times*, November 20, 2019, https://www.washingtontimes.com/news/2019/nov/20/impeachment-hearings-draw-low-ratings-most-america/; Mark Sumner, "Judiciary Committee Returns for Final Vote After Jerry Nadler Gives Republicans a Midnight Surprise," Daily Kos, December 13, 2019, https://www.dailykos.com/stories/2019/12/13/1905366/-Judiciary-Committee-returns-for-final-vote-after-Jerry-Nadler-gives-Republicans-a-midnight-surprise.

3   Adam Edelman, "Trump Impeachment: The 15 Best Lines from the House Debate," NBC News, December 18, 2019, https://www.nbcnews.com/politics/trump-impeachment-inquiry/trump-impeachment-10-best-lines-house-debate-so-far-n1104341.

4   Ibid.

5   Ibid.

6   Simon Tisdall, "It's Time to Throw the Kitchen Sink at Trump, and the Cutlery Too," *Guardian*, November 2, 2019, https://www.theguardian.com/commentisfree/2019/nov/02/its-time-to-throw-the-kitchen-sink-at-trump-impeachment; Charles Lipson, "The Democrats' High-Risk Gamble on Impeachment," Real Clear Politics, November 5, 2019, https://www.realclearpolitics.com/articles/2019/11/05/the_democrats_high-risk_gamble_on_impeachment_141655.html.

7   John Bowden, "FBI Agents in Texts: 'We'll Stop' Trump from Becoming President," *Hill*, June 14, 2018, https://thehill.com/policy/national-security/392284-fbi-agent-in-texts-well-stop-trump-from-becoming-president.

8   H. Res. 755, 116th Cong. (2019), https://www.congress.gov/116/crec/2019/12/18/modified/CREC-2019-12-18-pt1-PgH12130.htm; Tisdall, "It's Time to Throw the Kitchen Sink at Trump, and the Cutlery Too"; Lipson, "The Democrats' High-Risk Gamble on Impeachment."

9   Adam Entous, Devlin Barrett, and Rosalind S. Helderman, "Clinton Campaign, DNC Paid for Research That Led to Russia Dossier," *Washington Post*,

October 24, 2017, https://www.washingtonpost.com/world/national-security/ clinton-campaign-dnc-paid-for-research-that-led-to-russia-dossier/2017/10/24/ 226fabf0-b8e4-11e7-a908-a3470754bbb9_story.html; Paul R. Gregory, "Why Was the Steele Dossier Not Dismissed As Fake?," Hoover Institution, February 3, 2020, https://www.hoover.org/research/why-was-steele-dossier-not-dismissed-fake.

10 Scott Shane, Nicholas Confessore, and Matthew Rosenberg, "How a Sensational, Unverified Dossier Became a Crisis for Donald Trump," *New York Times*, January 11, 2017, https://www.nytimes.com/2017/01/11/us/politics/donald-trump-russia-in-telligence.html; Byron York, "New Report Details Comey Plan to Ambush Trump with Moscow Sex Allegation," *Washington Examiner*, August 29, 2019, https:// www.washingtonexaminer.com/opinion/columnists/new-report-details-comey -plan-to-ambush-trump-with-moscow-sex-allegation.

11 Jack Crowe, "Barr: Trump Did Not Obstruct Investigation Despite Being 'Frustrated and Angry,'" *National Review*, April 18, 2019, https://www.nationalreview.com/ news/william-barr-donald-trump-did-not-obstruct-investigation/; Monica Show-alter, "Did Ciaramella Have Conflict of Interest on Burisma?," American Thinker, January 30, 2020, https://www.americanthinker.com/blog/2020/01/witness_time_ did_eric_ciaramella_have_a_conflict_of_interest_on_ukraines_burisma.html.

12 Peter Baker, "Impeachment Trial Updates: Senate Acquits Trump, Ending Historic Trial," *New York Times*, February 6, 2020, https://www.nytimes.com/2020/02/05/ us/politics/impeachment-vote.html; H. Res. 755, "Final Vote Results for Roll Call 696," House.gov, December 18, 2019, http://clerk.house.gov/evs/2019/roll696.xml.

13 Frank Newport, "Partisan Polarization and Ratings of the Economy," Gallup, February 28, 2020, https://news.gallup.com/opinion/polling-matters/287105/ partisan-polarization-ratings-economy.aspx; Charlie Savage, "We Just Got a Rare Look at National Security Surveillance. It Was Ugly.," *New York Times*, Decem-ber 11, 2019, https://www.nytimes.com/2019/12/11/us/politics/fisa-surveillance-fbi. html; Glenn Greenwald, "The Inspector General's Report on 2016 FBI Spying Reveals a Scandal of Historic Magnitude: Not Only for the FBI but Also the U.S. Media," *Intercept*, December 12, 2019, https://theintercept.com/2019/12/12/ the-inspector-generals-report-on-2016-fb-i-spying-reveals-a-scandal-of-historic-magnitude-not-only-for-the-fbi-but-also-the-u-s-media/?comments=1.

14 David Von Drehle, "Vladimir Putin's Virus: How the Russian President Has Infected Our National Trust," *Washington Post*, March 2, 2020, https://www.washingtonpost. com/opinions/2020/03/02/did-vladimir-putin-turn-america-itself/?arc404=true.

15 Julia Ioffe, "What Putin Really Wants," *Atlantic*, January/February 2008, https:// www.theatlantic.com/magazine/archive/2018/01/putins-game/546548/; Darren Samuelsohn, "Facebook: Russian-linked Accounts Bought $150,000 in Ads During 2016 Race," *Politico*, September 6, 2017, https://www.politico.com/story/2017/09/06/ facebook-ads-russia-linked-accounts-242401; Jo Becker and Mike McIntire, "Cash Flowed to Clinton Foundation Amid Russian Uranium Deal," *New York Times*, April 23, 2015, https://www.nytimes.com/2015/04/24/us/cash-flowed-to-clinton-foundation-as-russians-pressed-for-control-of-uranium-company.html; James Surowiecki, "Putin's Power Play," *New Yorker*, March 17, 2014, https://www.newyo-rker.com/magazine/2014/03/24/putins-power-play.

16 Ioffe, "What Putin Really Wants"; Samuelsohn, "Facebook: Russian-linked Accounts Bought $150,000 in Ads During 2016 Race."

17 Ibid.

18 Memorandum from Cheryl Moss Herman to Vadim Mikerin, President, Tenam Corporation, "Policy/Legislative Issues Affecting the Business Climate in the U.S. for TENAM/Tenex," October 7, 2010; Dr. Tom Borelli, "Utility Industry Aids Putin's Stealth War on US Uranium Mining," Conservative Review, March 28, 2019, https://www.conservativereview.com/news/utility-industry-aids-putins-stealth-war-u-s-uranium-mining/; Surowiecki, "Putin's Power Play"; Madison Freeman, "How Russia, China Use Nuclear Reactors to Win Global Influence," Defense One, July 13, 2018, https://www.defenseone.com/ideas/2018/07/china-and-russia-look-dominate-global-nuclear-power/149642/.

19 Ibid.

20 Becker and McIntire, "Cash Flowed to Clinton Foundation Amid Russian Uranium Deal"; Robert Sam Anson, "Obama's Power Grid," Vanity Fair, October 13, 2011, https://www.vanityfair.com/news/2011/10/obama-nuclear-201110.

21 Mary Elise Sarotte, "Putin's View of Power Was Formed Watching East Germany Collapse," Guardian, October 1, 2014, https://www.theguardian.com/commentisfree/2014/oct/01/putin-power-east-germany-russia-kgb-dresden; Susan B. Glasser, "Putin the Great: Russia's Imperial Impostor," Foreign Affairs, September/October 2019, https://www.foreignaffairs.com/articles/russian-federation/2019-08-12/putin-great.

22 Glasser, "Putin the Great: Russia's Imperial Impostor"; Kim R. Holmes, "Putin's Asymmetrical War on the West," Foreign Policy, May 5, 2014, https://foreignpolicy.com/2014/05/05/putins-asymmetrical-war-on-the-west/; A Minority Staff Report Prepared for the Use of the Committee on Foreign Relations, United States Senate, "Putin's Asymmetric Assault on Democracy in Russia and Europe: Implications for U.S. National Security," 115th Cong. (2018), https://www.foreign.senate.gov/imo/media/doc/FinalRR.pdf; Andrew Meier, Black Earth: A Journey Through Russia After the Fall (New York: W. W. Norton & Company, 2005), 244.

23 Sarotte, "Putin's View of Power Was Formed Watching East Germany Collapse"; Evan Osnos, David Remnick, and Joshua Yaffa, "Trump, Putin, and the New Cold War," New Yorker, March 6, 2017, https://www.newyorker.com/magazine/2017/03/06/trump-putin-and-the-new-cold-war.

24 Michael Barbaro and Alison Smale, "Jeb Bush, on European Tour, Opens by Rebuking Putin," New York Times, June 9, 2015, https://www.nytimes.com/politics/first-draft/2015/06/09/jeb-bush-tells-germans-hed-confront-ruthless-putin/; Carlos Alberto Montaner, "Putin Wants to Follow Peter the Great," Real Clear Politics, September 30, 2008, https://www.realclearpolitics.com/articles/2008/09/putin_wants_to_follow_peter_th.html; Anna Ohanyan, "Why Russia Starts So Many Conflicts on Its Own Borders," Washington Post, September 12, 2018, https://www.washingtonpost.com/news/monkey-cage/wp/2018/09/12/russia-has-a-lot-of-conflicts-along-its-borders-thats-by-design/.

25 Robert W. Ortung and Indra Overland, "A Limited Toolbox: Explaining the Constraints on Russia's Foreign Energy Policy," Journal of Eurasian Studies 2, no. 1 (January

2011), https://www.sciencedirect.com/science/article/pii/S1879366510000394; Garrett M. Graff, "A Guide to Russia's High Tech Tool Box for Subverting US Democracy," *Wired*, August 13, 2017, https://www.wired.com/story/a-guide-to-russias-high-tech-tool-box-for-subverting-us-democracy/; Michael Crowley, "Putin's Revenge," *Politico*, December 16, 2016, https://www.politico.com/magazine/story/2016/12/russia-putin-hack-dnc-clinton-election-2016-cold-war-214532.

26   Steve Clemons, "US-Russian Relations After Crimea," Aspen Ideas Festival, 2014, https://www.aspenideas.org/sessions/us-russian-relations-after-crimea; Crowley, "Putin's Revenge."

27   Filip Novokmet, Thomas Piketty, and Gabriel Zucman, "From Soviets to Oligarchs: Inequality and Property in Russia, 1905-2016," VoxEU.org, November 9, 2017, https://voxeu.org/article/inequality-and-property-russia-1905-2016; Alan Cullison, "A Trio of Wealthy Russians Made an Enemy of Putin. Now They're All Dead.," *Wall Street Journal*, October 10, 2018, https://www.wsj.com/articles/a-trio-of-wealthy-russians-made-an-enemy-of-putin-now-theyre-all-dead-1539181416; Ariel Cohen, "A New Paradigm for U.S.-Russia Relations: Facing the Post-Cold War Reality," Heritage Foundation, March 6, 1997, https://www.heritage.org/europe/report/new-paradigm-us-russia-relations-facing-the-post-cold-warreality.

28   "U.S. Support for Perestroika," Roy Rosenzweig Center for History & New Media, accessed September 1, 2019, http://chnm.gmu.edu/1989/items/show/61; "Remarks and a Question-and-Answer Session with the Students and Faculty at Moscow State University," Roy Rosenzweig Center for History & New Media, Ronald Reagan interview, May 31, 1988, http://chnm.gmu.edu/1989/archive/files/reagan-interview-5-31-88_54d35167fe.pdf; Thomas L. Friedman, "How Washington Shifted to Embracing Gorbachev," *New York Times*, October 22, 1989, https://www.nytimes.com/1989/10/22/world/how-washington-shifted-to-embracing-gorbachev.html; Tom Parfitt, "Billionaires Boom As Putin Puts Oligarchs at No 2 in Global Rich List," *Guardian*, February 19, 2008, https://www.theguardian.com/world/2008/feb/19/russia; A Minority Staff Report Prepared for the Use of the Committee on Foreign Relations, United States Senate, "Putin's Asymmetric Assault on Democracy in Russia and Europe: Implications for U.S. National Security."

29   Daisy Sindelar, "Russia: Moscow Seeks to Reignite Nuclear Power Industry," Radio Free Europe/Radio Liberty, February 14, 2006, https://www.rferl.org/a/1065754.html; Becker and McIntire, "Cash Flowed to Clinton Foundation Amid Russian Uranium Deal."

30   Steven Lee Myers, "White House Unveils $1 Billion Georgia Aid Plan," *New York Times*, September 3, 2008, https://www.nytimes.com/2008/09/04/world/europe/04cheney.html.

31   "2008 Georgia Russia Conflict Fast Facts," CNN, last updated April 1, 2019, https://www.cnn.com/2014/03/13/world/europe/2008-georgia-russia-conflict/index.html; Mary Beth Nikitin, "U.S.-Russian Civilian Nuclear Cooperation Agreement: Issues for Congress," Congressional Research Service, January 11, 2011, https://fas.org/sgp/crs/nuke/RL34655.pdf.

32   Condoleezza Rice, "Russia Invaded Georgia 10 Years Ago. Don't Say America Didn't Respond," *Washington Post*, August 8, 2018, https://www.washingtonpost.

com/opinions/russia-invaded-georgia-10-years-ago-dont-say-america-didnt-re-spond/2018/08/08/ba4279d4-9b3e-11e8-8d5e-c6c594024954_story.html.

33 Ibid.

34 Jamie M. Putnam, "One Man's Reaction to NATO Expansion," *International Relations Honors Papers*, Ursinus College, April 25, 2016, https://digitalcommons. ursinus.edu/cgi/viewcontent.cgi?article=1000&context=int_hon; Steven Rosefielde and Daniel Quinn Mills, *The Trump Phenomenon and the Future of U.S. Policy* (New Jersey: World Scientific, 2016), 92.

35 Kathrin Hille, "Sanctions Extend Influence of Hardmen in Putin's Kremlin," *Financial Times*, September 18, 2014, https://www.ft.com/content/8fcc4068-3f49-11e4-a5f5-00144feabdc0; Ortung and Overland, "A Limited Toolbox: Explaining the Constraints on Russia's Foreign Energy Policy."

36 Julian Hans, "The Evidence is Strong," interview, Panama Papers, Suddeutsche Zeitung, April 15, 2016, https://panamapapers.sueddeutsche.de/ articles/57161f07a1bb8d3c3495bc36/; Jake Bernstein et al., "All Putin's Men: Secret Records Reveal Money Network Tied to Russian Leader," International Consortium of Investigative Journalists, April 3, 2016, https://www.icij.org/investigations/ panama-papers/20160403-putin-russia-offshore-network/; "Vladimir   Putin," OCCRP, accessed January 15, 2020, https://www.occrp.org/en/panamapapers/ persons/putin/.

37 Christian Lowe and Pavel Polityuk, "Russia Cuts Off Gas to Ukraine," Reuters, January 1, 2009, https://www.reuters.com/article/us-russia-ukraine-gas/russia-cuts-off-gas-to-ukraine-idUSTRE4BN32B20090101; David M. Herszenhorn and Andrew E. Kramer, "Russia Offers Cash Infusion for Ukraine," *New York Times*, December 17, 2013, https://www.nytimes.com/2013/12/18/world/europe/russia-of-fers-ukraine-financial-lifeline.html; Neil MacFarquhar, "Gazprom Cuts Russia's Natural Gas Supply to Ukraine," *New York Times*, June 16, 2014, https://www. nytimes.com/2014/06/17/world/europe/russia-gazprom-increases-pressure-on-ukraine-in-gas-dispute.html; Harvey Fierstein, "Russia's Anti-Gay Crackdown," *New York* Times, July 21, 2013, https://www.nytimes.com/2013/07/22/opinion/ russias-anti-gay-crackdown.html; Karoun Demirjian, "Meanwhile in Russia, Putin Passes Law Against Protests," *Washington Post*, July 22, 2014, https://www. washingtonpost.com/news/worldviews/wp/2014/07/22/meanwhile-in-russia-pu-tin-passes-law-against-protests/; Shaun Walker, "The Murder That Killed Free Media in Russia," *Guardian*, October 5, 2016, https://www.theguardian.com/ world/2016/oct/05/ten-years-putin-press-kremlin-grip-russia-media-tightens; Dave Davies, "In New Book, Journalist Alleges Russian Links to Mysterious Deaths Abroad," NPR, November 19, 2019, https://www.npr.org/2019/11/19/780759713/ in-new-book-journalists-alleges-russian-links-to-mysterious-deaths-abroad.

38 "Selected Maps and Schemes of Gas Pipelines of Russia and the FSU," Archipelago Gazprom, last updated November 2, 2019, https://eegas.com/maps.htm.

39 U.S. Senate, Hearing before the Committee on Armed Services, "Russian Strategy and Military Operations," 114th Cong. (2015), https://www.govinfo.gov/content/ pkg/CHRG-114shrg20922/html/CHRG-114shrg20922.htm; Borelli, "Utility Industry Aids Putin's Stealth War on US Uranium Mining."

40 U.S. Energy Information Administration, "Megatons to Megawatts Program Will Conclude at the End of 2013," September 24, 2013, https://www.eia.gov/todayinenergy/detail.php?id=13091.

41 Aleksandr Nikitin, "Rosatom State Corporation," Bellona, on Internet Archive, November 27, 2007, https://web.archive.org/web/20080705015311/https:/bellona.org/position_papers/rosatom_corporation (the screenshot of the site was captured on July 5, 2008); Sindelar, "Russia: Moscow Seeks to Reignite Nuclear Power Industry"; James A. Lyons, "The Criminalization of America's Government Agencies," *Washington Times*, November 14, 2017, https://www.washingtontimes.com/news/2017/nov/14/obama-officials-did-nothing-to-halt-uranium-deal-w/.

42 Becker and McIntire, "Cash Flowed to Clinton Foundation Amid Russian Uranium Deal"; Lyons, "The Criminalization of America's Government Agencies"; Paul Roderick Gregory, "Why Was Obama's Justice Department Silent on Criminal Activity by Russia's Nuclear Agency?," *Forbes*, October 25, 2017, https://www.forbes.com/sites/paulroderickgregory/2017/10/25/why-was-obamas-justice-department-silent-on-criminal-activity-by-russias-nuclear-agency/#427a7acebe17.

43 John Solomon and Alison Spann, "FBI Uncovered Russian Bribery Plot Before Obama Administration Approved Controversial Nuclear Deal with Moscow," *Hill*, October 17, 2017, https://thehill.com/policy/national-security/355749-fbi-uncovered-russian-bribery-plot-before-obama-administration; A Minority Staff Report Prepared for the Use of the Committee on Foreign Relations, United States Senate, "Putin's Asymmetric Assault on Democracy in Russia and Europe: Implications for U.S. National Security"; Borelli, "Utility Industry Aids Putin's Stealth War on US Uranium Mining."

44 John Solomon, "The Case for Russia Collusion… Against the Democrats," *Hill*, February 10, 2019, https://thehill.com/opinion/white-house/429292-the-case-for-russia-collusion-against-the-democrats.

45 Benjamin Haddad and Alina Polyakova, "Don't Rehabilitate Obama on Russia," Brookings Institution, March 5, 2018, https://www.brookings.edu/blog/order-from-chaos/2018/03/05/dont-rehabilitate-obama-on-russia/; Sara M. Birkenthal, "Grand Strategy in U.S. Foreign Policy: The Carter, Bush, and Obama Doctrines" (CMC Senior Theses, Claremont Colleges, 2013), Paper 598, https://scholarship.claremont.edu/cgi/viewcontent.cgi?article=1671&context=cmc_theses; Jeffrey Mankoff, "The Tricky U.S.-Russia 'Reset' Button," Council on Foreign Relations, February 17, 2009, https://www.cfr.org/expert-brief/tricky-us-russia-reset-button; Conor Lynch, "Why Neocons Really Hate Trump: He's Hastening the Deadline of American Empire," *Salon*, February 25, 2018, https://www.salon.com/2018/02/25/why-neocons-really-hate-trump-hes-hastening-the-decline-of-american-empire/.

46 Ibid.

47 James Blitz, "Biden Proposes to 'Press Reset Button' with Moscow," *Financial Times*, February 7, 2009, https://www.ft.com/content/21cb9768-f525-11dd-9e2e-0000779fd2ac; Peter Brookes, "Russian 'Reset' a Resounding Failure," Heritage Foundation, April 5, 2016, https://www.heritage.org/arms-control/commentary/russian-reset-resounding-failure; "Clinton, Lavrov Push Wrong Reset Button on Ties," Reuters, March 6, 2009, https://www.reuters.com/article/idUSN06402140;

Michael McFaul, "The Smear That Killed the 'Reset,'" *Washington Post*, May 11, 2018, https://www.washingtonpost.com/news/posteverything/wp/2018/05/11/feature/ putin-needed-an-american-enemy-he-picked-me/; Jim Geraghty, "The Infamous 'Reset' Button: Stolen from a Hotel Pool or Jacuzzi," *National Review*, March 3, 2014, https://www.nationalreview.com/the-campaign-spot/infamous-reset-button -stolen-hotel-pool-or-jacuzzi-jim-geraghty/.

48 Pavel K. Baev, "The Russia-US "Reset" and Medvedev's Non-Leadership," Jamestown Foundation, July 6, 2010, https://jamestown.org/program/the-russia- us-reset-and-medvedevs-non-leadership/; John R. Schindler, "Hillary's Secret Kremlin Connection Is Quickly Unraveling," *Observer*, August 25, 2016, https:// observer.com/2016/08/hillarys-secret-kremlin-connection-is-quickly-unraveling/; Solomon and Spann, "FBI Uncovered Russian Bribery Plot Before Obama Admin- istration Approved Controversial Nuclear Deal with Moscow."

49 Ibid.; Hearing Before the Committee on Foreign Affairs, U.S. House of Repre- sentatives, "Time to Pause the Reset? Defending U.S. Interests in the Face of Russian Aggression," 112th Cong. (2011), https://www.govinfo.gov/content/pkg/ CHRG-112hhrg67304/html/CHRG-112hhrg67304.htm; "Russian Foreign Direct Investment – Net Flows," Trading Economics, n.d., https://tradingeconomics.com/ russia/foreign-direct-investment.

50 Joel Schectman, "Exclusive: Secret Witness in Senate Clinton Probe Is Ex-Lobbyist for Russian Firm," Reuters, November 16, 2017, https://www.reuters.com/article/ us-usa-clinton-informant-exclusive/exclusive-secret-witness-in-senate-clinton- probe-is-ex-lobbyist-for-russian-firm-idUSKBN1DG1SB; Solomon and Spann, "FBI Uncovered Russian Bribery Plot Before Obama Administration Approved Controversial Nuclear Deal with Moscow"; John Solomon and Alison Spann, "FBI Watched, Then Acted As Russian Spy Moved Closer to Hillary Clinton," *Hill*, October 22, 2017, https://thehill.com/policy/national-security/356630-fbi- watched-then-acted-as-russian-spy-moved-closer-to-hillary.

51 Borelli, "Utility Industry Aids Putin's Stealth War on US Uranium Mining"; Luke O'Brien, "Putin's Washington," *Politico*, January/February 2015, https://www.polit- ico.com/magazine/story/2015/01/putins-washington-113894.

52 Becker and McIntire, "Cash Flowed to Clinton Foundation Amid Russian Uranium Deal"; Schindler, "Hillary's Secret Kremlin Connection Is Quickly Unraveling"; Solomon and Spann, "FBI Watched, Then Acted As Russian Spy Moved Closer to Hillary Clinton"; Kevin G. Hall, "WikiLeaks Emails Show How Clinton's Cam- paign Chief Once Opened Doors for Energy Firm," McClatchyDC, October 19, 2016, https://www.mcclatchydc.com/news/politics-government/election/ article109203352.html; Government Accountability Institute, "From Russia With Money: Hillary Clinton, the Russian Reset, and Cronyism," August 2016, https:// www.g-a-i.org/wp-content/uploads/2016/08/Report-Skolkvovo-08012016.pdf.

53 Ibid.

54 Ben Kamisar, "Clinton Slams 'Clinton Cash' on New Rapid-Response Site," *Hill*, May 5, 2015, https://thehill.com/blogs/ballot-box/presidential-races/241052-clin- ton-slams-clinton-cash-on-new-rapid-response-site; Clinton campaign insider, background interview with author.

55 Ibid.

56 E-mail message from MirandaL@dnc.org to PaustenbachM@dnc.org, "FW: You Saw This, Right?," Wikileaks, May 4, 2016, https://wikileaks.org/dnc-emails/ emailid/3962; Clinton campaign insider, background interview with author; Michelle Ye Hee Lee, "The Facts Behind Trump's Repeated Claim about Hillary Clinton's Role in the Russian Uranium Deal," *Washington Post*, October 26, 2016, https://www.washingtonpost.com/news/fact-checker/wp/2016/10/26/ the-facts-behind-trumps-repeated-claim-about-hillary-clintons-role-in-the-rus-sian-uranium-deal/.

57 E-mail message from MirandaL@dnc.org to PaustenbachM@dnc.org, "FW: You Saw This, Right?"

58 Glenn Simpson and Peter Fritsch, *Crime in Progress: Inside the Steele Dossier and the Fusion GPS Investigation of Donald Trump* (New York: Random House, 2019).

59 Ibid; Simpson and Fritsch, *Crime in Progress*; John Solomon, "Russian Oligarch, Justice Department and a Clear Case of Collusion," *Hill*, August 28, 2018, https:// thehill.com/hilltv/rising/404061-russian-oligarch-justice-department-and-a-clear-case-of-collusion; Olivia Beavers, "DOJ Releases Notes from Official Bruce Ohr's Russia Probe Interviews," *Hill*, August 9, 2019, https://thehill.com/policy/nation-al-security/456835-justice-department-releases-bruce-ohr-interviews-from-rus-sia-probe; Donald J. Trump (@realDonaldTrump), "Terrible! Just found out that Obama had my "wires tapped" in Trump Tower just before the victory. Nothing found. This is McCarthyism!," Twitter, March 4, 2017, 6:35 AM, https://twitter.com/ realDonaldTrump/status/837989835818287106; Philip Rucker, Ellen Nakashima, and Robert Costa, "Trump, Citing No Evidence, Accuses Obama of 'Nixon/Water-gate' Plot to Wiretap Trump Tower," *Washington Post*, March 4, 2017, https:// www.washingtonpost.com/news/post-politics/wp/2017/03/04/trump-accuses -obama-of-nixonwatergate-plot-to-wire-tap-trump-tower/.

60 Simpson and Fritsch, *Crime in Progress*.

61 Kimberley A. Strassel, "Mueller's Report Speaks Volumes," *Wall Street Journal*, April 18, 2019, https://www.wsj.com/articles/muellers-report-speaks-volumes-11555629994; Nicholas Kristof, "Dangerous Times for Trump and the Nation," *New York Times*, May 17, 2017, https://www.nytimes.com/2017/05/17/opinion/trump-rus-sia-mueller-special-counsel.html; Kimberley A. Strassel, "Schiffting to Phase 2 of Collusion," *Wall Street Journal*, February 21, 2019, https://www.wsj.com/arti-cles/schiffting-to-phase-2-of-collusion-11550794762; Ryan Teague Beckwith, "Here Are All of the Indictments, Guilty Pleas and Convictions from Robert Mueller's Investigation," *Time*, November 15, 2019, https://time.com/5556331/ mueller-investigation-indictments-guilty-pleas/.

62 Sharyl Attkisson, "The Curious Timeline for Taking Down Trump," *Hill*, November 8, 2019, https://thehill.com/opinion/white-house/469504-the-curious-timeline-for-taking-down-trump; Harriet Agerholm, "Donald Trump Told to 'Get Ready for Impeachment' by Senior Democrat Maxine Waters," *Independent*, March 22, 2017, https://www.independent.co.uk/news/world/americas/us-politics/maxine-waters -donald-trump-democrat-congresswoman-california-get-ready-impeach-ment-a7642681.html; Cameron Cawthorne, "Waters: Trump's Disclosure of Classified

Info to Russia Moves Us Closer to 'Impeachment,'" *Washington Free Beacon*, May 16, 2017, https://freebeacon.com/national-security/waters-trumps-disclosure-classified-info-russia-moves-closer-impeachment/; Kevin Daley, "Nadler: New Evidence from Michael Cohen Suggests Impeachable Offense Could Indict President Trump," NewsLI.com, December 9, 2018, https://www.newsli.com/2018/12/09/nadler-new-evidence-from-michael-cohen-suggests-impeachable-offense-could-indict-president-trump/; Alexandra Ma, "Incoming Top Democrats Talk of Impeachment and Jail Time for Trump with Increasing Confidence," Business Insider, December 10, 2018, https://www.businessinsider.com/schiff-nadler-predict-trump-impeachment-and-jail-over-illegal-payments-2018-12; "Three Top Democrats Warn Trump Not to Interfere with Michael Cohen Testimony," CBS News, January 14, 2019, https://www.cbsnews.com/news/three-top-democrats-warn-trump-not-to-interfere-with-michael-cohen-testimony/.

63 Ian Bateson, "What Rudy Giuliani's Version Reality Looks Like from Ukraine," *Washington Post*, December 27, 2019, https://www.washingtonpost.com/opinions/2019/12/27/what-rudy-giulianis-version-reality-looks-like-ukraine/.

64 Andrew E. Kramer, Mike McIntire, and Barry Meier, "Secret Ledger in Ukraine Lists Cash for Donald Trump's Campaign Chief," *New York Times*, August 14, 2016, https://www.nytimes.com/2016/08/15/us/politics/what-is-the-black-ledger.html; Nolan D. McCaskill, Alex Isenstadt, and Shane Goldmacher, "Paul Manafort Resigns from Trump Campaign," *Politico*, August 19, 2016, https://www.politico.com/story/2016/08/paul-manafort-resigns-from-trump-campaign-227197.

65 Jason Leopold et al., "The Mueller Report's Secret Memos," Buzzfeed News, November 2, 2019, https://www.buzzfeednews.com/article/jasonleopold/mueller-report-secret-memos-1; John Solomon, "Key Witness Told Team Mueller That Russia Collusion Evidence Found in Ukraine Was Fabricated," Just the News, last updated February 23, 2020, https://justthenews.com/accountability/political-ethics/key-witness-told-team-mueller-russia-collusion-evidence-found.

66 Rosalind S. Helderman, "How the Ukraine Pressure Campaign Began As an Effort to Undercut the Mueller Investigation," *Washington Post*, December 3, 2019, https://www.washingtonpost.com/politics/how-the-ukraine-pressure-campaign-began-as-an-effort-to-undercut-the-mueller-investigation/2019/12/02/208204c8-12c9-11ea-9cd7-a1becbc82f5e_story.html; Grace Panetta, "Rudy Giuliani Claims He's 'the Real Whistleblower' and That No One Will Know the Real Story on Trump and Ukraine 'If I Get Killed,'" Business Insider, September 27, 2019, https://www.businessinsider.com/rudy-giuliani-says-real-whistleblower-trump-ukraine-2019-9.

67 Becker and McIntire, "Cash Flowed to Clinton Foundation Amid Russian Uranium Deal"; Solomon and Spann, "FBI Uncovered Russian Bribery Plot Before Obama Administration Approved Controversial Nuclear Deal with Moscow"; John Solomon, "Five New Revelations in the Russian Uranium Case," *Hill*, November 20, 2017, https://thehill.com/homenews/administration/361290-five-new-revelations-in-the-russian-uranium-case.

68 Haddad and Polyakova, "Don't Rehabilitate Obama on Russia"; Tim Hains, "Montage: Mainstream Media Hype about Russia Collusion," Real Clear Politics, March 25, 2019, https://www.realclearpolitics.com/video/2019/03/25/montage_mainstream_media_hype_about_russia_collusion.html.

Chapter 2

1 Vladimir Putin, translated by Catherine A. Fitzpatrick, *First Person: An Astonishingly Frank Self-Portrait by Russia's President* (New York: PublicAffairs, 2000).

2 Dmitry Sudakov, "Russian Nuclear Energy Conquers the World," *Pravda*, January 22, 2013, https://www.pravdareport.com/russia/123551-russia_nuclear_energy/.

3 Ibid.; "Russia's Rosatom Is Aiming to Become the World's Largest Supplier of Uranium in the Coming Years," InvestorIntel, January 23, 2013, https://investorintel. com/sectors/uranium-energy/uranium-energy-intel/russias-rosatom-is-aiming-to-become-the-worlds-largest-supplier-of-uranium-in-the-coming-years/; Marin Katusa, *The Colder War: How the Global Energy Trade Slipped from America's Grasp* (Vermont: John Wiley & Sons, 2015), 90; Jo Becker and Mike McIntire, "Cash Flowed to Clinton Foundation Amid Russian Uranium Deal," *New York Times*, April 23, 2015, https://www.nytimes.com/2015/04/24/us/cash-flowed-to-clinton-foundation-as-russians-pressed-for-control-of-uranium-company.html.

4 John Solomon and Alison Spann, "FBI Uncovered Russian Bribery Plot Before Obama Administration Approved Controversial Nuclear Deal with Moscow," *Hill*, October 17, 2017, https://thehill.com/policy/national-security/355749-fbi-un-covered-russian-bribery-plot-before-obama-administration; John Solomon and Alison Spann, "Clintons Understated Support from Firm Hired by Russian Nuclear Company," *Hill*, November 28, 2017, https://thehill.com/homenews/news/362234-clintons-understated-support-from-firm-hired-by-russian-nuclear-company.

5 Hugo Driscoll, "Putin and the Tiger – Russian President's Four Best Photo-Ops," *Guardian*, August 1, 2014, https://www.theguardian.com/world/2014/aug/01/putin-and-the-tiger-russian-presidents-four-best-photo-ops.

6 Katusa, *The Colder War*, 133.

7 Becker and McIntire, "Cash Flowed to Clinton Foundation Amid Russian Uranium Deal"; U.S. International Trade Commission, "Uranium from Russia," Publication 3872, August 2006, https://www.usitc.gov/publications/701_731/pub3872.pdf.

8 Ned Mamula, "Russia's Uranium Gambit: The Real Uranium One Scandal," Capital Research Center, January 15, 2019, https://capitalresearch.org/article/russias-urani-um-gambit-part-4/; Dr. Tom Borelli, "Utility Industry Aids Putin's Stealth War on US Uranium Mining," Conservative Review, March 28, 2019, https://www.conservativer-eview.com/news/utility-industry-aids-putins-stealth-war-u-s-uranium-mining/.

9 Joe Weisenthal, "Interest Brews in the Other Yellow Metal: Uranium," Business Insider, December 1, 2009, https://www.businessinsider.com/interest-brews-in-the-other-yellow-metal-uranium-2009-12; Tom DiChristopher, "Nuclear Wasteland: The Explosive Boom and Long, Painful Bust of American Uranium Mining," CNBC, August 4, 2018, https://www.cnbc.com/2018/08/04/the-miners-that-fu-el-americas-nuclear-power-and-atomic-arsenal-are-di.html; 50th Anniversary Booklet, Tenex, accessed September 15, 2019, https://www.tenex.ru/download/201/booklet_for_tenex_50_sup_th__sup__anniversary.pdf.

10 Katusa, *The Colder War*, 128-129.

11 Sudakov, "Russian Nuclear Energy Conquers the World"; Becker and McIntire, "Cash Flowed to Clinton Foundation Amid Russian Uranium Deal."

12 Sudakov, "Russian Nuclear Energy Conquers the World"; Katusa, *The Colder War*, 90.

13 Geert De Clercq, Svetlana Burmistrova, and Jack Stubbs, "Rosatom's Global Nuclear Ambition Cramped by Kremlin Politics," Reuters, June 26, 2016, https://uk.reuters.com/article/us-russia-nuclear-rosatom-idUKKCN0ZC0QZ.

14 Ibid.; Vera Ponomareva, translated by Charles Digges, "As Russia's Nuclear Power Utility Goes Private, Who Will Actually Buy Nuclear Power Stations?," Bellona, August 29, 2008, https://bellona.org/news/nuclear-issues/2008-08-as-russias-nuclear-power-utility-goes-private-who-will-actually-buy-nuclear-power-stations; Aleksandr Nikitin, "Rosatom State Corporation," Bellona, November 27, 2007, on Internet Archive, https://web.archive.org/web/20080705015311/https:/bellona.org/position_papers/rosatom_corporation (the screenshot of the site was captured on July 5, 2008).

15 Sudakov, "Russian Nuclear Energy Conquers the World"; Becker and McIntire, "Cash Flowed to Clinton Foundation Amid Russian Uranium Deal"; Digges, "As Russia's Nuclear Power Utility Goes Private, Who Will Actually Buy Nuclear Power Stations?"; Nikitin, "Rosatom State Corporation"; Peter Schweizer, *Clinton Cash: The Untold Story of How Foreign Governments and Businesses Made Bill and Hillary Rich* (New York: HarperCollins, 2015), 48.

16 David Trifunov, "Iran Nuclear Power Plant at Bushehr Reaches Full Capacity," PRI, September 1, 2012, https://www.pri.org/stories/2012-09-01/iran-nuclear-power-plant-bushehr-reaches-full-capacity; Greg Bruno, "Iran's Nuclear Program," Council on Foreign Relations, March 10, 2010, https://www.cfr.org/backgrounder/irans-nuclear-program; Julian Borger, "Binyamin Netanyahu Demands 'Red Line' to Stop Iran Nuclear Programme," *Guardian*, September 28, 2012, https://www.theguardian.com/world/2012/sep/27/binyamin-netanyahu-iran-nuclear-programme.

17 Sun Shangwu, "Hu, Putin Promote Partnership," *China Daily*, last updated March 27, 2007, https://www.chinadaily.com.cn/china/2007-03/27/content_836856.htm; Simon Romero, "Putin Visits Venezuela to Discuss Oil and Arms," *New York Times*, April 2, 2010, https://www.nytimes.com/2010/04/03/world/americas/03venez.html; Letter from four House ranking members regarding CFIUS Case 10-40, to The Honorable Timothy F. Geithner, U.S. Department of the Treasury, Chairman, CFIUS, October 5, 2010, http://www.judicialwatch.org/wp-content/uploads/2018/10/JW-v-DOJ-Uranium-One-doc-00722.pdf.

18 Larry Bell, "Obama: Putin's Gift That Keeps on Giving," *Forbes*, September 17, 2013, https://www.forbes.com/sites/larrybell/2013/09/17/obama-putins-gift-that-keeps-on-giving/#1ecc8290a373; Lee Smith, "Framing Trump: The Russia Job," in *The Plot Against the President* (New York: Hachette Book Group, 2019).

19 John R. Schindler, "Hillary's Secret Kremlin Connection Is Quickly Unraveling," *Observer*, August 25, 2016, https://observer.com/2016/08/hillarys-secret-kremlin-connection-is-quickly-unraveling/; Peter Schweizer, "The Clinton Foundation, State and Kremlin Connections," *Wall Street Journal*, July 31, 2016, https://www.wsj.com/articles/the-clinton-foundation-state-and-kremlin-connections-1469997195.

20 Ibid.; Bell, "Obama: Putin's Gift That Keeps on Giving."

21 Mamula, "Russia's Uranium Gambit: The Real Uranium One Scandal."

22 "Statement by Boris Yeltsin," Kremlin.ru, December 31, 1999, http://en.kremlin.ru/events/president/transcripts/24080; Hans M. Kristensen and Matt Korda, "Status of

World Nuclear Forces," Federation of American Scientists, last updated May 2019, https://fas.org/issues/nuclear-weapons/status-world-nuclear-forces/; Mariel Synan, "What Is the Largest Country in the World?," History.com, last updated August 22, 2018, https://www.history.com/news/what-is-the-largest-country-in-the-world; Owen Matthews, "Vladimir Putin's New Plan for World Domination," *Spectator*, February 22, 2014, https://www.spectator.co.uk/2014/02/putins-masterplan/.

23 Áine Cain, "Before He Became the President of Russia, Vladimir Putin Was a KGB Spy – Take a Look at His Early Career," Business Insider, July 16, 2018, https://www.businessinsider.com/vladimir-putin-kgb-spy-2017-9; Celestine Bohlen, "Putin Tells Why He Became a Spy," *New York Times*, March 11, 2000, https://www.nytimes.com/2000/03/11/world/putin-tells-why-he-became-a-spy.html; Katusa, *The Colder War*, 58.

24 Ibid.

25 "Vladimir Putin: A Biographical Timeline," NPR, accessed September 1, 2019, https://www.npr.org/news/specials/putin/biotimeline.html; "Vladimir Putin," History.com, last updated August 21, 2018, https://www.history.com/topics/russia/vladimir-putin; "Vladimir Vladimirovich Putin – Early Life," GlobalSecurity.org, accessed September 1, 2017, https://www.globalsecurity.org/military/world/russia/putin-early.htm; Katusa, *The Colder War*, 58-59; David Hoffman, "Putin's Career Rooted in Russia's KGB," *Washington Post*, January 30, 2000, https://www.washingtonpost.com/wp-srv/inatl/longterm/russiagov/putin.htm.

26 Hoffman, "Putin's Career Rooted in Russia's KGB."

27 Karen Dawisha, *Putin's Kleptocracy: Who Owns Russia?* (New York: Simon & Schuster, 2014), 53; Hoffman, "Putin's Career Rooted in Russia's KGB"; Michael Wines, "PATH TO POWER: A Political Profile.; Putin Steering to Reform, but with Soviet Discipline," *New York Times*, February 20, 2000, https://www.nytimes.com/2000/02/20/world/path-power-political-profile-putin-steering-reform-but-with-soviet-discipline.html.

28 Andrew Osborn, "Vladimir Putin Saved KGB Offices from East German Looters," *Telegraph*, October 29, 2009, https://www.telegraph.co.uk/news/worldnews/europe/russia/6455858/Vladimir-Putin-saved-KGB-offices-from-East-German-looters.html; Dawisha, *Putin's Kleptocracy*, 116-117.

29 Pavel Felgenhauer, "Russian Military Reform: Ten Years of Failure," Federation of American Scientists, March 26 and 27, 1997, https://fas.org/nuke/guide/russia/agency/Felg.htm; Thomas E. Graham, Jr., *Russia's Decline and Uncertain Recovery* (Washington, D.C.: Carnegie Endowment for International Peace, 2002), https://carnegieendowment.org/files/RussiasDecline.pdf.

30 Ibid.; "The First Bloody Battle," BBC News, March 16, 2000, http://news.bbc.co.uk/2/hi/europe/482323.stm; Robert Coalson, "S Novym Godom! The New Year's Messages of Soviet and Russian Leaders over the Decades," Radio Free Europe/Radio Liberty, December 31, 2019, https://www.rferl.org/a/new-years-messages-of-soviet-and-russian-leaders-over-the-decades/30352967.html.

31 Dawisha, *Putin's Kleptocracy*, 29, 82, 104; "The Putin Interviews," Showtime, accessed September 1, 2019, https://www.sho.com/the-putin-interviews; Filip Novokmet, Thomas Piketty, and Gabriel Zucman, "From Soviets to Oligarchs:

Inequality and Property in Russia 1905-2016" (working paper, World Inequality Lab, April 6, 2018), 9, https://wid.world/document/soviets-oligarchs-inequality-property-russia-1905-2016/.

32 Dawisha, *Putin's Kleptocracy*, 78- 79.

33 Joe Barnes, "Putin's Rise to Power REVEALED: Does Newsnight Unearth Truth Behind Putin's Russian Rule?," *Daily Express*, March 1, 2018, https://www.express.co.uk/news/world/925683/BBC-Newsnight-Vladimir-Putin-Ksenia-Sobchak-Anatoly-Sobchak-Russia-election.

34 Dawisha, *Putin's Kleptocracy*, 5, 98, 133, 148.

35 Vladimir Putin, translated by Catherine A. Fitzpatrick, *First Person: An Astonishingly Frank Self-Portrait by Russia's President* (New York: PublicAffairs, 2000); Dawisha, *Putin's Kleptocracy*, 103, 150, 163, 175.

36 Putin, *First Person*, 113; Roberto Petitpas, "2015 President – EN," Vimeo, accessed September 1, 2019, https://tributetoapresident.blogspot.com/2017/05/bfirst-person-part-6-democrat.html; Dawisha, *Putin's Kleptocracy*, 121.

37 Dawisha, *Putin's Kleptocracy*, 95.

38 Fiona Hill and Clifford G. Gaddy, "How the 1980s Explains Vladimir Putin," *Atlantic*, February 14, 2013, https://www.theatlantic.com/international/archive/2013/02/how-the-1980s-explains-vladimir-putin/273135/#; Dawisha, *Putin's Kleptocracy*, 94-99.

39 V. Milov, B. Nemtsov, V. Ryzhkov, and O. Shorina, translated by Dave Essel, "Putin. Corruption. An Independent White Paper," Putin-itogi.ru, 2011, https://www.putin-itogi.ru/putin-corruption-an-independent-white-paper/; Dawisha, *Putin's Kleptocracy*, 127, 165.

40 Dawisha, *Putin's Kleptocracy*, 165.

41 Ibid.

42 Katusa, *The Colder War*, 8; Dawisha, *Putin's Kleptocracy*, 163-165.

43 Katusa, *The Colder War*, 8.

44 Ibid., 6-10.

45 "Yeltsin: I Knew about Lewinsky Plot Before Clinton," UPI (archives), October 7, 2000, https://www.upi.com/Archives/2000/10/07/Yeltsin-I-knew-about-Lewinsky-plot-before-Clinton/1451970891200/.

46 *Testimony of Anne Williamson Before the House Banking Committee, House of Representatives,* "The Rape of Russia" (106th Cong., 1999); John Lloyd, "The Russian Devolution," *New York Times*, August 15, 1999, https://www.nytimes.com/1999/08/15/magazine/the-russian-devolution.html; Liam Anderson, "Corruption in Russia: Past, Present, and Future," in *Corruption in Comparative Perspective: Sources, Status and Prospects* (United Kingdom: Ashgate, 2012), 15, https://www.researchgate.net/publication/289020599_Corruption_in_Russia_Past_present_and_future; *Testimony of Anne Williamson Before the House Banking Committee, House of Representatives,* "The Rape of Russia."

47 Bernard Black, Reinier Kraakman, and Anna Tarassova, "Russian Privatization and Corporate Governance: What Went Wrong?," *Stanford Law Review* 52, no. 6 (July 2000): 1731-808, https://www.jstor.org/stable/1229501?; *Testimony of Anne Williamson Before the House Banking Committee, House of Representatives,* "The

Rape of Russia"; Janine R. Wedel, "How the Chubais Clan, Harvard Fed Corruption," *Los Angeles Times*, September 12, 1999, https://www.latimes.com/archives/la-xpm-1999-sep-12-op-9170-story.html; "The Humbling of Chubais," *Economist*, November 20, 1997, https://www.economist.com/special/1997/11/20/the-humbling-of-chubais; "To the Rescue," *Economist*, July 16, 1998, https://www.economist.com/finance-and-economics/1998/07/16/to-the-rescue; Ariel Cohen, "No IMF Loans to Russia," Heritage Foundation, February 16, 1996, https://www.heritage.org/europe/report/no-imf-loans-russia.

48   Black, Kraakman, and Tarassova, "Russian Privatization and Corporate Governance: What Went Wrong?," 12; Anderson, "Corruption in Russia: Past, Present, and Future," in *Corruption in Comparative Perspective: Sources, Status and Prospects.*

49   Marshall I. Goldman, "Putin and the Oligarchs," *Foreign Affairs*, November/December 2004, https://www.cfr.org/world/putin-oligarchs/p7517; Alessandra Stanley, "Russian Reformer's Credibility Undercut by Scandal," *New York Times*, November 17, 1997, https://www.nytimes.com/1997/11/17/world/russian-reformer-s-credibility-undercut-by-scandal.html; Committee to Protect Journalists, "Attacks on the Press in 1997 - Russia," United Nations High Commissioner for Refugees, February 1998, https://www.refworld.org/docid/47c5654923.html.

50   "Finance Minister of the Year 1997: Chubais Forces the Pace," Euromoney, August 31, 1997, http://www.euromoney.com/Article/1005909/Category/774/Channel-Page/10685/Finance-Minister-of-the-Year-1997-Chubais-forces-the-pace.html; Nick Timothy, Kate McCann, Claire Newell, and Luke Heighton, "George Soros, the Man Who 'Broke the Bank of England', Backing Secret Plot to Thwart Brexit," *Telegraph*, February 8, 2018, https://www.telegraph.co.uk/politics/2018/02/07/george-soros-man-broke-bank-england-backing-secret-plot-thwart/.

51   Janine R. Wedel, "The Harvard Boys Do Russia," *Nation*, May 14, 1998, https://www.thenation.com/article/harvard-boys-do-russia/.

52   "Finance Minister of the Year 1997: Chubais Forces the Pace"; Guy Chazan, "George Soros Works to Rescue Investment in Russia's Svyazinvest," *Wall Street Journal*, April 30, 2001, https://www.wsj.com/articles/SB988575067628109309.

53   "The Humbling of Chubais"; David Hoffman, "Kremlin Strips Reformer of Finance Post," *Washington Post*, November 20, 1997, https://www.washingtonpost.com/wp-srv/inatl/longterm/russiagov/stories/chubais112097.htm; Alessandra Stanley, "Russian Banking Scandal Poses Threat to Future of Privatization," *New York Times*, January 28, 1996, https://www.nytimes.com/1996/01/28/world/russian-banking-scandal-poses-threat-to-future-of-privatization.html; Peter Reddaway, "Beware the Russian Reformer," *Washington Post*, August 24, 1997, http://www.washingtonpost.com/wp-srv/inatl/exussr/sep/16/chubais.htm.

54   Peter Beinart, "The U.S. Needs to Face Up to Its Long History of Election Meddling," *Atlantic*, July 22, 2018, https://www.theatlantic.com/ideas/archive/2018/07/the-us-has-a-long-history-of-election-meddling/565538/; Alessandra Stanley, "Moscow Journal; The Americans Who Saved Yeltsin (Or Did They?)," *New York Times*, July 9, 1996, https://www.nytimes.com/1996/07/09/world/moscow-journal-the-americans-who-saved-yeltsin-or-did-they.html.

55 Alessandra Stanley, "TV WEEKEND; Courting Voters in Moscow? It Just Takes Yankee Ingenuity," *New York Times*, March 12, 2004, https://www.nytimes.com/2004/03/12/movies/tv-weekend-courting-voters-in-moscow-it-just-takes-yankee-ingenuity.html; Beinart, "The U.S. Needs to Face Up to Its Long History of Election Meddling."

56 Fred Gardner, "Irrefutable Proof: Russian Election Meddling Documented!," CounterPunch, May 19, 2017, https://www.counterpunch.org/2017/05/19/irrefutable-proof-russian-election-meddling-documented/; Axel Dreher, Valentin Lang, B. Peter Rosendorff, and James Raymond Vreeland, "Dirty Work: Buying Votes at the UN Security Council," VoxEU.org, November 24, 2018, https://voxeu.org/article/buying-votes-un-security-council.

57 Ariel Cohen, "The IMF's $22.6 Billion Failure in Russia," Heritage Foundation, August 24, 1998, https://www.heritage.org/report/the-imfs-226-billion-failure-russia; Simon Pirani and Paul Farrely, "IMF Knew about Russian Aid Scam," *Guardian*, October 16, 1999, https://www.theguardian.com/world/1999/oct/17/russia.business; Reddaway, "Beware the Russian Reformer"; Michael R. Gordon and David E. Sanger, "RESCUING RUSSIA: A Special Report.; The Bailout of the Kremlin: How U.S. Pressed the I.M.F.," *New York Times*, July 17, 1998, https://www.nytimes.com/1998/07/17/world/rescuing-russia-special-report-bailout-kremlin-us-pressed-imf.html; Sean Guillory, "Dermokratiya, USA," *Jacobin*, March 13, 2017, https://www.jacobinmag.com/2017/03/russia-us-clinton-boris-yeltsin-elections-interference-trump/.

58 Reddaway, "Beware the Russian Reformer."

59 Richard C. Paddock, "Russia Lied to Get Loans, Says Aide to Yeltsin," *Los Angeles Times*, September 9, 1998, https://www.latimes.com/archives/la-xpm-1998-sep-09-mn-21002-story.html.

60 Simon Shuster, "Rewriting Russian History: Did Boris Yeltsin Steal the 1996 Presidential Election?," *Time*, February 24, 2012, http://content.time.com/time/world/article/0,8599,2107565,00.html; Sarah Mendelson, "Democracy Assistance and Political Transition in Russia: Between Success and Failure," *Quarterly Journal: International Security* 25, no. 4 (Spring 2001): 68-106, https://www.belfercenter.org/publication/democracy-assistance-and-political-transition-russia-between-success-and-failure.

61 Michael R. Gordon, "SHAKE-UP IN RUSSIA: THE KREMLIN DRAMA; In Russia Reformer's Fall, Wealthy Insider Triumphs," *New York Times*, August 27, 1998, https://www.nytimes.com/1998/08/27/world/shake-up-russia-kremlin-drama-russia-reformer-s-fall-wealthy-insider-triumphs.html; Reddaway, "Beware the Russian Reformer"; Edward Lucas, *Deception: The Untold Story of East-West Espionage Today* (New York: Bloomsbury Publishing USA, 2012).

62 "Finance Minister of the Year 1997: Chubais Forces the Pace"; Sharon Lafraniere, "Yeltsin Dismisses Premier," *Washington Post*, August 24, 1998, https://www.washingtonpost.com/wp-srv/inatl/longterm/russiagov/stories/dismiss082498.htm.

63 Lafraniere, "Yeltsin Dismisses Premier."

64 "Yeltsins's Man Wins Approval," BBC News, August 16, 1999, http://news.bbc.co.uk/2/hi/europe/422001.stm.

65 Katusa, *The Colder War*, 8; Dawisha, *Putin's Kleptocracy*, 182; Lucas, *Deception*.

66 Dawisha, *Putin's Kleptocracy,* 182-183.

67 Ibid.; "The Making of a Neo-KGB State," *Economist,* August 23, 2007, https://www.economist.com/briefing/2007/08/23/the-making-of-a-neo-kgb-state.

68 Lucas, *Deception;* "Andrei Illarionov," Cato Institute, accessed September 1, 2019, https://www.cato.org/people/andrei-illarionov; Andrei Illarionov, "The Siloviki in Charge," *Journal of Democracy* 20, no. 2 (April 2009), 70, https://www.cato.org/sites/cato.org/files/articles/andrei_illarionov_the_siloviki_in_charge.pdf; Paddy Rawlinson, "Corruption, Organised Crime and the Free Market in Russia," in *Corruption and Organized Crime in Europe: Illegal Partnerships* (Abingdon: Routledge, 2012), 168; Dawisha, *Putin's Kleptocracy,* 264, 335.

69 Dawisha, *Putin's Kleptocracy,* 187.

70 Ibid., 182-183, 187.

71 Ibid., 188, 210-211; Mary Dejevsky, "Russian Mafia 'Laundered $10bn at Bank of New York,'" *Independent,* August 20, 1999, https://www.independent.co.uk/news/world/russian-mafia-laundered-10bn-at-bank-of-new-york-p-1113796.html.

72 Dawisha, *Putin's Kleptocracy,* 187-188.

73 "Timeline: Vladimir Putin – 20 Tumultuous Years As Russian President or PM," Reuters, August 19, 2019, https://www.reuters.com/article/us-russia-putin-timeline/timeline-vladimir-putin-20-tumultuous-years-as-russian-president-or-pm-idUSKCN1UZ185; Floriana Fossato, "Russia: Duma Approves Putin As Prime Minister," Radio Free Europe/Radio Liberty, August 9, 1999, https://www.rferl.org/a/1091966.html.

74 Mark Tran, "Yeltsin Sacks Prime Minister," *Guardian,* August 9, 1999, https://www.theguardian.com/world/1999/aug/09/russia.marktran.

75 Katusa, *The Colder War,* 8-14.

76 Ibid.

77 Dawisha, *Putin's Kleptocracy,* 207-208.

78 Ibid., 208; Katusa, *The Colder War,* 9; David Holley, "Separatists Tied to '99 Bombings. Announcement Doesn't Quell Suspicion That Russia Officials Were Behind the Blasts.," *Los Angeles* Times, May 1, 2003, on Internet Archive, https://web.archive.org/web/20060719174541/http://eng.terror99.ru/publications/094.htm (the screenshot of the site was captured on July 19, 2006); "Russia Hit by New Islamic Offensive," BBC News, September 5, 1999, http://news.bbc.co.uk/2/hi/europe/438691.stm.

79 Preeti Bhattacharji, "Chechen Terrorism (Russia, Chechnya, Separatist)," Council on Foreign Relations, April 8, 2010, https://www.cfr.org/backgrounder/chechen-terrorism-russia-chechnya-separatist; "Dozens Dead in Moscow Blast," BBC News, September 13, 1999, http://news.bbc.co.uk/2/hi/europe/445529.stm; Katusa, *The Colder War,* 9; Dawisha, *Putin's Kleptocracy,* 208.

80 Katusa, *The Colder War,* 10; Dawisha, *Putin's Kleptocracy,* 208.

81 Ibid.

82 Dawisha, *Putin's Kleptocracy,* 212; Katusa, *The Colder War,* 11.

83 Lucas, *Deception;* Katusa, *The Colder War,* 11; Dawisha, *Putin's Kleptocracy,* 212-213.

84 David Satter, "The Mystery of Russia's 1999 Apartment Bombings Lingers – the CIA Could Clear It Up," *National Review,* February 2, 2017, https://www.nationalreview

.com/2017/02/russia-apartment-bombings-september-1999-vladimir-putin-fsb-cia/; Katusa, *The Colder War*, 14.

85 Katusa, *The Colder War*, 11-12; Dawisha, *Putin's Kleptocracy*, 212-214, 218.

86 Katusa, *The Colder War*, 9-12; Satter, "The Mystery of Russia's 1999 Apartment Bombings Lingers – the CIA Could Clear It Up."

87 Dawisha, *Putin's Kleptocracy*, 209, 213-214; Katusa, *The Colder War*, 11-13.

88 Anne Speckhard, "Sochi's Grim Reapers," *Daily News*, February 9, 2014, https://www.nydailynews.com/opinion/sochi-grim-reapers-article-1.1606377; Katusa, *The Colder War*, 12.

89 Katusa, *The Colder War*, 13; Lucas, *Deception*.

90 Lucas, *Deception*.

91 Dawisha, *Putin's Kleptocracy*, 272; "Russia Appoints Chechen Leader," BBC News, June 12, 2000, http://news.bbc.co.uk/2/hi/europe/787811.stm; Bhattacharji, "Chechen Terrorism (Russia, Chechnya, Separatist)"; Katusa, *The Colder War*, 13-14.

92 Dawisha, *Putin's Kleptocracy*, 220.

93 Ibid., 210-211; Strobe Talbott, interview, *Frontline*, PBS, accessed September 1, 2019, https://www.pbs.org/wgbh/pages/frontline/shows/kosovo/interviews/talbott.html.

94 Dawisha, *Putin's Kleptocracy*, 210; Strobe Talbott, interview, *Frontline*; *Prepared Testimony of Strobe Talbott, Deputy Secretary of State, Before the Senate Appropriations Committee, Subcommittee on Foreign Operations*, "Pursuing U.S. Interests with Russia & with President-Elect Putin," the 107th Cong. (2000), on Frontline, https://www.pbs.org/wgbh/pages/frontline/shows/yeltsin/putin/talbott00.html.

95 Lucas, *Deception*.

96 Ibid.

97 Guy Chazan, "Russian Government Adopts Proposal to Break Up Unified Energy System," *Wall Street Journal*, May 21, 2001, https://www.wsj.com/articles/SB990392286777881144.

98 Ibid.; Cynthia Romero, "Russia's Latin Affections?," Atlantic Council, February 13, 2009, https://www.atlanticcouncil.org/blogs/new-atlanticist/russia-s-latin-affections/.

99 "HEU Achievement," Tenex, accessed September 27, 2019, https://www.tenex.ru/resources/ca5a980045a8aa1b89f0bb470124f4f9/HEU_Book_Final.pdf; Lucas, *Deception*; Dawisha, *Putin's Kleptocracy*, 98.

100 Dawisha, *Putin's Kleptocracy*, 98, 133, 139-140, 305.

101 Ibid., 65, 95-97; 95.

102 Ibid., 64; "Minchenko Consulting Group: Politburo 2.0: Dismantling or Reset?," Institute of Modern Russia, November 11, 2016, https://imrussia.org/en/the-rundown/research-recaps/2665-minchenko-consulting-group-politburo-2-0-dismantling-or-reset,-7-november-2016; Stephen Grey, Andrey Kuzmin, and Elizabeth Piper, "Putin's Daughter, a Young Billionaire and the President's Friends," Reuters, November 10, 2015, https://www.reuters.com/investigates/special-report/russia-capitalism-daughters/; United States Securities and Exchange Commission, Form CB, JSC OGK-1, March 19, 2012, https://www.interrao.ru/upload/docs/2SEC2012.pdf; "Inter RAO UES PJSC," Bloomberg, accessed October 2, 2019, https://www.bloomberg.com/quote/IRAO:RU.

103 Grey, Kuzmin, and Piper, "Putin's Daughter, a Young Billionaire and the President's Friends"; "Rossiya Bank," OCCRP, June 3, 2016, https://www.occrp.org/documents/bank-rossiya/5_Rossiya-bank-founded-in-1990.pdf; Dawisha, *Putin's Kleptocracy*, 66; Danilo Elia, "Bank Rossiya, Putin's Bank," eastwest.eu, June 18, 2016, https://eastwest.eu/en/opinions/riding-the-russian-rollercoaster/bank-rossiya-putin-s-bank.

104 Dawisha, *Putin's Kleptocracy*, 70.

105 "Alexey Miller: Gazprom," European CEO, profiles, August 4, 2014, https://www.europeanceo.com/profiles/alexey-miller-gazprom/; "Alexey Miller," Gazprom, accessed October 3, 2019, https://www.gazprom.com/about/management/board/miller/; Amelia Gentleman, "Putin Puts Old Crony in to Shake Up Huge Gas Firm Racked by Scandals," *Guardian*, May 30, 2001, https://www.theguardian.com/world/2001/may/31/russia.ameliagentleman.

106 Bill Gertz, "Putin Corruption Network Revealed," *Washington Free Beacon*, April 7, 2014, https://freebeacon.com/national-security/putin-corruption-network-revealed/; M. Garside, "Gazprom's Net Revenue from 2011 to 2018 (in Billion U.S. Dollars)*," Statista, June 24, 2019, https://www.statista.com/statistics/350719/net-revenue-gazprom-worldwide/.

107 Grey, Kuzmin, and Piper, "Putin's Daughter, a Young Billionaire and the President's Friends."

108 Ibid.; Luke Harding, "The Russian President's Best Friend Portrays Himself As a Modest Musician, but Leaked Documents Reveal His Role in a Secret Money-go-round," *Guardian*, April 3, 2016, https://www.theguardian.com/news/2016/apr/03/sergei-roldugin-the-cellist-who-holds-the-key-to-tracing-putins-hidden-fortune; Stella Roque, "New Investigation Sheds Light on Putin's Eldest Daughter," OCCRP, February 1, 2016, https://www.occrp.org/en/daily/4877-new-investigation-sheds-light-on-putin-s-eldest-daughter.

109 Dawisha, *Putin's Kleptocracy*, 5, 98, 133, 141.

110 Ibid., 80-81, 133.

111 Ibid., 83-84, 87.

112 Ibid., 32-33.

113 Ibid., 132-133, 141-142.

114 Ibid., 132-133, 134, 136, 141-142; Luke Harding, "Revealed: The $2bn Offshore Trail That Leads to Vladimir Putin," *Guardian*, April 3, 2016, https://www.theguardian.com/news/2016/apr/03/panama-papers-money-hidden-offshore.

115 "People of Interest: Vladimir Sergeevich Kumarin," OCCRP, accessed August 28, 2019, https://www.reportingproject.net/peopleofinterest/profil.php?profil=49; McKenzie O'Brien, "Organization Attributes Sheet – Tambovskaya," Matthew B. Ridgway Center for International Security Studies, http://research.ridgway.pitt.edu/wp-content/uploads/2012/05/TambovskayaPROFILEFINAL.pdf; Dawisha, *Putin's Kleptocracy*, 79, 127, 134.

116 Dawisha, *Putin's Kleptocracy*, 134.

117 Ibid., 142.

118 Ibid., 133, 142, 145-152, 86.

119 Derek Scally, "Putin Sat on Board of Firm in Russian Mafia Inquiry," *Irish Times*, May 15, 2003, https://www.irishtimes.com/business/putin-sat-on-board

-of-firm-in-russian-mafia-inquiry-1.359050; Екип на Бивол, "Juergen Roth: Putin Is KGB Product and Works with Criminal Groups When He Needs It," Бивол, October 13, 2017, https://bivol.bg/en/juergen-roth-putin-is-kgb-product-and-works-with-criminal-groups-when-he-needs-it.html; Dawisha, *Putin's Kleptocracy*, 120-135, 138-140.

120 Dawisha, *Putin's Kleptocracy*, 132, 141 , 147-151.

121 "Our History," Gunvor, accessed October 3, 2019, https://gunvorgroup.com/our-history/; Dawisha, *Putin's Kleptocracy*, 6, 68, 112-113.

122 Dawisha, *Putin's Kleptocracy*, 6; Gertz, "Putin Corruption Network Revealed"; Andy Bloxham, "WikiLeaks: Putin's 'Secret Billions,'" Wikileaks, December 2, 2010, on Internet Archive, https://web.archive.org/web/20110128115530/http://www.telegraph.co.uk/news/worldnews/wikileaks/8175406/WikiLeaks-Putins-secret-billions.html (the screenshot of the site was captured on January 28, 2011).

123 Dawisha, *Putin's Kleptocracy*, 139-140; "Rogatory Letter on SPAG to Liechtenstein," Transborder Corruption Archive, November 14, 2018, https://tbcarchives.org/rogatory-letter-on-spag-to-liechtenstein/; Scally, "Putin Sat on Board of Firm in Russian Mafia Inquiry"; Sarah-Christian Müller and Dr. Karen Dawisha, *Appendices of Stasi Documents from Vladimir Putin, Operation LUCH and Matthias Warnig: The Secret KGB-Stasi Relationship*, Miami University, 2014, http://miamioh.edu/cas/_files/documents/havighurst/stasi-documents.pdf; Mark Hosenball, "A Stain on Mr. Clean," *Newsweek*, September 2, 2001, https://www.newsweek.com/stain-mr-clean-152259.

124 Dawisha, *Putin's Kleptocracy*, 140-141.

125 Ibid., 52-55.

126 Jules Gray, "Banking's Golden Age: Six Institutions That Shaped Europe," European CEO, September 7, 2015, https://www.europeanceo.com/business-and-management/bankings-golden-age-six-institutions-that-shaped-europe/.

127 Dawisha, *Putin's Kleptocracy*, 54-55.

128 Ibid., 55.

129 Ibid., 5-6; Katusa, *The Colder War*, 19-20; Alan Cullison, "Off to the Gulag: A Day in the Life of a Russian Tycoon," *Wall Street Journal*, November 30, 2005, https://www.wsj.com/articles/SB113331623541309782.

130 Kenneth P. Vogel and Matthew Rosenberg, "Agents Tried to Flip Russian Oligarchs. The Fallout Spread to Trump," *New York Times*, September 1, 2018, https://www.nytimes.com/2018/09/01/us/politics/deripaska-ohr-steele-fbi.html; "Russian Oligarch Has London Extradition Hearing Halted After His Mother Is 'Murdered' in Moscow," *Daily Mail*, August 6, 2010, https://www.dailymail.co.uk/news/article-1300934/Extradition-Russian-oligarch-halted-mother-murdered-Moscow.html; Alan Cullison, "In Russian Murder Case, a Long List of Enemies," *Wall Street Journal*, May 23, 2007, https://www.wsj.com/articles/SB117982581360410657; Katusa, *The Colder War*, 20.

131 Dawisha, *Putin's Kleptocracy*, 194-195; Katusa, *The Colder War*, 19-20.

132 Katusa, *The Colder War*, 22.

133 Ibid.

134 Ibid., 22-23.

135 Ibid., 25.

136 Ibid., 25-26.

137 Ibid.

138 Ibid., 26-27.

139 Ibid., 25; Nicole Sinclair, "Fund Manager Explains Why He Estimates Putin's Net Worth to Be $200 Billion," Yahoo Finance, July 20, 2017, https://finance.yahoo.com/news/fund-manager-explains-estimates-putins-net-worth-200-billion-105932448.html.

140 Katusa, *The Colder War*, 28-29.

141 Ibid., 30; Timothy L. O'Brien, "The Capitalist in the Cage," *New York Times*, June 20, 2004, https://www.nytimes.com/2004/06/20/business/the-capitalist-in-the-cage.html; Sinclair, "Fund Manager Explains Why He Estimates Putin's Net Worth to Be $200 Billion."

142 "The Russian Federal Property Fund (Hereinafter – the Seller) Announces a Tender for the Sale of the Arrested Shares of OAO Yuganskneftegaz," Rossiyskaya Gazeta, November 19, 2004, https://rg.ru/2004/11/19/ugansknefegaz-dok.html; Andrew E. Kramer, "Bankruptcy Auction Closes Book on Yukos," *New York Times*, May 11, 2007, https://www.nytimes.com/2007/05/11/business/worldbusiness/11iht-yukos.4.5672974.html.

143 Katusa, *The Colder War*, 29; "The Russian Federal Property Fund (Hereinafter – the Seller) Announces a Tender for the Sale of the Arrested Shares of OAO Yuganskneftegaz."

144 Katusa, *The Colder War*, 29; "Yukos Unit Fetches $9bn at Sale," BBC News, last updated December 20, 2004, http://news.bbc.co.uk/2/hi/business/4108509.stm; "Rosneft Wins First Yukos Auction," BBC News, last updated March 27, 2007, http://news.bbc.co.uk/2/hi/business/6498163.stm; MosNews, "Russia's State-Owned Rosneft Bought Baikal Finance Group for $350 – Newspaper," CbondS, December 29, 2004, http://cbonds.com/news/item/306146.

145 "The Last Days of Yukos," *Economist*, July 29, 2004, https://www.economist.com/business/2004/07/29/the-last-days-of-yukos; Steven Lee Myers and Andrew E. Kramer, "From Ashes of Yukos, New Russian Oil Giant Emerges," *New York Times*, March 27, 2007, https://www.nytimes.com/2007/03/27/world/europe/27russia.html.

146 Katusa, *The Colder War*, 20.

147 Ian Jeffries, *Political Developments in Contemporary Russia* (Abingdon: Routledge, 2011), 147.

Chapter 3

1 Mary Ann Koruth, "Russia's Would-Be Masters," *Atlantic*, March 2005, https://www.theatlantic.com/magazine/archive/2005/03/russias-would-be-masters/303878/.

2 Ministry of Energy of the Russian Federation, "The Summary of the Energy Strategy of Russia for the Period of up to 2020," 2003, on Internet Archive, https://web.archive.org/web/20071129125038/http://ec.europa.eu/energy/russia/events/doc/2003_strategy_2020_en.pdf (the screenshot of the site was captured on November 29, 2007).

3 Ibid.

4   "The Mystery of Vladimir Putin's Dissertation," Brookings Institution, March 30, 2006, https://www.brookings.edu/events/the-mystery-of-vladimir-putins-dissertation/; "The Mystery of Vladimir Putin's Dissertation," Edited versions of presentations by the authors at a Brookings Institution, Foreign Policy Program panel, March 30, 2006, https://www.brookings.edu/wp-content/uploads/2012/09/Putin-Dissertation-Event-remarks-with-slides.pdf; Dmitry Volchek and Robert Coalson, "Cut-and-Paste Job: 'My Father Wrote Putin's Dissertation,'" Radio Free Europe/Radio Liberty, March 7, 2018, https://www.rferl.org/a/russia-litvinenko-olga-says-father-wrote-putins-dissertation/29085343.html.

5   "History of the Company," Rosoboronexport, accessed October 3, 2019, http://roe.ru/eng/rosoboronexport/history/; Karen Dawisha, *Putin's Kleptocracy: Who Owns Russia* (New York: Simon & Schuster, 2014), 183, 338; Guy Chazan, "Russian Car Maker Comes Under Sway of Old Pal of Putin," *Wall Street Journal*, May 19, 2006, https://www.wsj.com/articles/SB114800303736957408; Polina Beliakova and Sam Perlo-Freeman, "Corruption in the Russian Defense Sector," World Peace Foundation, May 11, 2018, https://sites.tufts.edu/wpf/files/2018/05/Russian-Defense-Corruption-Report-Beliakova-Perlo-Freeman-20180502-final.pdf.

6   Brookings Institution, "The Brookings Foreign Policy Studies Energy Security Series: The Russian Federation," October 2006, https://www.brookings.edu/wp-content/uploads/2016/06/2006russia.pdf; Marshall I. Goldman, *Petrostate: Putin, Power, and the New Russia* (New York: Oxford University Press, 2008), 49, http://willzuzak.ca/cl/putin/Goldman2008PetrostatePutinPower.pdf; Craig E. Levitt, "Yugoslavia and the Soviet Union," CIA.gov, approved for release on September 8, 2000, https://www.cia.gov/library/readingroom/docs/CIA-RDP78-01634R000100060001-4.pdf.

7   Goldman, *Petrostate*, 2, 49; Sunita Meena, "Energy As a Political Weapon of Foreign Policy: The Russian Case," *International Journal of Academic Research and Development* 3, no. 5 (September 2018), https://www.academia.edu/37645461/Energy_as_a_political_weapon_of_foreign_policy_The_Russian_case.

8   Dawisha, *Putin's Kleptocracy*, 83; "Key Kremlin Figure Removed," BBC News, last updated October 30, 2003, http://news.bbc.co.uk/2/hi/europe/3229107.stm; Goldman, *Petrostate*, 104, 140.

9   Josh Cohen, "Vladimir Putin's Most Effective Weapon Is Gas - but Not the Poison Kind," Reuters, July 28, 2015, https://www.reuters.com/article/us-cohen-gazprom-idUSKCN0Q302820150729.

10   "Delivery Statistics," Gazprom Export, accessed October 3, 2019, http://www.gazpromexport.ru/en/statistics/; Steven Woehrel, "Russian Energy Policy Toward Neighboring Countries," Congressional Research Service, September 2, 2009, https://fas.org/sgp/crs/row/RL34261.pdf; Goldman, *Petrostate*.

11   Steven Erlanger, "Russia and Ukraine Settle Dispute over Black Sea Fleet," *New York Times*, June 10, 1995, https://www.nytimes.com/1995/06/10/world/russia-and-ukraine-settle-dispute-over-black-sea-fleet.html; Major S.B. Carr, *Nato Enlargement and Russia: The Need for a Dual-Track Policy*, Canadian Forces College, April 21, 2008, https://www.cfc.forces.gc.ca/259/290/294/286/carr.pdf; Graeme P. Herd and Jennifer D.P. Moroney, *Security Dynamics in the Former Soviet Bloc* (London: RoutledgeCurzon, 2003), 107; Viktor Luhovyk, "Ukraine

Pressed for Debt Payments," Associated Press, July 15, 1999, https://apnews. com/3c7d1272f079588532c548cfc2a6c05a.

12 Ibid.

13 Ibid.

14 Dawisha, *Putin's Kleptocracy*, 239-240.

15 Ibid.

16 Cohen, "Vladimir Putin's Most Effective Weapon Is Gas - but Not the Poison Kind"; "Russia Report: November 18, 2004," Radio Free Europe/Radio Liberty, reports archive, November 18, 2004, https://www.rferl.org/a/1344329.html.

17 Simon Jenkins, "What Is David Cameron Doing in Kazakhstan?," *Guardian*, July 1, 2013, https://www.theguardian.com/commentisfree/2013/jul/01/david-cameron-kaszakhstan-britain; Nate Schenkkan, "Customs Disunion: Putin's Plans for Regional Integration Go Boom," *Foreign Affairs*, May 12, 2014, https://www.foreignaffairs.com/articles/armenia/2014-05-12/customs-disunion; "Russia Report: November 18, 2004"; Paul Wasserman, "Between a Bear and a Dragon: New Challenges for Kazakhstan," Global Risk Insights, March 26, 2019, https://globalriskinsights.com/2019/03/kazakhstan-china-russia-leader/.

18 "Russia Report: November 18, 2004"; Goldman, *Petrostate*, 7.

19 Ian Traynor, "US Campaign Behind the Turmoil in Kiev," *Guardian*, November 25, 2004, https://www.theguardian.com/world/2004/nov/26/ukraine.usa.

20 Marin Katusa, *The Colder War: How the Global Energy Trade Slipped from America's Grasp* (Vermont: John Wiley & Sons, 2015), 62, 72-73; Traynor, "US Campaign Behind the Turmoil in Kiev"; "A Chestnut Revolution," *Wall Street Journal*, February 11, 2004, https://www.wsj.com/articles/SB107645635194826171; "Chestnuts and Revolutions," *Wall Street Journal*, November 15, 2004, https://www.wsj.com/articles/SB110047360291873634; Katherine T. Hinkle, "Russia's Reactions to the Color Revolutions" (master's thesis, Naval Postgraduate School, 2017), https://calhoun.nps.edu/bitstream/handle/10945/52991/17Mar_Hinkle_Katherine.pdf?sequence=1&isAllowed=y.

21 Katusa, *The Colder War*, 73; "Russia: Putin Defends Reforms, Condemns 'Revolutions,'" Radio Free Europe/Radio Liberty, December 23, 2004, https://www.rferl.org/a/1056558.html; Fiona Hill, "Putin and Bush in Common Cause? Russia's View of the Terrorist Threat After September 11," Brookings Institute, June 1, 2002, https://www.brookings.edu/articles/putin-and-bush-in-common-cause-russias-view-of-the-terrorist-threat-after-september-11/; "Russia's Western Neighbours: Ukraine Comes to the Forefront," *Economist*, September 11, 2008, https://www.economist.com/taxonomy/term/122?page=35.

22 Gerard Toal and John O'Loughlin, "How People in South Ossetia, Abkhazia and Transnistria Feel about Annexation by Russia," *Washington Post*, March 20, 2014, https://www.washingtonpost.com/news/monkey-cage/wp/2014/03/20/how-people-in-south-ossetia-abkhazia-and-transnistria-feel-about-annexation-by-russia/.

23 Dawisha, *Putin's Kleptocracy*, 345.

24 "Scenesetter for Visit of FBI Director Mueller to Moscow, November 15-17, 2009," Wikileaks, November 9, 2009, https://wikileaks.org/plusd/cables/09MOSCOW2749_a.html.

25 "FACTBOX: Russian Oil and Gas Export Interruptions," Reuters, August 29, 2008, https://www.reuters.com/article/us-energy-russia-cutoffs/factbox-russian-oil-and-gas-export-interruptions-idUSLS57897220080829; R. L. Larsson, "Russia's Energy Policy: Security Dimensions and Russia's Reliability As an Energy Supplier," National Technical Reports Library, 2006, https://ntrl.ntis.gov/NTRL/dashboard/searchResults/titleDetail/PB2007106453.xhtml; Robert W. Ortung and Indra Overland, "A Limited Toolbox: Explaining the Constraints on Russia's Foreign Energy Policy," *Journal of Eurasian Studies* 2, no. 1 (January 2011), 74-85, https://www.sciencedirect.com/science/article/pii/S1879366510000394#bbib26.

26 Ministry of Energy of the Russian Federation, "The Summary of the Energy Strategy of Russia for the Period of up to 2020."

27 "Russia Report: November 18, 2004."

28 "TENEX Ceded All Its Shares to the State," Tenex, June 29, 2001, on Internet Archive, https://web.archive.org/web/20100505002931/http://www.tenex.ru/en/press/events/?id=145 (the screenshot of the site was captured on May 5, 2010).

29 Ibid.; "Russian Spent Nuclear Fuel," Nuclear Threat Initiative, February 1, 2003, https://www.nti.org/analysis/articles/russian-spent-nuclear-fuel/; C.M. Johnson, "The Russian Federation's Ministry of Atomic Energy: Programs and Developments," International Atomic Energy Agency, Prepared for the U.S. Department of Energy, February 2000, https://inis.iaea.org/collection/NCLCollectionStore/_Public/31/051/31051595.pdf.

30 "Russia Close to Accepting World's Nuclear Waste," Environment News Service, December 22, 2000, http://www.ens-newswire.com/ens/dec2000/2000-12-22-12.html.

31 Charles Digges, "World Funding Pours into Russia for Nuclear Cleanup and Sub Dismantling," Bellona, July 16, 2003, https://bellona.org/news/nuclear-issues/radioactive-waste-and-spent-nuclear-fuel/2003-07-world-funding-pours-into-russia-for-nuclear-cleanup-and-sub-dismantling; Gregory Palast, "To Russia with Love and $15bn," *Guardian*, July 28, 2001, https://www.theguardian.com/business/2001/jul/29/columnists.theobserver1.

32 Ibid.; "Russian Spent Nuclear Fuel"; "Minatom Official Discusses Attempted Thefts of Fissile Materials," Nuclear Threat Initiative, September 28, 2000, https://www.nti.org/analysis/articles/minatom-official-discusses-attempted-thefts-fissile-materials/.

33 Dawisha, *Putin's Kleptocracy*, 97-98.

34 Ibid., 139-140; Mark Hosenball, "A Stain on Mr. Clean," *Newsweek*, September 2, 2001, https://www.newsweek.com/stain-mr-clean-152259; Edward Lucas, *Deception: The Untold Story of East-West Espionage Today* (New York: Bloomsbury Publishing USA, 2012).

35 Ibid.

36 Dawisha, *Putin's Kleptocracy*, 140; Roman Shleinov, "Seated Father: One Person Owns Russia – Its Manager," NovayaGazeta.ru, February 7, 2005, https://web.archive.org/web/20060213091039/http://2005.novayagazeta.ru/nomer/2005/09n/n09n-s26.shtml (the screenshot of the site was captured on February 13, 2006).

37 Alexander Litvinenko, "Why I Believe Putin Wanted Me Dead…," *Daily Mail*, November 25, 2006, https://www.mailonsunday.co.uk/news/article-418652/Why-I-

believe-Putin-wanted-dead-.html; Dawisha, *Putin's Kleptocracy*, 13, 187; Ben Judah, "Grinda's War," *American Interest*, June 12, 2018, https://www.the-american-interest.com/2018/06/12/grindas-war/; Alex Goldfarb and Anastasia Kirilenko, "Fresh Evidence Suggests Litvinenko Was Killed to Keep Him Quiet," *Guardian*, January 12, 2016, https://www.theguardian.com/world/2016/jan/12/alexander-litvinenko-russia-murder; Luke Harding, *A Very Expensive Poison: The Assassination of Alexander Litvinenko and Putin's War in the West* (New York: Vintage Books, 2016).

38 Alessandra Stanley, "After Yeltsin Shake-Up, Business As Usual," *New York Times*, March 25, 1998, https://www.nytimes.com/1998/03/25/world/after-yeltsin-shake-up-business-as-usual.html; Dawisha, *Putin's Kleptocracy*, 228.

39 "Kiriyenko, Sergei," Kremlin.ru, accessed October 3, 2019, http://en.kremlin.ru/catalog/persons/175/biography; Ministry of Energy of the Russian Federation, "The Summary of the Energy Strategy of Russia for the Period of up to 2020"; Jonathan B. Tucker, "Russia's New Plan for Chemical Weapons Destruction," Arms Control Association, accessed October 1, 2019, https://www.armscontrol.org/act/2001-07/features/russia%E2%80%99s-new-plan-chemical-weapons-destruction.

40 Alexander Nikitin, "Rosatom State Corporation," Bellona, November 26, 2007, https://bellona.org/news/nuclear-issues/nuclear-russia/2007-11-rosatom-state-corporation.

41 Ibid.

42 Stanley, "After Yeltsin Shake-Up, Business As Usual"; Alessandra Stanley, "Threatening Parliament, Yeltsin Names Neophyte Premier," *New York Times*, March 28, 1998, https://www.nytimes.com/1998/03/28/world/threatening-parliament-yeltsin-names-neophyte-premier.html.

43 "HEU Achievement," Tenex, accessed September 27, 2019, https://www.tenex.ru/resources/ca5a980045a8aa1b89f0bb470124f4f9/HEU_Book_Final.pdf.

44 "History," Tenex, accessed October 1, 2019, https://tenex.ru/en/about/history/; Behnam Ben Taleblu and Andrea Stricker, "Washington Must Revoke Sanctions Waiver After Latest Nuclear Violation," *Hill*, November 16, 2019, https://thehill.com/opinion/international/470781-washington-must-revoke-sanctions-waiver-after-latest-nuclear-violation; "Russia and China Deal on Uranium, Enrichment and Power," World Nuclear News, November 8, 2007, https://www.world-nuclear-news.org/Articles/Russia-and-China-deal-on-uranium,-enrichment-and-p.

45 50th Anniversary Booklet, Tenex, accessed September 15, 2019, https://www.tenex.ru/download/201/booklet_for_tenex_50_sup_th_sup_anniversary.pdf; Anton Khlopkov and Valeriya Chekina, "Governing Uranium in Russia," Danish Institute for International Studies (DIIS), DIIS Report No. 2014:19, https://www.econstor.eu/bitstream/10419/120406/1/818453915.pdf.

46 William J. Broad, "From Warheads to Cheap Energy," *New York Times*, January 27, 2014, https://www.nytimes.com/2014/01/28/science/thomas-l-neffs-idea-turned-russian-warheads-into-american-electricity.html.

47 John Ritch, "This Uranium Deal Was No Scandal," *New York Times*, November 21, 2017, https://www.nytimes.com/2017/11/21/opinion/uranium-deal-clinton-russia.html%20(1993);%20; U.S. House of Representatives, Hearing Before the Subcommittee on Oversight and Investigations of the Committee on Commerce,

"Privatization of the U.S. Enrichment Corporation and Its Impact on the Domestic Uranium Industry," 106th Cong. (2000), https://www.govinfo.gov/content/pkg/CHRG-106hhrg64028/html/CHRG-106hhrg64028.htm.

48 "Megatons to Megawatts Program: Hard Lessons and New Opportunities for US-Russian Nuclear Cooperation," *Russia Direct*, no. 4 (March 2014); Fern Shen, "Uranium, Converted from Russian Nuclear Warheads, Comes Through Baltimore's Port," Baltimore Brew, December 10, 2013, https://www.baltimorebrew.com/2013/12/10/uranium-converted-from-russian-nuclear-warheads-comes-through-baltimores-port/; Seamus Bruner, *Compromised* (New York: Post Hill Press, 2018), 58-63.

49 "UxC Published Interview with TENEX Director General," Oreanda-News, October 2, 2012, https://www.oreanda.ru/en/promyshlennost/article660259/; John Solomon and Alison Spann, "FBI Uncovered Russian Bribery Plot Before Obama Administration Approved Controversial Nuclear Deal with Moscow," *Hill*, October 17, 2017, https://thehill.com/policy/national-security/355749-fbi-uncovered-russian-bribery-plot-before-obama-administration%20.

50 "UxC Published Interview with TENEX Director General"; "Interview with TENEX Director General, Alexei Grigoriev," TENEX, September 24, 2012, https://tenex.ru/en/media-center/coverage/interview-with-tenex-director-general-alexei-grigoriev/.

51 Paul Kerr, "Iran, Russia Reach Nuclear Agreement," Arms Control Association, accessed October 3, 2019, https://www.armscontrol.org/act/2005-04/iran-nuclear-briefs/iran-russia-reach-nuclear-agreement; Lionel Beehner, "Russia's Nuclear Deal with Iran," Council on Foreign Relations, February 28, 2006, https://www.cfr.org/backgrounder/russias-nuclear-deal-iran; Anton Khlopkov, "Iran Breakthrough for Russian Nuclear Industry," Moscow Defense Brief, 2010, on Internet Archive, https://web.archive.org/web/20100309020452/http:/mdb.cast.ru/mdb/1-2010/item2/article2/ (the screenshot of the site was captured on March 9, 2010).

52 Beehner, "Russia's Nuclear Deal with Iran"; U.S. Energy Information Administration, "Megatons to Megawatts Program Will Conclude at the End of 2013," September 24, 2013, https://www.eia.gov/todayinenergy/detail.php?id=13091.

53 Ned Mamula, "Russia's Uranium Gambit: The Real Uranium One Scandal," Capital Research Center, January 15, 2019, https://capitalresearch.org/article/russias-uranium-gambit-part-4/; Dr. Tom Borelli, "Utility Industry Aids Putin's Stealth War on US Uranium Mining," Conservative Review, March 28, 2019, https://www.conservativereview.com/news/utility-industry-aids-putins-stealth-war-u-s-uranium-mining/.

54 Peter Baker, "The Seduction of George W. Bush," *Foreign Policy*, November 6, 2013, https://foreignpolicy.com/2013/11/06/the-seduction-of-george-w-bush/; Andrew Glass, "President Bush Cites 'Axis of Evil,' Jan. 29, 2002," *Politico*, January 29, 2019, https://www.politico.com/story/2019/01/29/bush-axis-of-evil-2002-1127725; "Kremlin Releases New Footage of Putin's 2001 Visit to Bush in Texas," *Moscow Times*, January 29, 2020, https://www.themoscowtimes.com/2020/01/29/kremlin-releases-new-footage-of-putins-2001-visit-to-bush-in-texas-a69089; "User Clip: Bush Saw Putin's Soul," C-SPAN, March 9, 2018, video, https://www.c-span.org/video/?c4718091/user-clip-bush-putins-soul.

55   Kim Murphy, "U.S. Slaps Sanctions on Russian Arms Maker for Sales to Tehran," *Los Angeles Times*, September 17, 2013, https://www.latimes.com/archives/la-xpm-2003-sep-17-fg-russarms17-story.html; Alex Wagner, "Bush, Putin Disagree on Russia-Iran Nuclear, Missile Cooperation," Arms Control Association, June 2002, https://www.armscontrol.org/act/2002-06/news/bush-putin-disagree-russia-iran-nuclear-missile-cooperation.

56   Khlopkov, "Iran Breakthrough for Russian Nuclear Industry."

57   Sara A. Carter, "Treasure Trove of Documents Tying Russia to Uranium One," Sean Hannity Show, November 21, 2017, on Internet Archive, https://web.archive.org/web/20171121024416/https://hannity.com/content/2017-11-20-sara-carter/ (the screenshot of the site was captured on November 21, 2017); Sara Carter, "FBI Informant on Uranium One Breaks Silence," Sara Carter's website, on Internet Archive, February 7, 2018, https://web.archive.org/web/20180209211913/https:/saraacarter.com/fbi-informant-uranium-one-breaks-silence-today/ (the screenshot of the site was captured on February 9, 2018).

58   Baker, "The Seduction of George W. Bush"; Jim Rutenberg, "Putin Arrives in Kennebunkport for 2-Day Visit with the Bushes," *New York Times*, July 2, 2007, https://www.nytimes.com/2007/07/02/washington/02putin.html; Gregory L. White, "Putin Woos Evans for Rosneft Job," *Wall Street Journal*, December 16, 2005, https://www.wsj.com/articles/SB113468313847923770.

59   David E. Sanger and Elaine Sciolino, "Bush and China Endorse Russia's Nuclear Plan for Iran," *New York Times*, January 27, 2006, https://www.nytimes.com/2006/01/27/politics/bush-and-china-endorse-russias-nuclear-plan-for-iran.html; Susan Cornwell, "Lawmakers Urge Bush to Shelve Russia Nuclear Deal," Reuters, May 7, 2008, https://www.reuters.com/article/us-nuclear-russia-usa/lawmakers-urge-bush-to-shelve-russia-nuclear-deal-idUSL0659405920080507.

60   Baker, "The Seduction of George W. Bush."

61   North Atlantic Treaty Organization, "Bucharest Summit Declaration," press release, April 3, 2008, https://www.nato.int/cps/en/natolive/official_texts_8443.htm; John J. Mearsheimer, "Getting Ukraine Wrong," *New York Times*, March 13, 2014, https://www.nytimes.com/2014/03/14/opinion/getting-ukraine-wrong.html.

62   Katusa, *The Colder War*, 63.

63   Ibid.; Amnesty International, "Civilians in the Line of Fire: The Georgia-Russia Conflict," November 2008, https://web.archive.org/web/20081212205224/http://amnesty.org/en/library/asset/EUR04/005/2008/en/d9908665-ab55-11dd-a4cd-bfa0fdea9647/eur040052008eng.pdf (the screenshot of the report was captured on December 12, 2008).

64   Mary Beth Nikitin, "U.S.-Russian Civilian Nuclear Cooperation Agreement: Issues for Congress," Congressional Research Service, January 11, 2011, https://fas.org/sgp/crs/nuke/RL34655.pdf; Thom Shanker and Nicholas Kulish, "Russia Lashes Out on Missile Deal," *New York Times*, August 15, 2008, https://www.nytimes.com/2008/08/15/world/europe/16poland.html?hp.

65   "Russian Rules Out Any War with U.S.," *New York Times*, October 1, 2008, https://www.nytimes.com/2008/10/01/world/europe/01iht-georgia.4.16622086.html.

66   Baker, "The Seduction of George W. Bush."

67 "Putin Ratifies Law on Formation of Rosatom," World Nuclear News, December 3, 2007, http://www.world-nuclear-news.org/Articles/Putin-ratifies-law-on-formation-of-Rosatom; Nikitin, "Rosatom State Corporation"; Tatiana Kachalina, "Employee Ownership in Russia: Evolution and Current Status," in *Sharing Ownership, Profits, and Decision-making in the 21st Century* (Bingley: Emerald Group Publishing, 2013), 184.

68 Nikitin, "Rosatom State Corporation."

69 Ibid.; "National Operator for Radioactive Waste Management," Rosatom, accessed October 16, 2019, https://www.rosatom.ru/en/rosatom-group/back-end/national-operator-for-radioactive-waste-management/.

70 Nikitin, "Rosatom State Corporation."

71 Oksana Boyko and Darya Pushkova, "Prominent Russians: Sergey Kiriyenko," Russiapedia, accessed October 16, 2019, https://russiapedia.rt.com/prominent-russians/politics-and-society/sergey-kirienko/; Daisy Sindelar, "Russia: Moscow Seeks to Reignite Nuclear Power Industry," Radio Free Europe/Radio Liberty, February 14, 2006, https://www.rferl.org/a/1065754.html; Victor Yasmann, "Russia: Sergei Kiriyenko – Russia's 'Kinder Surprise,'" Radio Free Europe/Radio Liberty, February 15, 2006, https://www.rferl.org/a/1065790.html; Victor Yasmann, "Russia: Moscow's New Nuclear Strategy," Radio Free Europe/Radio Liberty, February 15, 2006, https://www.rferl.org/a/1065789.html.

72 Lucy Martirosyan, "20 Years of Putin in Power: A Timeline," PRI, January 15, 2020, https://www.pri.org/stories/2019-08-09/20-years-putin-power-timeline; Will Englund and Kathy Lally, "Medvedev Confirms He Will Step Aside for Putin to Return to Russia's Presidency," *Washington Post*, September 24, 2011, https://www.washingtonpost.com/world/europe/dmitry-medvedev-asks-putin-to-run-for-president-of-russia/2011/09/24/gIQAXGwpsK_story.html; Adrian Blomfield, "Dmitry Medvedev Wins Russian Election," *Telegraph*, March 3, 2008, https://www.telegraph.co.uk/news/worldnews/1580592/Dmitry-Medvedev-wins-Russian-election.html.

73 Katusa, *The Colder War*, 63.

74 Ian Bremmer, "Putin Won. But Russia Is Losing," *Time*, March 22, 2018, https://time.com/5210520/putin-won-but-russia-is-losing/.

75 "The 'Illegals': Russian Spies Living in America?," *Week*, June 29, 2010, https://theweek.com/articles/493105/illegals-russian-spies-living-america.

76 Peter Foster, "US Isn't Global Policeman but We Must Lead by Diplomacy – Obama," Independent.ie, May 28, 2014, https://www.independent.ie/world-news/americas/us-isnt-global-policeman-but-we-must-lead-by-diplomacy-obama-30313633.html.

77 Richard Prince, "In Putin's Circle, Obama Was the 'N-Word,'" Root, March 16, 2018, https://journalisms.theroot.com/putins-circle-considered-obama-the-n-word-1823832442.

78 Dan Bilefsky, "Bulgaria, a Russian Ally, Is Left Cold and Angry," *New York Times*, January 12, 2009, https://www.nytimes.com/2009/01/12/world/europe/12iht-bulgaria.3.19283860.html; Luke Harding and Dan McLaughlin, "Deal to Resume Russian Gas Eludes EU As 11 People Die in Big Freeze-Up," *Guardian*, January 10, 2009, https://www.theguardian.com/world/2009/jan/11/russia-ukraine-gas-supplies-dispute;

Simon Pirani, Jonathan Stern, and Katja Yafimava, "The Russo-Ukrainian Gas Dispute of January 2009: A Comprehensive Assessment," Oxford Institute for Energy Studies, February 2009, https://www.oxfordenergy.org/wpcms/wp-content/uploads/2010/11/NG27-TheRussoUkrainianGasDisputeofJanuary2009ACompre-hensiveAssessment-JonathanSternSimonPiraniKatjaYafimava-2009.pdf.

79 Ibid.

80 Robert Coalson, "Russia Steps Up Cooperation with Breakaway Georgian Regions," Radio Free Europe/Radio Liberty, April 30, 2009, https://www.rferl.org/a/Russia_Steps_Up_Cooperation_With_Breakaway_Georgian_Regions/1619281.html.

81 David J. Kramer, "Resetting U.S.-Russian Relations: It Takes Two," *Washington Quarterly* 33, no. 1 (2010): 63, https://www.tandfonline.com/doi/pdf/10.1080/01636600903418694; Jesse Lee, "A Hopeful Reset," Obama White House (archive), speech, July 7, 2009, https://obamawhitehouse.archives.gov/blog/2009/07/07/a-hopeful-reset.

82 Pat Ralph, "What Happened Every Other Time Putin Met with US Presidents," Business Insider, July 17, 2018, https://www.businessinsider.com/putin-met-obama-bush-trump-clinton-us-presidents-2018-7; I. Lee, "President Barack Obama's Moscow Speech: President Addresses New Economic School Graduation," Bydewey.com, July 7, 2009, https://www.bydewey.com/obamamoscowspeech09.html.

83 Ibid.

84 "David J. Kramer," McCain Institute, accessed October 15, 2019, https://www.mccaininstitute.org/staff/david-j-kramer/; Kramer, "Resetting U.S.-Russian Relations: It Takes Two."

85 Marc A. Thiessen, "Obama Took Lying to New Heights with the Iran Deal," *Washington Post*, June 8, 2018, https://www.washingtonpost.com/opinions/obama-took-lying-to-new-heights-with-the-iran-deal/2018/06/07/b75f72d2-6a7c-11e8-9e38-24e693b38637_story.html; Lee Smith, *The Plot Against the President* (New York: Hachette Book Group, 2019), 31-32; Vladimir Frolov, "Why Russia Wants the Iran Nuclear Deal (Op-ed)," *Moscow Times*, May 8, 2018, https://www.themoscowtimes.com/2018/05/08/why-russia-wants-the-iran-deal-op-ed-a61386; Alla Eshchenko, "Obama, Putin Congratulate Each Other for Iran Deal," CNN, July 16, 2015, https://www.cnn.com/2015/07/16/politics/obama-putin-iran-nuclear-deal/index.html.

86 Ibid.

Chapter 4

1 "Remarks by President Barack Obama in Prague As Delivered," Obama White House (archive), press release, April 5, 2009, https://obamawhitehouse.archives.gov/the-press-office/remarks-president-barack-obama-prague-delivered.

2 "Birth of the Atomic Bomb," Multiwavelength Astronomy, accessed November 1, 2019, http://ecuip.lib.uchicago.edu/multiwavelength-astronomy/gamma-ray/history/.

3 "USEC, Tenex, ConverDyn Sign Agreement on Uranium Shipments to Russia," Centrus, news release, March 15, 2001, http://investors.centrusenergy.com/news-releases/news-release-details/usec-tenex-converdyn-sign-agreement-ura-nium-shipments-russia; Opensecrets.org, "Honeywell International: Summary,"

profile for all cycles, accessed November 1, 2019, https://www.opensecrets.org/orgs/summary.php?id=D000000334&cycle=A; "Obama's Crony Capitalism Posts More Pitiful Results," *Washington Examiner*, April 22, 2013, https://www.washingtonexaminer.com/examiner-editorial-obamas-crony-capitalism-posts-more-pitiful-results.

4   Ben Smith, "Cashing in on 'CHANGE,'" *Politico*, July 16, 2008, https://www.politico.com/blogs/ben-smith/2008/07/cashing-in-on-change-010324.

5   Opensecrets.org, "Client Profile: Honeywell International," summary, 2008, https://www.opensecrets.org/federal-lobbying/clients/summary?cycle=2008&id=D000000334; Opensecrets.org, "Client Profile: Exelon Corp," summary, 2009, https://www.opensecrets.org/federal-lobbying/clients/summary?cycle=2009&id=D000000368.

6   Oliver Staley, "All the Benefits Corporate Executives Unlock When They Get Access to the White House," *Quartz*, May 3, 2017, https://qz.com/974629/all-the-benefits-ceos-from-companies-like-ge-and-honeywell-hon-unlock-when-they-get-access-to-the-white-house/; Dr. Tom Borelli, "Utility Industry Aids Putin's Stealth War on US Uranium Mining," Conservative Review, March 28, 2019, https://www.conservativereview.com/news/utility-industry-aids-putins-stealth-war-u-s-uranium-mining/.

7   Ibid.; Jo Becker and Mike McIntire, "Cash Flowed to Clinton Foundation Amid Russian Uranium Deal," *New York Times*, April 23, 2015, https://www.nytimes.com/2015/04/24/us/cash-flowed-to-clinton-foundation-as-russians-pressed-for-control-of-uranium-company.html.

8   William J. Broad and David E. Sanger, "Obama's Youth Shaped His Nuclear-Free Vision," *New York Times*, July 4, 2009, https://www.nytimes.com/2009/07/05/world/05nuclear.html; Barack Obama, "Breaking the War Mentality," *Sundial*, March 10, 1983, http://www.columbia.edu/cu/computinghistory/obama-sundial.pdf.

9   Joint Subcommittee Hearing, U.S. House of Representatives, "Russian Arms Control Cheating: Violation of INF Treaty and the Administration's Responses One Year Later," 114th Cong. (2015), on Internet Archive, https://web.archive.org/web/20170430153234/https://foreignaffairs.house.gov/hearing/joint-subcommittee-hearing-russian-arms-control-cheating-violation-of-the-inf-treaty-and-the-administrations-responses-one-year-later/ (the screenshot of the site was captured on April 30, 2017); Borelli, "Utility Industry Aids Putin's Stealth War on US Uranium Mining."

10 Broad and Sanger, "Obama's Youth Shaped His Nuclear-Free Vision."

11 Mara D. Bellaby, "Russia Apologizes to Lugar, Obama After Detention at Airport," Nwi.com, August 29, 2005, https://www.nwitimes.com/news/state-and-regional/russia-apologizes-to-lugar-obama-after-detention-at-airport/article_39f411de-2421-587e-bcfc-bde7613e546f.html; Jeff Zeleny, "A Foreign Classroom for Junior Senator," *Chicago Tribune*, September 23, 2005, https://www.chicagotribune.com/nation-world/chi-0509230360sep23-story.html.

12 Zeleny, "A Foreign Classroom for Junior Senator"; Joint Subcommittee Hearing, U.S. House of Representatives, "Russian Arms Control Cheating: Violation of INF Treaty and the Administration's Responses One Year Later."

13 Lucy Martirosyan, "20 Years of Putin in Power: A Timeline," PRI, January 15, 2020, https://www.pri.org/stories/2019-08-09/20-years-putin-power-timeline; Adrian Blomfield, "Dmitry Medvedev Wins Russian Election," *Telegraph*, March 3, 2008, https://www.telegraph.co.uk/news/worldnews/1580592/Dmitry-Medvedev-wins-Russian-election.html; Will Englund and Kathy Lally, "Medvedev Confirms He Will Step Aside for Putin to Return to Russia's Presidency," *Washington Post*, September 24, 2011, https://www.washingtonpost.com/world/europe/dmitry-medvedev-asks-putin-to-run-for-president-of-russia/2011/09/24/gIQAXGwpsK_story.html.

14 Sam Savage, "Latvian Commentary Says Recognition of Abkhazia, S Ossetia Hurts Russia," RedOrbit, August 28, 2008, https://www.redorbit.com/news/international/1536309/latvian_commentary_says_recognition_of_abkhazia_s_ossetia_hurts_russia/; Englund and Lally, "Medvedev Confirms He Will Step Aside for Putin to Return to Russia's Presidency"; Hillary Rodham Clinton, *Hard Choices* (London: Simon and Schuster, 2014), 222.

15 Mark Tran, Julian Borger, and Ian Traynor, "EU Threatens Sanctions Against Russia," *Guardian*, August 28, 2008, https://www.theguardian.com/world/2008/aug/28/eu.russia; Brookings Institution, "The Brookings Foreign Policy Studies Energy Security Series: The Russian Federation," October 2006, https://www.brookings.edu/wp-content/uploads/2016/06/2006russia.pdf.

16 Mark Landler, "How Hillary Clinton Became a Hawk," *New York Times*, April 21, 2016, https://www.nytimes.com/2016/04/24/magazine/how-hillary-clinton-became-a-hawk.html; Ognyan Minchev, "Why Russia Distrusts America," Real Clear World, June 27, 2012, https://www.realclearworld.com/2012/06/27/why_russia_distrusts_america_137477.html; Erick Erickson, "Barack Obama's Post-Modern Liberal Syllogisms Keep Falling Apart," RedState, December 27, 2009, https://www.redstate.com/diary/erick/2009/12/27/barack-obamas-post-modern-liberal-syllogisms-keep-falling-apart/; Salena Zito, "Elite Democrats Lose," Real Clear Politics, April 20, 2008, https://www.realclearpolitics.com/articles/2008/04/elite_democrats_historically_los.html; John Cassidy, "What Kind of Liberal Is Obama? An Increasingly Crafty One," *New Yorker*, January 22, 2013, https://www.newyorker.com/news/john-cassidy/what-kind-of-liberal-is-obama-an-increasingly-crafty-one; Douglas Perry, "Hillary Clinton's 'Goldwater Girl' Days Unnerve Progressives, Fail to Convince Republicans," *Oregonian*, September 16, 2016, https://www.oregonlive.com/history/2016/09/hillary_clintons_goldwater_gir.html.

17 Toby Harnden, "Barack Obama: 'Arrogant US Has Been Dismissive' to Allies," *Telegraph*, April 3, 2009, https://www.telegraph.co.uk/news/worldnews/barackobama/5100338/Barack-Obama-arrogant-US-has-been-dismissive-to-allies.html.

18 Gordon Lubold, "Obama Says U.S. Will No Longer Be the World's Policeman," *Foreign Policy*, May 28, 2014, https://foreignpolicy.com/2014/05/28/obama-says-u-s-will-no-longer-be-the-worlds-policeman/; Ryan Lizza, "Leading from Behind," *New Yorker*, April 26, 2011, https://www.newyorker.com/news/news-desk/leading-from-behind.

19 David Remnick, *The Bridge: The Life and Rise of Barack Obama* (New York: Alfred A. Knopf, 2010), 81, 125-126; Eric Lipton, "Ties to Obama Aided in Access for Big

Utility," *New York Times*, August 22, 2012, https://www.nytimes.com/2012/08/23/us/politics/ties-to-obama-aided-in-access-for-exelon-corporation.html.

20 U.S. Mission to International Organizations in Geneva, "Geneva Press Briefing by Secretary of State Clinton and Foreign Minister Lavrov," March 6, 2009, https://geneva.usmission.gov/2009/03/06/clintonlavrov/.

21 Jim Geraghty, "The Infamous 'Reset' Button: Stolen from a Hotel Pool or Jacuzzi," *National Review*, March 3, 2014, https://www.nationalreview.com/the-campaign-spot/infamous-reset-button-stolen-hotel-pool-or-jacuzzi-jim-geraghty/; Eli Lake, "Russia Uses Dirty Tricks Despite U.S. 'Reset,'" *Washington Times*, August 4, 2011, https://www.washingtontimes.com/news/2011/aug/4/russia-uses-dirty-tricks-despite-us-reset/.

22 Jill Dougherty, "Clinton 'Reset Button' Gift to Russian FM Gets Lost in Translation," Political Ticker (blog), March 6, 2009, http://politicalticker.blogs.cnn.com/2009/03/06/clinton-reset-button-gift-to-russian-fm-gets-lost-in-translation/.

23 Abby Ohlheiser, "A Not-So-Brief List of All the Things President Obama Has Bowed to," *Atlantic*, April 24, 2014, https://www.theatlantic.com/politics/archive/2014/04/a-not-so-brief-list-of-all-the-things-president-obama-has-bowed-to/361160/.

24 Robert M. Gates, *Duty: Memoirs of a Secretary at War* (New York: Alfred A. Knopf, 2014), 261; Associated Press, "Russian Spies Receive Top Honours."

25 Gates, *Duty*, 261.

26 Ibid.

27 "Suspected Russian Spies Charged in US," BBC News, June 29, 2010, https://www.bbc.com/news/10442223; Seamus Bruner, *Compromised* (New York: Post Hill Press, 2018), 16, 59, 65.

28 Gates, *Duty*, 261.

29 Ibid.

30 Ibid.; Bruner, *Compromised*, 65.

31 Gates, *Duty*, 261.

32 Ibid.

33 Ibid.; Associated Press, "Russian Spies Receive Top Honours," *Guardian*, October 19, 2010, https://www.theguardian.com/world/2010/oct/19/russian-spies-receive-top-honours; Shaun Walker, "The Russian Spy Who Posed As a Canadian for More Than 20 Years," *Guardian*, August 23, 2019, https://www.theguardian.com/world/2019/aug/23/russian-spy-elena-vavilova-posed-as-a-canadian-estate-agent-for-over-20-years.

34 Associated Press, "Russian Spies Receive Top Honours"; Edecio Martinez, "Anna Chapman (PICTURES): Who Is the Russian "Femme Fatale"?," CBS News, June 30, 2010, https://www.cbsnews.com/news/anna-chapman-pictures-who-is-the-russian-femme-fatale/.

35 Associated Press, "Russian Spies Receive Top Honours"; "Elena Vavilova: Writer, Speaker, and Ex-Spy," Elenavavilova.ru, accessed on October 29, 2019.

36 Tom Parfitt, "Vladimir Putin Consoles Exposed Russian Spies with 'Singalong,'" *Guardian*, July 25, 2010, https://www.theguardian.com/world/2010/jul/25/vladimir-putin-russian-spy-ring.

37 Monica Showalter, "Putincide? Quite a Few Russian Diplomats Meeting Untimely Ends," American Thinker, February 27, 2017, https://www.americanthinker.com/

blog/2017/02/putincide_quite_a_few_russian_diplomats_meeting_untimely_
ends.html; Former National Intelligence Council Chairman Fritz Ermarth,
interview with author.

38 Ken Dilanian, "Obama Scraps Bush Missile-Defense Plan," ABC News, September 17,
2009, https://abcnews.go.com/Politics/obama-scraps-bush-missile-defense-plan/
story?id=8604357.

39 "Russia's Western Neighbours: Ukraine Comes to the Forefront," *Economist*, September 11, 2008, https://www.economist.com/taxonomy/term/122?page=35.

40 David J. Kramer, "Resetting U.S.-Russian Relations: It Takes Two," *Washington
Quarterly* 33, no. 1 (2010): 65-68, https://www.tandfonline.com/doi/pdf/10.1080/
01636600903418694; Thom Shanker and Nicholas Kulish, "U.S. and Poland Set Missile
Deal," *New York Times*, August 14, 2008, https://www.nytimes.com/2008/08/15
/world/europe/15poland.html; Gates, *Duty*, 254.

41 Peter Baker, "Obama Offered Deal to Russia in Secret Letter," *New York Times*,
March 2, 2009, https://www.nytimes.com/2009/03/03/washington/03prexy.html;
"Obama Explains Medvedev Missile Letter," YouTube video, posted by "Theman-
tesdotcom," March 3, 2009, https://www.youtube.com/watch?v=Bg2rBa7miqI.

42 Gates, *Duty*, 256-257.

43 Ibid., 254-256.

44 Central Intelligence Agency, "Biography of Mr. Robert M. Gates," August 19, 2011, https://
www.cia.gov/library/readingroom/docs/CIA-RDP90G00152R000801530018
-4.pdf.

45 "Timeline: Missile Defense, 1944-2002," *Frontline*, PBS, accessed October 14, 2019,
https://www.pbs.org/wgbh/pages/frontline/shows/missile/etc/cron.html.

46 "Robert M. Gates Oral History," Miller Center, transcript, July 23-24, 2000, https://
millercenter.org/the-presidency/presidential-oral-histories/robert-m-gates-deputy
-director-central.

47 "Timeline: Missile Defense, 1944-2002."

48 Gates, *Duty*, 104, 254; "Strategic Defense Initiative (SDI)," Atomic Heritage Foundation, July 18, 2018, https://www.atomicheritage.org/history/strategic-defense
-initiative-sdi.

49 Michael Frane, "Providing Adequate Funding for Defense," Heritage Foundation,
January 24, 2007, https://www.heritage.org/defense/commentary/providing-ad-
equate-funding-defense; Baker Spring, "Clinton's Failed Missile Defense Policy:
A Legacy of Missed Opportunities," Heritage Foundation, September 21, 2000,
https://www.heritage.org/defense/report/clintons-failed-missile-defense-policy
-legacy-missedopportunities.

50 Gates, *Duty*, 104, 254; "Strategic Defense Initiative (SDI)," Atomic Heritage
Foundation.

51 Gates, *Duty*, 254.

52 Terence Neilan, "Bush Pulls Out of ABM Treaty; Putin Calls Move a Mistake,"
New York Times, December 13, 2001, https://www.nytimes.com/2001/12/13/inter-
national/bush-pulls-out-of-abm-treaty-putin-calls-move-a-mistake.html; World
Freedom Foundation, *Vladimir Putin – Direct Speech Without Cuts: Russian Strategy for Winning the Geopolitical Game* (Int'l Business Publications: 2015), 168;

Cadence Quaranta, "Former U.S. Ambassador to Russia Michael McFaul Says U.S. and Russia Are Not Natural Enemies," *Daily Northwestern*, May 17, 2019, https://dailynorthwestern.com/2019/05/17/campus/former-u-s-ambassador-to-russia-michael-mcfaul-says-u-s-and-russia-are-not-natural-enemies/; Amber Phillips, "18 Not-So-Nice Things U.S. Politicians Have Said about Vladimir Putin," *Washington Post*, June 10, 2015, https://www.washingtonpost.com/news/the-fix/wp/2015/06/10/from-honest-to-killer-u-s-leaders-have-said-many-disparate-things-about-putin/.

53 "President Obama's Remarks in Turkey," *New York Times*, April 6, 2009, https://www.nytimes.com/2009/04/06/us/politics/06obama-text.html; "Barack Obama Tells Muslims 'Americans Are Not Your Enemy,'" *Telegraph*, January 27, 2009, https://www.telegraph.co.uk/news/worldnews/barackobama/4354579/Barack-Obama-tells-Muslims-Americans-are-not-your-enemy.html.

54 Nile Gardiner and Morgan Lorraine Roach, "Barack Obama's Top 10 Apologies: How the President Has Humiliated a Superpower," Heritage Foundation, June 2, 2009, https://www.heritage.org/node/14384/print-display; "Obama's G20 Press Conference," CBS News, transcript, April 2, 2009, https://www.cbsnews.com/news/transcript-obamas-g20-press-conference/.

55 Jaime Sneider, "Obama's Missing Thesis," *Washington Examiner*, July 25, 2008, https://www.washingtonexaminer.com/weekly-standard/obamas-missing-thesis; Broad and Sanger, "Obama's Youth Shaped His Nuclear-Free Vision"; Obama, "Breaking the War Mentality"; Joby Warrick, "Obama's Policy on Iran Bears Some Fruit but Nuclear Program Still Advances," *Washington Post*, September 24, 2012, https://www.washingtonpost.com/world/national-security/obamas-policy-on-iran-bears-some-fruit-but-nuclear-program-still-advances/2012/09/24/f51f9a04-fc21-11e1-a31e-804fccb658f9_story.html; Jacqueline Cabasso, "Atoms for Peace, Then and Now," Western States Legal Foundation, Summer 2012, http://www.wslfweb.org/docs/atomsforpeace2012.pdf.

56 Cabasso, "Atoms for Peace, Then and Now"; Emily B. Landau and Azriel Bermant, "The Nuclear Nonproliferation Regime at a Crossroads," Institute for National Security Studies, Memo No. 137, May 2014, https://www.files.ethz.ch/isn/180773/memo137%20(5)_May%2020.pdf; Alexander Mooney, "Obama Says Time to Rid World of Nuclear Weapons," CNN, accessed November 2, 2019, https://www.cnn.com/2008/POLITICS/07/16/obama.speech/.

57 U.S. Department of Defense, "New START Treaty: Executive Summary," Active Strategic Treaties, accessed October 14, 2019, https://www.acq.osd.mil/tc/nst/NSTexecsum.htm.

58 Gates, *Duty*, 259.

59 Mary Beth Nikitin, "U.S.-Russian Civilian Nuclear Cooperation Agreement: Issues for Congress," Congressional Research Service, January 11, 2011, https://fas.org/sgp/crs/nuke/RL34655.pdf; U.S. Nuclear Regulatory Commission, "Nuclear Regulatory Legislation," 112th Cong. (September 2013), https://www.nrc.gov/docs/ML1327/ML13274A489.pdf.

60 Nikitin, "U.S.-Russian Civilian Nuclear Cooperation Agreement: Issues for Congress"; Holly Ellyatt, "Russia Is Still Occupying 20% of Our Country, Georgia's Prime Minister Says," CNBC, January 22, 2019, https://www.cnbc.com/2019/01/22/russia-is-still-occupying-20percent-of-our-country-georgias-leader-says.html.

61 "The U.S.-Russian Agreement for Peaceful Nuclear Cooperation," Nuclear Threat Initiative, June 22, 2010, https://www.nti.org/analysis/articles/us-russian-peaceful-cooperation/; Nikitin, "U.S.-Russian Civilian Nuclear Cooperation Agreement: Issues for Congress."

62 "Russian Spent Nuclear Fuel," Nuclear Threat Initiative, February 1, 2003, https://www.nti.org/analysis/articles/russian-spent-nuclear-fuel/; "The U.S.-Russian Agreement for Peaceful Nuclear Cooperation."

63 Bureau of Public Affairs, "The Agreement Between the Government of the United States of America and the Government of the Russian Federation… (U.S.-Russia 123 Agreement)," U.S. Department of State, press release, January 12, 2011, https://2009-2017.state.gov/r/pa/prs/ps/2011/01/154318.htm; Zeba Reyahzuddin, e-mail message to Nathan P. Lane, "CFIUS Certification to Congress," U.S. Department of State, November 4, 2010; Jessica Kwong, "Russia Routed Millions to Influence Clinton in Uranium Deal, Informant Tells Congress," *Newsweek*, February 8, 2018, https://www.newsweek.com/russia-routed-millions-influence-clinton-uranium-deal-informant-tells-congress-801686.

64 Lake, "Russia Uses Dirty Tricks Despite U.S. 'Reset'"; John R. Schindler, "Hillary's Secret Kremlin Connection Is Quickly Unraveling," *Observer*, August 25, 2016, https://observer.com/2016/08/hillarys-secret-kremlin-connection-is-quickly-unraveling/; Andrew C. McCarthy, "The Obama Administration's Uranium One Scandal," *National Review*, October 21, 2017, https://www.nationalreview.com/2017/10/uranium-one-deal-obama-administration-doj-hillary-clinton-racketeering/; Benjamin Haddad and Alina Polyakova, "Don't Rehabilitate Obama on Russia," Brookings Institution, March 5, 2018, https://www.brookings.edu/blog/order-from-chaos/2018/03/05/dont-rehabilitate-obama-on-russia/.

65 Ibid.

66 John Judis, "Creation Myth," *New Republic*, September 10, 2008, https://carnegieendowment.org/2008/09/10/creation-myth-pub-20444; Remnick, *The Bridge*, 40.

67 Broad and Sanger, "Obama's Youth Shaped His Nuclear-Free Vision"; Jeremy Kuzmaro, *Obama's Unending Wars: Fronting the Foreign Policy of the Permanent Warfare State* (Atlanta: Clarity Press, 2019).

68 Sneider, "Obama's Missing Thesis."

69 Obama, "Breaking the War Mentality"; Jonah Goldberg, "Obama in Denial on Russia," *National Review*, March 6, 2014, https://www.nationalreview.com/2014/03/obama-denial-russia-jonah-goldberg/.

70 Remnick, *The Bridge*, 76.

71 "U.S. Public Interest Research Group (US-PIRG)," Influence Watch, accessed October 23, 2019, https://www.influencewatch.org/non-profit/u-s-public-interest-research-group/; "About Us," U.S. PIRG, accessed October 23, 2019, https://uspirg.org/page/usp/about-us-pirg-0.

72 Remnick, *The Bridge*, 76.

73 Ibid., 76, 80-82, 86.

74 Ibid., 80-82.

75 Ibid., 81-83.

76 Lipton, "Ties to Obama Aided in Access for Big Utility"; Remnick, *The Bridge*, 81.

77 Kimberley A. Strassel, "Obama and the Chicago Machine," *Wall Street Journal*, July 9, 2010, https://www.wsj.com/articles/SB10001424052748704111704575355222465098664.

78 Remnick, *The Bridge*, 125-126.

79 Ibid., 81, 126; James Warren, "Rahm the Screwup," *Politico*, April 8, 2015, https://www.politico.com/magazine/story/2015/04/rahm-emanuel-election-chicago-116765.

80 Lachlan Markay, "Obama Hails Green Energy Profit Potential at Environmental Business Summit," Washington Free Beacon, August 25, 2015, https://freebeacon.com/issues/obama-hails-green-energy-profit-potential-at-environmental-business-summit/.

81 Remnick, *The Bridge*, 59, 73, 83.

82 Ibid., 64, 123, 126; Binyamin Appelbaum, "Obama Haunted by Friend's Help Securing Dream House," Boston.com (archive), March 16, 2008, http://archive.boston.com/news/nation/articles/2008/03/16/obama_haunted_by_friends_help_securing_dream_house/; Bob Goldsborough, "Obama Foundation CEO Buys Kenwood House Near Barack Obama's for $900,000," *Hartford Courant*, June 22, 2018, https://www.courant.com/ct-re-elite-street-david-simas-20180622-story.html.

83 Appelbaum, "Obama Haunted by Friend's Help Securing Dream House"; Brian Ross and Rhonda Schwartz, "The Rezko Connection: Obama's Achilles Heel?," ABC News, January 9, 2008, https://abcnews.go.com/Blotter/rezko-connection-obamas-achilles-heel/story?id=4111483.

84 Appelbaum, "Obama Haunted by Friend's Help Securing Dream House"; Remnick, *The Bridge*, 146-147.

85 Appelbaum, "Obama Haunted by Friend's Help Securing Dream House"; Tim Novak, "Broken Promises, Broken Homes," *Chicago Sun Times*, on Internet Archive, April 24, 2007, https://web.archive.org/web/20080324131917/http://www.suntimes.com/news/metro/355099,cst-nws-rez24a.article (the screenshot of the site was captured on Mach 24, 2008).

86 Andrew Stern, "One-time Obama Fundraiser Guilty in Corruption Trial," Reuters, June 4, 2008, https://www.reuters.com/article/us-crime-rezko/one-time-obama-fundraiser-guilty-in-corruption-trial-idUSN0539204420080605; "Tony Rezko Gets 10½ Years," NBC Chicago, November 22, 2011, https://www.nbcchicago.com/blogs/ward-room/Tony-Rezko-Gets-10-and-a-Half-Years-134329878.html; Patrick J. Fitzgerald, "Businessman and Political Fundraiser Antoin Rezko Indicted in Two Fraud Cases, Including Scheme to Extort Millions of Dollars from Firms Seeking Teachers' Pension Fund Investments," U.S. Department of Justice, press release, October 11, 2006, https://www.justice.gov/archive/usao/iln/chicago/2006/pr1011_01.pdf; Mike Parker, Dana Kozlov, and the Associated Press, "Jury Finds Tony Rezko Guilty on 16 of 24 Charges," CBS2 Chicago, on Internet Archive, June 4, 2008, https://web.archive.org/web/20080605063726/http://cbs2chicago.com/local/rezko.trial.verdict.2.740375.html (the screenshot of the site was captured on June 5, 2008); Ray Long and Rick Pearson, "Impeached Illinois Gov. Rod Blagojevich Has Been Removed from Office," *Chicago Tribune*, January 30, 2009, https://www.chicagotribune.com/news/chi-blagojevich-impeachment-removal-story.html.

87 Ibid.

88 "Exelon Generation: Nuclear," Exelon, accessed November 1, 2019, https://www.exeloncorp.com/companies/exelon-generation/nuclear; Thomas Heath and Aaron C. Davis, "D.C. Regulators Give Green Light to Pepco-Exelon Merger, Creating Largest Utility in the Nation," *Washington Post*, March 23, 2016, https://www.washingtonpost.com/local/dc-politics/in-a-surprise-move-dc-regulators-give-green-light-to-pepco-exelon-merger/2016/03/23/4ace2bc0-f10e-11e5-89c3-a647fcce95e0_story.html.

89 U.S. Nuclear Regulatory Commission, "Operating Nuclear Power Reactors," accessed November 2, 2019, https://www.nrc.gov/info-finder/reactors/; "Nuclear Share of Electricity Generation in 2018," International Atomic Energy Agency, last updated February 29, 2020, https://pris.iaea.org/PRIS/WorldStatistics/NuclearShareofElectricityGeneration.aspx; Ed Lasky, "The President's Utility: Crony Capitalism in Chicago Turns "Green" into Greenbacks," Capital Research Center, September 10, 2013, https://capitalresearch.org/article/14995/; "Nuclear Power in the European Union," World Nuclear Association, last updated February 2020, https://www.world-nuclear.org/information-library/country-profiles/others/european-union.aspx.

90 Ibid.; "Exelon Generation: Nuclear"; "Powering a Cleaner and Brighter Future for Our Customers and Communities," Exelon, 2018 Summary Annual Report, https://www.exeloncorp.com/company/Documents/Exelon-Annual-Report-2018.pdf; "About Exelon: America's Leading Energy Power," Exelon, accessed November 1, 2019, https://www.exeloncorp.com/company/about-exelon.

91 Stacie Babula, "Clinton Backs Deregulation * Large Power Providers Divided on How to Promote Nationwide Measure," *Morning Call*, April 16, 1999, https://www.mcall.com/news/mc-xpm-1999-04-16-3255468-story.html.

92 Leonard S. Hyman, "The Best Laid Schemes…," mThink, accessed November 1, 2019, https://mthink.com/legacy/www.utilitiesproject.com/content/pdf/UTP2_wp_hyman.pdf; Lucas W. Davis and Catherine Wolfram, "Deregulation, Consolidation, and Efficiency: Evidence from U.S. Nuclear Power," Stanford University, August 2011, https://web.stanford.edu/group/SITE/archive/SITE_2011/2011_segment_6/2011_segment_6_papers/wolfram.pdf; W.M. Warwick, "A Primer on Electric Utilities, Deregulation, and Restructuring of U.S. Electricity Markets," Prepared for the U.S. Department of Energy Federal Energy Management Program, July 2000, https://www.pnnl.gov/main/publications/external/technical_reports/PNNL-13906.pdf; Travis Hoium, "Why Consolidation is the Name of the Game in the Utility Space," Motley Fool, June 4, 2016, https://www.fool.com/investing/2016/06/04/why-consolidation-is-the-name-of-the-game-in-the-u.aspx.

93 "Exelon Executive Wins Lifetime Achievement Award for Contributions to the Energy Industry," Exelon, December 3, 2010, https://www.exeloncorp.com/newsroom/Pages/pr_20101203_EXC_MolerLifetimeAchievement.aspx; United States Securities and Exchange Commission, Form 8-K, Exelon Corporation, June 20, 2002, https://www.sec.gov/Archives/edgar/data/22606/000095015902000382/ex99-7.txt; Eamon Javers, "How Rahm Got Rich," *Politico*, November 19, 2008, https://www.politico.com/story/2008/11/how-rahm-got-rich-015760.

94 Javers, "How Rahm Got Rich"; Curtis Black, "Chicago's Violence Tied to Policies of Rahm's Past," *Chicago Reporter*, April 23, 2014, https://www.chicagoreporter.com/chicagos-violence-tied-policies-rahms-past/; Lasky, "The President's Utility."

95 Javers, "How Rahm Got Rich."

96 Michael Luo, "In Banking, Emanuel Made Money and Connections," *New York Times*, December 3, 2008, https://www.nytimes.com/2008/12/04/us/politics/04emanuel.html.

97 Ibid.; Remnick, *The Bridge*.

98 Javers, "How Rahm Got Rich."

99 "Order No. 888," Federal Energy Regulatory Commission; "Order No. 888," Federal Energy Regulatory Commission, issued April 24, 1996, https://www.ferc.gov/legal/maj-ord-reg/land-docs/rm95-8-00w.txt; "Order No. 889," Federal Energy Regulatory Commission; "Order No. 889," Federal Energy Regulatory Commission, issued April 24, 1996, https://www.ferc.gov/legal/maj-ord-reg/land-docs/rm95-9-00k.txt; Martha M. Hamilton, "Clinton to Offer Plan to Deregulate Power," *Washington Post*, March 25, 1998, https://www.washingtonpost.com/wp-srv/politics/govt/admin/stories/pena032598.htm; "Energy Incentives Reborn: Deregulation Driven Funding for Energy-Efficiency Strategies," GreenBiz, May 13, 2002, https://www.greenbiz.com/news/2002/05/13/energy-incentives-reborn-deregulation-driven-funding-energy-efficiency-strategies; Javers, "How Rahm Got Rich."

100 Javers, "How Rahm Got Rich"; "ComEd, Peco Expect Rapid Merger Review," Natural Gas Intelligence, November 29, 1999, https://www.naturalgasintel.com/articles/94299-comed-peco-expect-rapid-merger-review.

101 "Dresdner Buys Wasserstein," CNN Money, September 18, 2000, https://money.cnn.com/2000/09/18/deals/dresdner_wasserstein/index.htm; Javers, "How Rahm Got Rich"; "Dresdner Closes Its Acquisition of U.S. Firm Wasserstein Perella," *Wall Street Journal*, January 5, 2001, https://www.wsj.com/articles/SB978639345602612988; United States Securities and Exchange Commission, Form 8-K, Exelon Corporation, October 26, 2006, https://www.sec.gov/Archives/edgar/data/78100/000095013706011523/c09463e8vk.htm; Edward A. Weihman, "Gasification Technologies 2004" (presentation, Washington, DC, October 3-6, 2004), https://www.globalsyngas.org/uploads/eventLibrary/15WEIH.pdf.

102 Ibid.; David Crawford, "Dresdner's Man in Russia," *Wall Street Journal*, April 26, 2005, https://www.wsj.com/articles/SB111446508809216383.

103 Kathy Bergen, "One Year In: Mayor Rahm Emanuel Tightens Ties with Business," *Chicago Tribune*, May 14, 2012, https://www.chicagotribune.com/business/ct-xpm-2012-05-14-ct-biz-0511-rahm-business-20120514-story.html; Aaron Cynic, "Rahm's Email Dump Pulls Back the Curtain on Top Donor Interests," Chicagoist, December 22, 2016, https://chicagoist.com/2016/12/22/emanuels_emails_reveal_interests_of.php; Michael Dobbs, "Obama's 'Backroom Deal'?," *Washington Post*, February 14, 2008, http://voices.washingtonpost.com/fact-checker/2008/02/obamas_backroom_deal.html; Lipton, "Ties to Obama Aided in Access for Big Utility"; Lasky, "The President's Utility"; Mike McIntire, "Nuclear Leaks and Response Tested Obama in Senate," *New York Times*, February 3, 2008, https://www.nytimes.com/2008/02/03/us/politics/03exelon.html?_r=1&hp&oref=slogin.

104 Lasky, "The President's Utility."

105 Ibid.

106 Ibid.; Rich Miller, "Rate Freeze Updates...UPDATE: Forby Shafted by Jones," Capitol Fax, April 20, 2007, https://capitolfax.com/wp-mobile.php?p=3465&more=1;

"ECON, ComEd Rate Increases," Proviso Probe (blog), September 15, 2006, http://provisoprobe.blogspot.com/2006/09/econ-comed-rate-increases.html; Crystal Yednak, "ComEd Is Behind 'Consumer' Warning," *Chicago Tribune*, on Internet Archive, January 5, 2007, https://web.archive.org/web/20070228000945/http://www.chicagotribune.com/news/nationworld/chi-0701050175jan05,0,719876,print.story (the screenshot of the site was captured on February 28, 2007).

107 "Exelon Corp," LittleSis, accessed November 1, 2019, https://littlesis.org/org/283561-Exelon_Corporation/political; Eric Lipton, "Ties to Obama Aided in Access for Big Utility."

108 "Christopher M. Crane," LittleSis, profile, accessed November 1, 2019, https://littlesis.org/person/2840-Christopher_M_Crane/political; Lasky, "The President's Utility"; Opensecrets.org, "Barack Obama's Bundlers," accessed November 1, 2019, https://www.opensecrets.org/pres12/bundlers.php.

109 Robert Sam Anson, "Obama's Power Grid," *Vanity Fair*, October 13, 2011, https://www.vanityfair.com/news/2011/10/obama-nuclear-201110; Opensecrets.org, "Barack Obama (D)," accessed November 1, 2019, https://www.opensecrets.org/pres08/bundlers.php?id=N00009638; "Frank M. Clark," LittleSis, accessed November 1, 2019, https://littlesis.org/person/2333-Frank_M_Clark/political; Steve Daniels, "ComEd CEO Frank Clark Sets Retirement," *Crain's Chicago Business*, September 8, 2011, https://www.chicagobusiness.com/article/20110908/NEWS11/110909911/comed-ceo-frank-clark-sets-retirement.

110 Eloise Harper and Tahman Bradley, "Clinton Accuses Obama of Cutting Deals with Contributor," ABC News, April 14, 2009, https://abcnews.go.com/Politics/Vote2008/story?id=4275897&page=1; "Irony Alert: Clinton Criticized Obama over Backroom Nuclear Deals in 2008," *Week*, April 27, 2015, https://theweek.com/speedreads/551824/irony-alert-clinton-criticized-obama-over-backroom-nuclear-deals-2008; Dobbs, "Obama's 'Backroom Deal'?"

111 "Illinois Sues Exelon for Radioactive Tritium Releases Since 1996," Environment News Service, March 21, 2006, http://www.ens-newswire.com/ens/mar2006/2006-03-21-02.asp.

112 Dobbs, "Obama's 'Backroom Deal'?"; Robyn Monaghan, "Exelon's Cover-up," *Daily Journal*, January 29, 2006, https://www.daily-journal.com/news/local/exelon-s-cover-up/article_64b1d6b7-2616-59d7-95e5-d009746fcd0f.html.

113 Dobbs, "Obama's 'Backroom Deal'?"

114 McIntire, "Nuclear Leaks and Response Tested Obama in Senate"; Taylor Marsh, "Obama Hearts Nuke Giant Exelon," *Huffington Post*, February 4, 2008, https://www.huffpost.com/entry/obama-hearts-nuke-giant-e_b_84824; Dobbs, "Obama's 'Backroom Deal'?"

115 "Irony Alert: Clinton Criticized Obama over Backroom Nuclear Deals in 2008"; Lisa Lerer, "Obamamania Verges on Obsession," *Politico*, February 20, 2008, https://www.politico.com/story/2008/02/obamamania-verges-on-obsession-008605; Becker and McIntire, "Cash Flowed to Clinton Foundation Amid Russian Uranium Deal"; McCarthy, "The Obama Administration's Uranium One Scandal."

116 LD-2 lobbying disclosure form for Exelon Business Services, LLC, for 2008, quarter 4, https://soprweb.senate.gov/index.cfm?event=getFilingDetails&filingID=1B-F930B1-826B-4A68-9A87-B83A07DA0F7D&filingTypeID=78.

117 Opensecrets.org, "Client Profile: Exelon Corp."

118 Lasky, "The President's Utility."

119 Lipton, "Ties to Obama Aided in Access for Big Utility."

120 Ibid.; Nancy Pfotenhauer, "Solyndra, Cronyism, and Double-Dipping on the Tax-payers' Dime," U.S. News, July 23, 2012, https://www.usnews.com/opinion/blogs/nancy-pfotenhauer/2012/07/23/solyndra-cronyism-and-double-dipping-on-the-taxpayers-dime-; Lasky, "The President's Utility"; Charles Herrick, "President Obama's War on Coal? Some Historical Perspective," Issues XXXIV, no. 2 (Winter 2018), https://issues.org/real-numbers-president-obamas-war-on-coal/.

121 Deborah Zabarenko, "Rift at U.S. Chamber of Commerce over Climate Change," Reuters, September 30, 2009, https://www.reuters.com/article/us-climate-usa-commerce/rift-at-u-s-chamber-of-commerce-over-climate-change-idUS-TRE58S5XH20090930; "NRG Energy, Inc. Joins United States Climate Action Partnership," Business Wire, press release, July 18, 2007, https://investors.nrg.com/node/10911/pdf.

122 Pfotenhauer, "Solyndra, Cronyism, and Double-Dipping on the Taxpayers' Dime"; Kellan Howell and Stephen Dinan, "Solyndra Misled Government to Get $535M Solar Project Loan: Report," Washington Times, August 26, 2015, https://www.washingtontimes.com/news/2015/aug/26/solyndra-misled-govern-ment-get-535-million-solar-p/; Kristen Lombardi, "Stimulus Recipient, Polluter Gives Dems $10 Million Credit Line," Public Integrity, March 17, 2011, https://publicin-tegrity.org/politics/stimulus-recipient-polluter-gives-dems-10-million-credit-line/.

123 Charles Digges, "Russia Secures America's Exelon As Its Fourth Customer in Growing Number of Commercial Uranium Deals," Bellona, June 9, 2009, https://bellona.org/news/nuclear-issues/radioactive-waste-and-spent-nuclear-fuel/2009-06-russia-secures-americas-exelon-as-its-fourth-customer-in-growing-number-of-commercial-uranium-deals; "Exelon Corp Signs Uranium Supply Deal with Russia," Reuters, June 3, 2009, https://www.reuters.com/article/us-exelon-rus-sia-uranium-idUSTRE5522VB20090603; "Exelon and Tenex Sign Long-Term Enrichment Contract in Edinburgh During WNFM," Tenex, February 6, 2009, https://tenex.ru/en/media-center/news/exelon-and-tenex-sign-long-term-enrich-ment-contract-in-edinburgh-during-wnfm/.

124 Anson, "Obama's Power Grid."

125 U.S. International Trade Commission, "Uranium from Russia," Investigation No. 731-TA-539-C, February 2012, https://www.usitc.gov/publications/701_731/pub4307.pdf; Techsnabexport v. United States, 515 F. Supp. 2d 1363 (Ct. Intl. Trade 2007), https://www.courtlistener.com/opinion/818162/techsnabexport-v-united-states/.

126 Ibid.

127 Borelli, "Utility Industry Aids Putin's Stealth War on US Uranium Mining."

128 Keith B. Payne and Mark B. Schneider, "The Nuclear Treaty Russia Won't Stop Violating," Wall Street Journal, February 11, 2014, https://www.wsj.com/arti-cles/the-nuclear-treaty-russia-won8217t-stop-violating-1392166706; Becker and McIntire, "Cash Flowed to Clinton Foundation Amid Russian Uranium Deal"; Samuel Charap, "Obama's Russia Reset Is Crucial for European Security," Guardian, November 18, 2010, https://www.theguardian.com/commentisfree/

cifamerica/2010/nov/18/barack-obama-russia-reset-european-security; Polina Sinovets, "Why Russia Undermines the Norm of Nuclear Disarmament," PONARS Eurasia, Memo No. 305, December 2013, http://www.ponarseurasia.org/memo/ why-russia-undermines-norm-nuclear-disarmament.

129 U.S. International Trade Commission, "Uranium from Russia."

130 Dmitry Sudakov, "Russian Nuclear Energy Conquers the World," Pravda.ru, January 22, 2013, https://www.pravdareport.com/russia/123551-russia_nuclear_energy/.

131 Steve Gutterman, "U.S.-Russian Civilian Nuclear Deal Boosts," Reuters, January 11, 2011, https://www.reuters.com/article/us-russia-usa-nuclear/u-s-russian-civilian-nuclear-deal-boosts-reset-idUSTRE70A5LB20110111; Borelli, "Utility Industry Aids Putin's Stealth War on US Uranium Mining."

132 U.S. International Trade Commission, "Uranium from Russia"; Ben Goldey, "50 Members of Congress and Stakeholders Urge the President to Make American Uranium Great Again," Congressional Western Caucus, press release, July 12, 2019, https://westerncaucus.house.gov/news/documentsingle.aspx?DocumentID=3082; Ana Swanson, "Trump Backs Away from Barriers on Foreign Uranium," *New York Times*, July 13, 2019, https://www.nytimes.com/2019/07/13/us/politics/trump-uranium-trade.html.

133 Ibid.; Borelli, "Utility Industry Aids Putin's Stealth War on US Uranium Mining."

134 Lynn Sweet, "Obama Foundation First Corporate Donors: Exelon, Microsoft Give $1 Mil," *Chicago Sun Times*, July 14, 2017, https://chicago.suntimes.com/2017/7/14/18350402/obama-foundation-first-corporate-donors-exelon-microsoft-give-1-mil; Manya Brachear Pashman, "Exelon, Microsoft Among Latest Donors to Obama Foundation," *Chicago Tribune*, July 14, 2017, https://www.chicagotribune.com/news/obama-center/ct-obama-foundation-donors-met-0714-20170714-story.html.

135 Ibid.; "Contributors," Obama.org, accessed November 2, 2019, https://www.obama.org/contributors/; Diana Stancy Correll, "Obama Delivers Speech to Boeing After $10M Donation Made to His Presidential Center," *Washington Examiner*, January 28, 2019, https://www.washingtonexaminer.com/news/obama-delivers-speech-to-boeing-after-10m-donation-made-to-his-presidential-center.

136 Charles D'agata, "Putin's Poll Numbers Plummet, But He's Still on Top," CBS News, December 16, 2011, https://www.cbsnews.com/news/putins-poll-numbers-plummet-but-hes-still-on-top/; Joshua Keating, "Vova and Dima 4eva?," *Foreign Policy*, September 16, 2019, https://foreignpolicy.com/slideshow/vova-and-dima-4eva/.

137 Clinton, *Hard Choices*, 222.

138 Gates, *Duty*, 259.

139 "Obama Tells Russia's Medvedev More Flexibility After Election," Reuters, March 26, 2012, https://www.reuters.com/article/us-nuclear-summit-obama-medvedev/obama-tells-russias-medvedev-more-flexibility-after-election-idUSBRE82P0JI20120326; Jillian Rayfield, "Obama: The '80s Called, They Want Their Foreign Policy Back," *Salon*, October 23, 2012, https://www.salon.com/2012/10/23/obama_the_80s_called_they_want_their_foreign_policy_back/.

140 "Barack Obama: The Changes of the Human Spirit Make This World a Better Place," Russia House, August 4, 2011, http://russiahouse.org/current_news. php?language=eng&id_current=91.

141 Haddad and Polyakova, "Don't Rehabilitate Obama on Russia"; Lake, "Russia Uses Dirty Tricks Despite U.S. 'Reset.'"

142 Harnden, "Barack Obama: 'Arrogant US Has Been Dismissive' to Allies."

143 Chris Cillizza, "President Obama Admits His Biggest Mistake: Arrogance," *Washington Post*, November 17, 2015, https://www.washingtonpost.com/news/the-fix/wp/2015/11/17/president-obamas-biggest-mistake-in-office-thinking-you-can-separate-politics-from-policy/; Karl Rove, "The President's Apology Tour," *Wall Street Journal*, April 23, 2009, https://www.wsj.com/articles/SB124044156269345357; Gates, *Duty*, 256.

144 Stephen Greenspan, "Foolish Arrogance: When High Self-Esteem Blinds You to Risk," *Psychology Today*, January 9, 2012, https://www.psychologytoday.com/us/blog/incompetence/201201/foolish-arrogance; Jonathan A. Knee, *The Accidental Investment Banker: Inside the Decade that Transformed Wall Street* (New York: Oxford University Press, 2006), 190.

145 Ester Bloom, "4 Celebrities Who Didn't Pay Off Their Student Loans Until Their 40s," CNBC, May 12, 2017, https://www.cnbc.com/2017/05/12/4-celebrities-who-didnt-pay-off-their-student-loans-until-their-40s.html; Rachel Wallace, "Barack and Michelle Obama Buy an $11.75 Million Home on Martha's Vineyard," *Architectural Digest*, December 6, 2019, https://www.architecturaldigest.com/story/barack-and-michelle-obama-buy-a-home-on-marthas-vineyard.

Chapter 5

1 "$100,000,000 Donation by Vancouver Tycoon," *Vancouver Sun*, June 22, 2007; James Rickards, *Aftermath: Seven Secrets of Wealth Preservation in the Coming Chaos* (New York: Penguin, 2019).

2 "HarperCollins Announces Publication of Peter Schweizer's Explosive Clinton Expose," HarperCollins Publishers, press release, March 5, 2015; "Clinton Cash," HarperCollins Publishers, on sale May 5, 2015, https://www.harpercollins.com/9780062369284/clinton-cash/.

3 E-mail message from robbymook2015@gmail.com to john.podesta@gmail.com and melias@perkinscoie.com, "Re: SCHWEIZER / Clinton Cash," Wikileaks, March 21, 2015, https://wikileaks.org/podesta-emails/emailid/29; Meghan Daum, "These Two Sisters Couldn't Be Closer – Or More Politically Opposed," *Vogue*, December 15, 2015, https://www.vogue.com/article/sisters-kori-kristina-schake-politics-liberal-democrat-republican/.

4 Ibid.; Anne Gearan and Philip Rucker, "Hillary Clinton Recruits Chief Strategist, Media Adviser for 2016 Effort," *Washington Post*, January 13, 2015, https://www.washingtonpost.com/news/post-politics/wp/2015/01/13/hillary-clinton-recruits-chief-strategist-media-advisor-for-2016-effort/.

5 Ibid.

6 Ibid.

7 Ibid.

8 E-mail message from robbymook2015@gmail.com to MElias@perkinscoie.com, "Re: BROCK," Wikileaks, March 21, 2015, https://wikileaks.org/podesta-emails/emailid/1560; E-mail message from robbymook2015@gmail.com to john.podesta@gmail.com and melias@perkinscoie.com, "Re: SCHWEIZER / Clinton Cash."

9 Michael Sainato, "Hillary Clinton Must Sever Ties to Psycho Dirty Tricks Hitman David Brock," *Observer*, March 31, 2016, https://observer.com/2016/03/hillary-clinton-must-sever-ties-with-dirty-tricks-hitman-david-brock/; Robert L. Borosage, "The Poisonous Politics of David Brock," *Nation*, January 19, 2017, https://www.thenation.com/article/archive/the-poisonous-politics-of-david-brock/.

10 Daniel Halper, "Blunt Clinton Aide Calls Her Loyal Attack Dog 'Bats-t Crazy,'" *New York Post*, November 4, 2016, https://nypost.com/2016/11/04/blunt-clinton-aide-calls-her-loyal-attack-dog-bats-t-crazy/; E-mail message from ntanden@americanprogress.org to john.podesta@gmail.com, "I hope," Wikileaks, February 11, 2015, https://wikileaks.org/podesta-emails/emailid/43904.

11 Borosage, "The Poisonous Politics of David Brock."

12 Ibid.; Kenneth P. Vogel, "David Brock Expands Empire," *Politico*, August 13, 2014, https://www.politico.com/story/2014/08/david-brock-citizens-for-responsibility-and-ethics-in-washington-110003; Jason Horowitz, "Inside Hillary Clinton's Outrage Machine, Allies Push the Buttons," *New York Times*, September 22, 2016, https://www.nytimes.com/2016/09/23/us/politics/hillary-clinton-media-david-brock.html.

13 Jane Mayer, "Abramson and Anita Hill," *New Yorker*, June 3, 2011, https://www.newyorker.com/news/news-desk/abramson-and-anita-hill; Tod Lindberg, "Strange Justice, by Jane Mayer and Jill Abramson," *Commentary*, February 1995, https://www.commentarymagazine.com/articles/tod-lindberg-3/strange-justice-by-jane-mayer-and-jill-abramson/.

14 E-mail message from kristinakschake@gmail.com to robbymook2015@gmail.com, "Re: DRAFT Questions for HRC Media Prepare," Wikileaks, March 22, 2015, https://wikileaks.org/podesta-emails/emailid/1903; E-mail message from nmerrill@hroffice.com to kristinakschake@gmail.com, "Re: DRAFT Questions for HRC Media Prepare," *Wikileaks*, March 22, 2015, https://wikileaks.org/podesta-emails/emailid/313.

15 E-mail message from nmerrill@hrcoffice.com to kristinakschake@gmail.com, "Re: DRAFT Questions for HRC Media Prepare."

16 E-mail message from Jennifer.m.palmieri@gmail.com to john.podesta@gmail.com, "Re: DRAFT Questions for HRC Media Prepare," Wikileaks, March 23, 2015, https://wikileaks.org/podesta-emails/emailid/820.

17 E-mail message from brentbbi@webtv.net to john.podesta@gmail.com, "Warning to Hillary Clinton," Wikileaks, March 21, 2015, https://wikileaks.org/podesta-emails/emailid/6900; "Contributor: Brent Budowsky," *Huffington Post*, accessed November 1, 2019, https://www.huffpost.com/author/brent-budowsky?guccounter=1&guce_referrer=aHR0cHM6Ly93d3cuZ29vZ2xlLmNvbS8&guce_referrer_sig=AQA-AAGuHQcmbTm_d8wpTNPvsWF0QK9t-HzefUjNuUzih5gLYTToLqYLx5V2_bxvxDrsa9-Od6vDPqaQyMRdPFTArGRWhRIMnFwfSb0loz4SSR1cnNQcu9X-SsH3ZYzjrA8COKRpetF-M_Jb6VJuteDsaCsKaarVj0HrY1iSMxKBCRwDFj; Brent

Budowsky, "Big Truths about Hillary," *Hill*, September 9, 2015, https://thehill. com/opinion/brent-budowsky/253154-brent-budowsky-big-truths-about-hillary; Tyler O'Neil, "Wikileaks Bombshell: Clinton Relied on Trump Primary Win, GOP Obliged," PJ Media, October 10, 2016, https://pjmedia.com/trending/2016/10/10/ wikileaks-bombshell-clinton-relied-on-trump-primary-win-gop-obliged/.

18 Ibid.

19 E-mail message from JFernandez@gibsondunn.com to john.podesta@gmail.com, "Helping with the Campaign," Wikileaks, April 17, 2015, https://wikileaks.org/ podesta-emails//emailid/2053.

20 Written Statement of Mr. Jose W. Fernandez, Nominee, Assistant Secretary of State for Economic, Energy and Business Affairs, Senate Committee on Foreign Relations, September 15, 2009, https://www.foreign.senate.gov/imo/media/doc/Fernandez-Testimony090915a.pdf; U.S. Department of State, "2011 Economic, Energy and Business Affairs Remarks," accessed November 1, 2019, https://2009-2017.state. gov/e/eb/rls/rm/2011/index.htm; "Jose W. Fernandez," Gibson Dunn, accessed November 1, 2019, https://www.gibsondunn.com/lawyer/fernandez-jose-w/.

21 Lachlan Markay, "Podesta Group Clients Donated to Podesta's Center for American Progress," *Washington Free Beacon*, December 17, 2013, https://freebeacon.com/pol-itics/podesta-group-clients-donated-to-podestas-center-for-american-progress/; E-mail message from JFernandez@gibsondunn.com to john.podesta@gmail.com, "Meeting," March 30, 2015, https://wikileaks.org/podesta-emails/emailid/2055.

22 E-mail message from JFernandez@gibsondunn.com to john.podesta@gmail.com, "Meeting."

23 "The Podesta Emails," Wikileaks, accessed November 1, 2019, https://wikileaks. org/podesta-emails/?q=&mfrom=JFernandez%40gibsondunn.com&mto=&ti-tle=&notitle=&date_from=&date_to=&nofrom=&noto=&count=50&sort=6#-searchresult.

24 Jennifer Epstein, "Hillary Clinton Inks Deal for 'Brooklyn Cool' Offices," *Bloomberg*, April 3, 2015, https://www.bloomberg.com/news/articles/2015-04-03/ hillary-clinton-inks-deal-for-brooklyn-cool-offices.

25 E-mail message from milia.fisher@gmail.com to john.podesta@gmail.com, "Logis-tics for Tomorrow @HQ," Wikileaks, April 16, 2015, https://wikileaks.org/podesta -emails/emailid/2054.

26 E-mail message from JFernandez@gibsondunn.com to john.podesta@gmail.com, "Helping with the Campaign," Wikileaks, April 17, 2015, https://wikileaks.org/podesta -emails/emailid/2053.

27 Ibid.

28 "Clinton Cash: The Untold Story of How and Why Foreign Governments and Busi-nesses Helped Make Bill and Hillary Rich," Goodreads, first published January 1, 2015, https://www.goodreads.com/book/show/25163753-clinton-cash?ac=1&from_ search=true&qid=XVaXZj4Vy5&rank=3.

29 Becker and McIntire, "Cash Flowed to Clinton Foundation Amid Russian Uranium Deal."

30 E-mail message from ha16@hillaryclinton.com to re47@hillaryclinton.com, "Re: The Book," Wikileaks, April 18, 2015, https://wikileaks.org/podesta-emails/emailid /44729.

31 Ibid.; E-mail message from jferguson@hillaryclinton.com to Jesse@jesseferguson. com, "4 23 Friends and Allies TP - Clinton Cash," Wikileaks, April 23, 2015, https:// wikileaks.org/podesta-emails/emailid/860.

32 E-mail message from bfallon@hillaryclinton.com to ha16@hillaryclinton.com, john.podesta@gmail.com, cheryl.mills@gmail.com, craig@minassianmedia.com, mpally@clintonfoundation.org, "FOR REVIEW: Statement for NYT Story on Clinton Cash," Wikileaks, April 19, 2015, https://wikileaks.org/podesta-emails/ emailid/1330; "BLOOMBERG: Will Clinton Cash Consume Hillary's Campaign," YouTube video, posted by "Government Accountability Institute," June 30, 2015, https://www.youtube.com/watch?v=H8YsDW9l_k0.

33 Jonathan S. Tobin, "Remember the Clinton Cash Scandals?," *Commentary*, May 13, 2016, https://www.commentarymagazine.com/politics-ideas/campaigns-elections/ remember-clinton-cash-scandals/.

34 E-mail message from john.podesta@gmail.com to John.Hardwood@nbcuni.com, "Re:," Wikileaks, April 20, 2015, https://wikileaks.org/podesta-emails/emailid /57691.

35 E-mail message from jpalmieri@hillaryclinton.com to hdr29@hrcoffice.com, ha16@ hillaryclinton.com, nmerrill@hillaryclinton.com, jp66@hillaryclinton.com, and john.podesta@gmail.com, "Fwd: Formal Response from Me," Wikileaks, April 23, 2015, https://wikileaks.org/podesta-emails//emailid/1489; Colin Campbell, "This is the 'Blockbuster Exposé' Rand Paul Says Will Wreck Hillary Clinton's Campaign," Business Insider, April 20, 2015, https://www.businessinsider.com/this-is-the-blockbuster-expos-rand-paul-says-will-wreck-hillary-clintons-campaign-2015-4.

36 E-mail message from jpalmieri@hillaryclinton.com to hdr29@hrcoffice.com, ha16@hillaryclinton.com, nmerrill@hillaryclinton.com, jp66@hillaryclinton.com, and john.podesta@gmail.com, "Fwd: Formal Response from Me."

37 E-mail message from jpalmieri@hillaryclinton.com to hdr29@hrcoffice.com, ha16@ hillaryclinton.com, nmerrill@hillaryclinton.com, jp66@hillaryclinton.com, and john.podesta@gmail.com, "Fwd: Formal Response from Me"; Memo from Brian Fallon, Hillary for America National Press Secretary, to Friends and Allies, "Re: It's Official: Book Attacking Hillary Clinton Full of Discredited, Disproved Attacks," Wikileaks, April 23, 2015, https://wikileaks.org/podesta-emails/fileid/972/201.

38 "Peter Schweizer Appears on ABC's This Week with George Stephanopoulos to Discuss CLINTON CASH," YouTube video, posted by "Government Accountability Institute," April 26, 2015, https://www.youtube.com/watch?v=8hc6ESwRf8c.

39 E-mail message from nmerrill@hillaryclinton.com to kfinney@hillaryclinton.com, "Re: 'This Week' Transcript: 'Clinton Cash' Author Peter Schweizer," Wikileaks, April 26, 2015, https://wikileaks.org/podesta-emails/emailid/1986.

40 E-mail message from aphillips@hillaryclinton.com to aphillips@hillaryclinton. com, "H4A News Clips 5.15.15.," Wikileaks, May 15, 2015, https://wikileaks.org/ podesta-emails/emailid/1668; "BIAS ALERT: Stephanopoulos Gets Tough on Clinton Foundation, Leaves out His Own Donations," Fox News, August 22, 2016, https://www.foxnews.com/us/bias-alert-stephanopoulos-gets-tough-on-clinton-foundation-leaves-out-his-own-donations; Eric Wemple, "Donation Disclosure Issue Snowballing for ABC News, Stephanopoulos," *Washington Post*, May 14, 2015, https://

www.washingtonpost.com/blogs/erik-wemple/wp/2015/05/14/donation-disclosure
-issue-snowballing-for-abc-news-stephanopoulos/.

41 "George Stephanopoulos Apologizes Again for Clinton Donations," YouTube video,
posted by "Fox Business," May 19, 2015, https://www.youtube.com/watch?v=fvEb-
bl0Z1s8; "George Stephanopoulos Apologizes for Keeping Clinton Donations
a Secret," YouTube video, posted by "Inside Edition," May 15, 2015, https://www.
youtube.com/watch?v=XzfEM44uN9U; Wemple, "Donation Disclosure Issue
Snowballing for ABC News, Stephanopoulos"; Mark Hensch, "'Clinton Cash'
Author: Stephanopoulos 'Favorable' to Clintons," *Hill*, May 17, 2015, https://thehill.
com/blogs/blog-briefing-room/news/242337-clinton-cash-author-stephanopoulos
-favorable-to-clintons.

42 Doyle McManus, "Column: Hillary Clinton's Conflict-of-Interest Problems," *Los
Angeles Times*, May 2, 2015, https://www.latimes.com/nation/la-oe-0503-mcma-
nus-clinton-foundation-20150503-column.html; David A. Graham, "Hillary's
Campaign Is Built on a Shaky Foundation," *Atlantic*, March 20, 2015, https://www.
theatlantic.com/politics/archive/2015/03/hillarys-campaign-is-built-on-a-shaky
-foundation/388324/.

43 Peter Schweizer, *Clinton Cash: The Untold Story of How Foreign Governments
and Businesses Made Bill and Hillary Rich* (New York: HarperCollins, 2015),
44; Rosalind S. Helderman and Tom Hamburger, "1,100 Donors to a Canadian Charity Tied to Clinton Foundation Remain Secret," *Washington Post*,
April 28, 2015, https://www.washingtonpost.com/politics/1100-donors-to-a-ca-
nadian-charity-tied-to-clinton-foundation-remain-secret/2015/04/28/
c3c0f374-edbc-11e4-8666-a1d756d0218e_story.html; Michael Patrick Leahy, "Clinton
Foundation Refuses to Release Names of 1,076 Secret Foreign Donors," Breitbart, June
3, 2015, https://www.breitbart.com/politics/2015/06/03/clinton-foundation-refuses
-to-release-names-of-1076-secret-foreign-donors/.

44 "The Podesta Emails; Part One," Wikileaks, accessed May 22, 2018, https://wikileaks.
org/podesta-emails/press-release.

45 Ibid.

46 Ibid.

47 E-mail message from oshur@hillaryclinton.com to jbenenson@bsgco.com,
gruncom@aol.com, Jim.margolis@gmmb.com, re47@hillaryclinton.com, David@
db-research.com, john@algpolling.com…, "RE: NH Primary Toplines and Memo,"
Wikileaks, June 28, 2015, https://wikileaks.org/podesta-emails/emailid/692;
Devlin Barrett, "FBI in Internal Feud over Hillary Clinton Probe," *Wall Street
Journal*, October 30, 2016, https://www.wsj.com/articles/laptop-may-include-
thousands-of-emails-linked-to-hillary-clintons-private-server-1477854957;
Devlin Barrett, "Secret Recordings Fueled FBI Feud in Clinton Probe," *Wall
Street Journal*, November 2, 2016, https://www.wsj.com/articles/secret-record-
ings-fueled-fbi-feud-in-clinton-probe-1478135518; "Rep. Sean Duffy on the
Possible Prosecutions of Clinton; Rep. Tim Ryan Speaks out about Challenging Pelosi," Fox News, November 22, 2016, https://www.foxnews.com/transcript/
rep-sean-duffy-on-the-possible-prosecutions-of-clinton-rep-tim-ryan-speaks-
out-about-challenging-pelosi; "The Corruption of Hillary Clinton," *FrontPage*

Magazine Archive, November 28, 2016, https://archives.frontpagemag.com/fpm/corruption-hillary-clinton-frontpagemagcom/.

48 E-mail message from oshur@hillaryclinton.com to jbenenson@bsgco.com, gruncom@aol.com, Jim.margolis@gmmb.com, re47@hillaryclinton.com, David@db-research.com, john@algpolling.com..., "RE: NH Primary Toplines and Memo."

49 Seamus Bruner, "7 Reasons Why the Uranium One Scandal Won't Go Away," *Epoch Times*, May 9, 2019, https://www.theepochtimes.com/7-reasons-why-the-uranium-one-scandal-wont-go-away_2914343.html.

50 Schweizer, *Clinton Cash*, 54-55.

51 Letter from Terry Krinvic, Director of Scheduling and Advance, to Jim Thessin, "RE: Speech Host for State Department Conflict of Interest Review," Judicial Watch, April 5, 2010, https://www.judicialwatch.org/wp-content/uploads/2014/07/Clinton-Inc-February-25-2014-pg-192-196.pdf; Letter from Terry Krinvic, Director of Scheduling and Advance, to Richard Visek, "RE: Speech Host for State Department Conflict of Interest Review," Judicial Watch, January 9, 2012, https://www.judicialwatch.org/wp-content/uploads/2014/07/Clinton-Inc-February-25-2014-pg-657-667.pdf.

52 Ibid.

53 Ibid.

54 John Solomon and Alison Spann, "Bill Clinton Sought State's Permission to Meet with Russian Nuclear Official During Obama Uranium Decision," *Hill*, October 19, 2017, https://thehill.com/policy/national-security/356323-bill-clinton-sought-states-permission-to-meet-with-russian-nuclear; Schweizer, *Clinton Cash*, 51.

55 Ibid.; Ben Geier, "Here's How Much the Clintons Earn from Paid Speeches," *Fortune*, February 4, 2016, https://fortune.com/2016/02/04/clinton-family-values/; Robert Yoon, "$153 Million in Bill and Hillary Clinton Speaking Fees, Documented," CNN, February 6, 2016, https://www.cnn.com/2016/02/05/politics/hillary-clinton-bill-clinton-paid-speeches/index.html.

56 "State Dept. Emails Raise Questions about Vetting Process, Conflicts for Pres. Clinton Speeches," Chuck Grassley's Senate page, August 28, 2015, https://www.grassley.senate.gov/news/news-releases/state-dept-emails-raise-questions-about-vetting-process-conflicts-pres-clinton; Kimberley A. Strassel, "The Clinton 'Charity' Begins at Home," *Wall Street Journal*, June 4, 2015, https://www.wsj.com/articles/the-clinton-charity-begins-at-home-1433459849; Solomon and Spann, "Bill Clinton Sought State's Permission to Meet with Russian Nuclear Official During Obama Uranium Decision"; Rachael Bade, "Hillary Named on Document Formalizing Abedin Job Change," *Politico*, September 24, 2015, https://www.politico.com/story/2015/09/clinton-abedin-state-job-approved-214038.

57 Strassel, "The Clinton 'Charity' Begins at Home"; Solomon and Spann, "Bill Clinton Sought State's Permission to Meet with Russian Nuclear Official During Obama Uranium Decision."

58 Solomon and Spann, "Bill Clinton Sought State's Permission to Meet with Russian Nuclear Official During Obama Uranium Decision."

59 Ibid.; 14th Annual Investor Conference, Renaissance Capital, June 28-29, 2010; Conference Agenda, Renaissance Capital, June 28-29, 2010.

60 Solomon and Spann, "Bill Clinton Sought State's Permission to Meet with Russian Nuclear Official During Obama Uranium Decision."

61 Message from the President of the United States, "Treaty with Russia on Measures for Further Reduction and Limitation of Strategic Offensive Arms," 111th Cong. (2013), https://www.congress.gov/111/cdoc/tdoc5/CDOC-111tdoc5.pdf; Bill Gertz, "Uranium One and New START," *Washington Times*, November 1, 2017, https://www.washingtontimes.com/news/2017/nov/1/uranium-one-new-start -investigations-urged/.

62 Robert M. Gates, *Duty: Memoirs of a Secretary at War* (New York: Alfred A. Knopf, 2014), 259.

63 Peter Baker, "Obama Expands Modernization of Nuclear Arsenal," *New York Times*, May 13, 2010, https://www.nytimes.com/2010/05/14/us/politics/14treaty. html; Ken Dilanian, "Obama Scraps Bush Missile-Defense Plan," ABC News, September 17, 2009, https://abcnews.go.com/Politics/obama-scraps-bush-missile-defense-plan/story?id=8604357; Katrina Heikkinen, "New START: 564th MS Silos Being Eliminated," U.S. Air Force, March 4, 2014, https://www.afgsc.af.mil/News/ Article-Display/Article/629635/new-start-564th-ms-silos-being-eliminated/.

64 Gates, *Duty*, 260; Secretary of State Hillary Rodham Clinton, *Congressional Testimony on the on the New START Treaty, Senate Foreign Relations Committee*, May 18, 2010, https://www.foreign.senate.gov/imo/media/doc/ClintonTestimony100518a.pdf.

65 Ben Smith, "Clinton Toils in the Shadows," *Politico*, June 23, 2009, https://www. politico.com/story/2009/06/clinton-toils-in-the-shadows-024067; Gates, *Duty*, 259-260.

66 Gates, *Duty*, 260.

67 Secretary of State Hillary Rodham Clinton, *Congressional Testimony on the on the New START Treaty, Senate Foreign Relations Committee*, May 18, 2010.

68 Keith B. Payne and Mark B. Schneider, "The Nuclear Treaty Russia Won't Stop Violating," *Wall Street Journal*, February 11, 2014, https://www.wsj.com/articles/ the-nuclear-treaty-russia-won8217t-stop-violating-1392166706; Secretary of State Hillary Rodham Clinton, *Congressional Testimony on the on the New START Treaty, Senate Foreign Relations Committee*, May 18, 2010.

69 Secretary of State Hillary Rodham Clinton, *Congressional Testimony on the on the New START Treaty, Senate Foreign Relations Committee*, May 18, 2010; Bill Gertz, "Uranium One and New START"; "Clinton Urges Early Senate Action on Arms Treaty with Russia," VOA News, August 10, 2010, https://www.voanews.com/usa/ clinton-urges-early-senate-action-arms-treaty-russia.

70 Solomon and Spann, "Bill Clinton Sought State's Permission to Meet with Russian Nuclear Official During Obama Uranium Decision."

71 John Solomon and Alison Spann, "FBI Watched, then Acted As Russian Spy Moved Closer to Hillary Clinton," *Hill*, October 22, 2017, https://thehill.com/policy/ national-security/356630-fbi-watched-then-acted-as-russian-spy-moved-closer-to-hillary; Dan Farber, "Former Presidents Putin and Clinton Talk Russian Spy Arrests," CBS News, June 29, 2010, https://www.cbsnews.com/news/former-presidents-putin-and-clinton-talk-russian-spy-arrests/; "Espionage: Spies Like Us," *Economist*, July 1, 2010, https://www.economist.com/node/16486569/all-comments;

Solomon and Spann, "Bill Clinton Sought State's Permission to Meet with Russian Nuclear Official During Obama Uranium Decision."

72 Gates, *Duty*, 260-261.

73 U.S. Department of State, "Secretary Clinton's Daily Calendar," November 5, 2015, https://foia.state.gov/search/results.aspx?searchText=marty+torrey+chris&beginDate=&endDate=&publishedBeginDate=7-15-2018&publishedEndDate=&caseNumber=.

74 Gates, *Duty*; Leon Panetta, *Worthy Fights* (New York: Penguin Press, 2014); McFaul, *From Cold War to Hot Peace*; Hillary Rodham Clinton, *Hard Choices* (London: Simon and Schuster, 2014).

75 Letter from Donna L. Wichers, Senior Vice President, ISR Operations, to Keith McConnell, Deputy Director, Decommissioning and Uranium Recovery Licensing Directorate, U.S. Nuclear Regulatory Commission, Uranium One, July 20, 2010, https://www.nrc.gov/docs/ML1020/ML102090404.pdf.

76 Solomon and Spann, "Bill Clinton Sought State's Permission to Meet with Russian Nuclear Official During Obama Uranium Decision."

77 U.S. Department of Justice, Executive Office for United States Attorneys, "Export Control Laws," November 2013, vol. 61, no. 6, https://www.justice.gov/sites/default/files/usao/legacy/2014/10/01/usab6106.pdf; Rickards, *Aftermath*; Becker and McIntire, "Cash Flowed to Clinton Foundation Amid Russian Uranium Deal."

78 Becker and McIntire, "Cash Flowed to Clinton Foundation Amid Russian Uranium Deal."

79 Ibid.

80 Andy Hoffman, "Renaissance Man," *Globe and Mail*, Jun 27, 2008, http://www.theglobeandmail.com/report-on-business/renaissance-man/article17988489/?page=all; "Mining Magnate Frank Giustra Takes a Break from Producing Blade Runner Sequel to Return to His First Love – Mining," *Financial Post*, May 19, 2017, https://business.financialpost.com/personal-finance/high-net-worth/frank-giustra-takes-a-break-from-the-blade-runner-sequel-and-an-italian-olive-estate-to-return-to-his-first-love-a-gold-mine; Miro Cernetig, "Frank Giustra: A Man of Many Hats," *BCBusiness*, November 5, 2012, http://www.bcbusiness.ca/people/frank-giustra-a-man-of-many-hats; Jo Becker and Don Van Natta Jr., "After Mining Deal, Financier Donated to Clinton," *New York Times*, January 31, 2008, http://www.nytimes.com/2008/01/31/us/politics/31donor.html?pagewanted=all&_r=0.

81 "How Canadian Tycoon Giustra Builds Ten Baggers in Mining and Energy," Mining.com, July 17, 2014, https://www.mining.com/web/how-canadian-tycoon-giustra-builds-ten-baggers-in-mining-and-energy/.

82 Becker and Van Natta Jr., "After Mining Deal, Financier Donated to Clinton."

83 Hobart M. King, "Diamond Mines in the United States," Geology.com, accessed November 4, 2019, https://geology.com/gemstones/united-states-diamond-production.shtml.

84 "History of the Diamond Mine," Arkansas State Parks, accessed November 4, 2019, https://www.arkansasstateparks.com/parks/crater-diamonds-state-park/history/history-of-the-diamond-mine; Jacquie McNish, *The Big Score: Robert Friedland and the Voisey's Bay Hustle* (Doubleday Canada, 1998), 38-52.

85 McNish, *The Big Score*, 36-52; Paul Waldie, "Mining Promoter Boulle Hit with Huge Tax Bill," *Globe and Mail*, May 8, 2006, https://www.theglobeandmail.com/report-on-business/mining-promoter-boulle-hit-with-huge-tax-bill/article708526/; "About Us," Jean Boulle Group, accessed November 4, 2019, https://jeanboulle-group.com/about-us/.

86 "Top Arkansas Lawyer Helped Hillary Clinton Turn Big Profit," *New York Times*, March 18, 1994, http://www.nytimes.com/1994/03/18/us/top-arkansas-lawyer-helped-hillary-clinton-turn-big-profit.html; Richard C. Morais, "Friends in High Places," *Forbes*, August 10, 1998, http://www.forbes.com/global/1998/0810/0109038a.html; McNish, *The Big Score*, ix, 40; Dick Morris and Eileen McGann, *Armageddon: How Trump Can Beat Hillary* (West Palm Beach: Humanix Books, 2016), 53.

87 Morais, "Friends in High Places."

88 Ibid.; McNish, *The Big Score*, ix, 40.

89 Morais, "Friends in High Places"; "Board of Directors," Clinton Foundation, accessed 2014, https://www.clintonfoundation.org/about/board-directors; Schweizer, *Clinton Cash*, 24-25; Jeffrey St. Clair, "Diamond Dogs: Clinton Family Jewels," CounterPunch, June 3, 2016, https://www.counterpunch.org/2016/06/03/diamond-dogs-clinton-family-jewels/.

90 McNish, *The Big Score*, 11-15; Dylan Love, "Steve Jobs' College Mentor Was a Drug Dealer Turned Billionaire Mining Magnate*," Business Insider, October 24, 2011, https://www.businessinsider.com/steve-jobs-robert-friedland-2011-10.

91 McNish, *The Big Score*, 7; Robert Weller, "Miner Agrees to Pay $30M in Spill," Associated Press, December 22, 2000, https://apnews.com/0bf12eb3b5564e-0134b9797257e0c36c; "Cyanide-Spill Suit Is Settled in Colorado," *New York Times*, December 24, 2000, https://www.nytimes.com/2000/12/24/us/cyanide-spill-suit-is-settled-in-colorado.html; Joshua Zapf, "Robert Friedland," Mining.com, June 29, 2012, https://www.mining.com/robert-toxic-bob-friedland-49502/; Robert McClure, "Innocent Financier or Irresponsible Polluter?," Seattle Post-Intelligence Reporter, June 12, 2001, https://www.seattlepi.com/news/article/Innocent-finan-cier-or-irresponsible-polluter-1057037.php.

92 McNish, *The Big Score*, 206-207; "The View from the Goldcorp Chairman's Office," Mining.com, November 3, 2017, http://www.mining.com/web/view-goldcorp-chairmans-office/.

93 McNish, *The Big Score*, ix, 45; Schweizer, *Clinton Cash*, 35-36; Becker and McIntire, "Cash Flowed to Clinton Foundation Amid Russian Uranium Deal."

94 "The View from the Goldcorp Chairman's Office," Mining.com; McNish, *The Big Score*, 206-207; Conference Agenda, Renaissance Capital, June 28-29, 2010.

95 Anu Narayanswamy, "Travels with Bill and Frank: A Look at the Clinton-Giustra Friendship," *Washington Post*, May 3, 2015, https://www.washingtonpost.com/news/post-politics/wp/2015/05/03/travels-with-bill-and-frank-a-look-at-the-clinton-giustra-friendship/; Hoffman, "Renaissance Man"; Becker and Van Natta Jr., "After Mining Deal, Financier Donated to Clinton"; Washington Post, "The Clinton Family, a Luxury Jet and Their US$100 Million Canadian Donors," *Financial Post*, May 4, 2015, https://business.financialpost.com/news/fp-street/the-clinton-family-a-luxury-jet-and-their-us100-million-canadian-donors.

96 NYS Board of Elections for U.S. Senate, November 7, 2000, https://www.elections. ny.gov/NYSBOE/elections/2000/wussen2000.pdf;NYS Board of Elections for U.S. Senate, November 7, 2006, http://www.elections.ny.gov/NYSBOE/elections/2006/ general/2006_ussen.pdf; Philip Rucker, Tom Hamburger, and Alexander Becker, "How the Clintons Went from Dead Broke to Rich: Bill Earned $104.9 Million for Speeches," *Washington Post*, June 26, 2014, https://www.washingtonpost.com/ politics/how-the-clintons-went-from-dead-broke-to-rich-bill-earned-1049-mil-lion-for-speeches/2014/06/26/8fa0b372-fd3a-11e3-8176-f2c941cf35fl_story.html.

97 Becker and Van Natta Jr., "After Mining Deal, Financier Donated to Clinton."

98 "How to Make Money in Kazakhstan," TheNewswire.ca, October 14, 2011, https:// web.archive.org/web/20130923061726/http://www.metalinvestmentnews.com:80/ how-to-make-money-in-kazakhstan/; "Kazakhstan: Mining, Minerals and Fuel Resources," AZoMining, August 1, 2012, https://www.azomining.com/Article.aspx? ArticleID=64.

99 Becker and Van Natta Jr., "After Mining Deal, Financier Donated to Clinton."

100 World Health Organization, "Summary Country Profile For HIV/AIDS Treat-ment Scale-Up," December 2005, http://www.who.int/hiv/HIVCP_KAZ.pdf; UNAIDS, *Sub-Saharan Africa Fact Sheet*, May 25, 2006, http://data.unaids.org/ pub/GlobalReport/2006/200605-fs_subsaharanafrica_en.pdf.

101 Simon Jenkins, "What Is David Cameron Doing in Kazakhstan?," *Guardian*, July 1, 2013, https://www.theguardian.com/commentisfree/2013/jul/01/david-camer-on-kaszakhstan-britain; Jim Nichol, "Kazakhstan: Recent Developments and U.S. Interests," Congressional Research Service, June 20, 2008; Joshua Foust, "The Gilded Cage of Asia," *Foreign Policy*, April 11, 2013, http://www.foreignpolicy.com/ articles/2013/04/11/the_gilded_cage_of_asia; Nicholas Watt, "Kazakhstan's Auto-cratic President Tells David Cameron: I Would Vote for You," *Guardian*, July 1, 2013, http://www.theguardian.com/world/2013/jul/01/kazakhstan-president-david-cam-eron-vote; *Encyclopedia Britannica Online*, s.v. "Nursultan Nazarbayev," accessed November 2, 2019, https://www.britannica.com/biography/Nursultan-Nazarbayev.

102 Walter Mayr, "Ex-Stepson Talks in Family Feud: Tapping Kazakhstan's Natural Resources," Spiegel, May 19, 2009; Vlad Lavrov and Irene Velska, "Kazakhstan: President's Grandson Hid Assets Offshore," OCCRP, April 4, 2016, https://www. occrp.org/en/panamapapers/kazakh-presidents-grandson-offshores/; "#715 Dinara Kulibaeva," *Forbes*, last updated February 28, 2020, https://www.forbes.com/profile/ dinara-kulibaeva/#22d8b0547a01; "#715 Timur Kulibaev," *Forbes*, last updated Feb-ruary 28, 2020, https://www.forbes.com/profile/timur-kulibaev/#bd9408d329f5; James Love, "The Well-Connected Dictator," *Huffington Post*, October 6, 2007, http://www.huffingtonpost.com/james-love/the-wellconnected-dictato_b_67423. html; James Kilner, "Copper Tycoon Tops Kazakhstan's Rich List," *Telegraph*, May 15, 2012, http://www.telegraph.co.uk/news/worldnews/asia/kazakhstan/9268133/ Copper-tycoon-tops-Kazakhstans-rich-list.html; Neil Buckley, "ENRC Founders Made Good in Kazakhstan," *Financial Times*, May 2, 2013, http://www.ft.com/intl/ cms/s/0/71a13774-b3e0-11e2-ace9-00144feabdc0.html#axzz351P7vNvu; "Billion-aires: The Richest People in the World," *Forbes*, March 5, 2019, https://www.forbes. com/billionaires/#24f2ca0625lc.

103 Nichol, "Kazakhstan: Recent Developments and U.S. Interests"; Joanna Lillis, "Kazakhstan: UK Courts Nazarbayev amid Human Rights Concerns," Eurasianet, July 1, 2013, http://www.eurasianet.org/node/67200; Schweizer, *Clinton Cash*, 22; United States Diplomatic Mission to Kazakhstan, U.S. Embassy, "Trafficking in Persons Report 2013"; "Kazakhstan: Events of 2018," Human Rights Watch, accessed November 7, 2019, https://www.hrw.org/world-report/2019/country-chapters/kazakhstan.

104 Becker and Van Natta Jr., "After Mining Deal, Financier Donated to Clinton."

105 Nichol, "Kazakhstan: Recent Developments and U.S. Interests."

106 Becker and Van Natta Jr., "After Mining Deal, Financier Donated to Clinton"; "The Organization for Security and Cooperation in Europe," Icelandic Human Rights Centre, accessed November 1, 2019, http://www.humanrights.is/en/human-rights-education-project/human-rights-concepts-ideas-and-fora/human-rights-fora/the-organization-for-security-and-cooperation-in-europe; Schweizer, *Clinton Cash*, 30.

107 Elliot Blair Smith, "Clinton Used Giustra's Plane, Opened Doors for Deals (Correct)," *Bloomberg*, February 22, 2008, http://www.bloomberg.com/apps/news?pid=news archive&sid=aa2b8Mj3NEWQ; Embassy of the Republic of Kazakhstan, "Weekly News Bulletin," September 7, 2005, http://web.archive.org/web/20060324003505/http://www.kazakhembus.com/090705.html.

108 Smith, "Clinton Used Giustra's Plane, Opened Doors for Deals (Correct)"; Schweizer, *Clinton Cash*, 34.

109 Schweizer, *Clinton Cash*, 30-31.

110 Hoffman, "Renaissance Man"; Cernetig, "Frank Giustra: A Man of Many Hats"; Becker and Van Natta Jr., "After Mining Deal, Financier Donated to Clinton."

111 Hoffman, "Renaissance Man"; Smith, "Clinton Used Giustra's Plane, Opened Doors for Deals (Correct)"; Peter Baker, "The Mellowing of William Jefferson Clinton," *New York Times*, May 26, 2009, http://www.nytimes.com/2009/05/31/magazine/31clinton-t.html?pagewanted=all.

112 Hoffman, "Renaissance Man"; Tommy Humphreys, "Stop Taking Yourself So Seriously, Says Tycoon Frank Giustra," Mining.com, June 28, 2013, http://www.mining.com/web/stop-taking-yourself-so-seriously-says-tycoon-frank-giustra/; Schweizer, *Clinton Cash*, 23.

113 Hoffman, "Renaissance Man."

114 Cernetig, "Frank Giustra: A Man of Many Hats"; Smith, "Clinton Used Giustra's Plane, Opened Doors for Deals (Correct)."

115 Andy Hoffman and Sinclair Stewart, "How to (Still) Get Rich in Mining," *Globe and Mail*, May 19, 2007, https://www.theglobeandmail.com/report-on-business/how-to-still-get-rich-in-mining/article18139221/; Hoffman, "Renaissance Man"; Schweizer, *Clinton Cash*, 24.

116 Ibid.

117 Schweizer, *Clinton Cash*, 25.

118 Jessica Taylor, "More Surprises: FBI Releases Files on Bill Clinton's Pardon of Marc Rich," NPR, November 1, 2016, https://www.npr.org/2016/11/01/500297580/more-surprises-fbi-releases-files-on-bill-clintons-pardon-of-marc-rich; Peter Schweizer, "Bill Clinton's Pardon of Fugitive March Rich Continues to Pay Big," *New York Post*,

January 17, 2016, https://nypost.com/2016/01/17/after-pardoning-criminal-marc-rich-clintons-made-millions-off-friends/.

119 Becker and Van Natta Jr., "After Mining Deal, Financier Donated to Clinton."

120 Ibid.

121 Schweizer, *Clinton Cash*, 25.

122 Becker and Van Natta Jr., "After Mining Deal, Financier Donated to Clinton"; Signature Resources Ltd, "Signature Enters into Acquisition Agreement with UrAsia Energy (B.V.I.) Ltd," September 20, 2005, http://www.infomine.com/index/pr/Pa299684.PDF; Schweizer, *Clinton Cash*, 27-28; "Uranium and Nuclear Power in Kazakhstan," World Nuclear Association, last updated March 2020, https://www.world-nuclear.org/information-library/country-profiles/countries-g-n/kazakhstan.aspx.

123 Becker and Van Natta Jr., "After Mining Deal, Financier Donated to Clinton"; Hoffman, "Renaissance Man."

124 Human Rights Watch, "Kazakhstan: Events of 2005," World Report 2006, http://www.hrw.org/world-report-2006/kazakhstan; Schweizer, *Clinton Cash*, 32; Joel Brinkley, "Rice Takes Democracy Call to Central Asians," *New York Times*, October 14, 2005, http://www.nytimes.com/2005/10/14/international/asia/14rice.html?_r=0.

125 Becker and Van Natta Jr., "After Mining Deal, Financier Donated to Clinton"; "Kazakhstan President Nursultan Nazarbayev," About Kazakhstan, accessed November 1, 2019, http://aboutkazakhstan.com/about-kazakhstan-government/kazakhstan-president.

126 Schweizer, *Clinton Cash*, 32.

127 Becker and Van Natta Jr., "After Mining Deal, Financier Donated to Clinton."

128 Signature Resources Ltd, "Signature Enters into Acquisition Agreement with UrAsia Energy (B.V.I.) Ltd"; Schweizer, *Clinton Cash*, 32-33.

129 Schweizer, *Clinton Cash*, 32; Hoffman and Stewart, "How to (Still) Get Rich in Mining"; Bob Moriarty, "Girls and Peak Gold: Wheaton River Jr.," 321gold.com (archives), October 7, 2007, accessed November 2, 2014, http://www.321gold.com/editorials/moriarty/moriarty103007.html; Andy Hoffman, "Ian Telfer: 'I'm More of an Opportunist Than a Visionary,'" *Globe and Mail*, May 27, 2011, http://www.theglobeandmail.com/report-on-business/careers/careers-leadership/ian-telfer-im-more-of-an-opportunist-than-a-visionary/article582085/?page=all.

130 Becker and Van Natta Jr., "After Mining Deal, Financier Donated to Clinton"; Jason Kirby, "Uranium Blockbuster," *National Post*, January 31, 2006; Schweizer, *Clinton Cash*, 33.

131 "Coming Soon! A New Uranium Stock," Morningstar, November 7, 2005, accessed November 2, 2014; "Uranium Mining and Exploration Post # 2119," Investors Hub, November 7, 2005, accessed November 2, 2014, http://investorshub.advfn.com/boards/read_msg.aspx?message_id=8398619; Kirby, "Uranium Blockbuster"; Schweizer, *Clinton Cash*, 33.

132 "Uranium One and UrAsia Energy Announce Combination to Create Emerging Senior Uranium Company," Investegate, news release, February 12, 2007, https://www.investegate.co.uk/urasia-energy-ltd--uuu-/rns/plans-merger-with-sxr-uranium/200702120726400752R/; Schweizer, *Clinton Cash*, 33.

133 Sinclair Stewart and Andy Hoffman, "Uranium One Ensnared in Kazakh Scandal," *Globe and Mail*, May 27, 2009, https://www.theglobeandmail.com/globe-investor/uranium-one-ensnared-in-kazakh-scandal/article4211504/; Becker and Van Natta Jr., "After Mining Deal, Financier Donated to Clinton"; Schweizer, *Clinton Cash*, 28.

134 Robert Lenzner, "Clinton Commits No Foul in Kazakhstan Uranium Deal," *Forbes*, January 12, 2009, http://www.forbes.com/2009/01/12/giustra-clinton-kazakhstan-pf-ii-in_rl_0912croesus_inl.html; Becker and Van Natta Jr., "After Mining Deal, Financier Donated to Clinton."

135 Becker and Van Natta, Jr., "After Mining Deal, Financier Donated to Clinton"; Lenzner, "Clinton Commits No Foul in Kazakhstan Uranium Deal"; Peter Baker and Helene Cooper, "Clinton Vetting Includes Look at Mr. Clinton," *New York Times*, November 16, 2008, http://www.nytimes.com/2008/11/17/us/politics/17memo.html?pagewanted=all&_r=0.

136 Love, "The Well-Connected Dictator"; Schweizer, *Clinton Cash*, 34; "President Nursultan Nazarbayev Takes Part in the Clinton Global Initiative Forum in New York," Official Site of the President of the Republic of Kazakhstan, September 26, 2007.

137 Sarah Westwood, "Clinton 'Fact-Check' Under Fire," *Washington Examiner*, May 7, 2015, https://www.washingtonexaminer.com/clinton-fact-check-under-fire; "Uranium One and UrAsia Energy Announce Combination to Create Emerging Senior Uranium Company."

138 Westwood, "Clinton 'Fact-Check' Under Fire"; "Uranium One and UrAsia Energy Announce Combination to Create Emerging Senior Uranium Company"; Liezel Hill, "Uranium One Wraps Up UrAsia Acquisition, Eyes London Listing," *Engineering News*, April 23, 2007, http://www.engineeringnews.co.za/article/uranium-one-wraps-up-urasia-acquisition-eyes-london-listing-2007-04-23; Schweizer, *Clinton Cash*, 34, 196-197; *Uranium One Inc. Annual Information Form 2007*, March 31, 2008; David Stellfox, "Uranium One's Russian Deals Pushes Kazakh Probes to the Background," Platts Nucleonics Week, June 18, 2009; "UrAsia Energy Ltd Plans Merger with SXR Uranium," London Stock Exchange Aggregated Regulatory News Service, February 17, 2007.

139 "Uranium One Signs US$100 Million Credit Facility," Norton Rose Fulbright, June 27, 2008, on Internet Archive, https://web.archive.org/web/20160318062912/http://www.nortonrosefulbright.com/ca/en/about-us/client-work/ca-uranium-one-signs-us100-million-credit-facility-49178.aspx (the screenshot of the site was captured on March 18, 2016); Rickards, *Aftermath*.

140 "Uranium One to Buy Energy Metals," World Nuclear News, June 4, 2007, on Internet Archive, https://web.archive.org/web/20110324020545/http://www.world-nuclear-news.org/newsarticle.aspx?id=13506 (the screenshot of the site was captured on March 24, 2011).

141 Rickards, *Aftermath*; "Uranium One to Buy Energy Metals."

142 "Uranium One and UrAsia Energy Announce Combination to Create Emerging Senior Uranium Company."

143 Energy Metals Corporation, "Uranium One and Energy Metals Receive CFIUS Approval for Proposed Arrangement," news release, July 31, 2007, https://www.sec.gov/Archives/edgar/data/1361605/000106299307002905/rule425.htm.

144 "Uranium One and UrAsia Energy Announce Combination to Create Emerging Senior Uranium Company"; Hill, "Uranium One Wraps Up UrAsia Acquisition, Eyes London Listing."

145 Becker and McIntire, "Cash Flowed to Clinton Foundation Amid Russian Uranium Deal."

146 U.S. Energy Information Administration, "U.S. Uranium Concentrate Production in 2017 Was the Lowest Since 2004," February 26, 2018, https://www.eia.gov/today-inenergy/detail.php?id=35092; Schweizer, *Clinton Cash*, 34; "The Next Trade War Commodity: Uranium," Pinnacle Digest, July 28, 2018, https://www.pinnacledigest.com/uncategorized/nuclear-power-relies-foreign-imports/.

147 Becker and McIntire, "Cash Flowed to Clinton Foundation Amid Russian Uranium Deal"; Judy Fahys, "How a Tiny Utah Town Got Thrown into the 'Real' Russia Scandal," Keur 90.1, December 15, 2017, https://www.kuer.org/post/how-tiny-utah-town-got-thrown-real-russia-scandal#stream/0.

148 Ned Mamula, "Russia's Uranium Gambit: The Real Uranium One Scandal," Capital Research Center, January 15, 2019, https://capitalresearch.org/article/russias-uranium-gambit-part-4/.

149 Ibid.; Seamus Bruner, *Compromised* (New York: Post Hill Press, 2018), 100.

150 Correspondence from Senator Richard G. Lugar to Rebecca Schmidt, "Sale of Uranium Mines in Wyoming to a Russian Company," December 22, 2010, https://adamswebsearch2.nrc.gov/webSearch2/view?AccessionNumber=ML103570140.

151 Becker and Van Natta, "After Mining Deal, Financier Donated to Clinton"; Schweizer, *Clinton Cash*, 35, 198; Hoffman, "Renaissance Man."

152 "Contributor Information," Clinton Foundation, accessed 2014, https://www.clintonfoundation.org/contributors?category=%24250%2C001+to+%24500%2C000; Schweizer, *Clinton Cash*, 35, 198; "Frank Edward Holmes," *Bloomberg*, accessed November 2, 2019, https://www.bloomberg.com/profile/person/14001742.

153 JT Long, "Is It 2003 All Over Again? U.S. Global Investors' Frank Holmes Predicts a Resurgence of the Love Trade for Gold," Kitco News, June 19, 2014, http://www.kitco.com/ind/GoldReport/2014-06-19-Is-It-2003-All-Over-Again-U-S-Global-Investors-Frank-Holmes-Predicts-a-Resurgence-of-the-Love-Trade-for-Gold.html; Schweizer, *Clinton Cash*, 35, 198; "Frank Edward Holmes," *Bloomberg*.

154 Hoffman, "Renaissance Man"; "Press Release: President Clinton and Business Leaders Launch Sustainable Development Initiative in the Developing World," Clinton Foundation, June 21, 2007, https://www.clintonfoundation.org/main/news-and-media/press-releases-and-statements/press-release-president-clinton-and-business-leaders-launch-sustainable-developm.html; Schweizer, *Clinton Cash*, 35, 198; "Management," Endeavour Mining Corporation, accessed November 1, 2019.

155 "Clinton Foundation Donors," *The Wall Street Journal*, December 18, 2008, http://online.wsj.com/public/resources/documents/st_clintondonor_20081218.html; Schweizer, *Clinton Cash*, 35, 198; "Transactions (Page 2)," Haywood Securities Inc, accessed 2014.

156 "Clinton Foundation Donors"; "Paul D. Reynolds," *Bloomberg*, accessed November 1, 2019, https://www.bloomberg.com/profile/person/6250118; Schweizer, *Clinton Cash*, 35, 198.

157 Andy Hoffman, "Clinton Charities Take Hit from Mining Bust," *Globe and Mail*, December 19, 2008, http://www.theglobeandmail.com/report-on-business/clinton-charities-take-hit-from-mining-bust/article665023/; Schweizer, *Clinton Cash*, 35, 198; Signature Resources Ltd, "Signature Enters into Acquisition Agreement with UrAsia Energy (B.V.I.) Ltd"; Canaccord Capital Inc., "Canaccord Capital Inc. Reports Record Third Quarter Results," news release, February 8, 2006, http://www.canaccordgenuitygroup.com/EN/IR/FinReports/Documents/Q3%2006_Earnings%20Release.pdf.

158 "Press Release: President Clinton and Business Leaders Launch Sustainable Development Initiative in the Developing World"; Schweizer, *Clinton Cash*, 35, 198; Hoffman, "Renaissance Man"; Kirby, "Uranium Blockbuster."

159 "Press Release: President Clinton and Business Leaders Launch Sustainable Development Initiative in the Developing World"; Schweizer, *Clinton Cash*, 36, 198; "Robert Melvin Douglas Cross MBA," Investing.businessweek.com, accessed November 1, 2019.

160 "Global Metals & Mining Biographies," BMO Capital Markets, accessed 2014; Schweizer, *Clinton Cash*, 36, 198; "Uranium One and UrAsia Energy Announce Combination to Create Emerging Senior Uranium Company."

161 Hoffman, "Renaissance Man"; Kirby, "Uranium Blockbuster"; Schweizer, *Clinton Cash*, 36, 198.

162 Hoffman, "Renaissance Man"; "Sergey Vladimirovich Kurzin Ph.D." Investing.businessweek.com, accessed November 1, 2014; Schweizer, *Clinton Cash*, 36, 198; Dmitry Sidorov, "An Interview With Sergei Kurzin," *Forbes*, April 20, 2009, http://www.forbes.com/2009/04/17/clinton-sergei-kurzin-opinions-contributors-sidorov.html.

163 Hoffman, "Renaissance Man"; "Board of Directors," Uranium One, accessed 2014; Schweizer, *Clinton Cash*, 36, 199.

Chapter 6

1 William D. Campbell, interview with author; John Solomon and Alison Spann, "FBI Uncovered Russian Bribery Plot Before Obama Administration Approved Controversial Nuclear Deal with Moscow," *Hill*, October 17, 2017, https://thehill.com/policy/national-security/355749-fbi-uncovered-russian-bribery-plot-before-obama-administration.

2 Campbell v. Mikerin, 1:16—cv-01888 (D. Maryland 2016), https://www.courtlistener.com/docket/8423862/campbell-v-mikerin/; John Solomon, "FBI Informant Gathered Years of Evidence on Russian Push for US Nuclear Fuel Deals, Including Uranium One, Memos Show," *Hill*, November 20, 2017, https://thehill.com/homenews/administration/361276-fbi-informant-gathered-years-of-evidence-on-russian-push-for-us.

3 CNN, "DOJ Gives FBI Informant Green Light to Testify on Russian Uranium Efforts," RTV6 Indianapolis, October 26, 2017, https://www.theindychannel.com/news/national/doj-gives-fbi-informant-green-light-to-testify-on-russian-uranium-efforts; Solomon and Spann, "FBI Uncovered Russian Bribery Plot Before Obama Administration Approved Controversial Nuclear Deal with Moscow"; Sara A. Carter, "Treasure Trove of Documents Tying Russia to Uranium One," Sean

Hannity Show, on Internet Archive, https://web.archive.org/web/20171121024416/
https://hannity.com/content/2017-11-20-sara-carter/ (the screenshot of the site was
captured on November 21, 2017).

4   "FBI Informant Opens Up about Russia-Uranium Controversy," YouTube video,
     posted by "Fox News," March 28, 2018, https://www.youtube.com/watch?v=
     2fIk0haqdwg.

5   Campbell *v.* Mikerin, 1:16—cv-01888 (D. Maryland 2016); William D. Campbell,
     interview with author.

6   Letter from Charles E. Grassley, Chairman, Committee on the Judiciary, to The
     Honorable Rex W. Tillerson, Secretary, U.S. Department of State, October 12, 2017,
     https://www.judiciary.senate.gov/imo/media/doc/2017-10-12%20CEG%20to%20
     DOS%20(Uranium%20One%20Follow%20up).pdf; "House Also Probing Obama-
     Era Uranium One Deal, DeSantis Says," Fox News, October 22, 2017, https://www.
     foxnews.com/politics/house-also-probing-obama-era-uranium-one-deal-desan-
     tis-says; Interview Summary, To: Members of the House Committee on Oversight
     and Government Reform, Members of the House Permanent Select Committee
     on Intelligence, Members of the Senate Committee on the Judiciary, Fr: Demo-
     cratic Staff, "Re: Interview Summary of Uranium One 'Confidential Informant'
     William Campbell," Congress of the United States, March 8, 2018, https://oversight.
     house.gov/sites/democrats.oversight.house.gov/files/2018-03-08.Interview%20
     Summary%20of%20Campbell%20Interview%20for%20Members-2.pdf.

7   U.S. Department of Justice, "Russian Nuclear Energy Official Pleads Guilty to
     Money Laundering Conspiracy Involving Violations of the Foreign Corrupt
     Practices Act," press release, August 31, 2015, https://www.justice.gov/opa/pr/
     russian-nuclear-energy-official-pleads-guilty-money-laundering-conspiracy-in-
     volving; United States of America v. Vadim Mikerin, August 27, 2015, https://www.
     justice.gov/criminal-fraud/file/782186/download; "Affidavit in Support of an Appli-
     cation Under Rule 41 for a Warrant to Search 2/6/15," Scribd, https://www.scribd.
     com/document/361793720/Affidavit-in-support-of-an-application-under-rule-
     41-for-a-warrant-to-search-2-6-15 (uploaded by Caroline McKee on October 17,
     2017); "United States of America v. Vadim Mikerin – Original Indictment 11/12/14,"
     Scribd,   https://www.scribd.com/document/361793697/United-States-of-Ameri-
     ca-v-Vadim-Mikerin-Original-Indictment-11-12-14 (uploaded by Caroline McKee
     on October 17, 2017); "Evidence Exhibits for Uranium One and Mark Lambert
     Uranium One Trial 159-Pages Filed April 26th 2019," Scribd, https://www.scribd.
     com/document/408071998/Evidence-exhibits-for-Uranium-One-and-Mark-Lam-
     bert-Uranium-One-trial-159-pages-filed-April-26th-2019 (uploaded by Harry
     the Greek on April 29, 2019); John Solomon, "FBI's 37 Secret Pages of Memos
     about Russia, Clintons and Uranium One," *Hill*, October 1, 2018, https://thehill.
     com/opinion/white-house/409356-fbis-37-secret-pages-of-memos-about-russia-
     clintons-and-uranium-one.

8   Michael Isikoff, "Doubts Surface about Key Witness in Uranium One Probe
     of Clinton," Yahoo News, November 17, 2017, https://www.yahoo.com/news/
     doubts-surface-key-witness-uranium-one-probe-clinton-203614558.html; Joel
     Schectman, "Exclusive: Secret Witness in Senate Clinton Probe Is Ex-Lobbyist

for Russian Firm," Reuters, November 16, 2017, https://www.reuters.com/article/us-usa-clinton-informant-exclusive/exclusive-secret-witness-in-senate-clinton-probe-is-ex-lobbyist-for-russian-firm-idUSKBN1DG1SB; Sophie Tatum, "DOJ Gives FBI Informant Green Light to Testify on Russian Uranium Efforts," CNN, October 27, 2017, https://www.cnn.com/2017/10/26/politics/doj-fbi-informant-uranium-congress/index.html; Interview Summary, "Re: Interview Summary of Uranium One 'Confidential Informant' William Campbell," Congress of the United States, March 8, 2018.

9   Michael Isikoff, "Doubts Surface about Key Witness in Uranium One Probe of Clinton"; Joel Schectman, "Exclusive: Secret Witness in Senate Clinton Probe Is Ex-Lobbyist for Russian Firm."

10   William D. Campbell, interview with author.

11   Ibid.

12   Ibid.

13   "Evidence Exhibits for Uranium One and Mark Lambert Uranium One Trial 159-Pages Filed April 26th 2019"; William D. Campbell, interview with author.

14   Ibid.

15   Ibid.

16   Ibid.

17   Ibid.

18   Sara Carter, "FBI Informant on Uranium One Breaks Silence," Sara Carter's website, on Internet Archive, February 7, 2018, https://web.archive.org/web/20180209211913/https://saraacarter.com/fbi-informant-uranium-one-breaks-silence-today/ (the screenshot of the site was captured on February 9, 2018); William D. Campbell, interview with author; "FBI Informant: Russians Bragged Clintons Had Influence over CFIUS in Uranium One," People's Pundit Daily, February 8, 2018, https://www.peoplespunditdaily.com/news/politics/2018/02/08/fbi-informant-russians-bragged-clintons-influence-cifius-uranium-one/.

19   Ibid.

20   Anthony C. Cain, John Gearson, and Lee Willett, eds., "Deterrence in the Twenty-First Century," September 2010, https://media.defense.gov/2017/Apr/05/2001727306/-1/-1/0/B_0118_DETERRENCE_TWENTYFIRST_CENTURY.PDF; Carter, "FBI Informant on Uranium One Breaks Silence"; Jo Becker and Mike McIntire, "Cash Flowed to Clinton Foundation Amid Russian Uranium Deal," New York Times, April 23, 2015, https://www.nytimes.com/2015/04/24/us/cash-flowed-to-clinton-foundation-as-russians-pressed-for-control-of-uranium-company.html; Alexander Nikitin, "Rosatom State Corporation," Bellona, November 26, 2007, https://bellona.org/news/nuclear-issues/nuclear-russia/2007-11-rosatom-state-corporation.

21   Becker and McIntire, "Cash Flowed to Clinton Foundation Amid Russian Uranium Deal"; Carter, "FBI Informant on Uranium One Breaks Silence"; William D. Campbell, interview with author.

22   "Mr. Rod Fisk," Daher-TLI, August 12, 2011, https://www.tliusa.com/index.php/about/news/67-mr-rod-fisk; William D. Campbell, interview with author; "Evidence Exhibits for Uranium One and Mark Lambert Uranium One Trial 159-Pages Filed April 26th 2019."

23 Cristiano Lima, "Sessions Praises Lifting of Gag Order on FBI Informant in Uranium Probe," *Politico*, October 27, 2017, https://www.politico.com/story/2017/10/27/jeff-sessions-doj-gag-order-fbi-informant-uranium-244262; "Evidence Exhibits for Uranium One and Mark Lambert Uranium One Trial 159-Pages Filed April 26th 2019"; Julie Hirschfeld Davis, "Trump Urged Gag Order to Be Lifted on Federal Informant," *New York Times*, October 27, 2017, https://www.nytimes.com/2017/10/27/us/politics/trump-gag-order-justice-department.html.

24 Solomon and Spann, "FBI Uncovered Russian Bribery Plot Before Obama Administration Approved Controversial Nuclear Deal with Moscow"; William D. Campbell, interview with author.

25 Taylor Marsh, "Obama Hearts Nuke Giant Exelon," *Huffington Post*, February 4, 2008, https://www.huffpost.com/entry/obama-hearts-nuke-giant-e_b_84824; Robert Sam Anson, "Obama's Power Grid," *Vanity Fair*, October 13, 2011, https://www.vanityfair.com/news/2011/10/obama-nuclear-201110; Mikheil Saakashvili, "When Russia Invaded Georgia," *Wall Street Journal*, August 7, 2018, https://www.wsj.com/articles/when-russia-invaded-georgia-1533682576.

26 Campbell v. Mikerin, 1:16—cv-01888 (D. Maryland 2016), document 1, filed June 6, 2016, Scribd, https://www.scribd.com/document/369163681/Document (uploaded by DownTheRabbitHole on January 15, 2018); William D. Campbell, interview with author.

27 William D. Campbell, interview with author; Campbell v. Mikerin, 1:16—cv-01888 (D. Maryland 2016), document 1.

28 Ibid.; "Affidavit in Support of an Application Under Rule 41 for a Warrant to Search 2/6/15"; "Evidence Exhibits for Uranium One and Mark Lambert Uranium One Trial 159-Pages Filed April 26th 2019"; "Indictment Affidavit," Scribd, https://www.scribd.com/document/361782806/Indictment-Affidavit (uploaded by M Mali on October 17, 2017); "A Russian Nuclear Firm Under FBI Investigation Was Allowed to Purchase US Uranium Supply," Circa, on Internet Archive, October 17, 2017, https://web.archive.org/web/20180122094147/https://www.circa.com/story/2017/10/17/national-security/the-fbi-uncovered-russian-nuclear-kickback-scheme-months-before-the-obama-administration-passed-uranium-one-deal-with-moscow (the screenshot of the site was captured on January 22, 2018).

29 Ibid.

30 Ibid.

31 William D. Campbell, interview with author.

32 Ibid.

33 Ibid.

34 Ibid.

35 Ibid.

36 Ibid.

37 Ibid.

38 Ibid.

39 Ibid.

40 Ibid.; Campbell v. Mikerin, 1:16—cv-01888 (D. Maryland 2016), document 1.

41 William D. Campbell, interview with author.

42 Ibid.

43 Ibid.

44 Ibid.

45 Andrew C. McCarthy, "Collusion with Russia, a Bipartisan Affair," in *Ball of Collusion: The Plot to Rig an Election and Destroy a Presidency* (New York: Encounter Books, 2019).

46 William D. Campbell, interview with author.

47 Jill Dougherty, "Clinton to Meet Medvedev for Wide-Ranging Talks," CNN, 2009, https://www.cnn.com/2009/WORLD/europe/10/12/us.russia.clinton.medvedev/index.html; Jeff Mason, "Clinton Fails to Win Russia Pledge on Iran Sanctions," Reuters, October 13, 2009, https://www.reuters.com/article/us-russia-clinton/clinton-fails-to-win-russia-pledge-on-iran-sanctions-idUSTRE59B5JB20091013; "Dmitry Medvedev Met with U.S. Secretary of State Hillary Clinton," Kremlin.ru, October 13, 2009, http://en.kremlin.ru/events/president/news/5728.

48 "US and Russia Seek to Show Unity on Iran," Times of Malta, October 14, 2009, https://timesofmalta.com/articles/view/us-and-russia-seek-to-show-unity-on-iran.277373; "Beginning of Meeting with U.S. Secretary of State Hillary Clinton," Kremlin.ru, October 13, 2009, http://en.kremlin.ru/events/president/transcripts/48482.

49 U.S. Department of State, "Secretary Clinton's Interview with Ekho Moskvy Radio," interview, October 14, 2009, https://2009-2017.state.gov/secretary/20092013clinton/rm/2009a/10/130546.htm; Charles Digges, "UPDATE: Reports That New Megatons to Megawatts Deal Is Being Brokered on Sidelines of Start Talks Met with Scepticism from Nuke Industry Experts," Bellona, November 10, 2009, https://bellona.org/news/nuclear-issues/nuclear-agreements/2009-11-update-reports-that-new-megatons-to-megawatts-deal-is-being-brokered-on-sidelines-of-start-talks-met-with-scepticism-from-nuke-industry-experts.

50 Charles Digges, "US and Russia Ink First Ever Completely Commercial Uranium Sales Deal Estimated at $1 Billion," Bellona, May 26, 2009, https://bellona.org/news/nuclear-issues/nuclear-russia/2009-05-us-and-russia-ink-first-ever-completely-commercial-uranium-sales-deal-estimated-at-1-billion; U.S. Energy Information Administration, "Megatons to Megawatts Program Will Conclude at the End of 2013," September 24, 2013, https://www.eia.gov/todayinenergy/detail.php?id=13091.

51 Mary Beth Nikitin, "U.S.-Russian Civilian Nuclear Cooperation Agreement: Issues for Congress," Congressional Research Service, January 11, 2011, https://fas.org/sgp/crs/nuke/RL34655.pdf.

52 "The U.S.-Russian Agreement for Peaceful Nuclear Cooperation," Nuclear Threat Initiative, accessed January 15, 2020, https://www.nti.org/analysis/articles/us-russian-peaceful-cooperation/; Steve Gutterman, "U.S.-Russian Civilian Nuclear Deal Enters Force," Reuters, January 11, 2011, https://www.reuters.com/article/us-russia-usa-nuclear/u-s-russian-civilian-nuclear-deal-enters-force-idUSTRE70A1SF20110111.

53 U.S. Department of State, "Secretary Clinton's Interview with Ekho Moskvy Radio"; U.S. Department of State, "Arms Control and International Security: Releases," n.d., https://2009-2017.state.gov/p/eur/ci/rs/usrussiabilat/c37593.htm; Andrea

Noble, "Uranium One Deal Informant Sued to Recoup More than $700K Lost in Bribes," *Washington Times*, November 16, 2017, https://m.washingtontimes.com/news/2017/nov/16/uranium-one-deal-informant-sued-recoup-more-700k/; Solomon, "FBI Informant Gathered Years of Evidence on Russian Push for US Nuclear Fuel Deals, Including Uranium One, Memos Show"; "A Russian Nuclear Firm Under FBI Investigation Was Allowed to Purchase US Uranium Supply," Circa, on Internet Archive, October 17, 2017, https://web.archive.org/web/20180122094147/http://www.circa.com/story/2017/10/17/national-security/the-fbi-uncovered-russian-nuclear-kickback-scheme-months-before-the-obama-administration-passed-uranium-one-deal-with-moscow (the screenshot of the site was captured on January 22, 2018).

54 Solomon, "FBI Informant Gathered Years of Evidence on Russian Push for US Nuclear Fuel Deals, Including Uranium One, Memos Show."

55 Bureau of Public Affairs, "The Agreement Between the Government of the United States of America and the Government of the Russian Federation… (U.S.-Russia 123 Agreement)," U.S. Department of State, press release, January 12, 2011, https://2009-2017.state.gov/r/pa/prs/ps/2011/01/154318.htm; "Russia, U.S. Sign Deal to Reduce Nuclear Risk," Reuters, December 7, 2010, https://www.reuters.com/article/us-russia-usa-nuclear/russia-u-s-sign-deal-to-reduce-nuclear-risk-idUSTRE6B61T820101207; Michael McFaul, *From Cold War to Hot Peace: An American Ambassador in Putin's Russia* (Boston: Houghton Mifflin Harcourt, 2018).

56 "The U.S.-Russian Agreement for Peaceful Nuclear Cooperation"; Eli Lake, "4 GOP Leaders Warn of Uranium Mine Sale," *Washington Times*, October 5, 2010, https://www.washingtontimes.com/news/2010/oct/5/4-gop-leaders-warn-of-uranium-mine-sale/; E-mail message from Carol Gallagher to Rulemaking Comments, "FW: National Security Concerns with Uranium Mines in Wyoming," Nuclear Regulatory Commission, January 20, 2011, https://www.nrc.gov/docs/ML1102/ML110250286.pdf; "Pentagon Wanted Longer Review of U.S.-Russian Nuclear Trade Pact," Nuclear Threat Initiative, September 22, 2010, https://www.nti.org/gsn/article/pentagon-wanted-longer-review-of-us-russian-nuclear-trade-pact/.

57 Michael Mariotte, "Is U.S. Nuclear Energy or Isn't It Dependent on Russian Enriched Uranium? (Part 2)," Foreign Policy in Focus, April 9, 2014, https://fpif.org/u-s-nuclear-energy-isnt-dependent-russian-enriched-uranium-part-2/; "Putin Admits Russian Forces Were Deployed to Crimea," Reuters, April 17, 2014, https://www.reuters.com/article/russia-putin-crimea/putin-admits-russian-forces-were-deployed-to-crimea-idUSL6N0N921H20140417.

58 William D. Campbell, interview with author; Becker and McIntire, "Cash Flowed to Clinton Foundation Amid Russian Uranium Deal."

59 Carter, "Treasure Trove of Documents Tying Russia to Uranium One"; William D. Campbell, interview with author.

60 Ibid.

61 E-mail message from Rod Fisk to William D. Campbell, "Russian Uranium," June 24, 2010.

62 Ibid.

63 William D. Campbell, interview with author; Lake, "4 GOP Leaders Warn of Uranium Mine Sale."

64 Lake, "4 GOP Leaders Warn of Uranium Mine Sale."

65 E-mail message from Rod Fisk to William D. Campbell, "ARMZ + Uranium One," October 6, 2010.

66 E-mail message from William D. Campbell to MikerinV@tenex.ru and Fefelov.V.I@tenex.ru, "C.M. Herman-Sigma Transnational Report," October 7, 2010; Memorandum from Cheryl Moss Herman to Vadim Mikerin, President, Tenam Corporation, "Policy/Legislative Issues Affecting the Business Climate in the U.S. for TENAM/Tenex," October 7, 2010; Sara A. Carter, "Current DOE Official Once Consulted for Russian Nuclear Companies," Sara A. Carter's website, November 3, 2017, http://s698055499.onlinehome.us/2017/11/03/; Carter, "Treasure Trove of Documents Tying Russia to Uranium One"; William D. Campbell, interview with author.

67 "Policy/Legislative Issues Affecting the Business Climate in the U.S. for TENAM/Tenex."

68 Ibid.

69 Ibid.

70 "Evidence Exhibits for Uranium One and Mark Lambert Uranium One Trial 159-Pages Filed April 26th 2019"; William D. Campbell, interview with author.

71 Solomon, "FBI's 37 Secret Pages of Memos about Russia, Clintons and Uranium One"; William D. Campbell, interview with author.

72 Ibid.

73 "Russia Boosts Nuclear Fuel Exports," World Nuclear News, October 6, 2010, https://www.world-nuclear-news.org/ENF-Russia_boosts_nuclear_fuel_exports-0610104.html; Jeb Handwerger, "Is America Falling Asleep at the Switch with Uranium?," Seeking Alpha, December 16, 2020, https://seekingalpha.com/article/242340-is-america-falling-asleep-at-the-switch-with-uranium.

74 William D. Campbell, interview with author.

75 John Solomon, "Uranium One Informant Makes Clinton Allegations to Congress," Hill, February 7, 2018, https://thehill.com/homenews/administration/372861-uranium-one-informant-makes-clinton-allegations-in-testimony; William D. Campbell, interview with author.

76 Interview Summary, "Re: Interview Summary of Uranium One 'Confidential Informant' William Campbell," Congress of the United States, March 8, 2018; Katie Bo Williams, "Dems: Uranium One Informant Provided 'No Evidence' of Clinton 'Quid Pro Quo,'" Hill, March 8, 2018, https://thehill.com/policy/national-security/377404-dems-uranium-one-informant-provided-no-evidence-of-wrongdoing-by; Paul Waldman, "Democrats Strike a Blow Against GOP Efforts to Shield Trump," Washington Post, March 8, 2018, https://www.washingtonpost.com/blogs/plum-line/wp/2018/03/08/democrats-strike-a-blow-against-gop-efforts-to-shield-trump/; Jonah Goldberg, "Good for Shep Smith," National Review, November 15, 2017, https://www.nationalreview.com/corner/shep-smith-uranium-one-hillary-clinton-story-not-treason/.

77 Paul Rosenzweig, "Unpacking Uranium One: Hype and Law," Lawfare, October 27, 2017, https://www.lawfareblog.com/unpacking-uranium-one-hype-and-law;

Solomon, "FBI's 37 Secret Pages of Memos about Russia, Clintons and Uranium One."

78 Nuclear Regulatory Commission, "Response to Request for Information, Senator John Barrasso, Letter Dated December 11, 2017," https://www.nrc.gov/docs/ML1802/ML18023B016.pdf; Letter from Donna Wichers, President, Uranium One USA, Inc., to Andrew Persinko, Deputy Director, Nuclear Regulatory Commission, and Robert J. Torres, Senior Health Physicist, Nuclear Regulatory Commission, January 29, 2013, https://www.nrc.gov/docs/ML1304/ML13043A505.pdf.

79 Ibid.

80 Ibid.

81 Joseph Tipograph and Lisha Zhou, "US-China Trade War: New Risks for Dealmakers," PaRR, September 2018, https://www.dealreporter.com/assets/PaR-RUSChinaTradeWarFinal_0.pdf; William D. Campbell, interview with author; Carter, "Treasure Trove of Documents Tying Russia to Uranium One."

82 Solomon, "Uranium One Informant Makes Clinton Allegations to Congress"; William D. Campbell, interview with author.

83 William D. Campbell, interview with author.

84 Ibid.

85 Brooke Singman, "Uranium One Informant Says Moscow Paid Millions in Bid to Influence Clinton," Fox News, February 8, 2018, https://www.foxnews.com/politics/uranium-one-informant-says-moscow-paid-millions-in-bid-to-influence-clinton; William D. Campbell, interview with author; Solomon, "Uranium One Informant Makes Clinton Allegations to Congress."

86 Ibid.

87 Dmitry Sudakov, "Russian Nuclear Energy Conquers the World," Pravda, January 22, 2013, https://www.pravdareport.com/russia/123551-russia_nuclear_energy/.

88 William D. Campbell, interview with author.

89 Solomon, "Uranium One Informant Makes Clinton Allegations to Congress."

90 European Court of Human Rights, Application #20914/07 by Maria Anna Carter against Russia, lodged on May 21, 2007, https://hudoc.echr.coe.int/eng-comold#{%22itemid%22:[%22003-3345303-3743418%22]}; Peter Finn, "Most Polonium Made Near the Volga River," *Moscow Times*, January 11, 2007, https://www.the-moscowtimes.com/archive/most-polonium-made-near-the-volga-river; William D. Campbell, interview with author; Luke Harding, chap. 15 in *A Very Expensive Poison: The Assassination of Alexander Litvinenko and Putin's War in the West* (New York: Vintage Books, 2016).

91 William D. Campbell, interview with author; Carter, "Treasure Trove of Documents Tying Russia to Uranium One"; Solomon, "Uranium One Informant Makes Clinton Allegations to Congress."

92 Ibid.

93 Ibid.

94 Ibid.

95 Memorandum from William D. Campbell to FBI Special Agent Tim Taylor, "Explanation of New Transfer Coordinates from Cyprus by Internal Tenex Network Directive," August 23, 2010.

96 William D. Campbell, interview with author.

97 Ibid.

98 Ibid.

99 Memorandum from William D. Campbell to FBI Special Agent Tim Taylor, "Explanation of New Transfer Coordinates from Cyprus by Internal Tenex Network Directive"; William D. Campbell, interview with author.

100 Memorandum from William D. Campbell to FBI Special Agent Tim Taylor, "Explanation of New Transfer Coordinates from Cyprus by Internal Tenex Network Directive."

101 William D. Campbell, interview with author.

102 Andis Kudors and Robert Orttung, "Russian Public Relations Activities and Soft Power," *Russian Analytical Digest* 81 (June 16, 2010), https://www.research-collection.ethz.ch/handle/20.500.11850/26212; William D. Campbell, interview with author.

103 Memorandum from William D. Campbell to FBI Special Agent Tim Taylor, "Explanation of New Transfer Coordinates from Cyprus by Internal Tenex Network Directive."

104 Ibid.

105 William D. Campbell, interview with author.

106 "Former Jockey for Vladimir Putin Moves Tack to U.S.," Paulick Report, November 11, 2013, https://www.paulickreport.com/news/people/former-jockey-for-vladimir-putin-moves-tack-to-u-s/; William D. Campbell, interview with author.

107 William D. Campbell, interview with author.

108 "About Us," Kentucky Colonels, n.d., https://www.kycolonels.org/about-us/; William D. Campbell, interview with author.

109 Official Kentucky Colonel certificate for Vladimir V. Putin, October 15, 2012.

110 Ibid.

111 William D. Campbell, memos to FBI Special Agent Tim Taylor, 2010-2012.

112 Lake, "4 GOP Leaders Warn of Uranium Mine Sale"; Memorandum from Cheryl Moss Herman to Vadim Mikerin, President, Tenam Corporation, "Policy/Legislative Issues Affecting the Business Climate in the U.S. for TENAM/Tenex"; William D. Campbell, interview with author.

113 Memorandum from William D. Campbell to FBI Special Agent Tim Taylor, "Explanation of New Transfer Coordinates from Cyprus by Internal Tenex Network Directive."

114 William D. Campbell, interview with author; "Timeline of Nuclear Diplomacy with Iran," Arms Control Association, March 2020, https://www.armscontrol.org/factsheet/Timeline-of-Nuclear-Diplomacy-With-Iran.

115 Restricted IAEA report, "Re: Iran Enrichment Activities - May 2010"; E-mail message from Rod Fisk to William D. Campbell, "Analysis of IAEA Report," May 31, 2010; Julian Borger, "Iran Lets in UN Inspectors Ahead of Nuclear Report," *Guardian*, August 20, 2009, https://www.theguardian.com/world/2009/aug/20/iran-un-nuclear-iaea-report.

116 Ibid.

117 Iran memo from FBI Special Agent Taylor to William D. Campbell, February 1, 2012; William D. Campbell, interview with author.

118 Ibid.
119 Ibid.
120 Ibid.
121 Ibid.
122 Ibid.
123 "Evidence Exhibits for Uranium One and Mark Lambert Uranium One Trial 159-Pages Filed April 26th 2019"; Carter, "Treasure Trove of Documents Tying Russia to Uranium One"; William D. Campbell, interview with author.
124 "FBI Informant: Russians Bragged Clintons Had Influence over CFIUS in Uranium One"; William D. Campbell, interview with author; Solomon, "Uranium One Informant Makes Clinton Allegations to Congress."
125 "Evidence Exhibits for Uranium One and Mark Lambert Uranium One Trial 159-Pages Filed April 26th 2019"; Carter, "Treasure Trove of Documents Tying Russia to Uranium One"; Ruben Castaneda, "Profile of Rod Rosenstein, U.S. Attorney for Maryland," *Washington Post*, October 9, 2011, https://www.washingtonpost.com/local/profile-of-rod-rosenstein-us-attorney-for-maryland/2011/09/29/gIQAfOT-WYL_story.html.
126 John Solomon, "DOJ Failed to Interview FBI Informant Before it Filed Charges in Russian Nuclear Bribery Case," *Hill*, December 4, 2017, https://thehill.com/homenews/news/363019-doj-failed-to-interview-fbi-informant-before-it-filed-charges-in-russian; Isikoff, "Doubts Surface about Key Witness in Uranium One Probe of Clinton"; William D. Campbell, interview with author.
127 Solomon, "FBI Informant Gathered Years of Evidence on Russian Push for US Nuclear Fuel Deals, Including Uranium One, Memos Show"; William D. Campbell, interview with author; United States of America v. Mark T. Lambert, Case No. TDC-18-0012, document 65, filed April 29, 2019, https://globalinvestigationsreview.com/digital_assets/2a9cde07-b000-4a68-a65b-585c85199444/D.-Md.-18-cr-00012-dckt-000065_000-filed-2019-04-29.pdf.
128 Ibid.
129 Ibid.
130 "Warrant Affidavit," Scribd, https://www.scribd.com/document/361783030/Warrant-Affidavit (uploaded by M Mali on October 17, 2017); United States v. Mikerin, Criminal Action No. TDC-14-0529 (D. Md. May. 7, 2015), https://casetext.com/case/united-states-v-mikerin.
131 "Warrant Affidavit," Scribd.
132 U.S. Department of Justice, "Russian National and Three Others Charged in Kickback Scheme to Obtain Contracts to Transport Russian Nuclear Fuel to the U.S.," press release, October 31, 2014, https://www.justice.gov/usao-md/pr/russian-national-and-three-others-charged-kickback-scheme-obtain-contracts-transport; U.S. Department of Justice, "Former Russian Nuclear Energy Official Sentenced to 48 Months in Prison for Money Laundering Conspiracy Involving Foreign Corrupt Practices Act Violations," press release, December 15, 2015, https://www.justice.gov/opa/pr/former-russian-nuclear-energy-official-sentenced-48-months-prison-money-laundering-conspiracy.
133 Joel Schectman, "U.S. Sentences Russian Nuclear Official to Four Years for Bribe Scheme," Reuters, December 15, 2015, https://www.reuters.com/article/

us-usa-crime-russia/u-s-sentences-russian-nuclear-official-to-four-years-for-bribe-scheme-idUSKBN0TY2V420151215.

134 Ibid.

135 William D. Campbell, photographer, check from Justice Federal Credit Union to William Douglas Campbell, January 7, 2016; William D. Campbell, interview with author.

136 E-mail message from David Gadren to William D. Campbell, "RE: ONGC Individuals," June 21, 2017.

137 Carter, "FBI Informant on Uranium One Breaks Silence."

138 Campbell v. Mikerin, 1:16—cv-01888 (D. Maryland 2016), document 1; William D. Campbell, interview with author.

139 Letter from Linda Dale Hoffa to William D. Campbell, "Re: William Douglas Campbell, et al. v. Vadim Mikerin, et al., Case No. 1:16-cv-01888-MJG (D. Md.) – Voluntarily Dismissing Suit," August 4, 2016.

140 Sara Carter, "Attorney for FBI Informant Presses DOJ for Leak Investigation," Sara A. Carter's website, on Internet Archive, February 21, 2018, https://web.archive.org/web/20180221174047/https://saraacarter.com/attorney-fbi-informant-presses-doj-leak-investigation/ (the screenshot of the site was captured on February 21, 2018); "FBI's 37 Secret Pages of Memos about Russia, Clintons and Uranium One."

141 United States of America v. Mark T. Lambert, Case No. TDC-18-0012, document 65; Carter, "FBI Informant on Uranium One Breaks Silence"; Solomon, "FBI's 37 Secret Pages of Memos about Russia, Clintons and Uranium One"; "Evidence Exhibits for Uranium One and Mark Lambert Uranium One Trial 159-Pages Filed April 26th 2019"; William D. Campbell, interview with author; Solomon, "Uranium One Informant Makes Clinton Allegations to Congress."

142 Ibid.

Chapter 7

1 Hillary Rodham Clinton, "Interview with Vladimir Pozner of First Channel Television," U.S. Department of State, March 19, 2010, https://2009-2017.state.gov/secretary/20092013clinton/rm/2010/03/138712.htm.

2 Hearing Before the Committee on Armed Services, United States Senate, "Briefing by Representatives from the Departments and Agencies Represented on the Committee on Foreign Investment in the United States (CFIUS) to Discuss the National Security Implications of the Acquisition of Peninsular and Oriental Steamship Navigation Company by Dubai Ports World, a Government-owned and –controlled Firm of the United Arab Emirates (UAE)," 109th Cong. (2006), http://www.gpo.gov/fdsys/pkg/CHRG-109shrg32744/html/CHRG-109shrg32744.htm.

3 Reid Pillifant, "Hillary Clinton Remembers 'Friend and Mentor' Robert Byrd," *Observer*, June 28, 2010, https://observer.com/2010/06/hillary-clinton-remembers-friend-and-mentor-robert-byrd/; Senate Armed Services Committee, "U.S. Seaport Security" C-SPAN, February 23, 2006, video, 14:11, https://www.c-span.org/video/?191340-1/us-seaport-security; "User Clip: 2006-02-23 – HRC CFIUS Dubai Ports," C-SPAN, December 10, 2019, video, https://www.c-span.org/video/?c4837338/user-clip-2006-02-23-hrc-cfius-dubai-ports.

4   Hearing Before the Committee on Armed Services, United States Senate, "Briefing by Representatives from the Departments and Agencies Represented on the Committee on Foreign Investment in the United States (CFIUS)...," 109th Cong. (2006).

5   Ibid.

6   Ibid.

7   Congressional Research Service, "Committee on Foreign Investment in the United States (CFIUS)," updated February 14, 2020, http://fas.org/sgp/crs/natsec/RL33388.pdf; "Executive Orders: Executive Order 11858—Foreign Investment in the United States," National Archives, last updated August 15, 2016, http://www.archives.gov/federal-register/codification/executive-order/11858.html.

8   Jill Priluck, "The Mysterious Agency That Can Block a Global Merger," *Reuters* (blog), July 8, 2013, http://blogs.reuters.com/great-debate/2013/07/08/the-mysterious-agency-that-can-block-a-global-merger/; Congressional Research Service, "Committee on Foreign Investment in the United States (CFIUS)."

9   Z. Byron Wolf, "Frist Joins Critics Opposing Port Deal As Bush Presses Forward," ABC News, February 22, 2006, http://abcnews.go.com/Politics/story?id=1645140; Peter Schweizer, *Clinton Cash* (New York: HarperCollins, 2015), 54; Associated Press, "Bush Backs Transfer of U.S. Ports to Dubai Firm," NBC News, February 21, 2006, http://www.nbcnews.com/id/11474440/ns/us_news-security/t/bush-backs-transfer-us-ports-dubai-firm/#.XkHNnBNKiDU.

10   Hearing Before the Committee on Armed Services, United States Senate, "Briefing by Representatives from the Departments and Agencies Represented on the Committee on Foreign Investment in the United States (CFIUS)...," 109th Cong. (2006); Stephanie Kirchgaessner, "Hillary Clinton 'Unaware' of Bill's Dubai Ties," MSNBC, on Internet Archive, March 4, 2006, https://web.archive.org/web/20060313171317/http://msnbc.msn.com/id/11657573 (the screenshot of the site was captured on March 13, 2006).

11   Stephanie Kirchgaessner, "Bill Clinton Helped Dubai on Ports Deal," *Financial Times*, March 1, 2006, https://www.ft.com/content/60414c4c-a95e-11da-a64b-0000779e2340; Dick Morris, "Clintons' UAE Quid Pro Quo," *Hill*, March 17, 2015, https://thehill.com/opinion/dick-morris/236033-dick-morris-clintons-uae-quid-pro-quo; Robert Novak, "The Clintons on Dubai," Real Clear Politics, March 2, 2006, https://www.realclearpolitics.com/Commentary/com-3_2_06_RN.html.

12   Ibid.

13   Morris, "Clintons' UAE Quid Pro Quo."

14   "The Clintons and the Emirates," *Wall Street Journal*, October 16, 2015, https://www.wsj.com/articles/the-clintons-and-the-emirates-1445036941.

15   Raphael Schweber-Koren, "Matthews Cut Short Schumer Quote, Omitting Gist of Schumer's Concern over Ports Deal," Media Matters for America, February 27, 2006, https://www.mediamatters.org/nbc/matthews-cut-short-schumer-quote-omitting-gist-schumers-concern-over-ports-deal.

16   Associated Press, "Bush Backs Transfer of U.S. Ports to Dubai Firm"; "Obama Statement on Administration's Approval of Plan to Outsource U.S. Ports to United Arab Emirates," Barack Obama's Senate page, on Internet Archive, February 21, 2006, https://web.archive.org/web/20080131080732/http://obama.senate.gov/

press/060221-obama_statement_17/ (the screenshot of the site was captured on January 31, 2008).

17 Hearing Before the Committee on Armed Services, United States Senate, "Briefing by Representatives from the Departments and Agencies Represented on the Committee on Foreign Investment in the United States (CFIUS)…," 109th Cong. (2006); Report on Legislative and Oversight Activities of the House Committee on Homeland Security, Together with Additional Views, House of Representatives, "Nomination of Hillary R. Clinton to Be Secretary of State," 109th Cong. (2006).

18 "Marketplace: Concern over Control of U.S. Ports," NPR, February 20, 2006, https://www.npr.org/templates/story/story.php?storyId=5225229.

19 "Five Years After 9/11 Attacks: U.S. Ports More Secure Than Ever; Progress Must Continue," American Association of Port Authorities, news release, September 1, 2006, https://www.aapa-ports.org/advocating/PRdetail.aspx?itemnumber=1092.

20 Simon Romero and Heather Timmons, "A Ship Already Sailed," *New York Times*, February 24, 2006, https://www.nytimes.com/2006/02/24/business/a-ship-already-sailed.html.

21 Neil King Jr. and Greg Hitt, "Dubai Ports World Sells U.S. Assets," *Wall Street Journal*, December 12, 2006, https://www.wsj.com/articles/SB116584567567746444.

22 "AIG Pledges $5.25 Million to Microfinance Project Headed by Ex-President Clinton," Insurance Journal, September 25, 2006, https://www.insurancejournal.com/news/international/2006/09/25/72757.htm.

23 "The Clintons and the Emirates"; James Rickards, *Aftermath: Seven Secrets of Wealth Preservation in the Coming Chaos* (New York: Penguin, 2019).

24 "Hillary Clinton Promotes Plan for Strong Defense and Good Jobs in Indiana," American Presidency Project, on Internet Archive, press release, April 12, 2008, https://web.archive.org/web/20150816160113/http://www.presidency.ucsb.edu/ws/?pid=96587 (the screenshot of the site was captured on August 16, 2015).

25 Jo Becker and Mike McIntire, "Cash Flowed to Clinton Foundation Amid Russian Uranium Deal," *New York Times*, April 23, 2015, https://www.nytimes.com/2015/04/24/us/cash-flowed-to-clinton-foundation-as-russians-pressed-for-control-of-uranium-company.html.

26 Hearing Before the Committee on Armed Services, United States Senate, "Briefing by Representatives from the Departments and Agencies Represented on the Committee on Foreign Investment in the United States (CFIUS)…," 109th Cong. (2006).

27 Morris, "Clintons' UAE Quid Pro Quo"; Rickards, *Aftermath*; Schweizer, *Clinton Cash*, 54.

28 "About Us," Clinton Global Initiative, Clinton Foundation, accessed November 15, 2019, https://www.clintonfoundation.org/clinton-global-initiative/about-us/cgi-mission; Anna Massoglia, "Clinton Foundation's Revenue Hit 15-Year Low After 2016 Presidential Election," Opensecrets.org, December 13, 2018, https://www.opensecrets.org/news/2018/12/clinton-foundation-revenue-low/.

29 Michael Sainato, "Exclusive: Wikileaks Guccifer 2.0 Teaser Exposes Pay-to-Play and Financial Data," *Observer*, October 5, 2016, https://observer.com/2016/10/exclusive-wikileaks-guccifer-2-0-teaser-exposes-pay-to-play-and-financial-data/; Tyler Durden, "Clinton Foundation Allegedly Hacked Exposing Thousands of Donor Databases; "Pay to Play" Folder," Zero Hedge,

October 4, 2016, https://www.zerohedge.com/news/2016-10-04/clinton-foundation
-hacked-exposing-thousands-donor-databases-pay-play-folder.

30 James V. Grimaldi and Anupreeta Das, "Clinton Foundation's Fundraisers Pressed
Donors to Steer Business to Former President," *Wall Street Journal*, October 26,
2016, https://www.wsj.com/articles/clinton-foundations-fundraisers-pressed-do-
nors-to-steer-business-to-former-president-1477527597.

31 Massoglia, "Clinton Foundation's Revenue Hit 15-Year Low After 2016 Presidential
Election"; Anna Massoglia and Yue Stella Yu, "Clinton Foundation Cash Flow Continues to Drop Years After 2016 Election Loss," Opensecrets.org, November 18, 2019,
https://www.opensecrets.org/news/2019/11/clinton-foundation-cash-flow-drop/.

32 Hearing Before the Committee on Foreign Relations, United States Senate, "Nomination of Hillary R. Clinton to be Secretary of State," 111th Cong. (2009), https://
www.govinfo.gov/content/pkg/CHRG-111shrg54615/html/CHRG-111shrg54615.
htm; Seamus Bruner, *Compromised* (New York: Post Hill Press, 2018), 78-79.

33 Bruner, *Compromised*, 80; Jonathan Swan, "Seven Ways the Clinton Foundation
Failed to Meet Its Transparency Promises," *Hill*, August 27, 2016, https://thehill.
com/homenews/campaign/293507-seven-ways-the-clinton-foundation-failed-to-
meet-its-transparency-promises.

34 Swan, "Seven Ways the Clinton Foundation Failed to Meet Its Transparency Promises"; Schweizer, *Clinton Cash*, 35-36, 45; Siobhan Hughes and James V. Grimaldi,
"Clinton Foundation Provides Details on Canadian Donation," *Wall Street Journal*,
April 26, 2015, https://www.wsj.com/articles/clinton-foundation-provides-de-
tails-on-canadian-donation-1430092540; "Revealed: Washington Post Uncovers
1,100 Hidden Foreign 'Clinton Cash' Donations," Breitbart, April 28, 2015, https://
www.breitbart.com/politics/2015/04/28/revealed-washington-post-uncov-
ers-1100-hidden-foreign-clinton-cash-donations/; Michael Patrick Leahy, "Clinton
Foundation Refuses to Release Names of 1,076 Secret Foreign Donors," Breitbart,
June 3, 2015, https://www.breitbart.com/politics/2015/06/03/clinton-foundation-
refuses-to-release-names-of-1076-secret-foreign-donors/; "The Clinton Giustra
Enterprise Partnership (Canada)," Clinton Global Initiative, Clinton Foundation,
accessed November 15, 2019, https://www.clintonfoundation.org/clinton-glob-
al-initiative/commitments/clinton-giustra-enterprise-partnership-canada; Claudia
Parsons, "Clinton, Mining Industry Launch Anti-Poverty Effort," Reuters, June 21,
2007, https://uk.reuters.com/article/environment-clinton-poverty-mining-dc/
clinton-mining-industry-launch-anti-poverty-effort-idUKN2139844220070621;
Rosalind S. Helderman and Tom Hamburger, "1,100 Donors to a Canadian
Charity Tied to Clinton Foundation Remain Secret," *Washington Post*, April
28, 2015, https://www.washingtonpost.com/politics/1100-donors-to-a-canadian
-charity-tied-to-clinton-foundation-remain-secret/2015/04/28/c3c0f374-ed-
bc-11e4-8666-a1d756d0218e_story.html; Energy Metals Corporation, "Uranium
One and Energy Metals Receive CFIUS Approval for Proposed Arrangement,"
news release, July 31, 2007, https://www.sec.gov/Archives/edgar/data/1361605
/000106299307002905/rule425.htm.

35 Uranium One Inc., "Uranium One Special Committee and Board Recommend Transaction with ARMZ," Cision, July 15, 2010, https://www.newswire.ca/

news-releases/uranium-one-special-committee-and-board-recommend-transac-tion-with-armz-544710692.html.

36 Rickards, *Aftermath*.

37 Ibid., 32.

38 Ibid., 31-32.

39 Ibid., 31-35.

40 Bruner, *Compromised*, 73; Becker and McIntire, "Cash Flowed to Clinton Founda-tion Amid Russian Uranium Deal."

41 Rickards, *Aftermath*.

42 U.S. Department of the Treasury, "CFIUS Overview," accessed November 2, 2019, https://home.treasury.gov/policy-issues/international/the-committee-on-foreign-investment-in-the-united-states-cfius/composition-of-cfius; Rickards, *Aftermath*.

43 Rickards, *Aftermath*.

44 Ibid.

45 E-mail message from Zeba Reyahzuddin to Nathan P. Lane, "CFIUS Certification to Congress," U.S. Department of State, November 4, 2010, https://foia.state.gov/Search/results.aspx?searchText=%2220101004+AM+CFIUS+10-40.doc%22&be-ginDate=&endDate=&publishedBeginDate=&publishedEndDate=&caseNumber=.

46 "FACT SHEET: U.S. – Russia Bilateral Presidential Commission," Obama White House (archive), press release, July 6, 2009, https://obamawhitehouse.archives.gov/the-press-office/fact-sheet-us russia-bilateral-presidential-commission; "Joint Statement by the Coordinators of the U.S.-Russia Presidential Commission," Obama White House (archive), accessed November 15, 2019, https://obamawhitehouse.archives.gov/sites/default/files/u.s.-russia_presidential_commission_joint_state-ment.pdf.

47 U.S. Department of State, "Economic Statecraft," Remarks by Hillary Rodham Clinton, October 14, 2011, https://2009-2017.state.gov/secretary/20092013clinton/rm/2011/10/175552.htm.

48 Ben Jacobs, "Hillary Clinton Aides' Wall Street Links Raise Economic Policy Doubts," *Guardian*, July 26, 2015, https://www.theguardian.com/us-news/2015/jul/26/wall-street-links-hillary-clinton-aides-economic-policy-doubts; U.S. Department of State, "Daily Appointments Schedule for June 18, 2010," June 18, 2010, https://2009-2017.state.gov/r/pa/prs/appt/2010/06/143304.htm.

49 "PART 2 RUSSIA – US BUSINESS DIALOGUE.mp4," YouTube video, posted by "SPIEF," October 14, 2010, https://youtu.be/ofsMBcSI80o?t=377; U.S. Department of State, "Daily Appointments Schedule for June 18, 2010."

50 Sarah Westwood, "Emails Show Clinton Ties to Russian Oligarch Under Investiga-tion," *Washington Examiner*, September 12, 2016, https://www.washingtonexaminer.com/emails-show-clinton-ties-to-russian-oligarch-under-investigation; "PART 2 RUSSIA – US BUSINESS DIALOGUE.mp4."

51 Owen Matthews, "How Obama Bought Russia's (Expensive) Friendship," *Newsweek*, June 24, 2010, https://www.newsweek.com/how-obama-bought-russias -expensive-friendship-73289; "Is Barack Obama Tough Enough?," *Economist*, Feb-ruary 25, 2010, https://www.economist.com/united-states/2010/02/25/is-barack

-obama-tough-enough; James Joyner, "Europe's Obama Fatigue," *Foreign Policy*, October 29, 2009, https://foreignpolicy.com/2009/10/29/europes-obama-fatigue/.

52 Letter from four House ranking members regarding CFIUS Case 10-40, to The Honorable Timothy F. Geithner, U.S. Department of the Treasury, Chairman, CFIUS, October 5, 2010, https://www.judicialwatch.org/wp-content/uploads/2018/12/JW-v-DOJ-Uranium-One-Treasury-doc-00722.pdf.

53 Letter from Charles E. Grassley, Chairman, Committee on the Judiciary, to The Honorable Rex W. Tillerson, Secretary, U.S. Department of State, October 12, 2017, https://www.judiciary.senate.gov/imo/media/doc/2017-10-12%20CEG%20to%20DOS%20(Uranium%20One%20Follow%20up).pdf; Letter from John Barrasso, M.D., Chairman, Committee on Environment and Public Works, to The Honorable Rick Perry, Secretary, U.S. Department of Energy, and to The Honorable Kristine Svinicki, Chairman, U.S. Nuclear Regulatory Commission, December 11, 2017, https://www.nrc.gov/docs/ML1734/ML17346A446.pdf.

54 E-mail message from Ari N. Sulby to Helen Recinos, "FW: Additional Information on Russian Nuclear Cooperation with Iran: CFIUS Case 10-40," U.S. Department of State, obtained by Judicial Watch, Inc., October 31, 2018, http://www.judicialwatch.org/wp-content/uploads/2018/12/JW-v-DOJ-Uranium-One-records-00722-production-3-pg-13.pdf/.

55 Ibid.

56 Letter from Eric F. Stein, Director, Office of Information Programs and Services, to Mr. William F. Marshall, Judicial Watch, August 31, 2018, http://www.judicialwatch.org/wp-content/uploads/2018/12/JW-v-DOJ-Uranium-One-records-00722.pdf.

57 Ibid.

58 Ibid

59 Ibid.

60 Letter from four House ranking members regarding CFIUS Case 10-40, to The Honorable Timothy F. Geithner, U.S. Department of the Treasury, Chairman, CFIUS, October 5, 2010.

61 Ibid.

62 Bureau of Counterterrorism, "State Sponsors of Terrorism," U.S. Department of State, accessed November 1, 2019, https://www.state.gov/state-sponsors-of-terrorism/.

63 Letter from four House ranking members regarding CFIUS Case 10-40, to The Honorable Timothy F. Geithner, U.S. Department of the Treasury, Chairman, CFIUS, October 5, 2010.

64 Rickards, *Aftermath*.

65 Letter from four House ranking members regarding CFIUS Case 10-40, to The Honorable Timothy F. Geithner, U.S. Department of the Treasury, Chairman, CFIUS, October 5, 2010; Nuclear Regulatory Commission, Response to Request for Information, Senator John Barrasso, Letter dated December 11, 2017, https://www.nrc.gov/docs/ML1802/ML18023B016.pdf.

66 Melissa Akin and Julie Gordon, "3-Russia's ARMZ to Take Uranium One Private for $1.3 Bln," Reuters, January 14, 2013, https://www.reuters.com/article/uranium-one-private/update-3-russias-armz-to-take-uranium-one-private-for-1-3-bln-idUSL6N0AJ0BA20130114.

67 Rickards, *Aftermath*.

68 Ibid.

69 Federal Bureau of Investigation, "Uranium One Transaction Part 01 of 01," accessed July 23, 2019, https://vault.fbi.gov/uranium-one-transaction/uranium-one-transaction-part-01-of-01/view; Letter from Charles E. Grassley, Chairman, Committee on the Judiciary, to The Honorable Daniel R. Coats, Director, Office of the Director of National Intelligence, October 12, 2017, https://www.judiciary.senate.gov/imo/media/doc/2017-10-12%20CEG%20to%20DNI%20(Uranium%20One%20Follow%20up).pdf.

70 John Solomon and Alison Spann, "FBI Uncovered Russian Bribery Plot Before Obama Administration Approved Controversial Nuclear Deal with Moscow," *Hill*, October 17, 2017, https://thehill.com/policy/national-security/355749-fbi-uncovered-russian-bribery-plot-before-obama-administration; Bruner, *Compromised*, 46.

71 Bruner, *Compromised*, 63-65.

72 William D. Campbell, interview with author.

73 Nuclear Regulatory Commission, Response to Request for Information, Senator John Barrasso, Letter dated December 11, 2017; Bruner, *Compromised*, 63-65.

74 Bruner, *Compromised*, 63-65.

75 Ibid., 63-64.

76 Nuclear Regulatory Commission, Response to Request for Information, Senator John Barrasso, Letter dated December 11, 2017; Bruner, *Compromised*, 57.

77 Letter from Donna I. Wichers, Senior Vice President, ISR Operations, to Keith McConnell, Deputy Director, Decommissioning and Uranium Recovery Licensing Directorate, U.S. Nuclear Regulatory Commission, Uranium One, July 20, 2010, https://www.nrc.gov/docs/ML1020/ML102090404.pdf; Uranium One, Notice of Change of Control and Ownership Information, NRC Form 313, https://www.nrc.gov/docs/ML1020/ML102090404.pdf.

78 Letter from Donna L. Wichers, Senior Vice President, ISR Operations, to Keith McConnell, Deputy Director, Decommissioning and Uranium Recovery Licensing Directorate, U.S. Nuclear Regulatory Commission, Uranium One, July 20, 2010.

79 Ibid.

80 Paul Rosenzweig, "Unpacking Uranium One: Hype and Law," Lawfare, October 27, 2017, https://www.lawfareblog.com/unpacking-uranium-one-hype-and-law.

81 Uranium One, Notice of Change of Control and Ownership Information, NRC Form 313.

82 Letter from Greg Kruse, Manager, US Operations, Uranium One Americas, Inc., to Andrew Persinko, Deputy Director, Decommissioning & Uranium Recovery Licensing Directorate, U.S. Nuclear Regulatory Commission, and Roberto J. Torres, Senior Health Physicist, Nuclear Materials Safety, Branch B, U.S. Nuclear Regulatory Commission, June 1, 2015, https://www.nrc.gov/docs/ML1518/ML15181A376.pdf;Letter from Greg Kruse, Manager, US Operations, Uranium One Americas, Inc., to Andrew Persinko, Deputy Director, Decommissioning & Uranium Recovery Licensing Directorate, U.S. Nuclear Regulatory Commission, and Roberto J. Torres, Senior Health Physicist, Nuclear Materials Safety, Branch B, U.S. Nuclear Regulatory Commission, September 14, 2016, https://www.nrc.gov/docs/ML1629/

ML16299A040.pdf; Letter from Janice Dunn Lee, Director, Office of International Programs, to Andre – Claude Lacoste, Director, Nuclear Installations, Nuclear Regulatory Commission, February 28, 2001, https://www.nrc.gov/docs/ML0106/ML010610358.pdf; E-mail message from Andrew Persinko to ForeignTravel, "Quick Look Report: Moscow May 19-30," Nuclear Regulatory Commission, June 3, 2003, https://www.nrc.gov/docs/ML0408/ML040890656.pdf.

83 Uranium One Inc., Quarterly Report, Quarter 2, translated, approved on August 15, 2018, http://www.uranium1.com/upload/iblock/5ac/5acd5fec499284 cf2e3e8e686124e014.pdf.

84 Ibid.; Letter from Donna L. Wichers, Senior Vice President, ISR Operations, to Keith McConnell, Deputy Director, Decommissioning and Uranium Recovery Licensing Directorate, U.S. Nuclear Regulatory Commission, Uranium One, July 20, 2010.

85 Uranium One, Notice of Change of Control and Ownership Information, NRC Form 313; Uranium One Inc., Quarterly Report, Quarter 4, approved on February 10, 2017, http://www.uranium1.com/upload/iblock/85c/85c15dd83c0e5a76ae6c 747980a006ca.pdf.

86 John Solomon and Alison Spann, "Uranium One Deal Led to Some Exports to Europe, Memos Show," *Hill*, November 2, 2017, https://thehill.com/policy/national-security/358339-uranium-one-deal-led-to-some-exports-to-europe-memos-show.

87 Letter from John Barrasso, M.D., Chairman, Committee on Environment and Public Works, to The Honorable Rick Perry, Secretary, U.S. Department of Energy, and to The Honorable Kristine Svinicki, Chairman, U.S. Nuclear Regulatory Commission, December 11, 2017.

88 Eugene Kiely, "The Facts on Uranium One," FactCheck.org, October 26, 2017, https://www.factcheck.org/2017/10/facts-uranium-one/; David Emery, "Did Hillary Clinton Give 20% of United States' Uranium to Russia in Exchange for Clinton Foundation Donations?," Snopes, October 25, 2016, https://www.snopes.com/fact-check/hillary-clinton-uranium-russia-deal/; Jack Holmes, "What Is the Uranium One 'Scandal?,'" *Esquire*, December 21, 2017, https://www.esquire.com/news-politics/a14477730/trump-uranium-one-republicans-russia/.

89 Rickards, *Aftermath*.

90 Dr. Tom Borelli, "Utility Industry Aids Putin's Stealth War on US Uranium Mining," Conservative Review, March 28, 2019, https://www.conservativereview.com/news/utility-industry-aids-putins-stealth-war-u-s-uranium-mining/; "US Uranium Mining and Exploration," World Nuclear Association, last updated February 2020, https://www.world-nuclear.org/information-library/country-profiles/countries-t-z/appendices/us-nuclear-fuel-cycle-appendix-1-us-uranium-mining.aspx; "Uranium One Mothballs US Mine," Nuclear Engineering International, August 21, 2018, https://www.neimagazine.com/news/newsuranium-one-mothballs-us-mine-6715119.

91 Borelli, "Utility Industry Aids Putin's Stealth War on US Uranium Mining."

92 Ned Mamula, "Russia's Uranium Gambit: The Real Uranium One Scandal," Capital Research Center, January 15, 2019, https://capitalresearch.org/article/russias-uranium-gambit-part-4/.

93 Rickards, *Aftermath.*

94 Borelli, "Utility Industry Aids Putin's Stealth War on US Uranium Mining";
Spencer Abraham, "Russian Control of US Uranium Supply Is a Huge National
Security Problem," Fox News, March 24, 2019, https://www.foxnews.com/opinion/
russian-control-of-us-uranium-supply-is-a-huge-national-security-problem.

95 William D. Campbell, interview with author.

96 Ibid.

97 Schweizer, *Clinton Cash*, 35-36.

98 Parsons, "Clinton, Mining Industry Launch Anti-Poverty Effort."

99 Energy Metals Corporation, Form 51-102F3, Material Change Report, June 8, 2007,
https://www.sec.gov/Archives/edgar/data/1361605/000106299307002200/exhibit
99-2.htm; Parsons, "Clinton, Mining Industry Launch Anti-Poverty Effort"; "The
Clinton Giustra Enterprise Partnership (Canada)," Clinton Foundation; Energy
Metals Corporation, "Uranium One and Energy Metals Receive CFIUS Approval
for Proposed Arrangement."

100 Helderman and Hamburger, "1,100 Donors to a Canadian Charity Tied to Clinton
Foundation Remain Secret"; Schweizer, *Clinton Cash*, 44-45.

101 Ibid.; Leahy, "Clinton Foundation Refuses to Release Names of 1,076 Secret Foreign
Donors."

102 Catherine Belton, "Rosatom Agrees Deal for Stake in Uranium One," *Financial Times*,
June 15, 2009, https://www.ft.com/content/5f23915a-59d5-11de-b687-00144feabdc0.

103 Schweizer, *Clinton Cash,* 50-51.

104 Ibid., 51; Bruner, *Compromised*, 65.

105 "Recognizing Our Generous Supporters," Clinton Foundation, accessed 2019,
https://www.clintonfoundation.org/contributors?category=%241%2C000%2C001+
to+%245%2C000%2C000.

106 John Solomon and Alison Spann, "Clintons Understated Support from Firm
Hired by Russian Nuclear Company," *Hill*, November 28, 2017, https://thehill.com/
homenews/news/362234-clintons-understated-support-from-firm-hired-by-rus-
sian-nuclear-company.

107 E-mail message from Cheryl D. Mills to H, "FW: economy speech," U.S. Department of State, October 3, 2011, https://foia.state.gov/searchapp/DOCUMENTS/
HRCEmail_SeptemberWeb/O-2015-08633-192/DOC_0C05782639/C05782639.
pdf; Cassidy & Associates, "A Nuclear Renaissance for Today" (presentation for
Tenex, July 25, 2007).

108 Tenex Contract for Lobbying Services and Consulting Services, April 12, 2010;
APCO Worldwide, Inc., Exhibit A, Pursuant to the Foreign Agents Registration
Act of 1938, as amended, received April 13, 2010; "CGI 2010 Annual Meeting:
Agenda," Clinton Global Initiative, Clinton Foundation, September 2010, https://
www.clintonfoundation.org/clinton-global-initiative/meetings/annual-meet-
ings/2010/agenda/day-1; "CGI 2010 Annual Meeting: Sponsors," Clinton Global
Initiative, Clinton Foundation, September 2010, https://www.clintonfoundation.
org/clinton-global-initiative/meetings/annual-meetings/2010/sponsors.

109 Opensecrets.org, "Bill Clinton's Foundation Discloses Diverse List of Donors," Open-
Secrets News, December 18, 2008, https://www.opensecrets.org/news/2008/12/
bill-clintons-foundation-discl/.

110 Solomon and Spann, "Clintons Understated Support from Firm Hired by Russian Nuclear Company."

111 "CGI 2010 Annual Meeting: Sponsors"; "Press Release: Secretary Geithner to Join President Clinton at CGI America," Clinton Foundation, June 16, 2011, https://www.clintonfoundation.org/main/news-and-media/press-releases-and-statements/press-release-secretary-geithner-to-join-president-clinton-at-cgi-america.html; "Press Release: President Clinton Announces Impact of Commitments Made at the Second Annual Clinton Global Initiative America Meeting," Clinton Foundation, June 8, 2012, https://www.clintonfoundation.org/main/news-and-media/press-releases-and-statements/president-clinton-announces-impact-of-commitments.html; "MEDIA ADVISORY: Program and Press Conference Schedule 2013 CGI Annual Meeting," Clinton Foundation, September 23, 2013, https://www.clintonfoundation.org/press-releases/media-advisory-program-and-press-conference-schedule-2013-cgi-annual-meeting.

112 APCO Worldwide, Inc., Supplemental Statement, Pursuant to the Foreign Agents Registration Act of 1938, as amended, received September 30, 2010.

113 Solomon and Spann, "Clintons Understated Support from Firm Hired by Russian Nuclear Company."

114 Bruner, *Compromised*, 68-69, 81, 198; Tenex Contract for Lobbying Services and Consulting Services, May 21, 2007; Tenex Contract for Lobbying Services and Consulting Services, June 24, 2008.

115 Bruner, *Compromised*, 68-69; Sara A. Carter, "Current DOE Official Once Consulted for Russian Nuclear Companies," Circa, November 2, 2017, on Internet Archive, https://web.archive.org/web/20171104021026/https://www.circa.com/story/2017/11/02/nation/current-doe-official-once-consulted-for-russian-nuclear-companies (the screenshot of the site was captured on November 4, 2017); "Cheryl Moss Herman," LinkedIn profile, accessed November 15, 2019, https://www.linkedin.com/in/cheryl-moss-herman-0112897.

116 David M. Marchick and Matthew J. Slaughter, "Global FDI Policy: Correcting a Protectionist Drift," Council on Foreign Relations, June 2008, https://cdn.cfr.org/sites/default/files/pdf/2008/06/FDI_CSR34.pdf; "Theodore W. Kassinger," O'Melveny, accessed November 15, 2019, https://www.omm.com/professionals/theodore-w-kassinger/.

117 Marchick and Slaughter, "Global FDI Policy: Correcting a Protectionist Drift"; "Protectionist Drift in Global FDI Policy Poses Threat to World Economy, Warns Council Special Report," Council on Foreign Relations, June 25, 2008, https://www.cfr.org/news-releases/protectionist-drift-global-fdi-policy-poses-threat-world-economy-warns-council.

118 Bureau of Economic, Energy and Business Affairs, "Summary of Discussions of September 30, 2009 Meeting of the Advisory Committee on International Economic Policy," U.S. Department of State, archives, September 30, 2009, https://2009-2017.state.gov/e/eb/adcom/aciep/mtg/130558.htm.

119 Bruner, *Compromised*, 68.

120 U.S. Department of State, "Photo Gallery: August 12, 2010 Meeting of the ACIEP," accessed April 11, 2018, https://2009-2017.state.gov/e/eb/adcom/aciep/2010/pg5/index.htm; "1-Uranium One Shareholders Approve ARMZ Deal," Reuters,

August 31, 2010, https://www.reuters.com/article/uraniumone-armz-idUKN31247 33820100831; Becker and McIntire, "Cash Flowed to Clinton Foundation Amid Russian Uranium Deal"; Bruner, *Compromised*, 68-69.

121 E-mail message from Rebecca H. Neff to Ari N. Sulby, "RE: CFIUS CASE: Rosatom / Uranium One," U.S. Department of State, November 2, 2010, https://foia.state. gov/Search/results.aspx?searchText=%22+Scanned+signed+closing+letter+to+- Theodore+W+Kassinger%22&beginDate=&endDate=&publishedBeginDate=&- publishedEndDate=&caseNumber=.

122 Chris Matthews, "Clinton Foundation Lawyers Thought Non-Profit Was Shady Too," *Fortune*, October 18, 2016, https://fortune.com/2016/10/18/clinton-foundation -conflicts/.

123 "Recognizing Our Generous Supporters," Clinton Foundation, accessed 2019, https://www.clintonfoundation.org/contributors.

124 Bruner, *Compromised*, 12-13, 56-57.

125 "Statement by the President on United States Commitment to Open Invest- ment Policy," Obama White House (archive), press release, June 20, 2011, https:// obamawhitehouse.archives.gov/the-press-office/2011/06/20/statement-president -united-states-commitment-open-investment-policy.

126 "Exelon Corp Signs Uranium Supply Deal with Russia," Reuters, June 3, 2009, https:// www.reuters.com/article/us-exelon-russia-uranium/exelon-corp-signs-uranium -supply-deal-with-russia-idUSTRE5522VB20090603.

127 Rickards, *Aftermath*.

Chapter 8

1 Michael McFaul, *From Cold War to Hot Peace: An American Ambassador in Putin's Russia* (Boston: Houghton Mifflin Harcourt, 2018).

2 Ibid.

3 Ibid.

4 U.S. Department of State, "Joint Report: 2009-2010 Results of the U.S.-Russia Pres- idential Commission," June 24, 2010, https://web.archive.org/web/20110228215504/ http://www.state.gov/documents/organization/143808.pdf (the screenshot of the site was captured on February 28, 2011); "Joint Statement by the Coordinators of the U.S.-Russia Presidential Commission," Obama White House (archive), n.d., https://obamawhitehouse.archives.gov/sites/default/files/u.s.-russia_presidential_ commission_joint_statement.pdf; McFaul, *From Cold War to Hot Peace*.

5 Ibid.; Hillary Rodham Clinton, *Hard Choices* (London: Simon and Schuster, 2014), 222.

6 McFaul, From Cold War to Hot Peace; Nicole Martinelli, "After Apple Visit, Russia Creating Copycat 4G Phone?," Cult of Mac, September 16, 2010, https://www.cul- tofmac.com/59401/after-apple-visit-russia-creating-copycat-4g-phone/59401/; Christian Zibreg, "Russian President Visits Apple and Tweets about iPhone 4 Before Meeting with Obama," Geek.com, June 25, 2010, https://www.geek.com/ apple/russian-president-visits-apple-and-tweets-about-iphone-4-before-meeting- with-obama-1266216/.

7 McFaul, *From Cold War to Hot Peace*; Government Accountability Institute, "From Russia With Money: Hillary Clinton, the Russian Reset, and Cronyism," August 2016,

https://www.g-a-i.org/wp-content/uploads/2016/08/Report-Skolkvovo-08012016
.pdf; "Medvedev Now on Twitter, 19,000 Follow," UPI, June 24, 2010, https://www.
upi.com/Top_News/US/2010/06/24/Medvedev-now-on-Twitter-19000-follow
/22061277390545/?ur3=1; Amie Ferris-Rotman, "New Year Ski Tweet for Medvedev and Schwarzenegger?," Reuters, January 4, 2011, https://uk.reuters.com
/article/oukoe-uk-russia-schwarzenegger-twitter/new-year-ski-tweet-for-med-
vedev-and-schwarzenegger-idUKTRE7032YW20110104; Dmitry Medvedev
(@MedvedevRussiaE), "My congratulations to @BarackObama on his birthday," Twitter, August 4, 2010, 12:12 PM, https://twitter.com/MedvedevRussiaE/
status/20315417480.

8   McFaul, *From Cold War to Hot Peace*.

9   Robert M. Gates, *Duty: Memoirs of a Secretary at War* (New York: Alfred A. Knopf,
    2014), 260-261; Leon Panetta, *Worthy Fights* (New York: Penguin Press, 2014), 164.

10 Thomas Grove, "Russia's 'Sexy Spy' in Provocative Photoshoot," Reuters,
    October 19, 2010, https://www.reuters.com/article/us-annachapman-photo/
    russias-sexy-spy-in-provocative-photoshoot-idUSTRE69I3LW20101019; Gov-
    ernment Accountability Institute, "From Russia With Money: Hillary Clinton,
    the Russian Reset, and Cronyism," 37; Julia Ioffe, "Anna Chapman Starts a Tech
    Venture Fund, and You Can Too," *Forbes*, June 8, ,2011, https://www.forbes.com/
    sites/juliaioffe/2011/06/08/anna-chapman-opens-a-tech-venture-fund-and-
    you-can-too/#73196f9a444c; Chris Matthews, "Russia's Anna Chapman Cashes
    In," *Newsweek*, February 13, 2011, https://www.newsweek.com/russias-anna
    -chapman-cashes-68751.

11 McFaul, *From Cold War to Hot Peace*.

12 Gates, *Duty*, 261-262; John Solomon and Alison Spann, "FBI Watched, Then Acted
    As Russian Spy Moved Closer to Hillary Clinton," *Hill*, October 22, 2017, https://
    thehill.com/policy/national-security/356630-fbi-watched-then-acted-as-russian-
    spy-moved-closer-to-hillary; McFaul, *From Cold War to Hot Peace*.

13 McFaul, *From Cold War to Hot Peace*.

14 Ibid.

15 Andrew Osborn, "Washington to Tone Down Criticism of Russian Human
    Rights Record," *Telegraph*, October 13, 2009, https://www.telegraph.co.uk/news/
    worldnews/barackobama/6318943/Washington-to-tone-down-criticism-of-Rus-
    sian-human-rights-record.html.

16 Philip Hanson, James Nixey, Lila Shevtsova, and Andrew Wood, "Putin Again:
    Implications for Russia and the West," Chatham House, February 2012, https://
    www.chathamhouse.org/sites/default/files/public/Research/Russia%20and%20
    Eurasia/r0212_putin.pdf.

17 "PART 2 RUSSIA – US BUSINESS DIALOGUE.mp4," YouTube video, posted
    by "SPIEF," October 14, 2010, https://youtu.be/ofsMBcSI80o?t=377; U.S. Depart-
    ment of State, "Daily Appointments Schedule for June 18, 2010," June 18, 2010,
    https://2009-2017.state.gov/r/pa/prs/appt/2010/06/143304.htm.

18 Dan Friedman, "Hillary Clinton's Campaign Lashes Back at Fund-Raising
    Charges, and President Obama Backs Her," *New York Daily News*, April 24, 2015,
    https://www.nydailynews.com/news/national/obama-backs-hillary-funds-flap
    -article-1.2198308#.

19 Robert Hormats, "The Future of Russian Innovation: A Conversation with Russia's Young Entrepreneurs," *Huffington Post*, July 8, 2010, https://www.huffpost.com/entry/the-future-of-russian-inn_b_639689.

20 Ibid.

21 "Robert Hormats," U.S. Chamber of Commerce, accessed January 1, 2020, https://www.uschamber.com/robert-hormats; "Robert Hormats," Carnegie Council, last updated August 17, 2017, https://www.carnegiecouncil.org/people/robert-hormats.

22 "Robert Hormats," Carnegie Council; Jeanne Whalen, "Russian Court Overturns Privatization; Court Says Key Documents Are Illegal," *Wall Street Journal*, October 12, 1999, https://www.wsj.com/articles/SB939687879194244568.

23 Ben Jacobs, "Hillary Clinton Aides' Wall Street Links Raise Economic Policy Doubts," *Guardian*, July 26, 2015, https://www.theguardian.com/us-news/2015/jul/26/wall-street-links-hillary-clinton-aides-economic-policy-doubts; Reginald Dale, "Thinking Ahead/Commentary: Clouds Loom for Global Economy," *New York Times*, April 9, 1996, https://www.nytimes.com/1996/04/09/business/world-business/IHT-thinking-ahead-commentary-clouds-loom-for-global.html; James K. Glassman, "Jim Glassman Interviews Robert Hormats," Ideas in Action, on Internet Archive, July 3, 2000, https://web.archive.org/web/20120519151436/http://www.ideasinactiontv.com/tcs_daily/2000/07/jimglassman-interviews-robert-hor-mats.html (the screenshot of the site was captured on May 19, 2012).

24 Council on Foreign Relations, Annual Report, July 1, 2005 – June 30, 2006, https://www.cfr.org/sites/default/files/report_pdf/CFR_annual_report_2006.pdf; Council on Foreign Relations, "U.S.-Latin America Relations: A New Direction for a New Reality," Independent Task Force Report No. 60, 2008, https://www.cfr.org/sites/default/files/report_pdf/LatinAmerica_TF%20final.pdf; Bureau of Public Affairs, "Assistant Secretary Jose W. Fernandez to Speak at the Council on Foreign Relations about the BRIDGE Initiative in Latin America," U.S. Department of State, press release, January 13, 2011, https://2009-2017.state.gov/r/pa/prs/ps/2011/01/154625.htm; "The Russian Economy and US-Russia Relations," Peterson Institute for International Economics, April 15, 2011, https://www.piie.com/events/russian-economy-and-us-russia-relations.

25 "Robert D. Hormats," Globalist, n.d., https://www.theglobalist.com/contributors/robert-d-hormats/; Stephan Richter, "Why Donald Trump Is Completely Wrong about Globalism," Globalist, September 30, 2018, https://www.theglobalist.com/globalism-patriotism-donald-trump-united-states/; Stephan Richter, "About Us," Globalist, n.d., https://www.theglobalist.com/about-us/.

26 "José W. Fernandez," World Economic Forum, n.d., https://www.weforum.org/people/jose-w-fernandez; "Robert Hormats," U.S. Chamber of Commerce, n.d., https://www.uschamber.com/robert-hormats; "Theodore W. Kassinger," O'Melveny, n.d., https://www.omm.com/professionals/theodore-w-kassinger/?generatePdf=1.

27 Council on Foreign Relations, Annual Report, July 1, 2005 – June 30, 2006, https://www.cfr.org/sites/default/files/report_pdf/CFR_annual_report_2006.pdf; Alan P. Larson and David M. Marchick, "Foreign Investment and National Security: Getting the Balance Right," Council on Foreign Relations, July 2006, https://cdn.cfr.org/sites/default/files/pdf/2006/07/CFIUSreport.pdf.

28 Larson and Marchick, "Foreign Investment and National Security: Getting the Balance Right."

29 Alston & Bird, Supplemental Statement, Pursuant to the Foreign Agents Registration Act of 1938, as amended, received November 30, 2011, for six month period ending October 31, 2011, https://efile.fara.gov/docs/5549-Supplemental-Statement -20111201-16.pdf.

30 A Minority Staff Report Prepared for the Use of the Committee on Foreign Relations, United States Senate, "Putin's Asymmetric Assault on Democracy in Russia and Europe: Implications for U.S. National Security," 115th Cong. (2018), https:// www.foreign.senate.gov/imo/media/doc/FinalRR.pdf.

31 Ibid.

32 A Minority Staff Report Prepared for the Use of the Committee on Foreign Relations, United States Senate, "Putin's Asymmetric Assault on Democracy in Russia and Europe: Implications for U.S. National Security"; Bill Alpert, "How a Putin Aide Gained $119 Million," Barron's, December 3, 2011, https://www.barrons.com/ articles/SB50001424052748703827804577056191874119450.

33 Bureau of Public Affairs, "U.S. and Russia Kick Off New Innovation Working Group on March 27 in Silicon Valley," U.S. Department of State, press release, March 26. 2012, https://2009-2017.state.gov/r/pa/prs/ps/2012/03/186815.htm; Bureau of Public Affairs, "U.S.-Russia Innovation Working Group Completes Inaugural Meeting in Silicon Valley, Memorandum of Understanding Signed on Skolkovo Innovation Center," U.S. Department of State, press release, March 28, 2012, https://2009-2017. state.gov/r/pa/prs/ps/2012/03/187016.htm.

34 "Governor Delivers Remarks at USRBC Annual Meeting," California Office of the Governor, on Internet Archive, October 21, 2010, https://web.archive.org/ web/20101103024149/https:/www.gov.ca.gov/speech/16296/ (the screenshot of the site was captured on November 3, 2010); "Governor Delivers Remarks at USRBC Annual Meeting," YouTube video, posted by "Yuri Mazur," November 1, 2010, https://www.youtube.com/watch?v=O7ancmFnZiQ; Appendix No. 5, to Contract No. 12-10 RIK MS dated April 30, 2010, September 15, 2010, https://efile.fara.gov/ docs/3634-Exhibit-AB-20101216-25.pdf; U.S.-Russia Business Council, "From Silicon Valley to Skolkovo: Forging Innovation Partnerships," Issuu, October 13, 2010, https://issuu.com/usrbc/docs/usrbc_annualmeeting2010.

35 "Governor Delivers Remarks at USRBC Annual Meeting."

36 Ibid.; Michael Schwirtz, "Russia Asks Schwarzenegger to Help in a Tough Task," New York Times, October 11, 2010, https://www.nytimes.com/2010/10/12/world/ europe/12russia.html; Kathy Lally, "Russia Nears Membership in World Economic Club," Washington Post, October 20, 2010, https://www.washingtonpost.com/ wp-dyn/content/article/2010/10/20/AR2010102006240.html.

37 McFaul, From Cold War to Hot Peace; Josh Gerstein, "2010 Complete Election Coverage: New U.S.-Russia Tone Proves Elusive," Politico, July 6, 2009, https:// www.politico.com/news/stories/0709/24608_Page2.html; Daniel J. Edelman, Inc., Exhibit A, Pursuant to the Foreign Agents Registration Act of 1938, as amended, November 18, 2010, https://efile.fara.gov/docs/3634-Exhibit-AB-20101123-23.pdf.

38 Schwirtz, "Russia Asks Schwarzenegger to Help in a Tough Task."

39 Andrew C. McCarthy, "Collusion with Russia; The Obama Reset," in *Ball of Collusion: The Plot to Rig an Election and Destroy a Presidency* (New York: Encounter Books, 2019).

40 Seth Elan, "Russia's Skolkovo Innovation Center," EUCOM Strategic Foresight, on Internet Archive, July 29, 2013, https://web.archive.org/web/20170627225836/http://fmso.leavenworth.army.mil/Collaboration/COCOM/EUCOM/Skolkovo.pdf (the screenshot of the site was captured on June 27, 2017).

41 Lucia Ziobro, "FBI's Boston Office Warns Businesses of Venture Capital Scams," *Boston Business Journal*, April 4, 2014, https://www.bizjournals.com/boston/blog/startups/2014/04/fbis-boston-office-warns-businesses-of-venture.html.

42 John Solomon, "The Case for Russia Collusion… Against the Democrats," *Hill*, February 10, 2019, https://thehill.com/opinion/white-house/429292-the-case-for-russia-collusion-against-the-democrats; Elan, "Russia's Skolkovo Innovation Center."

43 John R. Schindler, "Hillary's Secret Kremlin Connection Is Quickly Unraveling," *Observer*, August 25, 2016, https://observer.com/2016/08/hillarys-secret-kremlin-connection-is-quickly-unraveling/.

44 "The First Russian Industrial Design Hackathon Was Held at Skolkovo Robotics," Sk.ru, March 23, 2015, http://sk.ru/news/b/articles/archive/2015/03/23/pervyy-rossiyskiy-hakaton-po-promyshlennomu-dizaynu-proshel-na-skolkovo-robotics.aspx; "About Robocenter," Sk.ru, n.d., http://sk.ru/foundation/itc/robotics/; "Sk Robocenter," Robohub, n.d., https://robohub.org/author/skolkovo-robotics/; "Visiting Skolkovo. Coach Tours Around the Innovation Centre," Open Innovations, 2017, https://2017.openinnovations.ru/en/interestingexcursions-on-skolkovo.

45 "Positive Hack Days," Sk.ru, site search, n.d., http://sk.ru/search/default.aspx#q=%22positive+hack+days%22.

46 "Positive Hack Days St.-Petersburg 2012," HackSpace, on Internet Archive, https://web.archive.org/web/20160322084144/http://hackspb.ru/events/positive-hack-days-st-petersburg-2012/ (the screenshot of the site was captured on March 22, 2016).

47 Ibid.

48 Ibid.

49 "International Forum on Practical Information Security," Positive Technologies, May 30-31, 2012, on Internet Archive, https://web.archive.org/web/20120529044736/http://www.phdays.com:80/ (the screenshot of the site was captured on May 29, 2012); David Gilbert, "Russian Cybersecurity Firm Kaspersky Wants to Run Your Next Election," *Vice*, November 14, 2017, https://www.vice.com/en_us/article/5955k3/kaspersky-polys-election-voting.

50 "Sponsors," PHDays, n.d., http://2017.phdays.com/about/sponsors/; "Sberbank History," Sberbank, n.d., https://www.sberbank.com/about/history; "Yukos Unit Fetches $9bn at Sale," BBC News, December 20, 2004, http://news.bbc.co.uk/2/hi/business/4108509.stm; U.S. Department of State, "Joint Report: 2009-2010 Results of the U.S.-Russia Presidential Commission."

51 "The First Two Series of JSC Atomenergoprom's Bonds Have Been Placed on MICEX," Rustocks.com, November 30, 2009, http://local.rustocks.com/index.phtml/Pressreleases/0/11/22069?filter=2009.

52 Paul Roderick Gregory, "No One Mentions That the Russian Trail Leads to Democratic Lobbyists," *Forbes*, February 18, 2017, https://www.forbes.com/sites/paulroderickgregory/2017/02/18/no-one-mentions-that-the-russian-trail-leads-to-democratic-lobbyists/#7e4c5ee03991.

53 Jonathan Allen and Carrie Budoff Brown, "The Meaning of Podesta's Hire," *Politico*, December 10, 2013, https://www.politico.com/story/2013/12/john-podesta-hire-signals-a-more-aggressive-white-house-100961; Timothy P. Carney, "Obama Hires Revolving-Door Lobbyist and Clinton Fixer John Podesta," *Washington Examiner*, December 10, 2013, https://www.washingtonexaminer.com/obama-hires-revolving-door-lobbyist-and-clinton-fixer-john-podesta; Larry O'Connor, "How the Russian Collusion Myth Was Hatched by Team Hillary Immediately After Her Loss," *Washington Times*, May 4, 2018, https://www.washingtontimes.com/news/2018/may/4/how-russian-collusion-myth-was-hatched-team-hillar/.

54 Michael Doran, "The Real Collusion Story," *National Review*, March 13, 2018, https://www.nationalreview.com/2018/03/russia-collusion-real-story-hillary-clinton-dnc-fbi-media/.

55 Schindler, "Hillary's Secret Kremlin Connection Is Quickly Unraveling"; John R. Schindler, "Panama Papers Reveal Clinton's Kremlin Connection," *Observer*, April 7, 2016, https://observer.com/2016/04/panama-papers-reveal-clintons-kremlin-connection/.

56 Caleb Daniloff, "A Running Conversation with John Podesta," *Runner's World*, May 1, 2014, http://www.runnersworld.com/runners-stories/a-running-conversation-with-john-podesta.

57 E-mail message from eyrn.sepp@gmail.com to john.podesta@gmail.com, "Fwd: Podesta Outstanding Docs for Joule," Wikileaks, January 1, 2014, https://wikileaks.org/podesta-emails/emailid/4635; John Podesta, Public Financial Disclosure Report, February 21, 2014, https://s3.amazonaws.com/s3.documentcloud.org/documents/1227013/john-podesta-white-house-financial-disclosure-form.pdf; "Joule Unlimited, Inc.," Portfolio Companies, accessed April 6, 2016, http://en.rusnano.com/portfolio/companies/jouleunlimited; Richard Pollock, "EXCLUSIVE: Podesta Was Board Member of Firms Linked to Russian Investors," U.S. Congressman Louie Gohmert's website, March 22, 2017, https://gohmert.house.gov/news/documentsingle.aspx?DocumentID=398429; David Glass, "A Transformative Production Platform for Liquid Fuel from the Sun" (SAE Presentation, on Internet Archive, January 30, 2013), https://web.archive.org/web/20160429220825/http://www.sae.org/events/gim/presentations/2013/glass_david.pdf (the screenshot of the site was captured on April 29, 2016).

58 Richard Polluck, "Three People Died in Illegal Human Experiments Carried Out by John Podesta Backer's Firm," *Washington Examiner*, July 23, 2014, https://www.washingtonexaminer.com/three-people-died-in-illegal-human-experiments-carried-out-by-john-podesta-backers-firm; John Podesta, Public Financial Disclosure Report, February 21, 2014; "Contributor and Grantor Information," Clinton Foundation, accessed March 30, 2020, https://www.clintonfoundation.org/contributors?category=%241%2C000%2C001+to+%245%2C000%2C000&page=3.

59 James Freeman, "John Podesta and the Russians," *Wall Street Journal*, October 23, 2016, https://www.wsj.com/articles/john-podesta-and-the-russians-1477262565; John Podesta, Public Financial Disclosure Report, February 21, 2014; Mark Tapscott, "Podesta Still Hasn't Explained Where 41,000 Stock Shares Went," Daily Caller, April 2, 2017, https://dailycaller.com/2017/04/02/podesta-still-hasnt-explained-where-41000-stock-shares-went/; Richard Polluck, "EXCLUSIVE: John Podesta May Have Violated Federal Law by Not Disclosing 75,000 Stock Shares," Daily Caller, March 26, 2017, https://dailycaller.com/2017/03/26/exclusive-john-podesta-may-have-violated-federal-law-by-not-disclosing-75000-stock-shares/.

60 Ibid.

61 Freeman, "John Podesta and the Russians"; "Joule Elects Former White House Chief of Staff John Podesta to Board of Directors," Business Wire, January 18, 2011, https://www.businesswire.com/news/home/20110118006438/en/Joule-Elects-White-House-Chief-Staff-John; "Joule Biotechnologies Elects Graham Allison to Board of Directors," Joule Unlimited, accessed April 6, 2016.

62 Alex Philippidis, "From Russia with Drugs and Vaccines, as Federation and Big Pharma Drive Partnerships," Genetic Engineering & Biotechnology News, December 2, 2011, accessed April 10, 2016, http://www.genengnews.com/insight-and-intelligence/from-russia-with-drugs-and-vaccines-as-federation-and-big-pharma-drive-partnerships/77899504/; Pollock, "EXCLUSIVE: Podesta Was Board Member of Firms Linked to Russian Investors"; Government Accountability Institute, "From Russia With Money: Hillary Clinton, the Russian Reset, and Cronyism"; "Joule Elects Anatoly Chubais to Board of Directors," Joule Unlimited, February 2, 2012, accessed April 10, 2016.

63 Philippidis, "From Russia with Drugs and Vaccines, As Federation and Big Pharma Drive Partnerships"; Pollock, "EXCLUSIVE: Podesta Was Board Member of Firms Linked to Russian Investors."

64 Ziobro, "FBI's Boston Office Warns Businesses of Venture Capital Scams."

65 Ibid.

66 "RCNT and Rosatom Have Signed an Agreement for Cooperation," Rusnano, May 14, 2008, https://en.rusnano.com/press-centre/news/88144; Rusnano, Booklet, n.d., https://en.rusnano.com/upload/oldnews/Document/31815_1.pdf; Pollock, "EXCLUSIVE: Podesta Was Board Member of Firms Linked to Russian Investors"; "An R&D Center for Composite Materials Will Be Opened at Skolkovo," Rusnano, October 26, 2011, https://en.rusnano.com/press-centre/news/88588; State Atomic Energy Corporation, 2011 Public Annual Report, https://rosatom.ru/upload/iblock/249/24905d24266b5cea87be9127864972f1.pdf.

67 Freeman, "John Podesta and the Russians"; Government Accountability Institute, "From Russia With Money: Hillary Clinton, the Russian Reset, and Cronyism"; "Klein Ltd Certificate of Incorporation," Klein Ltd., March 11, 2011, http://freebeacon.com/wp-content/uploads/2013/08/klein-ltd-certificate.pdf; "Klein Ltd Memorandum of Association," March 11, 2011, accessed April 11, 2016, http://freebeacon.com/wp-content/uploads/2013/08/klein-ltd-articles.pdf; "Mr. Nicholas Hoskins Lawyer Profile," HG.org, accessed April 11, 2016, http://www.hg.org/lawyer/nicholas-hoskins/156993; "Marlies Smith," LinkedIn profile, accessed April 11, 2016, https://www.linkedin.com/in/marlies-smith-ab3a9621.

68 Julia Limitone, "Hillary Clinton Campaign Chair John Podesta on Alleged Kremlin-Backed Investment: It's Not True," Fox Business, on Internet Archive, June 28, 2017, https://web.archive.org/web/20170703100450/https://www.foxbusiness.com/politics/2017/06/28/hillary-clinton-campaign-chair-john-podesta-on-alleged-kremlin-backed-investment-it-s-not-true.html (the screenshot of the site was captured on July 3, 2017); "Maria Bartiromo vs John Podesta," YouTube video, posted by "LurkerDood," June 29, 2017, https://www.youtube.com/watch?v=u3CH6wZuiEA&feature=youtu.be.

69 Kevin G. Hall, "WikiLeaks Emails Show How Clinton's Campaign Chief Once Opened Doors for Energy Firm," McClatchyDC, October 19, 2016, https://www.mcclatchydc.com/news/politics-government/election/article109203352.html.

70 Catherine Herridge, Jake Gibson, and Edmund DeMarche, "Judge Orders Paul Manafort to Be Transferred to New York City's Notorious Rikers Island," Fox News, June 3, 2019, https://www.foxnews.com/politics/judge-orders-pul-manafort-to-be-transferred-to-new-york-citys-notorious-rikers-island.

71 Robert Pear and John M. Broder, "In a Lobby-Happy Washington, Politics Can Be Even Thicker Than Blood," *New York Times*, September 5, 2000, https://www.nytimes.com/2000/09/05/us/in-a-lobby-happy-washington-politics-can-be-even-thicker-than-blood.html; Matthew Vadum, "Manafort, Gates Indicted – But Not for Russian Shenanigans," FrontPage Magazine, October 31, 2017, https://archives.frontpagemag.com/fpm/manafort-gates-indicted-not-russian-shenanigans-matthew-vadum/; Chuck Ross, "Shady Foreign Lobbying Effort Implicates Trump and Clinton Campaign Chairmen," Daily Caller, August 17, 2016, https://dailycaller.com/2016/08/17/shady-foreign-lobbying-effort-implicates-trump-and-clinton-campaign-chairmen/; Paul Roderick Gregory, "No One Mentions That the Russian Trail Leads to Democratic Lobbyists," *Forbes*, February 18, 2017, https://www.forbes.com/sites/paulroderickgregory/2017/02/18/no-one-mentions-that-the-russian-trail-leads-to-democratic-lobbyists/#316bbff93991; J. Michael Waller, "13 Reasons Why the Russia Probes Must be Expanded," Center for Security Policy, May 3, 2017, https://www.centerforsecuritypolicy.org/2017/05/03/13-reasons-why-the-russia-probes-must-be-expanded/.

72 Mark Hosenball, "With Cash, Ukraine's Political Foes Bring Fight to Washington," Reuters, December 20, 2013, http://www.reuters.com/article/us-usa-ukraine-lobbying-idUSBRE9BJ1B220131220; Gregory, "No One Mentions That the Russian Trail Leads to Democratic Lobbyists"; Michal Kranz, "How a Prominent Democratic Lobbyist Got Swept Up in Mueller's Russia Probe," Business Insider, October 31, 2017, https://www.businessinsider.com/tony-podesta-russian-backed-lobbying-ukraine-manafort-mueller-russia-2017-10.

73 Isaac Arnsdorf, "Podesta Group Files New Disclosures in Manafort-linked Ukraine Lobbying," *Politico*, April 12, 2017, https://www.politico.com/story/2017/04/paul-manafort-lobbying-ukraine-podesta-group-237163; William J. Rashbaum, "New York Charges Manafort with 16 Crimes. If He's Convicted, Trump Can't Pardon Him.," *New York Times*, March 13, 2019, https://www.nytimes.com/2019/03/13/nyregion/manafort-indictment.html; Emily Jashinsky, "How Do You Say 'Whoops' in Russian? Podesta Group Retroactively Files More DOJ Disclosures for Pro-Putin Work," *Washington Examiner*, August 24, 2017, https://

www.washingtonexaminer.com/how-do-you-say-whoops-in-russian-podesta-group-retroactively-files-more-doj-disclosures-for-pro-putin-work; Jacqueline Thomsen, "Mueller Investigating Manafort for Decade-old Crimes: Report," *Hill*, September 19, 2017, https://thehill.com/homenews/administration/351472-mueller-investigating-manafort-for-decade-old-crimes-report; "FULL TEXT: Paul Manafort Indictment," *Politico*, October 30, 2017, https://www.politico.com/story/2017/10/30/full-text-paul-manafort-indictment-244307.

74 Ibid.; Herridge, Gibson, and DeMarche, "Judge Orders Paul Manafort to Be Transferred to New York City's Notorious Rikers Island."

75 Confidential/Sensitive Source, "U.S. Presidential Election: Republican Candidate Donald Trump's Activities in Russia and Compromising Relationship with the Kremlin," August 10, 2016, https://www.documentcloud.org/documents/3259984-Trump-Intelligence-Allegations.html; Isikoff, "U.S. Intel Officials Probe Ties Between Trump Adviser and Kremlin"; Glenn R. Simpson and Mary Jacoby, "How Lobbyists Help Ex-Soviets Woo Washington," *Wall Street Journal*, April 17, 2007, https://www.wsj.com/articles/SB117674837248471543; Paul Roderick Gregory, "The Trump Dossier Is Fake – and Here Are the Reasons Why," *Forbes*, January 13, 2017, https://www.forbes.com/sites/paulroderickgregory/2017/01/13/the-trump-dossier-is-false-news-and-heres-why/#140d13c16867; "Cleaning up After Comey," *Wall Street Journal*, January 23, 2020, https://www.wsj.com/articles/cleaning-up-after-comey-11579825303; John Solomon, "FBI's Spreadsheet Puts a Stake Through the Heart of the Steele's Dossier," *Hill*, July 16, 2019, https://thehill.com/opinion/white-house/453384-fbis-spreadsheet-puts-a-stake-through-the-heart-of-steeles-dossier; Rowan Scarborough, "0 for 12: Mueller Report Debunks Democrats' Entire Trump-Russia Dossier," *Washington Times* April 21, 2019, https://www.washingtontimes.com/news/2019/apr/21/robert-muellers-report-debunks-russia-dossier/.

76 Megan Slack, "President Obama Announces New Ukraine-Related Sanctions," Obama White House (archive), March 17, 2014, https://obamawhitehouse.archives.gov/blog/2014/03/17/president-obama-announces-new-ukraine-related-sanctions; E-mail message from Andrew N. Keller to Marquita L. Johnson and Kathleen A. Kavalec, "RE: Sberbank USA," July 12, 2016, https://foia.state.gov/searchapp/DOCUMENTS/Litigation_Mar2018/F-2017-12795/DOC_0C06493841/C06493841.pdf.

77 E-mail message from Kathleen A. Kavalec to Andrew N. Keller, Daniel Fried, and Robin L. Dunnigan, "RE: Sberbank USA," July 7, 2016, https://foia.state.gov/Search/results.aspx ?searchText=%22happy+to+meet+with+sberbank%22&beginDate=&endDate=&publishedBeginDate=&publishedEndDate=&caseNumber=.

78 John Solomon, "Steele's Stunning Pre-FISA Confession: Informant Needed to Air Trump Dirt Before Election," *Hill*, May 7, 2019, https://thehill.com/opinion/white-house/442592-steeles-stunning-pre-fisa-confession-informant-needed-to-air-trump-dirt.

79 Paul R. Gregory, "Why Was the Steele Dossier Not Dismissed As Fake?," Hoover Institution, February 3, 2020, https://www.hoover.org/research/why-was-steele-dossier-not-dismissed-fake; Ian Kullgren, "Podesta Suggests Trump Associates May Have Colluded with Russian Hackers," *Politico*, December 18, 2016, https://www.politico.com/story/2016/12/podesta-trump-russian-hackers-232786.

80   Ken Dilanian, "Clinton Ally Says Smoke, but No Fire: No Russia-Trump Collusion," NBC News, March 15, 2017, https://www.nbcnews.com/news/us-news/clinton-ally-says-smoke-no-fire-no-russia-trump-collusion-n734176; Lloyd Billingsley, "Kerry State Department Promoted Steele Dossier and Russia Collusion Fantasy," FrontPage Magazine, June 17, 2019, https://www.frontpagemag.com/fpm/2019/06/kerry-state-department-promoted-steele-dossier-and-lloyd-billingsley/; Julia Ainsley, Tom Winter, and Carol E. Lee, "Sources: Podesta Group, Mercury Are Companies 'A' and 'B' in Indictment," NBC News, October 30, 2017, https://www.nbcnews.com/news/investigations/sources-podesta-group-mercury-are-companies-b-indictment-n815721.

81   U.S. Attorney's Office, "Russian Agent Pleads Guilty to Leading Scheme to Illegally Export Controlled Technology to the Russian Military," Federal Bureau of Investigation, press release, September 9, 2015, https://www.fbi.gov/contact-us/field-offices/newyork/news/press-releases/russian-agent-pleads-guilty-to-leading-scheme-to-illegally-export-controlled-technology-to-the-russian-military.

82   U.S. Attorney's Office, "Russian Agent and 10 Other Members of Procurement Network for Russian Military and Intelligence Operating in the U.S. and Russia Indicted in New York," Federal Bureau of Investigation, press release, October 3, 2012, https://archives.fbi.gov/archives/houston/press-releases/2012/russian-agent-and-10-other-members-of-procurement-network-for-russian-military-and-intelligence-operating-in-the-u.s.-and-russia-indicted-in-new-york; McNabb Associates, P.C., "Federal Criminal Indictment," JD Supra, on Internet Archive, September 28, 2012, https://web.archive.org/web/20130617000020/https://www.jdsupra.com/legalnews/federal-criminal-indictment-usa-v-fishe-71053/ (the screenshot of the site was captured on June 17, 2013); Jeffrey Carr, "Breaking: Secret Russian Lab in the Fishenko Espionage Case Identified," SOFREP, June 21, 2013, https://sofrep.com/news/breaking-secret-russian-lab-in-the-fishenko-espionage-case-identified/?goback=.gde_2708813_member_253213262; Embassy of the United States, "Innovation Working Group of the U.S.-Russia Bilateral Presidential Commission Holds Its Second Meeting in Moscow," U.S. Department of State, press release, November 1, 2012, https://web.archive.org/web/20130403073443/http://moscow.usembassy.gov/pr-nov0112.html (the screenshot of the site was captured on April 3, 2013).

83   McFaul, *From Cold War to Hot Peace.*

84   Michael S. Schmidt and Eric Schmitt, "A Russian GPS Using U.S. Soil Stir Spy Fears," *New York Times*, November 16, 2013, https://www.nytimes.com/2013/11/17/world/europe/a-russian-gps-using-us-soil-stirs-spy-fears.html; John R. Schindler, "The Real Russian Mole Inside NSA," *Observer*, August 23, 2016, https://observer.com/2016/08/the-real-russian-mole-inside-nsa/; Keith B. Payne and Mark B. Schneider, "The Nuclear Treaty Russia Won't Stop Violating," *Wall Street Journal*, February 11, 2014, https://www.wsj.com/articles/the-nuclear-treaty-russia-won8217t-stop-violating-1392166706; Gates, *Duty*, 262-263; Aaron Blake, "'I Feel Like We Sort of Choked': Obama's No-Drama Approach to Russian Hacking Isn't Sitting Well," *Washington Post*, June 23, 2017, https://www.washingtonpost.com/news/the-fix/wp/2017/06/23/the-russia-2016-blame-game-finds-obama/; Benjamin Haddad and

Alina Polyakova, "Don't Rehabilitate Obama on Russia," Brookings Institution, March 5, 2018, https://www.brookings.edu/blog/order-from-chaos/2018/03/05/dont-rehabilitate-obama-on-russia/.

85 U.S.-Russia Bilateral Presidential Commission, Fall Newsletter, September-November 2013, https://2009-2017.state.gov/documents/organization/219290.pdf.

86 Carr, "Breaking: Secret Russian Lab in the Fishenko Espionage Case Identified"; U.S. Attorney's Office, "Russian Agent Pleads Guilty to Leading Scheme to Illegally Export Controlled Technology to the Russian Military"; "[OS] RUSSIA/SECURITY – Friction Between Russian Special Services Seen As Potentially "Very Dangerous,"" Wikileaks, March 4, 2013, https://wikileaks.org/gifiles/docs/13/133565-os-russia-security-friction-between-russian-special.html.

87 Evan Perez, "How the U.S. Thinks Russians Hacked the White House," CNN, April 8, 2015, https://edition.cnn.com/2015/04/07/politics/how-russians-hacked-the-wh/index.html.

88 Schmidt and Schmitt, "A Russian GPS Using U.S. Soil Stir Spy Fears."

89 Ibid.

90 Evan Perez, "Sources: State Dept. Hack the 'Worst Ever,'" CNN, March 10, 2015, https://www.cnn.com/2015/03/10/politics/state-department-hack-worst-ever/index.html; Perez, "How the U.S. Thinks Russians Hacked the White House."

91 U.S. Department of Justice, "Russian Agent Sentenced to 10 Years for Acting As Unregistered Russian Government Agent and Leading Scheme to Illegally Export Controlled Technology to Russian Military," press release, July 21, 2016, https://www.justice.gov/opa/pr/russian-agent-sentenced-10-years-acting-unregistered-russian-government-agent-and-leading; U.S. Attorney's Office, "Russian Agent Pleads Guilty to Leading Scheme to Illegally Export Controlled Technology to the Russian Military."

92 U.S. Department of Justice, "Russian Agent Sentenced to 10 Years for Acting as Unregistered Russian Government Agent and Leading Scheme to Illegally Export Controlled Technology to Russian Military."

93 Carr, "Breaking: Secret Russian Lab in the Fishenko Espionage Case Identified."

94 David Ignatius, "Russia's New Strategy for Information Warfare," *Washington Post*, January 18, 2017, https://www.washingtonpost.com/blogs/post-partisan/wp/2017/01/18/russias-radical-new-strategy-for-information-warfare/; U.S.-Russia Bilateral Presidential Commission, Fall Newsletter, September-November 2013.

95 Ignatius, "Russia's New Strategy for Information Warfare."

96 U.S.-Russia Bilateral Presidential Commission, Fall Newsletter, September-November 2013.

97 Carr, "Breaking: Secret Russian Lab in the Fishenko Espionage Case Identified; "[OS] RUSSIA/SECURITY – Friction Between Russian Special Services Seen As Potentially "Very Dangerous," Wikileaks, March 4, 2013.

98 U.S. Attorney's Office, "Russian Agent and 10 Other Members of Procurement Network for Russian Military and Intelligence Operating in the U.S. and Russia Indicted in New York."

99 U.S.-Russia Bilateral Presidential Commission, Fall Newsletter, September-November 2013; Schindler, "The Real Russian Mole Inside NSA"; Chantel McGee, "Here's What Keeps Obama's Former Cyber Policy Advisor up at Night," CNBC,

July 28, 2017, https://www.cnbc.com/2017/07/28/heres-what-keeps-obamas-former-cyber-policy-advisor-up-at-night.html; "R. David Edelman," Obama White House (archive), n.d., https://obamawhitehouse.archives.gov/blog/author/r-david-edelman; U.S.-Russia Bilateral Presidential Commission, Fall Newsletter, September-November 2013; "Michael Daniel," Cyber Threat Alliance, n.d., https://www.cyberthreatalliance.org/biography/michael-daniel/; Amy Knight, "Putin's Top Spy: We're Teaming up with D.C. on Cybersecurity," Daily Beast, November 4, 2019, https://www.thedailybeast.com/putins-top-spy-russian-fsb-chief-alexander-bortnikov-were-teaming-up-with-dc-on-cybersecurity; "Video: White House Cybersecurity Coordinator Michael Daniel on Russian Hacking," *Federal Times*, n.d., https://www.federaltimes.com/video/2014/08/07/white-house-cybersecurity-coordinator-michael-daniel-on-russian-hacking/.

Chapter 9

1 Tim Hains, "FLASHBACK, 2018: Joe Biden Brags at CFR Meeting about Withholding Aid to Ukraine to Force Firing of Prosecutor," Real Clear Politics, September 27, 2019, https://www.realclearpolitics.com/video/2019/09/27/flashback_2018_joe_biden_brags_at_cfr_meeting_about_withholding_aid_to_ukraine_to_force_firing_of_prosecutor.html.

2 Daniel Bush, "Romney's Surprise Vote Is Democrats' Impeachment Silver Lining," PBS, February 5, 2020, https://www.pbs.org/newshour/politics/romneys-surprise-vote-is-democrats-impeachment-silver-lining.

3 "Adam Schiff Closing Argument Transcript: Thursday Impeachment Trial," Rev.com, January 24, 2020, https://www.rev.com/blog/transcripts/adam-schiff-closing-argument-transcript-thursday-impeachment-trial; Sheryl Gay Stolberg, "Emotional Schiff Speech Goes Viral, Delighting the Left and Enraging the Right," *New York Times*, January 24, 2020, https://www.nytimes.com/2020/01/24/us/politics/adam-schiff-closing-remarks.html; "Media Fawns over Schiff During Impeachment Arguments," Fox News, transcript, January 24, 2020, https://www.foxnews.com/transcript/media-fawns-over-schiff-during-impeachment-arguments.

4 John Hudson, Rachael Bade, and Matt Viser, "Diplomat Tells Investigators He Raised Alarms in 2015 about Hunter Biden's Ukraine Work but Was Rebuffed," *Washington Post*, October 18, 2019, https://www.washingtonpost.com/politics/diplomat-tells-investigators-he-raised-alarms-in-2015-about-hunter-bidens-ukraine-work-but-was-rebuffed/2019/10/18/81e35be9-4f5a-4048-8520-0baabb18ab63_story.html; Tess Bonn, "GOP Lawmaker Blasts Democrats Hypocrisy Amid Impeachment Fallout," *Hill*, November 15, 2019, https://thehill.com/hilltv/rising/470632-gop-lawmaker-blasts-democrats-hypocrisy-amid-impeachment-fallout.

5 Ibid.

6 "Adam Schiff Closing Argument Transcript: Thursday Impeachment Trial."

7 Ibid.

8 Benjamin Haddad and Alina Polyakova, "Don't Rehabilitate Obama on Russia," Brookings Institution, March 5, 2018, https://www.brookings.edu/blog/order-from-chaos/2018/03/05/dont-rehabilitate-obama-on-russia/; Faculty of Science, Analysis of: John J. Mearsheimer, "Why the Ukraine Crisis Is the West's Fault: The Liberal Delusions That Provoked Putin," Charles University, September/October 2014,

https://www.natur.cuni.cz/geografie/socialni-geografie-a-regionalni-rozvoj/studium/doktorske-studium/kolokvium/kolokvium-2013-2014-materialy/ukrajina-a-rusko-mearsheimer-souleimanov.pdf; John Kruzel, "Trump, Democrats Risk Unintended Consequences with Impeachment Arguments," *Hill*, January 25, 2020, https://thehill.com/homenews/senate/479856-trump-democrats-risk-unintended-consequences-with-impeachment-arguments.

9   Ben Rhodes, *The World as It Is: A Memoir of the Obama White House* (New York: Perry Merrill LLC, 2018), Apple Books, 278.

10   Jeffrey Goldberg, "The Obama Doctrine," *Atlantic*, April 2016, https://www.theatlantic.com/magazine/archive/2016/04/the-obama-doctrine/471525/.

11   Peter Schweizer, "The Clinton Foundation, State and Kremlin Connections," *Wall Street Journal*, July 31, 2016, https://www.wsj.com/articles/the-clinton-foundation-state-and-kremlin-connections-1469997195; Deroy Murdock, "How the Clintons Sold out U.S. National Interests to the Putin Regime," *National Review*, April 7, 2017, https://www.nationalreview.com/2017/04/clinton-russia-ties-bill-hillary-sold-out-us-interests-putin-regime/.

12   Igor Kossov and Jack Laurenson, "Kolomoisky Rides High Again Despite $5.5 Billion Taxpayer Bailout of Bank," *Kyiv Post*, September 20, 2019, https://www.kyivpost.com/ukraine-politics/kolomoisky-rides-high-again-despite-5-5-billion-taxpayer-bailout-of-bank.html; Adrian Karatnycky, "To Save Ukraine, Pressure Its Oligarchs," *New Atlanticist*, February 8, 2014, https://www.atlanticcouncil.org/blogs/new-atlanticist/to-help-ukraine-pressure-its-oligarchs/; "The Mess that Nuland Made," Consortium News, July 13, 2015, https://consortiumnews.com/2015/07/13/the-mess-that-nuland-made/; Michael Carpenter, "The Oligarchs Who Lost Ukraine and Won Washington," *Foreign Affairs*, November 26, 2019, https://www.foreignaffairs.com/articles/russia-fsu/2019-11-26/oligarchs-who-lost-ukraine-and-won-washington; Mikhail Klikushin, "The New Ukraine Is Run by Rogues, Sexpots, Warlords, Lunatics and Oligarchs," *Observer*, January 14, 2015, https://observer.com/2015/01/the-new-ukraine-is-run-by-rogues-sexpots-warlords-lunatics-and-oligarchs/; Derek Monroe, "The U.S. Is 'Missing' Millions in Ukraine," *Observer*, May 17, 2016, https://observer.com/2016/05/the-u-s-is-missing-millions-in-ukraine/.

13   James V. Grimaldi and Rebecca Ballhaus, "Clinton Charity Tapped Foreign Friends," *Wall Street Journal*, March 19, 2015, https://www.wsj.com/articles/clinton-charity-tapped-foreign-friends-1426818602; Polina Ivanova, Maria Tsvetkova, Ilya Zhegulev, and Luke Baker, "What Hunter Biden Did on the Board of Ukrainian Energy Company Burisma," Reuters, October 19, 2019, https://www.reuters.com/article/us-hunter-biden-ukraine/what-hunter-biden-did-on-the-board-of-ukrainian-energy-company-burisma-idUSKBN1WX1P7; Jeff Carlson, "Biden, Obama Officials Stood to Gain from Ukraine Influence," *Epoch Times*, April 26, 2019, https://www.theepochtimes.com/joe-biden-obama-officials-influenced-ukraine-to-advance-own-interests_2896259.html.

14   Ellen Barry, "Russian Authorities Pressure Elections Watchdog," *New York Times*, December 1, 2011, https://www.nytimes.com/2011/12/02/world/europe/russia-puts-pressure-on-elections-monitor-golos.html; Gabriela Baczynska, "Russia Suspends

Vote Monitoring Group Under 'Foreign Agent' Law," Reuters, June 26, 2013, https://www.reuters.com/article/us-russia-ngos-golos/russia-suspends-vote-monitoring-group-under-foreign-agent-law-idUSBRE95P0ZV20130626; United States Agency for International Development, "Golos Impact Evaluation—Final Report," February 2013, https://www.usaid.gov/sites/default/files/documents/1866/Russia%20IE%20Final%20Report.pdf; Michael McFaul, *From Cold War to Hot Peace: An American Ambassador in Putin's Russia* (Boston: Houghton Mifflin Harcourt, 2018); Hillary Clinton, *Hard Choices* (London: Simon & Schuster, 2014), 222-223.

15   Andrey Kurkov, "Ukraine's Revolution: Making Sense of a Year of Chaos," BBC News, November 21, 2014, https://www.bbc.com/news/world-europe-30131108; Mike Eckel, "Top U.S. Official: Ukraine Reforms Endangered by Oligarchs Fighting Back," Radio Free Europe/Radio Liberty, March 15, 2016, https://www.rferl.org/a/ukraine-nuland-oligarchs-corruption/27615366.html.

16   Ted Galen Carpenter, "America's Ukraine Hypocrisy," CATO Institute, August 6, 2017, https://www.cato.org/publications/commentary/americas-ukraine-hypocrisy; "Ukraine Crisis: Transcript of Leaked Nuland-Pyatt Call," BBC News, February 7, 2014, https://www.bbc.com/news/world-europe-26079957; Renee Parsons, "Chronology of the Ukrainian Coup," Counter Punch, March 5, 2014, https://www.counterpunch.org/2014/03/05/chronology-of-the-ukrainian-coup/; "The Mess that Nuland Made"; "The Putin Files: Victoria Nuland," YouTube video, posted by "FRONTLINE PBS," October 25, 2017, https://www.youtube.com/watch?v=U2fYcHLouXY#t=504; "How Poroshenko Stole and Exported $8 Billion from Ukraine," Stalker Zone, August 26, 2019, https://www.stalkerzone.org/how-poroshenko-stole-and-exported-8-billion-from-ukraine/.

17   John J. Mearsheimer, "Why the Ukraine Crisis Is the West's Fault," *Foreign Affairs*, September/October 2014, https://www.foreignaffairs.com/articles/russia-fsu/2014-08-18/why-ukraine-crisis-west-s-fault; Haddad and Polyakova, "Don't Rehabilitate Obama on Russia"; Mikhail Zygar, "The Russian Reset That Never Was," *Foreign Policy*, December 9, 2016, https://foreignpolicy.com/2016/12/09/the-russian-reset-that-never-was-putin-obama-medvedev-libya-mikhail-zygar-all-the-kremlin-men/.

18   Ibid.; McFaul, *From Cold War to Hot Peace*; Will Englund, "Why Ukraine and Russia Are Still at War," *Washington Post*, November 13, 2019, https://www.washingtonpost.com/world/2019/11/13/why-ukraine-russia-are-still-war/.

19   Ibid.

20   Barry, "Russian Authorities Pressure Elections Watchdog"; Baczynska, "Russia Suspends Vote Monitoring Group Under 'Foreign Agent' Law"; United States Agency for International Development, "Golos Impact Evaluation—Final Report."

21   Natasha Abbakumova and Kathy Lally, "Russia Boosts out USAID," *Washington Post*, https://www.washingtonpost.com/world/russia-boots-out-usaid/2012/09/18/c2d185a8-01bc-11e2-b260-32f4a8db9b7e_story.html; Matthew Rojansky, "Why USAID Is Leaving Russia," Carnegie Endowment for International Peace, September 20, 2012, https://carnegieendowment.org/2012/09/20/why-usaid-is-leaving-russia-pub-49444; Kathy Lally, "As USAID Stops Work in Russia, Activists Wonder How

They Can Continue Operations," *Washington Post*, October 1, 2012, https://www.washingtonpost.com/world/us-aid-stops-work-in-russia/2012/10/01/90d4cbb2-0bcd-11e2-bb5e-492c0d30bff6_story.html; "Thousands in Moscow Protest Election Results Favoring Putin, United Russia," Radio Free Europe/Radio Liberty, December 5, 2011, https://www.rferl.org/a/moscow_protests_election/24412655.html; Andrew Roth, "Moscow Voters: 'Putin Has Silenced Our Protests, but We'll Take Revenge in 2021,'" *Guardian*, September 8, 2019, https://www.theguardian.com/world/2019/sep/08/putin-silenced-us-revenge-2021-elections.

22 Lally, "As USAID Stops Work in Russia, Activists Wonder How They Can Continue Operations."

23 "Mid-Term Performance Evaluation of the Ukraine Access to Justice and Legal Empowerment Project," USAID Ukraine, Final Report, February 2013, https://pdf.usaid.gov/pdf_docs/PDACX372.pdf; "OSI Condemns Takeover of Moscow Foundation," Open Society Foundations (archive), November 23, 2003, https://archive.fo/6lVz1 (the screenshot of the site was captured on June 28, 2018); Janine R. Wedel, "The Harvard Boys Do Russia," *Nation*, May 14, 1998, https://www.thenation.com/article/archive/harvard-boys-do-russia/; "Who Taught Crony Capitalism to Russia?," *Wall Street Journal*, last updated March 19, 2001, https://www.wsj.com/articles/SB984947892753855394.

24 Ibid.; Guy Chazan, "George Soros Works to Rescue Investment in Russia's Svyazinvest," *Wall Street Journal*, April 30, 2001, https://www.wsj.com/articles/SB988575067628109309; "Leaked Memos Show George Soros Plotted to Oust Putin, Destabilize Russia," Sputnik International, August 27, 2016, https://sputniknews.com/russia/201608271044703488-soros-memo-oust-putin-russia/.

25 OSF memo, November 16, 2012; "Leaked Memos Show George Soros Plotted to Oust Putin, Destabilize Russia."

26 OSF memo, March 31, 2014.

27 Evan Osnos, David Remnick, and Joshua Yaffa, "Trump, Putin, and the New Cold War," *New Yorker*, March 6, 2017, https://www.newyorker.com/magazine/2017/03/06/trump-putin-and-the-new-cold-war; James Carden, "Obama's Foreign Policy: A Hostage to Bipartisan Consensus," *Nation*, October 26, 2016, https://www.thenation.com/article/archive/obamas-foreign-policy-a-hostage-to-bipartisan-consensus/; John Glaser and Trevor Thrall, "Obama's Foreign Policy Legacy and the Myth of Retrenchment" (working paper, Cato Institute, April 24, 2017), https://www.cato.org/sites/cato.org/files/pubs/pdf/working-paper-43-updated.pdf.

28 OSF memo, March 31, 2014; Yuliya Talmazan, "Maidan Massacre Anniversary: Ukraine Remembers Bloody Day of Protests," NBC News, February 20, 2019, https://www.nbcnews.com/news/world/maidan-massacre-anniversary-ukraine-remembers-bloody-day-protests-n973156; Marc Young, "Did Uncle Sam Buy Off the Maidan?," Die Zeit, May 2015, https://www.zeit.de/politik/ausland/2015-05/ukraine-usa-maidan-finance/seite-2.

29 Ibid.

30 Ibid.; "Yanukovych, Fugitive Ex-President Wanted for Mass Murder, Remains Missing (UPDATE)," *Kyiv Post*, February 25, 2014, https://www.kyivpost.com/

article/content/ukraine-politics/arrest-warrant-issued-for-yanukovych-and-oth-er-former-officials-337482.html; Anthony Faiola and Terri Rupar, "People Haven't Left Kiev's Maidan. Here's What It Looks and Feels Like Now.," *Washington Post*, March 7, 2014, https://www.washingtonpost.com/news/worldviews/wp/2014/03/07/people-havent-left-kievs-maidan-heres-what-it-looks-and-feels-like-now/; Hanna Kozlowska, "The Revolution Has Not Been Finalized," *Foreign Policy*, May 23, 2014, https://foreignpolicy.com/2014/05/23/the-revolution-has-not-been-finalized/.

31 "Putin: Ouster of Ukrainian President Was an 'Unconstitutional Drop,'" DW News, April 3, 2014, https://www.dw.com/en/putin-ouster-of-ukrainian-president-was-an-unconstitutional-coup/a-17472054.

32 AFP, "Putin Describes Secret Operation to Seize Crimea," Yahoo News, March 8, 2015, https://news.yahoo.com/putin-describes-secret-operation-seize-crimea-212858356.html; Bonnie Malkin and Raziye Akkoc, "Vladimir Putin Saved My Life, Says Ousted Ukrainian President Viktor Yanukovych," *Telegraph*, June 22, 2015, https://www.telegraph.co.uk/news/worldnews/europe/russia/11692593/Vladimir-Putin-saved-my-life-says-ousted-Ukrainian-president-Viktor-Yanukovych.html.

33 Ibid.

34 "Putin: Ouster of Ukrainian President Was an 'Unconstitutional Drop'"; "Putin Admits Russian Forces Were Deployed to Crimea," Reuters, April 17, 2014, https://www.reuters.com/article/russia-putin-crimea/putin-admits-russian-forces-were-deployed-to-crimea-idUSL6N0N921H20140417; Carl Schreck, "From 'Not Us' to 'Why Hide It?': How Russia Denied Its Crimea Invasion, Then Admitted It," Radio Free Europe/Radio Liberty, February 26, 2019, https://www.rferl.org/a/from-not-us-to-why-hide-it-how-russia-denied-its-crimea-invasion-then-admit-ted-it/29791806.html.

35 Schreck, "From 'Not Us' to 'Why Hide It?': How Russia Denied Its Crimea Invasion, Then Admitted It"; "'Loss' of Colors," U.S. Army Center of Military History, January 6, 1994, https://history.army.mil/html/forcestruc/loss.html.

36 "Annexation of Crimea by the Russian Federation," Wikipedia, accessed January 15, 2020, https://en.wikipedia.org/wiki/Annexation_of_Crimea_by_the_Russian_Federation.

37 Bogdana Depo, *Goliath Versus Goliath: EU Democracy Promotion in the Eastern Neighbourhood and Russia's Alternative Agenda* (Germany: Nomos Verlag, 2019), 77, 204; Spencer Kimball, "Bound by Treaty: Russia, Ukraine and Crimea," DW News, November 3, 2014, https://www.dw.com/en/bound-by-treaty-russia-ukraine-and-crimea/a-17487632.

38 "Address by President of the Russian Federation," Kremlin.ru, March 18, 2014, http://en.kremlin.ru/events/president/news/20603; Mearsheimer, "Why the Ukraine Crisis Is the West's Fault"; "Putin Signs Laws on Reunification of Republic of Crimea and Sevastopol with Russia," Tass.com, March 21, 2014, https://tass.com/russia/724785.

39 Anna Nemtsova, "This Is What a War in Europe Really Looks Like," *Politico*, July 27, 2014, https://www.politico.com/magazine/story/2014/07/eastern-ukraine-civil-war-109388.

40 Ewen MacAskill, "Ukraine Crisis: Bugged Call Reveals Conspiracy Theory about Kiev Snipers," *Guardian*, March 5, 2014, https://www.theguardian.com/world/2014/

mar/05/ukraine-bugged-call-catherine-ashton-urmas-paet; Mattathias Schwartz, "Who Killed the Kiev Protesters? A 3-D Model Holds the Clues," New York Times, May 30, 2018, https://www.nytimes.com/2018/05/30/magazine/ukraine-protest-video.html; Talmazan, "Maidan Massacre Anniversary: Ukraine Remembers Bloody Day of Protests."

41 Mearsheimer, "Why the Ukraine Crisis Is the West's Fault."

42 Alan Cullison, "Bidens in Ukraine: An Explainer," *Wall Street Journal*, September 22, 2019, https://www.wsj.com/articles/bidens-anticorruption-effort-in-ukraine-over-lapped-with-sons-work-in-country-11569189782; "The Ukraine Scandal Timeline Democrats and Their Media Allies Don't Want America to See," John Solomon Reports, November 20, 2019, https://johnsolomonreports.com/the-ukraine-scandal-timeline-democrats-and-their-media-allies-dont-want-america-to-see/.

43 Tracy Wilkinson and Sergei L. Loiko, "Here Is What Joe Biden Actually Did in Ukraine," *Los Angeles Times*, October 5, 2019, https://www.latimes.com/politics/story/2019-10-05/bidens-visits-to-ukraine-under-scrutiny.

44 "The Russian Laundromat Exposed," OCCRP, March 20, 2017, https://www.occrp.org/en/laundromat/the-russian-laundromat-exposed/; "Ukraine's Overall Debt for Russian Gas Grows to $3.492 Billion," Institute of Energy for South-East Europe, April 30, 2014, https://www.iene.eu/ukraines-overall-debt-for-russian-gas-grows-to-3492-billion-p596.html; Derek Monroe, "The U.S. Is 'Missing' Millions in Ukraine"; Zachary Stieber, "Latvia Flagged 'Suspicious' Hunter Biden Payments in 2016," *Epoch Times*, December 17, 2019, https://www.theepochtimes.com/lat-via-flagged-suspicious-hunter-biden-payments-in-2016_3177002.html.

45 "FACTSHEET: U.S. Crisis Support Package for Ukraine," Obama White House (archive), press release, April 21, 2014, https://obamawhitehouse.archives.gov/the-press-office/2014/04/21/fact-sheet-us-crisis-support-package-ukraine.

46 "FACTSHEET: International Support for Ukraine," Obama White House (archive), press release, March 4, 2014, https://obamawhitehouse.archives.gov/the-press-of-fice/2014/03/04/fact-sheet-international-support-ukraine; "FACTSHEET: U.S. Assistance to Ukraine," Obama White House (archive), press release, June 7, 2014, https://obamawhitehouse.archives.gov/the-press-office/2014/06/07/fact-sheet-us-assistance-ukraine; Associated Press, "IMF Approves $17 Billion Loan Package for Ukraine," CNBC, April 30, 2014, https://www.cnbc.com/2014/04/30/imf-approves-17-billion-loan-package-for-ukraine.html.

47 "FACTSHEET: U.S. Assistance to Ukraine," Obama White House (archive), press release, June 7, 2014.

48 Julian Hattem, "Thousands of Soros Docs Released by Alleged Russian-Backed Hackers," *Hill*, August 15, 2016, https://thehill.com/policy/national-securi-ty/291486-thousands-of-soros-docs-released-by-alleged-russia-backed-hackers; OSF memo, March 31, 2014.

49 Glenn Beck, "'The Democrats' Hydra': Here are the FACTS about the Impeach-ment Inquiry, Soros, Ukraine," Glenn Beck's website, November 17, 2019, https://www.glennbeck.com/glenn-beck/the-democrats-hydra-here-are-the-facts-about-the-impeachment-inquiry-soros-ukraine; "The Future of Europe: An Interview with George Soros," interview by Gregor Peter Schmitz, Inter-national Renaissance Foundation, April 24, 2014, https://www.irf.ua/en/

the_future_of_europe_an_interview_with_george_soros/; OSF memo, March 31, 2014.

50 "The Future of Europe: An Interview with George Soros"; OSF memo, March 31, 2014.

51 Ibid.

52 Ibid.

53 "Ukraine Crisis: Transcript of Leaked Nuland-Pyatt Call"; "US-EU Clash on How to Install a Puppet Regime in Ukraine. Victoria Nuland.," Global Research News, February 7, 2014, https://www.globalresearch.ca/us-eu-clash-on-how-to-install-a-puppet-regime-in-ukraine-victoria-nuland/5367794.

54 "US-EU Clash on How to Install a Puppet Regime in Ukraine. Victoria Nuland."

55 "Ukraine Crisis: Transcript of Leaked Nuland-Pyatt Call."

56 OSF memo, March 31, 2014; "OSI Condemns Takeover of Moscow Foundation"; "Is AIDS US $90B Taxpayer Dollars a Global Slush Fund?," Corey's Digs, January 29, 2020, https://www.coreysdigs.com/health-science/is-aids-us-90b-taxpayer-dollars-a-global-slush-fund/.

57 "About Us," Clinton Health Access Initiative, n.d., https://clintonhealthaccess.org/about-us/#history; "Press Release: Clinton Foundation HIV/AIDS Initiative Announces Partnership with ANTIAIDS and the Victor Pinchuk Foundation," Clinton Foundation, press release, September 19, 2006, https://www.clintonfoundation.org/main/news-and-media/press-releases-and-statements/press-release-clinton-foundation-hiv-aids-initiative-announces-partnership-with.html; Grimaldi and Ballhaus, "Clinton Charity Tapped Foreign Friends"; "How a Small Core of Donors Supplied a Large Share of the Clintons' Political Support," *Washington Post*, accessed January 1, 2020, https://www.washingtonpost.com/graphics/politics/clinton-donors/; "About Victor Pinchuk," Victor Pinchuk Foundation, accessed on January 15, 2020, https://pinchukfund.org/en/about_pinchuk/biography/; "The Biggest Ukrainian Anti-AIDS Project with Private Financing Was Presented in Kiev," Elena Pinchuk Foundation, November 10, 2006, http://www.antiaids.org/eng/news/clinton/the-biggest-ukrainian-anti-aids-project-with-private-financing-was-presented-in-kiev-1910.html; "Our Partners," Elena Pinchuk Foundation, accessed January 15, 2020, http://www.antiaids.org/eng/about/partners.html.

58 Peter Schweizer, *Clinton Cash* (New York: HarperCollins, 2015) 21-22.

59 "U.S., Soros-Funded Ukrainian HIV Charity Under Criminal Probe for Embezzlement," Judicial Watch, February 26, 2020, https://www.judicialwatch.org/corruption-chronicles/u-s-soros-funded-ukrainian-hiv-charity-under-criminal-probe-for-embezzlement/; "National Police Launches Inquiry into Work of Ant-Corruption Action Center Under Appeal of MP Derkach," Interfax-Ukraine, February 17, 2020, https://en.interfax.com.ua/news/general/641802.html; РІЧНИЙ ЗВІТ (100% Life, formerly the All-Ukrainian Network of PLWH), Annual Report, 2007,https://network.org.ua/wp-content/uploads/2017/03/2007.pdf; "Our Partners," РІЧНИЙ ЗВІТ (100% Life, formerly the All-Ukrainian Network of PLWH), accessed January 15, 2020, https://network.org.ua/en/our-partners/.

60 March 31, 2014 OSF memo.

61 Ibid.

62 Ibid.

63 "Background Conference Call on Ukraine Sanctions," Obama White House (archive), press release, April 28, 2014, https://obamawhitehouse.archives.gov/the-press-office/2014/04/28/background-conference-call-ukraine-sanctions.

64 "Remarks by President Obama and President Poroshenko of Ukraine After Bilateral Meeting," Obama White House (archive), press release, September 18, 2014, https://obamawhitehouse.archives.gov/the-press-office/2014/09/18/remarks-president-obama-and-president-poroshenko-ukraine-after-bilateral; "President Obama Meets with the President of Ukraine," YouTube video, posted by "The Obama White House," September 18, 2014, https://www.youtube.com/watch?v=vxxmexUrluk.

65 Ibid.

66 Ibid; "President Obama Meets with the President of Ukraine."

67 Reuters, "IMF Signs Off $17.5bn Loan for Ukraine in Second Attempt to Stave Off Bankruptcy," *Guardian*, March 11, 2015, https://www.theguardian.com/world/2015/mar/11/imf-signs-off-175bn-loan-ukraine-second-attempt-bankruptcy-bailout; New York Review of Books, "A New Policy to Rescue Ukraine," George Soros's website, January 8, 2015, https://www.georgesoros.com/2015/01/08/a-new-policy-to-rescue-ukraine/; Reid Standish, "Russian Duma Dissident Believes West Must Save Ukraine to Defeat Putin," *Foreign Policy*, March 18, 2015, https://foreignpolicy.com/2015/03/18/russian-duma-dissident-believes-west-must-save-ukraine-to-defeat-putin/.

68 Soros, "A New Policy to Rescue Ukraine"; Sujata Rao, "Soros Urges Giving Ukraine $50 Billion of Aid to Foil Russia," Reuters, January 8, 2015, https://www.reuters.com/article/us-ukraine-crisis-soros/soros-urges-giving-ukraine-50-billion-of-aid-to-foil-russia-idUSKBN0KH0NQ20150108.

69 Ibid.

70 Ibid.

71 International Monetary Fund, "Statement by IMF Managing Director Christine Lagarde on Ukraine," press release no. 15/50, February 12, 2015, https://www.imf.org/en/News/Articles/2015/09/14/01/49/pr1550; Ingrid Melander, "Ukraine to Get $40 Billion, Including $17.5 Billion from IMF – Lagarde," Reuters, February 12, 2015, https://uk.reuters.com/article/uk-ukraine-crisis-imf/ukraine-to-get-40-billion-including-17-5-billion-from-imf-lagarde-idUKKBN0LG0Q420150212; Reuters, "IMF Signs Off $17.5bn Loan for Ukraine in Second Attempt to Stave Off Bankruptcy."

72 Standish, "Russian Duma Dissident Believes West Must Save Ukraine to Defeat Putin."

73 Ibid.

74 Ibid.

75 Mark Thompson, "George Soros: I May Invest $1 Billion in Ukraine," CNN, March 30, 2015, https://money.cnn.com/2015/03/30/investing/ukraine-soros-billion-russia/index.html.

76 Soros, "A New Policy to Rescue Ukraine."

77 Thomas Grove and Alan Cullison, "Ukraine Company's Campaign to Burnish Its Image Stretched Beyond Hunter Biden," *Wall Street Journal*, November 7, 2019, https://www.wsj.com/articles/ukraine-companys-campaign-to-burnish-its-image-stretched-beyond-hunter-biden-11573154199.

Endnotes

78 Serious Fraud Office v. Mykola Zlochevskyi, Case No. RSTO/7/2014, Final Judgment, January 21, 2015, https://www.justsecurity.org/wp-content/uploads/2019/09/Zlochevsky-SFO-v-MZ-Final-Judgment-Revised.doc; Ilya Timtchenko, "Prosecutors Put Zlochevsky, Multimillionaire Ex-Ecology Minister, on Wanted List," *Kyiv Post*, January 18, 2015, https://www.kyivpost.com/article/content/reform-watch/prosecutors-put-zlochevsky-multimillionaire-ex-ecology-minister-on-wanted-list-377719.html; Paul Sonne and Laura Mills, "Ukrainians See Conflict in Biden's Anticorruption Message," *Wall Street Journal*, December 7, 2015, https://www.wsj.com/articles/ukrainians-see-conflict-in-bidens-anticorruption-message-1449523458?mod=article_inline.

79 "American Financier Devon Archer Joined the Board of Directors of Burisma Holdings," Burisma, on Internet Archive, press release, April 22, 2014, https://web.archive.org/web/20140514174746/http://burisma.com/american-financier-devon-archer-joined-the-board-of-directors-of-burisma-holdings/ (the screenshot of the site was captured on May 14, 2014); "Echo Chambers," BBC News, May 14, 2014, https://www.bbc.com/news/blogs-echochambers-27403003; Peter Schweizer, *Secret Empires: How Our Politicians Hide Corruption and Enrich Their Family and Friends* (New York: HarperCollins, 2018), 60-61.

80 "Burisma Holdings Accounting Ledger," Scribd, https://www.scribd.com/document/436048670/Burisma-Holdings-Accounting-Ledger (uploaded by John Solomon on November 20, 2019); "Rosemont Seneca Partners Court File," Scribd, https://www.scribd.com/document/404001731/Rosemont-Seneca-Partners-Court-File (uploaded by John Solomon on April 1, 2019); Schweizer, *Secret Empires*, 60-61.

81 Schweizer, *Secret Empires*, 60-61; Secret Service entry logs (WAVES).

82 "Remarks to the Press by Vice President Joe Biden and Ukrainian Prime Minister Arseniy Yatsenyuk," Obama White House (archive), press release, April 22, 2014, https://obamawhitehouse.archives.gov/the-press-office/2014/04/22/remarks-press-vice-president-joe-biden-and-ukrainian-prime-minister-arse.

83 Serious Fraud Office (UK), "Ukraine Money Laundering Investigation," last updated October 1, 2018, https://www.sfo.gov.uk/cases/ukraine-money-laundering-investigation/; Serious Fraud Office (UK), "Money Laundering Investigation Opened," news release, April 28, 2014, https://www.sfo.gov.uk/2014/04/28/money-laundering-investigation-opened/; Serious Fraud Office v. Mykola Zlochevskyi, Case No. RSTO/7/2014, Final Judgment, January 21, 2015.

84 Javier E. David, "Ukraine Gas Producer Appoints Biden's Son to Board," CNBC, May 13, 2014, https://www.cnbc.com/2014/05/13/bidens-son-joins-ukraine-gas-companys-board-of-directors.html; "Hunter Biden," Burisma, on Internet Archive, https://web.archive.org/web/20190319041558/https://burisma-group.com/eng/director/hunter-biden/ (the screenshot of the site was captured on March 19, 2019).

85 "CU v. State FOIA Doc (Ukraine)," Scribd, https://www.scribd.com/document/433436789/CU-v-State-FOIA-Doc-Ukraine (uploaded by John Solomon on November 4, 2019).

86 "Burisma Holdings Accounting Ledger"; "Rosemont Seneca Partners Court File."

87 Daevum, "User Clip: Hunter Biden Ukraine / Joe Biden Conflict of Interest MAY 13, 2014," C-SPAN, September 29, 2019, video, https://www.c-span.org/video/?c4819961/user-clip-hunter-biden-ukraine-joe-biden-conflict-interest-13-2014.

88 Opensecrets.org, "Client Profile: Burisma Holdings," report images, 2014, https://www.opensecrets.org/lobby/client_reports.php?id=F212407&year=2014; Michael Scherer, "Ukrainian Employer of Joe Biden's Son Hires a D.C. Lobbyist," *Time*, July 7, 2014, https://time.com/2964493/ukraine-joe-biden-son-hunter-burisma/.

89 Jessica Donati, "Firm Hired by Ukraine's Burisma Tried to Use Hunter Biden As Leverage, Documents Show," *Wall Street Journal*, November 5, 2019, https://www.wsj.com/articles/firm-hired-by-ukraines-burisma-tried-to-use-hunter-biden-as-leverage-documents-show-11573009615.

90 Adam Entous, "Will Hunter Biden Jeopardize His Father's Campaign?," *New Yorker*, July 1, 2019, https://www.newyorker.com/magazine/2019/07/08/will-hunter-biden-jeopardize-his-fathers-campaign.

91 Ibid.; "Burisma Holdings Accounting Ledger"; Serious Fraud Office (UK), "Ukraine Money Laundering Investigation."

92 A Minority Staff Report Prepared for the use of the Committee on Foreign Relations, United States Senate, 112th Cong. (2012), https://www.foreign.senate.gov/imo/media/doc/Energy%20and%20Security%20from%20the%20Caspian%20to%20Europe.pdf.

93 Ibid.

94 Statement of Amos J. Hochstein, Deputy Assistant Secretary for Energy Diplomacy, Bureau of Energy Resources, U.S. Department of State, Before the Subcommittee on Energy Policy, Health Care & Entitlements, Committee on Oversight and Government Reform, U.S. House of Representatives, "U.S. Foreign Policy and the Export of Domestically Sourced Liquefied Natural Gas," April 30, 2014, https://oversight.house.gov/sites/democrats.oversight.house.gov/files/migrated/uploads/DAS%20Hochstein%20Testimony%204-30-14.pdf; Bureau of Public Affairs, "State Department Launches 'Bureau of Energy Resources,'" U.S. Department of State, press release, November 16, 2011, https://2009-2017.state.gov/r/pa/prs/ps/2011/11/177262.htm; Amy Harder, "State Department Names Acting Energy Envoy," *Wall Street Journal*, July 25, 2014, https://www.wsj.com/articles/state-department-names-new-energy-envoy-1406299086.

95 Ibid.

96 Ibid.; Hearings Before the Committee on Foreign Relations, United States Senate, "Nomination Hearings of the 114th Congress," 114th Cong. (2015-2016), https://www.foreign.senate.gov/imo/media/doc/12%2001%2015%20Nomination%20Gray%20Hochstein%20Marcil%20Feely%20Taglialatela%20Chapman%20Manes%20Transcript.pdf.

97 "European Energy Reliance on Russia," C-SPAN, July 8, 2014, video, https://www.c-span.org/video/?320330-1/hearing-european-energy-reliance-russia&start=469.

98 Ibid.; Hearing Before the Subcommittee on European Affairs of the Committee on Foreign Relations, United States Senate, "Renewed Focus on European Energy Security," 113th Cong. (2014), https://www.govinfo.gov/content/pkg/CHRG-113shrg91142/html/CHRG-113shrg91142.htm; Statement of Amos J. Hochstein, April 30, 2014.

99 "European Energy Reliance on Russia," C-SPAN, July 8, 2014, video, https://www.c-span.org/video/?320330-1/hearing-european-energy-reliance-russia&start=469;

Hearing Before the Subcommittee on European Affairs of the Committee on Foreign Relations, United States Senate, "Renewed Focus on European Energy Security."

100 Ibid.

101 Hearing Before the Subcommittee on International Development and Foreign Assistance, Economic Affairs, International Environmental Protection, and Peace Corps, of the Committee on Foreign Relations, "U.S. Security Implications of International Energy and Climate Policies and Issues," 113th Cong. (2014), https://www.govinfo.gov/content/pkg/CHRG-113shrg94134/html/CHRG-113shrg94134.htm.

102 Ibid.

103 Harder, "State Department Names Acting Energy Envoy"; Bureau of Public Affairs, "Amos J. Hochstein," U.S. Department of State, accessed January 14, 2020, https://2009-2017.state.gov/r/pa/ei/biog/230679.htm.

104 Josh Cohen, "COLUMN-Vladimir Putin's Most Effective Weapon Is Gas – But Not the Poison Kind," Reuters, July 28, 2015, https://www.reuters.com/article/cohen-gazprom/column-vladimir-putins-most-effective-weapon-is-gas-but-not-the-poison-kind-idUSL1N1082VT20150728.

105 Ibid.

106 Atlantic Council, "Honor Roll Contributors," n.d., https://www.atlanticcouncil.org/support-the-council/honor-roll-of-contributors/; "US Energy Diplomacy Priorities for 2015," Atlantic Council, transcript, January 14, 2015, https://www.atlanticcouncil.org/commentary/transcript/transcript-us-energy-diplomacy-priorities-for-2015/.

107 Entous, "Will Hunter Biden Jeopardize His Father's Campaign?"; Tiana Lowe, "Joe Biden Adviser Amos Hochstein Took Meetings with Burisma-hired Lobbying Firm," *Washington Examiner*, November 7, 2019, https://www.washingtonexaminer.com/opinion/joe-biden-adviser-amos-hochstein-took-meetings-with-burisma-hired-blue-star-strategies; Joint Hearing Before the Subcommittee on the Middle East and North Africa of the Committee on Foreign Affairs and the Subcommittee on Energy of the Committee on Science, Space, and Technology, U.S. House of Representatives, 114th Cong. (2016), https://www.govinfo.gov/content/pkg/CHRG-114hhrg21461/html/CHRG-114hhrg21461.htm.

108 "Amos Hochstein," C-SPAN, accessed on January 15, 2020, https://www.c-span.org/person/?amoshochstein; Hearing Before the Subcommittee on European Affairs of the Committee on Foreign Relations, United States Senate, "Renewed Focus on European Energy Security"; Hearing Before the Subcommittee on International Development and Foreign Assistance, Economic Affairs, International Environmental Protection, and Peace Corps, of the Committee on Foreign Relations, "U.S. Security Implications of International Energy and Climate Policies and Issues," 113th Cong. (2014); Joint Hearing Before the Subcommittee on the Middle East and North Africa of the Committee on Foreign Affairs and the Subcommittee on Energy of the Committee on Science, Space, and Technology, U.S. House of Representatives, 114th Cong. (2016).

109 Bureau of Public Affairs, "Amos J. Hochstein"; Opensecrets.org, "Hochstein, Amos," Employment History, accessed January 15, 2020, https://www.opensecrets.org/revolving/rev_summary.php?id=21321; Opensecrets.org, "Amos Hochstein," donor lookup, accessed January 15, 2020, https://www.opensecrets.org/donor-lookup/

results?name=amos+hochstein&order=asc&sort=D; "Amos Hochstein to Join Presidential Campaign," Cassidy & Associates, on Internet Archive, press release, January 16, 2007, https://web.archive.org/web/20070301175141/https://cassidy.com/press/pressdetail.asp?Id=61 (the screenshot of the site was captured on March 1, 2007).

110 "A Conversation with Amos Hochstein," interview by Michael Grunwald, *Washington Post*, April 23, 2006, https://www.washingtonpost.com/wp-dyn/content/article/2006/04/21/AR2006042101754_pf.html.

111 Joshua Kurlantzick, "Putting Lipstick on a Dictator," Mother Jones, May 7, 2007, https://www.motherjones.com/politics/2007/05/putting-lipstick-dictator/.

112 "A Conversation with Amos Hochstein," interview by Michael Grunwald.

113 "Amos Hochstein to Join Presidential Campaign," Cassidy & Associates, on Internet Archive, press release, January 16, 2007, https://web.archive.org/web/20070301175141/https://cassidy.com/press/pressdetail.asp?Id=61 (the screenshot of the site was captured on March 1, 2007); E-mail message from William D. Campbell to Amos Hochstein, March 1, 2006; Letter from Amos Hochstein to Alexei Grigoriev, April 9, 2007; Letter from Amos Hochstein to Vladimir Smirnov, August 1, 2007; Memo from Amos Hochstein to Vadim Mikerin, September 21, 2008; "Amos Hochstein," LinkedIn profile, accessed April 3, 2020, https://www.linkedin.com/in/amos-hochstein-a8639423/.

114 Ibid.

115 "Amos Hochstein," LinkedIn profile, https://ia601508.us.archive.org/34/items/2011archivedamoshochsteinlinkedin/2011--ARCHIVED%20Amos%20Hochstein%20_%20LinkedIn.pdf (screenshot of the site was captured on December 7, 2014); "Amos J. Hochstein," *Huffington Post*, accessed on December 15, 2019, https://www.huffpost.com/author/amos-j-hochstein; Harder, "State Department Names Acting Energy Envoy"; "Amos J Hochstein," U.S. House of Representatives, biography, n.d., https://docs.house.gov/meetings/GO/GO27/20140430/102182/HHRG-113-GO27-Bio-SmithC-20140430.pdf; Bureau of Public Affairs, "Amos J. Hochstein."

116 White House Visitors' Logs.

117 "Amos Hochstein," LinkedIn profile; "Team," Cassidy & Associates, on Internet Archive, https://web.archive.org/web/20110801031415/http://www.cassidy.com:80/team/ (the screenshot of the site was captured on August 1, 2011); E-mail message from Amos Hochstein to Cheryl Mills, "AS REQUESTED," May 10, 2011, https://foia.state.gov/Search/results.aspx?searchText=%22amos+hochstein%22&beginDate=&endDate=&publishedBeginDate=&publishedEndDate=&caseNumber=; "Amos Hochstein," Cassidy & Associates, on Internet Archive, https://web.archive.org/web/20110130073919/http://www.cassidy.com/team/41/ (the screenshot of the site was captured on January 30, 2011).

118 Office of Inspector General, "Inspection of the Bureau of Energy Resources," Office of Inspections, February 2016, https://www.stateoig.gov/system/files/isp-i-16-06.pdf; Statement of Amos J. Hochstein, April 30, 2014.

119 Bureau of Public Affairs, "Public Schedule," U.S. Department of State, December 3, 2014, https://2009-2017.state.gov/r/pa/prs/appt/2014/12/234631.htm.

120 Ibid.; Seamus Bruner, *Compromised* (New York: Post Hill Press, 2018), 113-114; "White House Visitor Logs Detail Meetings of Eric Ciaramella," Judicial Watch, press release, November 8, 2019, https://www.judicialwatch.org/press-releases/judicial-watch-white-house-visitor-logs-detail-meetings-of-eric-ciaramella/.

121 Atlantic Council, "US Energy Diplomacy Priorities for 2015"; "Remarks by Vice President Joe Biden on European Energy Security to the Atlantic Council Energy and Economic Summit," Obama White House (archive), press release, November 22, 2014, https://obamawhitehouse.archives.gov/the-press-office/2014/11/22/remarks-vice-president-joe-biden-european-energy-security-atlantic-counc; Kenneth P. Vogel and Iulia Mendel, "Biden Faces Conflict of Interest Questions That Are Being Promoted by Trump and Allies," *New York Times*, May 1, 2019, https://www.nytimes.com/2019/05/01/us/politics/biden-son-ukraine.html; Amos J. Hochstein, Deputy Assistant Secretary for Energy Diplomacy, Bureau of Energy Resources, written testimony, U.S. Senate, July 8, 2014, https://www.foreign.senate.gov/imo/media/doc/REVISED_Hochstein_Testimony1.pdf; Amos J. Hochstein, Deputy Assistant Secretary for Energy Diplomacy, Bureau of Energy Resources, written testimony, July 22, 2014, https://www.foreign.senate.gov/imo/media/doc/Hochstein_Testimony.pdf.

122 Ibid.; Bureau of Public Affairs, "Special Envoy Hochstein Travels to Bratislava for Meeting of EU Energy Ministers and to Athens," U.S. Department of State, press release, July 13, 2016, https://2009-2017.state.gov/r/pa/prs/ps/2016/07/259968.htm; Bureau of Public Affairs, "Special Envoy Amos J Hochstein Travels to Saudi Arabia and Lebanon," U.S. Department of State, press release, May 23, 2016, https://2009-2017.state.gov/r/pa/prs/ps/2016/05/257648.htm; Bureau of Public Affairs, "Special Envoy Amos J Hochstein Travels to Argentina," U.S. Department of State, press release, June 20, 2016, https://2009-2017.state.gov/r/pa/prs/ps/2016/06/258660.htm; Bureau of Public Affairs, "Special Envoy Hochstein Travels to Jerusalem, Cairo, Kuwait City, and Doha," U.S. Department of State, press release, April 18, 2016, https://2009-2017.state.gov/r/pa/prs/ps/2016/04/255943.htm; Bureau of Public Affairs, "Special Envoy and Coordinator for International Energy Affairs Amos J Hochstein Travels to Baku, Sofia, and Zagreb," U.S. Department of State, press release, February 29, 2016, https://2009-2017.state.gov/r/pa/prs/ps/2016/02/253773.htm; Bureau of Energy Resources, "Remarks at the Atlantic Council Energy & Economic Summit," U.S. Department of State, November 19, 2015, https://2009-2017.state.gov/e/enr/rls/250781.htm; Bureau of Public Affairs, "Special Envoy Hochstein Travels to Brussels, Zagreb, and Kyiv," U.S. Department of State, press release, November 28, 2016, https://2009-2017.state.gov/r/pa/prs/ps/2016/11/264590.htm.

123 Office of Inspector General, "Inspection of the Bureau of Energy Resources."

124 Ibid.

125 Ibid.

126 Tiana Lowe, "Subpoena Amos Hochstein to Get to the Bottom of Burisma Holdings and Trump's Quid Pro Quo," *Washington Examiner*, October 23, 2019, https://www.washingtonexaminer.com/opinion/subpoena-amos-hochstein-to-get-to-the-bottom-of-burisma-holdings-and-trumps-quid-pro-quo.

127 Wilkinson and Loiko, "Here Is What Joe Biden Actually Did in Ukraine"; Tim Hains, "FLASHBACK, 2018: Joe Biden Brags at CFR Meeting about Withholding Aid to Ukraine to Force Firing of Prosecutor," Real Clear Politics, September 27, 2019, https://www.realclearpolitics.com/video/2019/09/27/flashback_2018_joe_biden _brags_at_cfr_meeting_about_withholding_aid_to_ukraine_to_force_firing_of_ prosecutor.html.

128 Ibid.; Ryan Bort, "What Actually Happened Between Joe Biden and Ukraine, Explained," *Rolling Stone*, September 23, 2019, https://www.rollingstone.com/pol-itics/politics-news/biden-ukraine-prosecutor-trump-tweet-888662/; "Remarks by Vice President Joe Biden to the Ukrainian Rada," Obama White House (archive), December 9, 2015, https://obamawhitehouse.archives.gov/the-press-of-fice/2015/12/09/remarks-vice-president-joe-biden-ukrainian-rada; "Part 2 – Not So "Dormant" Investigations," UkraineGate, video, accessed January 15, 2020, https:// ukrainegate.info/part-2-not-so-dormant-investigations/.

129 James Risen, "Joe Biden, His Son and the Case Against a Ukrainian Oligarch," *New York Times*, December 8, 2015, https://www.nytimes.com/2015/12/09/world/ europe/corruption-ukraine-joe-biden-son-hunter-biden-ties.html; "Remarks by Vice President Joe Biden to the Ukrainian Rada."

130 Wilkinson and Loiko, "Here Is What Joe Biden Actually Did in Ukraine"; Hains, "FLASHBACK, 2018: Joe Biden Brags at CFR Meeting about Withholding Aid to Ukraine to Force Firing of Prosecutor"; Miriam Elder, "Joe Biden's Advis-ers Knew in 2018 His Comments about Ukraine Would Be a Problem," Buzzfeed News, October 5, 2019, https://www.buzzfeednews.com/article/miriamelder/joe-biden-ukraine-hunter; Adam Entous, "The Ukrainian Prosecutor Behind Trump's Impeachment," *New Yorker*, December 16, 2019, https://www.newyorker.com/ magazine/2019/12/23/the-ukrainian-prosecutor-behind-trumps-impeachment; John Solomon, "US Embassy Pressed Ukraine to Drop Probe of George Soros Group During 2016 Election," *Hill*, March 26, 2019, https://thehill.com/opinion/ campaign/435906-us-embassy-pressed-ukraine-to-drop-probe-of-george-soros-group-during-2016.

131 Hains, "FLASHBACK, 2018: Joe Biden Brags at CFR Meeting about Withholding Aid to Ukraine to Force Firing of Prosecutor."

132 Entous, "The Ukrainian Prosecutor Behind Trump's Impeachment."

133 Wilkinson and Loiko, "Here Is What Joe Biden Actually Did in Ukraine."

134 Hains, "FLASHBACK, 2018: Joe Biden Brags at CFR Meeting about Withholding Aid to Ukraine to Force Firing of Prosecutor."

135 Andrew E. Kramer, "Ukraine Ousts Viktor Shokin, Top Prosecutor, and Polit-ical Stability Hangs in the Balance," *New York Times*, March 29, 2016, https:// www.nytimes.com/2016/03/30/world/europe/political-stability-in-the-bal-ance-as-ukraine-ousts-top-prosecutor.html; U.S. Embassy in Ukraine, "U.S. Signs Loan Guarantee Agreement for Ukraine," press release, June 3, 2016, https:// ua.usembassy.gov/u-s-signs-loan-guarantee-agreement-ukraine/.

136 Entous, "The Ukrainian Prosecutor Behind Trump's Impeachment."

137 Ibid.; "Ukrainian Parliament Backs Nomination of Shokin As Prosecutor General," Interfax-Ukraine, October 2, 2015, https://en.interfax.com.ua/news/ general/249709.html; Interfax-Ukraine, "Lutsenko Becomes Ukraine's Prosecutor

General," *Kyiv Post*, May 12, 2016, https://www.kyivpost.com/article/content/ukraine-politics/lutsenko-becomes-ukraines-prosecutor-general-413608.html; "I Am Submitting My Resignation Today – Prosecutor General Lutsenko," Interfax-Ukraine, June 11, 2018, https://en.interfax.com.ua/news/general/543099.html.

138 Hains, "FLASHBACK, 2018: Joe Biden Brags at CFR Meeting about Withholding Aid to Ukraine to Force Firing of Prosecutor"; Lowe, "Subpoena Amos Hochstein to Get to the Bottom of Burisma Holdings and Trump's Quid Pro Quo."

139 Hains, "FLASHBACK, 2018: Joe Biden Brags at CFR Meeting about Withholding Aid to Ukraine to Force Firing of Prosecutor."

140 "Profile: Ukraine's Firebrand Ex-Minister Lutsenko," BBC News, January 11, 2014, https://www.bbc.com/news/world-europe-25695982; Jacob Comenetz, "Drunk Official Stopped at Airport," Reuters, May 7, 2009, https://www.reuters.com/article/us-minister-drunk/drunk-official-stopped-at-airport-idUSTRE5465KK20090507; Interfax Ukraine, "Ukrainian Foreign Ministry Investigating Incident with Lutsenko at Frankfurt airport," *Kyiv Post*, May 7, 2009, https://www.kyivpost.com/article/content/ukraine-politics/ukrainian-foreign-ministry-investigating-incident-40998.html.

141 Associated Press, "Opposition Leader Yuri Lutsenko Injured in Clashes in Ukrainian Capital," CTV News, January 11, 2014, https://www.ctvnews.ca/world/opposition-leader-yuri-lutsenko-injured-in-clashes-in-ukrainian-capital-1.1634667.

142 "Former Interior Minister Lutsenko Appointed As Non-Staff Adviser to Ukrainian President," Interfax-Ukraine, June 17, 2014, https://en.interfax.com.ua/news/general/209626.html; "Klitschko Becomes Leader of Petro Poroshenko Bloc 'Solidarity' Party," Interfax-Ukraine, August 28, 2015, https://en.interfax.com.ua/news/general/286616.html; Olena Makarenko, "A New General Prosecutor for Poroshenko," Euromaidan Press, May 13, 2016, http://euromaidanpress.com/2016/05/13/new-general-prosecutor-for-poroshenko/.

143 "Summary – Part 2 – Not So "Dormant" Investigations," Ukraine Gate, video, accessed January 15, 2020, https://ukrainegate.info/summary-part-2-not-so-dormant-investigations/.

144 Memorandum of Telephone Conversation, "Telephone Conversation with President Zelenskyy of Ukraine," July 25, 2019, https://www.whitehouse.gov/wp-content/uploads/2019/09/Unclassified09.2019.pdf.

145 U.S. House of Representatives, Permanent Select Committee on Intelligence, "The Trump-Ukraine Impeachment Inquiry Report," accessed January 15, 2020, https://intelligence.house.gov/report/.

146 "Poroshenko Asks Obama for Weapons, Obtains Blankets," Euractiv, September 19, 2014, https://www.euractiv.com/section/europe-s-east/news/poroshenko-asks-obama-for-weapons-obtains-blankets/; Madison Dibble, "Ambassador Taylor Urged Obama to Provide Ukraine with Lethal Weapons, Was 'Pleased' When Trump Did," *Washington Examiner*, November 13, 2019, https://www.washingtonexaminer.com/news/ambassador-taylor-urged-obama-to-provide-ukraine-with-lethal-weapons-was-pleased-when-trump-did.

147 H.R. 955, 114th Cong. (2015), cosponsors, https://www.congress.gov/bill/114th-congress/house-bill/955/cosponsors?searchResultViewType=expanded&KWICView=false; Alex Pappas, "Adam Schiff-Ukraine Connection Comes Under

Scrutiny," Fox News, October 3, 2019, https://www.foxnews.com/politics/adam-schiffs-own-ukraine-connection-comes-under-scrutiny.

148 H.R. 955, 114th Cong. (2015), cosponsors; John Kiriakou, "The Military Industrial Complex Loves Left Wing Hawk Adam Schiff," Mint Press News, June 28, 2019, https://www.mintpressnews.com/why-the-military-industrial-complex-loves-left-wing-hawk-adam-schiff/260069/; Branko Marcetic, "Who Is Adam Schiff?," *Jacobin*, May 15, 2018, https://jacobinmag.com/2018/02/adam-schiff-russia-in-tervention-raytheon-parsons; Michael Sainato, "Adam Schiff Is a Moderate War Hawk, Not the Liberal Hero Democrats Need," *Observer*, March 24, 2017, https://observer.com/2017/03/democrat-adam-schiff-russia-war-hawk/; "Adam Schiff on War & Peace," OnTheIssues, last updated January 17, 2017, https://www.ontheissues.org/CA/Adam_Schiff_War_+_Peace.htm.

149 H.R. 955, 114th Cong. (2015), cosponsors.

150 John Kiehle and Erica Irigoyen, "Ukrainian American Business Leader Honored by Ukrainian Embassy for Recent Diplomatic Efforts," Cision, press release, March 27, 2014, https://www.prweb.com/releases/2014/03/prweb11709226.htm; Yuliana Romanyshyn, "Airship Producer Igor Pasternak Building Blimps for Whole World (GRAPHICS)," *Kyiv Post*, July 12, 2016, https://www.kyivpost.com/article/content/business/airship-producer-igor-pasternak-building-blimps-for-whole-world-418133.html; "Aeros History," Aeroscraft.com, last updated 2019, http://aeroscraft.com/history/4575665539.

151 Ibid.; "Ukroboronprom Will Produce Unique Border Control Systems Using American Technology," Ukroboronprom, February 16, 2016, https://ukroboronprom.com.ua/en/pro-golovne/ukroboronprom-vyroblyatyme-unikalni-systemy-kontrolyu-kor-donu-za-amerykanskymy-tehnologiyamy.html; "Military-Industrial Complex; Schiff & Co. Making Bank in Ukraine," Tore Says, December 2, 2019, https://toresays.com/2019/12/02/military-industrial-complex-schiff-co-making-bank-in-ukraine/.

152 Kiehle and Irigoyen, "Ukrainian American Business Leader Honored by Ukrainian Embassy for Recent Diplomatic Efforts"; Romanyshyn, "Airship Producer Igor Pasternak Building Blimps for Whole World (GRAPHICS)"; "Aeros History."

153 Courtney E. Howard, "Aeros Patents Cargo Airship Technology," Intelligent Aerospace, May 12, 2015, https://www.intelligent-aerospace.com/military/article/16538488/aeros-patents-cargo-airship-technology; Kiehle and Irigoyen, "Ukrainian American Business Leader Honored by Ukrainian Embassy for Recent Diplomatic Efforts"; "Aeros History"; "Aeroscraft Media Kit," Aeros, accessed January 8, 2020, http://aeroscraft.com/download/i/mark_dl/u/4011780344/4604005480/AeroscraftMediaKit.pdf; Aarian Marshall, "The Flying Bum Just Crashed – So Why Are We Building Airships?," *Wired*, August 25, 2016, https://www.wired.com/2016/08/airlander-flying-bum-crash-airships-advantages/; Michael Walsh, "NASA, Pentagon Sponsor $35 Million High-Tech Zeppelin That Could Be Key Aircraft of the Future," *New York Daily News*, January 4, 2013, https://www.nydailynews.com/news/national/high-tech-zeppelin-key-aircraft-future-article-1.1233523; "Military-Industrial Complex; Schiff & Co. Making Bank in Ukraine."

154 LD-2 lobbying disclosure form for Worldwide Aeros Corp., for 2014, quarter 1, https://soprweb.senate.gov/index.cfm?event=getFilingDetails&filingID=4E6596E6-CD34-421D-A8B9-FA009C18E501&filingTypeID=51; LD-2 lobbying disclosure

form for Worldwide Aeros Corp., for 2014, quarter 2, https://soprweb.senate.gov
/index.cfm?event=getFilingDetails&filingID=AA04149C-7DD8-4E5B
-97B4-B63B974BF3E2&filingTypeID=61; LD-2 lobbying disclosure form for
Worldwide Aeros Corp., for 2015, quarter 1, https://soprweb.senate.gov/index.
cfm?event=getFilingDetails&filingID=4CFDB39B-5101-4C00-9DF7-B0824B-
1683B2&filingTypeID=51; LD-2 lobbying disclosure form for Worldwide Aeros
Corp., for 2014, quarter 4, https://soprweb.senate.gov/index.cfm?event=getFiling-
Details&filingID=2E80B474-132E-4735-A51C-EE60C84F5BFF&filingTypeID=78;
LD-2 lobbying disclosure form for Worldwide Aeros Corp., for 2016, quarter 3,
https://soprweb.senate.gov/index.cfm?event=getFilingDetails&filingID=AB-
7C1EB6-2F07-4953-912B-C040657190DB&filingTypeID=73.

155 LD-2 lobbying disclosure form for Worldwide Aeros Corp., for 2015, quarter 1; "In
1.5 Years We Regained Trust in Ukrainian Defense Industry and Attracted Investors," Ukroboronprom, March 1, 2017, https://ukroboronprom.com.ua/en/media/
za-1-5-roky-vidnovyly-doviru-ukrayinskoyiyi-oboronky-ta-zaluchyly-inves-
toriv-ukroboronprom.html.

156 "In 1.5 Years We Regained Trust in Ukrainian Defense Industry and Attracted
Investors."

157 Illia Ponomarenko, "New Ukrainian M4-WAC47 Rifle 'A Strong Political Message
to Russia,'" *Kyiv Post*, January 28, 2018, https://www.kyivpost.com/ukraine-politics/
new-ukrainian-m4-wac47-rifle-strong-political-message-russia.html.

158 "In 1.5 Years We Regained Trust in Ukrainian Defense Industry and Attracted
Investors."

159 Alexandra Mclees and Eugene Rumer, "Saving Ukraine's Defense Industry," Carnegie Endowment for International Peace, July 30, 2014, https://carnegieendowment.
org/2014/07/30/saving-ukraine-s-defense-industry-pub-56282; "Outlook 2018,"
Defense News, January 2018, https://www.dau.edu/cop/iam/DAU%20Sponsored
%20Documents/Defense%20News%202018%20Outlook%20-%20Jan%2018.pdf;
"Ukroboronprom Started "Day of Defense Industry of Ukraine" at NATO HQ,"
Ukroboronprom, accessed January 15, 2020, https://ukroboronprom.com.ua/
en/media/ukroboronprom-rozpochav-den-oboronnoyi-promyslovosti-ukray-
iny-u-shtab-kvartyri-nato.html; Ukraine Embassy Facebook photo, Embassy of
Ukraine in the USA, accessed on January 15, 2020, https://www.facebook.com/ukr.
embassy.usa/photos/a.437547496288488/1192579027451994/?type=3; "Ukroboronprom in 2017: Cooperation with NATO and Joint Developments," Ukroboronprom,
March 1, 2018, https://ukroboronprom.com.ua/en/media/ukroboronprom-u-2017-
rotsi-spivpratsya-z-nato-ta-spilni-rozrobky.html.

160 Valeriy Akimenko, "Ukraine's Toughest Fight: The Challenge of Military
Reform," Carnegie Endowment for International Peace, February 22, 2018,
https://carnegieendowment.org/2018/02/22/ukraine-s-toughest-fight-challenge
-of-military-reform-pub-75609.

161 Commission on Security & Cooperation in Europe: U.S. Helsinki Commission,
"Ukraine's Fight Against Corruption," transcript by Superior Transcriptions
LLC, November 29, 2017, https://www.csce.gov/sites/helsinkicommission.house.
gov/files/unofficial-transcript/1129%20Ukraines%20Fight%20Against%20Cor-
ruption%20FINAL%20SCRUBBED.pdf; Larry Elliott and Patrick Wintour,

"IMF Warns Ukraine It Will Halt $40bn Bailout Unless Corruption Stops," *Guardian*, February 10, 2016, https://www.theguardian.com/world/2016/feb/10/imf-warns-ukraine-halt-40bn-bailout-corruption-christine-lagarde.

162 Commission on Security & Cooperation in Europe: U.S. Helsinki Commission, "Ukraine's Fight Against Corruption."

163 "Financial Information," Center for International Policy, accessed January 15, 2020, https://www.internationalpolicy.org/financial-information; "Honor Roll of Contributors," Atlantic Council, accessed January 15, 2020, https://www.atlanticcouncil.org/support-the-council/honor-roll-of-contributors/; "Open Society Foundations," National Center for Public Policy Research, October 14, 2011, https://nationalcenter.org/ncppr/2011/10/14/open-society-foundations/; Commission on Security & Cooperation in Europe: U.S. Helsinki Commission, "Ukraine's Fight Against Corruption"; "Organizations Funded Directly by George Soros and His Open Society Institute," Key Wiki, last updated October 16, 2011, https://www.keywiki.org/Organizations_Funded_Directly_by_George_Soros_and_his_Open_Society_Institute.

164 Commission on Security & Cooperation in Europe: U.S. Helsinki Commission, "Ukraine's Fight Against Corruption."

165 Ibid.

166 Ibid.

167 Akimenko, "Ukraine's Toughest Fight: The Challenge of Military Reform."

168 Ibid.

169 Jorgan K. Andrews, "U.S. Goals and Expectations for the Ukraine Reform Conference in Denmark," U.S. Department of State, June 26, 2018, https://www.state.gov/u-s-goals-and-expectations-for-the-ukraine-reform-conference-in-denmark/; In Proceedings Before the United States Senate, Trial Memorandum of President Donald J. Trump, January 20, 2020, https://www.whitehouse.gov/wp-content/uploads/2020/01/Trial-Memorandum-of-President-Donald-J.-Trump.pdf.

170 Ibid.

171 Ibid.

172 Andrew E. Kramer, Mike McIntire, and Barry Meier, "Secret Ledger in Ukraine Lists Cash for Donald Trump's Campaign Chief," *New York Times*, August 14, 2016, https://www.nytimes.com/2016/08/15/us/politics/what-is-the-black-ledger.html; "Secret Ledgers Found in Ukraine List Millions in Cash Payments for Trump's Campaign Chairman," *Week*, August 15, 2016, https://theweek.com/speedreads/642929/secret-ledgers-found-ukraine-list-millions-cash-payments-trumps-campaign-chairman; Jeff Carlson, "Ties to Ukrainian National a Unifying Theme in Early Attacks on Trump," *Epoch Times*, April 10, 2019, https://www.theepochtimes.com/ties-to-ukrainian-national-a-unifying-theme-in-early-attacks-on-trump_2872609.html; *New York Times*, "Secret Ledger in Ukraine Lists Cash for Donald Trump's Campaign Chief," *Kyiv Post*, August 15, 2016, https://www.kyivpost.com/article/content/ukraine-politics/the-new-york-times-secret-ledger-in-ukraine-lists-cash-for-donald-trumps-campaign-chief-421022.html.

173 Tucker Carlson, "We're Becoming an Authoritarian Society - and the Group in Charge is Coming After Fox News," Fox News, March 13, 2019, https://www.foxnews.com/opinion/tucker-carlson-were-becoming-an-authoritarian

-society-and-the-group-in-charge-is-coming-after-fox-news; Nick Fernandez, "Fox News Virtually Silent on NY Times Report Detailing Trump Campaign Chairman's Ties to Pro-Russian Ukrainian Politicians," Media Matters, August 15, 2016, https://www.mediamatters.org/donald-trump/fox-news-virtually-silent-ny-times-report-detailing-trump-campaign-chairmans-ties-pro; "CBS This Morning: Paul Manafort May Be Guilty of 'Tax Evasion, Money Laundering, and Illegally Providing Funds for Lobbyists,'" Media Matters, August 19, 2016, https://www. mediamatters.org/donald-trump/cbs-morning-paul-manafort-may-be-guilty-tax-evasion-money-laundering-and-illegally; "CBS This Morning Examines Alleged Payments to Trump Campaign Chairman from Pro-Russian Ukrainian Politicians," Media Matters, August 18, 2016,https://www.mediamatters.org/donald-trump/ cbs-morning-examines-alleged-payments-trump-campaign-chairman-pro-rus-sian-ukrainian; "CNN's Clarissa Ward Explains the Problematic Ties Between Paul Manafort and Ukraine's Former Pro-Russian President," Media Matters, August 16, 2016, https://www.mediamatters.org/donald-trump/cnns-clarissa-ward-explains-problematic-ties-between-paul-manafort-and-ukraines-former.

174 Kenneth P. Vogel and David Stern, "Ukrainian Efforts to Sabotage Trump Backfire," *Politico*, January 11, 2017, https://www.politico.com/story/2017/01/ukraine-sab-otage-trump-backfire-233446; Carlson, "Ties to Ukrainian National a Unifying Theme in Early Attacks on Trump"; Sergii Leshchenko, Facebook post, August 19, 2016, https://archive.is/YD7KK; OSF memo, March 31, 2014; "CBS This Morning: Paul Manafort May Be Guilty of 'Tax Evasion, Money Laundering, and Illegally Providing Funds for Lobbyists.'"

175 Sergii Leshchenko, Facebook post, August 19, 2016; "CBS This Morning: Paul Manafort May Be Guilty of 'Tax Evasion, Money Laundering, and Illegally Provid-ing Funds for Lobbyists.'"

176 Nolan D. McCaskill, Alex Isenstadt, and Shane Goldmacher, "Paul Manafort Resigns from Trump Campaign," *Politico*, August 19, 2016, https://www.politico. com/story/2016/08/paul-manafort-resigns-from-trump-campaign-227197.

177 "Hacked Emails from US State Dept's Top Russian Intel Official Robert Otto Matching Trump1," Scribd, https://www.scribd.com/document/368348458/ Hacked-Emails-From-US-State-Dept-s-Top-Russian-Intel-Official-Robert-Otto-Matching-Trump1-pdf (uploaded by Special Ops on January 3, 2018).

178 Tristan Justice, "FBI Blows Off Senators' Request on Materials Related to Ukrainian DNC Contractor in 2016," *Federalist*, December 18, 2019, https:// thefederalist.com/2019/12/18/fbi-blows-off-senators-request-on-materials-relat-ed-to-ukrainian-dnc-contractor-in-2016/; Ivan Pentchoukov, "Top Prosecutor Probing Ukrainian Plot to Boost Clinton in 2016 Election," *Epoch Times*, March 21, 2019, https://www.theepochtimes.com/top-prosecutor-probing-ukrainian-plot-to-boost-clinton-in-2016-election_2847598.html; "Hannity: Another Stinging Setback for the Special Counsel," Fox News, May 16, 2018, https://www.foxnews. com/transcript/hannity-another-stinging-setback-for-the-special-counsel.

179 Todd Ruger, "House Democrats Abandon Crimes in Trump Impeachment Articles," *Roll Call*, December 11, 2019, https://www.rollcall.com/2019/12/11/house-dem-ocrats-abandon-crimes-in-trump-impeachment-articles/; Elizabeth Janowski,

"Timeline: Trump Impeachment Inquiry," NBC News, October 16, 2019, https://www.nbcnews.com/politics/trump-impeachment-inquiry/timeline-trump-impeachment-inquiry-n1066691; Adriana Cohen, "It's High Time to End This Schiff Show," Real Clear Politics, January 31, 2020, https://www.realclearpolitics.com/articles/2020/01/31/its_high_time_to_end_this_schiff_show_142278.html.

180 Elizabeth Janowski, "Timeline: Trump Impeachment Inquiry"; Matea Gold, "The Campaign to Impeach President Trump Has Begun," *Washington Post*, January 20, 2017, https://www.washingtonpost.com/news/post-politics/wp/2017/01/20/the-campaign-to-impeach-president-trump-has-begun/.

181 Morgan Chalfant, "Trump Demands Schiff Resign over Account of Ukraine Call," *Hill*, September 27, 2019, https://thehill.com/homenews/administration/463344-trump-demands-schiff-resign; Donald J. Trump (@realDonaldTrump), "I JUST GOT IMPEACHED FOR MAKING A PERFECT PHONE CALL!," Twitter, January 16, 2020, 3:39 PM, https://twitter.com/realDonaldTrump/status/1217909231946477575.

182 Entous, "The Ukrainian Prosecutor Behind Trump's Impeachment."

183 Vogel and Stern, "Ukrainian Efforts to Sabotage Trump Backfire"; Vogel and Mendel, "Biden Faces Conflict of Interest Questions That Are Being Promoted by Trump and Allies"; Glenn Thrush and Kenneth P. Vogel, "What Joe Biden Actually Did in Ukraine," *New York Times*, November 10, 2019, https://www.nytimes.com/2019/11/10/us/politics/joe-biden-ukraine.html.

184 Vogel and Stern, "Ukrainian Efforts to Sabotage Trump Backfire"; John Solomon, "The Case for Russia Collusion… against the Democrats," *Hill*, February 10, 2019, https://thehill.com/opinion/white-house/429292-the-case-for-russia-collusion-against-the-democrats; Dan Merica, "First on CNN: Former DNC Contractor Denies Working with Ukrainian Officials on Anti-Trump Research," CNN, July 14, 2017, https://www.cnn.com/2017/07/14/politics/dnc-contractor-ukraine-alexandra-chalupa-trump/index.html; Monica Showalter, "Witness Time: Did Eric Ciaramella Have a Conflict of Interest on Ukraine's Burisma?," American Thinker, January 30, 2020, https://www.americanthinker.com/blog/2020/01/witness_time_did_eric_ciaramella_have_a_conflict_of_interest_on_ukraines_burisma.html; Paul Sperry, "Whistleblower Was Overheard in '17 Discussing with Ally How to Remove Trump," Real Clear Investigations, January 22, 2020, https://www.realclearinvestigations.com/articles/2020/01/22/whistleblower_was_overheard_in_17_discussing_with_ally_how_to_remove_trump_121701.html; Grassley, Johnson Want Details of FBI Interactions with 2016 DNC Contractor," Chuck Grassley's Senate page, November 22, 2019, https://www.grassley.senate.gov/news/news-releases/grassley-johnson-want-details-fbi-interactions-2016-dnc-contractor.

185 Sperry, "Whistleblower Was Overheard in '17 Discussing with Ally How to Remove Trump"; Sara Carter, "Whistleblower and DNC Contractor Visited Obama WH. It Must Be Investigated," Sara Carter's website, November 8, 2019, https://saraacarter.com/whistleblower-and-dnc-contractor-visited-obama-wh-it-must-be-investigated/; Ian Schwartz, "Rand Paul: Alleged Whistleblower, Friend Plotted for over a Year to Bring Down Trump," Real Clear Politics, video, January 31, 2020, https://www.realclearpolitics.com/video/2020/01/31/rand_paul_alleged_whistleblower_friend_plotted_for_over_a_year_to_bring_down_trump.html; Betsy

McCaughey, "Why Adam Schiff Doesn't Want Anyone Talking to the Whistleblower," *New York Post*, December 30, 2019, https://nypost.com/2019/12/30/why-adam-schiff-doesnt-want-anyone-talking-to-the-whistleblower/; Mike Brest, "GOP Lawmaker Demands Alleged Whistleblower Eric Ciaramella Testify," *Washington Examiner*, December 11, 2019, https://www.washingtonexaminer.com/news/gop-lawmaker-demands-alleged-whistleblower-eric-ciaramella-testify; "Judicial Watch Sues CIA and DOJ for Communications of Eric Ciaramella," Judicial Watch, press release, December 26, 2019, https://www.judicialwatch.org/press-releases/judicial-watch-sues-cia-and-doj-communications-of-eric-ciaramella/.

186 Ibid.

187 Ginger Gibson, "Clinton Accuses Trump of Being Putin's 'Puppet,'" Reuters, October 20, 2016, https://www.reuters.com/article/us-usa-election-debate-russia-idUSKCN12K0E7; Brooke Seipel, "Clinton Calls Trump 'Putin's Puppet' amid Reports of Russian Interference in 2020 Election," *Hill*, February 21, 2020, https://thehill.com/homenews/news/484105-clinton-calls-trump-putins-puppet-amid-reports-that-russia-is-interfering-in; John Solomon, "How the Clinton Machine Flooded the FBI with Trump-Russia Dirt…Until Agents Bit," *Hill*, January 22, 2019, https://thehill.com/opinion/white-house/426464-how-the-clinton-machine-flooded-the-fbi-with-trump-russia-dirt-until; Jeff Carlson, "UK, Australia Have Reason to Be Concerned about Declassification," *Epoch Times*, September 26, 2018, https://www.theepochtimes.com/the-uk-and-australia-have-reason-to-be-concerned-about-declassification_2671461.html.

Chapter 10

1 Brennan Weiss, Ellen Cranley, and Grace Panetta, "Everything You Should Know about Robert Mueller, Who Led the Government's 2-year Investigation into Trump and Russia," Business Insider, July 23, 2019, https://www.businessinsider.com/robert-mueller-bio-photos-trump-russia-investigator-history-2017-10.

2 Former Special Counsel Robert S. Mueller III, on the Investigation into Russian Interference in the 2016 Presidential Election, U.S. House of Representatives, Permanent Select Committee on the Intelligence, July 24, 2019, https://docs.house.gov/meetings/IG/IG00/20190724/109808/HHRG-116-IG00-Transcript-20190724.pdf.

3 Ibid.

4 Ibid.; "About," Representative Will Hurd's website, accessed January 15, 2020, https://hurd.house.gov/about.

5 Special Counsel Robert S. Mueller, III, "Report on the Investigation into Russian Interference in the 2016 Presidential Election," March 2019, U.S. Department of Justice, https://www.justice.gov/storage/report.pdf.

6 Former Special Counsel Robert S. Mueller III, on the Investigation into Russian Interference in the 2016 Presidential Election, U.S. House of Representatives, Permanent Select Committee on the Intelligence, July 24, 2019; John Solomon, "Move Over 'Grassy Knoll,' the Trump-Russia Bank Tale Joins Unproven Conspiracies List," *Hill*, October 14, 2018, https://thehill.com/opinion/white-house/411209-move-over-grassy-knoll-the-trump-russia-bank-tale-joins-unproven.

7 Rowan Scarborough, "Hillary Clinton Operatives Pushed Now-Debunked Trump-Alfa Server Conspiracy, Testimony Reveals," Associated Press, January

23, 2019, https://apnews.com/cd2da448a9db6af11d8c10e9c3f3495b; Franklin Foer, "Trump's Server, Revisited," Slate, November 2, 2016, https://slate.com/news-and-politics/2016/11/the-trump-server-evaluating-new-evidence-and-countertheories.html; Franklin Foer, "Was a Trump Server Communicating with Russia?," Slate, October 31, 2016, http://www.slate.com/articles/news_and_politics/cover_story/2016/10/was_a_server_registered_to_the_trump_organization_communicating_with_russia.html; Sam Biddle, "Russian Bank Accused of Trump Connection Tries to Clear Name by Pressuring U.S. Computer Researcher," *Intercept*, October 26, 2016, https://theintercept.com/2017/10/26/russian-bank-accused-of-trump-connection-tries-to-clear-name-by-pressuring-u-s-computer-researcher/; Solomon, "Move Over 'Grassy Knoll,' the Trump-Russia Bank Tale Joins Unproven Conspiracies List"; "A Clinton Supporter Pushed the Trump-Russia Computer Narrative Investigated by the FBI," Circa, on Internet Archive, March 15, 2017, https://web.archive.org/web/20190403211129/https://www.circa.com/story/2017/03/15/a-clinton-supporter-pushed-the-trump-russia-computer-narrative-investigated-by-the-fbi (the screenshot of the site was captured on April 3, 2019).

8 Solomon, "Move Over 'Grassy Knoll,' the Trump-Russia Bank Tale Joins Unproven Conspiracies List."

9 John Solomon, "FBI's Steele Story Falls Apart: False Intel and Media Contacts Were Flagged Before FISA," *Hill*, May 9, 2019, https://thehill.com/opinion/white-house/442944-fbis-steele-story-falls-apart-false-intel-and-media-contacts-were-flagged.

10 Solomon, "Move Over 'Grassy Knoll,' the Trump-Russia Bank Tale Joins Unproven Conspiracies List."

11 Ibid.

12 Ibid.; Former Special Counsel Robert S. Mueller III, on the Investigation into Russian Interference in the 2016 Presidential Election, U.S. House of Representatives, Permanent Select Committee on the Intelligence, July 24, 2019.

13 Ibid.

14 Desmond Butler, "Obama: U.S. Has 'Reset' Relations with Russia," NBC News, June 24, 2010, http://www.nbcnews.com/id/37892671/ns/politics-white_house/t/obama-us-has-reset-relations-russia/; Hillary Rodham Clinton, "Trade With Russia Is a Win-Win," *Wall Street Journal*, June 20, 2012, https://2009-2017.state.gov/secretary/20092013clinton/rm/2012/06/193475.htm; "U.S.-Russia Relations: "Reset" Fact Sheet," Obama White House (archive), June 24, 2010, https://obamawhitehouse.archives.gov/realitycheck/the-press-office/us-russia-relations-reset-fact-sheet; Peter Brookes, "Russian 'Reset' a Resounding Failure," Heritage Foundation, April 5, 2016, https://www.heritage.org/arms-control/commentary/russian-reset-resounding-failure; Rich Lowry, "The Reset Failure," *National Review*, January 10, 2017, https://www.nationalreview.com/2017/01/barack-obama-vladimir-putin-russian-reset-failure/; "Text: Obama's Speech at the New Economic School," *New York Times*, July 7, 2009, https://www.nytimes.com/2009/07/07/world/europe/07prexy.text.html; Lara Jakes, "US, Europeans Try to Rally Western Front vs Russia," Associated Press, March 3, 2014, https://apnews.com/ed84f287ae5a431eb5a97334df0062c5.

15 U.S. Department of State, "Interview with Vladimir Pozner of First Channel Television," March 19, 2010, https://2009-2017.state.gov/secretary/20092013clinton/rm/2010/03/138712.htm; Michael McFaul, *From Cold War to Hot Peace: An American Ambassador in Putin's Russia* (Boston: Houghton Mifflin Harcourt, 2018); "US Ambassador Meets with Skolkovo Tech Students," Skolkovo Foundation, July 23, 2012, https://old.sk.ru/news/b/press/archive/2012/07/23/us-ambassador-meets-with-skolkovo-tech-students.aspx; "From Cold War to Hot Peace," Medium, May 2, 2018, https://medium.com/freeman-spogli-institute-for-international-studies/from-cold-war-to-hot-peace-3856bb902eed; Peter Schweizer, "The Clinton Foundation, State and Kremlin Connections," *Wall Street Journal*, July 31, 2016, https://www.wsj.com/articles/the-clinton-foundation-state-and-kremlin-connections-1469997195; Deroy Murdock, "How the Clintons Sold Out U.S. National Interests to the Putin Regime," *National Review*, April 7, 2017, https://www.nationalreview.com/2017/04/clinton-russia-ties-bill-hillary-sold-out-us-interests-putin-regime/.

16 Confidential/Sensitive Source, "U.S. Presidential Election: Republican Candidate Donald Trump's Activities in Russia and Compromising Relationship with the Kremlin," August 10, 2016, https://www.documentcloud.org/documents/3259984-Trump-Intelligence-Allegations.html.

17 U.S. Department of Justice, "Review of Four FISA Applications and Other Aspects of the FBI's Crossfire Hurricane Investigation," Office of the Inspector General, December 2019, https://www.justice.gov/storage/120919-examination.pdf.

18 Olivia Beavers, "Rosenstein Knocks Republicans Who Want to Impeach Him: 'They Can't Even Resist Leaking Their Own Drafts,'" *Hill*, May 1, 2018, https://thehill.com/policy/national-security/385713-rosenstein-knocks-republicans-who-wrote-draft-calling-for-his; Rachel Maddow, "Comey: Criticism of Carter Page FISA Warrant 'A Political Deal,'" NBC News, April 19, 2018, https://www.nbcnews.com/video/comey-criticism-of-carter-page-fisa-warrant-a-political-deal-1215189059764; Ronn Blitzer, "Comey Admits 'I Was Wrong' on FISA Conduct, Remains Defiant on Dossier in Tense Interview," Fox News, December 15, 2019, https://www.foxnews.com/politics/comey-defends-fbis-fisa-process-after-scathing-ig-report.

19 U.S. Department of Justice, "Review of Four FISA Applications and Other Aspects of the FBI's Crossfire Hurricane Investigation"; "Just How Bad Was the FBI's Russia FISA? 51 Violations and 9 False Statements," John Solomon Reports, December 9, 2019, https://johnsolomonreports.com/just-how-bad-was-the-fbis-russia-fisa-51-violations-and-9-false-statements/.

20 Jonathan Turley, "Horowitz Report Is Damning for the FBI and Unsettling for the Rest of Us," *Hill*, December 9, 2019, https://thehill.com/opinion/judiciary/473709-horowitz-report-is-damning-for-the-fbi-and-unsettling-for-the-rest-of-us; U.S. Department of Justice, "Review of Four FISA Applications and Other Aspects of the FBI's Crossfire Hurricane Investigation."

21 Emily Larsen, "Joe Biden Admits Burisma Board Position for Son Hunter Was 'A Bad Image,'" *Washington Examiner*, February 3, 2020, https://www.washingtonexaminer.com/news/joe-biden-agrees-burisma-board-position-for-hunter-biden-set-a-bad-image.

22 Marty Johnson, "Career State Official Warned about Biden's Son: Report," *Hill*, October 18, 2019, https://thehill.com/homenews/campaign/466493-career-state-official-warned-about-bidens-son-report; "Testimony Bombshell: Obama Administration Tried to Partner with Hunter Biden's Ukrainian Gas Firm but Was Blocked over Corruption Concerns," John Solomon Reports, November 7, 2019, https://johnsolomonreports.com/testimony-bombshell-obama-administration-tried-to-partner-with-hunter-bidens-ukrainian-gas-firm-but-was-blocked-over-corruption-concerns/.

23 Zachary B. Wolf and Sean O'Key, "The Trump-Ukraine Impeachment Inquiry Report, Annotated," CNN, December 3, 2019, https://www.cnn.com/interactive/2019/12/politics/trump-ukraine-impeachment-inquiry-report-annotated/.

24 Charles Creitz, "Document Reveals Ukraine Had Already Reopened Probe of Hunter Biden-Linked Firm Months Before Trump Phone Call," Fox News, October 9, 2019, https://www.foxnews.com/media/john-solomon-says-new-hunter-biden-related-doc-shows-significant-shift-in-factual-timeline.

25 Ann M. Simmons, "Russia's Meddling in on Other Nations' Elections Is Nothing New. Just Ask the Europeans," *Los Angeles Times*, March 30, 2017, https://www.latimes.com/world/europe/la-fg-russia-election-meddling-20170330-story.html; Eli Lake, "Obama Choked on Russia Long Before the 2016 Election," *Pioneer Press*, June 29, 2017, https://www.twincities.com/2017/06/29/eli-lake-obama-choked-on-russia-long-before-the-2016-election/; Eli Lake, "Russia Uses Dirty Tricks Despite U.S. 'Reset,'" *Washington Times*, August 4, 2011, https://www.washingtontimes.com/news/2011/aug/4/russia-uses-dirty-tricks-despite-us-reset/.

26 Turley, "Horowitz Report Is Damning for the FBI and Unsettling for the Rest of Us"; Josh Gerstein, "Report Slams State Department FOIA Process," *Politico*, January 7, 2016, https://www.politico.com/story/2016/01/report-slams-state-department-foia-process-217436.

27 Turley, "Horowitz Report Is Damning for the FBI and Unsettling for the Rest of Us."

28 Kelly Riddell, "Ideological Billionaires Sway Universities' Agendas with Big Bucks," *Washington Times*, August 26, 2015, https://www.washingtontimes.com/news/2015/aug/26/george-soros-tom-steyer-michael-bloomberg-koch-bro/; Nancy Smith, "Billionaire Leftist George Soros Bought America's Media. Why Hasn't Anybody Noticed?" Sunshine State News, October 17, 2019, http://www.sunshinestatenews.com/story/billionaire-george-soros-bought-and-paid-americas-media.

29 Turley, "Horowitz Report Is Damning for the FBI and Unsettling for the Rest of Us."

30 U.S. Department of Justice, "Review of Four FISA Applications and Other Aspects of the FBI's Crossfire Hurricane Investigation."

31 Ibid.

32 Ibid.

33 Ibid.

34 Erik Wemple, Horowitz Report Confirms John Solomon's Scoop on FBI 'Spreadsheet' Regarding Steele Dossier," *Washington Post*, December 16, 2019, https://www.washingtonpost.com/opinions/2019/12/16/horowitz-report-confirms-john-solomons-scoop-fbi-spreadsheet-regarding-steele-dossier/; John Solomon, "FBI Email Chain May Provide Most Damning Evidence of FISA Abuses Yet," *Hill*, December 5, 2018, https://thehill.com/hilltv/rising/419901-fbi-email-chain

-may-provide-most-damning-evidence-of-fisa-abuses-yet; John Solomon, "Silence of 'the Lambs': The Deadening Quietude of the FISA Court and John Roberts," *Hill*, October 30, 2018, https://thehill.com/opinion/white-house/413854-silence-of-the-lambs-the-deafening-quietude-of-the-fisa-court-and-john.

35 Michael S. Schmidt, Mark Mazzetti, and Matt Apuzzo, "Trump Campaign Aides Had Repeated Contacts with Russian Intelligence," *New York Times*, February 14, 2017, https://www.nytimes.com/2017/02/14/us/politics/russia-intelligence-com-munications-trump.html; Michael S. Schmidt, Mark Mazzetti, and Matt Apuzzo, "Comey Disputes New York Times Article about Russia Investigation," *New York Times*, June 8, 2017, https://www.nytimes.com/2017/06/08/us/politics/james-com-ey-new-york-times-article-russia.html; David Cohen, "Schiff: 'Ample Evidence of Collusion in Plain Sight,'" *Politico*, April 21, 2019, https://www.politico.com/story/2019/04/21/adam-schiff-collusion-trump-1283786; Karoun Demirjian, "Schiff Doubles Down on Trump Despite Russia Report: 'Undoubtedly There Is Collusion,'" *Los Angeles Times*, March 27, 2019, https://www.latimes.com/nation/politics/la-na-pol-russia-investigation-schiff-trump-20190327-story.html; Kimber-ley Strassel, "Inside the Media's Relentless Crusade to Destroy President Trump," *New York Post*, October 13, 2019, https://nypost.com/2019/10/13/inside-the-me-dias-relentless-crusade-to-destroy-president-trump/; Tim Hains, "Montage: Mainstream Media Hype about Russia Collusion," Real Clear Politics, March 25, 2019, https://www.realclearpolitics.com/video/2019/03/25/montage_main-stream_media_hype_about_russia_collusion.html; Byron York, "Nunes Blows up, Threatens Contempt After FBI Stonewalls House on Russia Investigator Demoted for Anti-Trump Bias," *Washington Examiner*, https://www.washingtonexaminer.com/byron-york-nunes-blows-up-threatens-contempt-after-fbi-stonewalls-house-on-russia-investigator-demoted-for-anti-trump-bias.

36 Abigail Abrams, "Here's What We Know So Far about Russia's 2016 Meddling," *Time*, April 18, 2019, https://time.com/5565991/russia-influence-2016-election/; Scott Shane, "The Fake Americans Russia Created to Influence the Election," *New York Times*, September 7, 2017, https://www.nytimes.com/2017/09/07/us/politics/russia-facebook-twitter-election.html; Darren Samuelsohn, "Facebook: Russian-linked Accounts Bought $15,000 in Ads during 2016 Race," *Politico*, Sep-tember 6, 2017, https://www.politico.com/story/2017/09/06/facebook-ads-russia-linked-accounts-242401.

37 Schweizer, "The Clinton Foundation, State and Kremlin Connections"; Vladimir Isa-chenkov, "Russia: New Weapon Can Travel 27 Times the Speed of Sound," *Navy Times*, December 27, 2019, https://www.navytimes.com/news/your-navy/2019/12/28/rus-sia-new-weapon-can-travel-27-times-the-speed-of-sound/; Vladimir Isachenkov, "Putin Says Russia Is Leading in Hypersonic Weapons," Associated Press, Decem-ber 24, 2019, https://apnews.com/d4e05956217d895594bcef491083e950.

38 Benjamin Haddad and Alina Polyakova, "Don't Rehabilitate Obama on Russia," Brookings Institute, March 5, 2018, https://www.brookings.edu/blog/order-from-chaos/2018/03/05/dont-rehabilitate-obama-on-russia/.

39 Glenn Kessler, "Flashback: Obama's Debate Zinger on Romney's '1980s' Foreign Policy," *Washington Post*, March 20, 2014, https://www.washingtonpost.com/news/

fact-checker/wp/2014/03/20/flashback-obamas-debate-zinger-on-romneys-1980s-foreign-policy/?utm_term=.00fa183d823d.

40 Marc A. Thiessen, "Joe Biden Is a Hypocrite on Ukraine," *Washington Post*, October 8, 2019, https://www.washingtonpost.com/opinions/2019/10/08/joe-biden-is-hypocrite-ukraine/; Tim Hains, "FLASHBACK, 2018: Joe Biden Brags at CFR Meeting about Withholding Aid to Ukraine to Force Firing of Prosecutor," Real Clear Politics, September 27, 2019, https://www.realclearpolitics.com/video/2019/09/27/flashback_2018_joe_biden_brags_at_cfr_meeting_about_withholding_aid_to_ukraine_to_force_firing_of_prosecutor.html; "GOP Lawmaker Blasts Democrats Hypocrisy amid Impeachment Fallout," *Hill*, November 15, 2019, https://thehill.com/hilltv/rising/470632-gop-lawmaker-blasts-democrats-hypocrisy-amid-impeachment-fallout.

41 Joe Gould, "Trump to Seek $250M in New Lethal Aid to Ukraine," *Defense News*, December 4, 2019, https://www.defensenews.com/congress/2019/12/04/trump-to-seek-250m-in-new-lethal-aid-to-ukraine/.

42 Michael Crowley, Falih Hassan, and Eric Schmitt, "U.S. Strike in Iraq Kills Qassim Suleimani, Commander of Iranian Forces," *New York Times*, January 2, 2020, https://www.nytimes.com/2020/01/02/world/middleeast/qassem-soleimani-iraq-iran-attack.html.

43 Julie Allen, "NATO Members Increase Defence Spending by $100 Billion after Donald Trump Called Them 'Delinquents,'" *Telegraph*, January 27, 2019, https://www.telegraph.co.uk/news/2019/01/27/nato-members-increase-defence-spending-100-billion-donald-trump/; Tony Shaffer, "Donald Trump Is Ending Endless War," *Hill*, February 19, 2020, https://thehill.com/opinion/international/483676-donald-trump-is-ending-endless-war.

44 Jordan Fabian and Kyle Balluck, "Trump Enters North Korea, Announces Nuclear Talks Will Resume," Hill, June 30, 2019, https://thehill.com/homenews/administration/451044-trump-makes-history-crossing-into-north-korea-before-announcing.

45 David Rothkopf, "Obama's 'Don't Do Stupid Shit' Foreign Policy," *Foreign Policy*, June 4, 2014, https://foreignpolicy.com/2014/06/04/obamas-dont-do-stupid-shit-foreign-policy/.

46 Ibid.; Jeffrey Goldberg, "The Obama Doctrine," *Atlantic*, April 2016, https://www.theatlantic.com/magazine/archive/2016/04/the-obama-doctrine/471525/; Stephen M. Walt, "Barack Obama Was a Foreign-Policy Failure," *Foreign Policy*, January 18, 2017, https://foreignpolicy.com/2017/01/18/barack-obama-was-a-foreign-policy-failure/.

ACKNOWLEDGMENTS

The authors would first like to thank Doug Campbell for his bravery, integrity, and his many years of service to our country. Thank you to Victoria Toensing and Joe di Genova for their assistance with this project. We are looking forward to many more years of friendship with you all.

We appreciate Adam Bellow, Michael Wilson, Anthony Ziccardi, and the entire team at Post Hill Press for giving us this opportunity and for being a pleasure to work with.

A special thanks to the JustTheNews.com team for their hard work and support during the book writing process. We are grateful to Peter Schweizer and our friends at the Government Accountability Institute: first and foremost, to Tarik Noriega, whose efforts were nothing short of herculean; to Joe Duffus, for his expertise and clever wit; to Steve Post, for his fastidious style and especially for the last minute scrubs; and to Steven Richards and Corey Adamyk for their brilliant research and incredible organization skills. This book would not have been possible without this team's exhaustive research, thorough editing, careful fact checking, and incredible attention to detail. Thank you, all.

Sincere thanks go to Winston Lambert, Jeff Walburn, Chick Lawson, Bobby Vaughn Jr., Steele Lancaster, M.D., Scott Melbye, and James Rickards (among so many others) for lending their strategic insights. Their help elucidating the extraordinarily complex world that is the international uranium industry was invaluable.

Finally, many thanks and immense gratitude go to our families, for their patience and much needed encouragement. The Solomons (Judy, Josh, Jack, and Marcia Olsen for their unwavering support in the pursuit of truth), and the Bruners (James, Gretchen, Meredith, Julia, Sally, Teddy, and Faith + the Schwarzs, especially Bob and Muriel a.k.a Grand & Grand, for their wisdom, inspiration, and mentorship).

We know it's not easy being an author's or a journalist's "widow." To Judy and Jillian, our absolute most heartfelt appreciation goes to both of you, with much love.

329

INDEX

Index

Index

Index

Toronto Stock Exchange (TSX), 95, 142, 143
Transport Logistics International, 123
Trump, Donald J., 1, 2, 3, 4, 8, 10, 11, 12, 13, 53, 77, 102,
    103, 106, 115, 123, 125, 162, 166, 168, 171, 172, 173,
    174, 192, 196, 197, 199, 200, 201, 202, 203, 204,
    205, 206, 207, 208, 209, 210, 211, 212, 213, 214,
    215, 216, 217
Turkey, 178, 192
    Istanbul, 192
Turkmenistan, 41
TVEL, 120
Twentieth Trust, 32
Twitter, 153

U
U.S. Agency for International Development
    (USAID), 176, 177, 188, 198
U.S. Air Force, 198
U.S. Army Foreign Military Studies Program, 159
U.S. Chamber of Commerce, 154
U.S. Climate Action Partnership, 74
U.S. International Trade Commission (USITC), 76
U.S. PIRG, 66
U.S.-Russia Business Council, 158
Ukraine, 3, 4, 5, 6, 7, 9, 11, 12, 39, 40, 41, 42, 49, 52, 53,
    87, 105, 111, 166, 167, 172, 174, 175, 176, 177, 178,
    179, 180, 181, 182, 183, 184, 185, 186, 188, 189, 190,
    192, 193, 194, 195, 196, 197, 198, 199, 200, 201, 202,
    203, 204, 205, 210, 213, 214, 215, 219
    Donbass Region, 176, 179
    Kiev, 7, 177, 178, 179, 180, 184, 185, 186, 193, 194, 195,
        196, 197, 202
Ukroboronprom, 198, 199, 200, 201
Unified Energy System (UES), 29
    Inter RAO UES, 30
Union of Soviet Socialist Republics, 6, 7, 15, 17, 27, 39,
    40, 46, 63, 66, 94, 106, 171, 203
United Airlines, 68
United Arab Emirates (UAE), 127, 128, 129, 130, 131
United Kingdom, 43, 186, 205
United Nations (UN), 120, 137, 138, 181
    UN Security Council (UNSC), 137, 138
United States Enrichment Corporation (USEC),
    46, 145
United States of America, 7, 9, 14, 44, 46, 49, 51, 53,
    55, 58, 61, 63, 64, 68, 69, 78, 88, 91, 98, 99, 105,
    106, 109, 110, 111, 113, 118, 119, 127, 129, 136, 137,
    138, 142, 144, 146, 151, 154, 157, 170, 172, 175, 187,
    199, 210, 213, 214
University of Chicago, 55
Uranium One, 4, 8, 9, 10, 13, 14, 15, 16, 43, 47, 56, 62,
    65, 73, 76, 82, 84, 85, 86, 87, 90, 91, 93, 97, 98, 99,
    100, 101, 103, 106, 111, 112, 113, 114, 115, 119, 125,
    129, 131, 132, 133, 134, 135, 136, 137, 138, 139, 140,
    141, 142, 143, 144, 145, 146, 147, 149, 150, 151, 152,
    155, 156, 158, 161, 166, 168, 172, 182, 212, 215

Uranium Producers of America (UPA), 99
UrAsia Engery Ltd., 95, 96, 97, 98, 99, 100, 101
Urenco, 145
Utah, 15, 98, 99, 173

V
Vancouver Stock Exchange (VSE), 95
Vekselberg, Viktor, 136
Venezuela, 16
Vezdekhod, 26
Vindman, Alexander, 204
Vogel, Ken, 203, 204
Volgodonsk, Russia, 26
von Hoffer, Eugene, 33

W
Walgreens, 68
Wall Street Journal, 89, 167, 207
Warner, Mark, 190, 191
Warnig, Matthias, 18, 33, 70
Washington Post, 6, 171, 172, 190
Wasserstein Parella & Co., 69, 70
Watergate, 1
Waters, Maxine, 12
Weissmann, Andrew, 141
Westinghouse, 15
Winer, Jonathan, 192
Woodyer, Neil, 100
World Trade Organization (WTO), 156, 158, 159
Wyoming, USA, 15, 98, 142, 144, 145
Wyss, Hansjörg, 163

Y
Yahoo, 103, 117
Yahoo! News, 103
Yakunin, Vladimir, 29
Yale University, 185
Yanukovych, Viktor, 166, 167, 168, 175, 176, 177, 178,
    179, 180, 189, 196, 197, 202
Yatsenyuk, Artseniy, 180, 185, 194
Yeltsin, Boris, 5, 17, 18, 20, 21, 22, 23, 24, 25, 27, 28,
    34, 40, 43, 45, 47, 111, 156
Yucaipa Companies LLC, 130
Yugoslavia, 39, 42
Yukos, 21, 34, 35, 36, 37, 70, 161
YukosSibneft, 35

Z
Zelensky, Volodymyr, 12, 203, 204
Ziobro, Lucia, 160
Zlochevsky, Mykola, 185, 186, 195
Zyuganov, Gennady, 22

ABOUT THE AUTHORS

John Solomon is an award-winning journalist and the author of *DSK: The Scandal that Brought Down Dominique Strauss-Kahn*. During his quarter-century career in print and broadcast media, Solomon has covered a variety of issues, from the convicted serial killer Jeffrey Dahmer to an in-depth look at teachers who returned to classrooms after child molestation convictions. In 2008, Solomon joined the *Washington Times* as executive editor.

Before joining the *Times*, Solomon was a national investigative correspondent at the *Washington Post*, where he uncovered former New York Mayor Rudolph Giuliani's secret security firm clients, former Senator John Edwards' relationship with a controversial hedge fund, and the FBI's misuse of an anti-terrorism tool that allowed agents to gather phone and computer records of Americans without court approval.

Seamus Bruner is the author of *Compromised: How Money and Politics Drive FBI Corruption* and the Associate Director of Research at the Government Accountability Institute. Bruner has worked with Peter Schweizer since 2011 and GAI since 2013 providing research and support for numerous *N.Y. Times* bestsellers.

Bruner's research has been featured on the front page of top publications like the *New York Times*, *Wall Street Journal*, and *Washington Post* and resulted in multiple *60 Minutes* exposés. Bruner has discussed the results of his findings on national TV and radio.